AUGUST STRINDBERG

Self-portrait, 1886

AUGUST STRINDBERG
OLOF LAGERCRANTZ
TRANSLATED BY ANSELM HOLLO

FARRAR STRAUS GIROUX
New York

CONTENTS

ILLUSTRATIONS

FOREWORD

This book could not have been written without the Strindberg scholarship that has been vigorously pursued both in Sweden and elsewhere during the last thirty years. Distinguished representatives of this line of studies have been acknowledged in my text, although not as frequently as they deserve, considering how much I have learned from them. Wherever I have arrived at conclusions differing from theirs, I have refrained from polemical discussion, which would have caused this book to extend to an inordinate length.

I am particularly indebted to Torsten Eklund. The abundance of information on Strindberg provided by his monumental edition of Strindberg's letters, and by his dissertation and other writings has been of invaluable assistance to me throughout my work on this book. In addition, Torsten Eklund has very generously given me advice and special information on the subject.

A great part of my work was done at the Royal Library in Stockholm where Strindberg was once employed and where the majority of his posthumous papers and manuscripts are preserved. The director of the manuscript collection, Harry Järv, himself a distinguished Strindberg expert and his staff have been tireless in their goodwill and readiness to assist me.

Lars Dahlbäck, whose fine study of *The People of Hemsö* is occasionally cited in the present work, was kind enough to read it in manuscript form. He saved me from a number of factual errors and provoked stimulating discussion from which the book has greatly benefited.

When quoting from Strindberg, I have normally referred to John Landquist's edition of *Collected Writings* 1912–1919. Not infrequently, however, I have used the original editions. The quotation from *A Fool's*

Apology on page 169 is taken from the version of the novel—probably the original—which was discovered in Oslo in 1973.

OLOF LAGERCRANTZ
April 1984

Chapter One

CHILDHOOD AND YOUTH

I

JOHAN AUGUST STRINDBERG was born in Stockholm on 22 January 1849, only a few days after the end of the year of the February Revolution and the *Communist Manifesto*. Yet if one bases his astrological chart not on his birth-date but, as he himself insists one should do, on the date of his conception, he is indeed a child of that year of upheaval.

'I was born under the sign of the Ram,' he writes from Paris on 20 July 1896, to his Theosophist friend Torsten Hedlund. 'That sign represents Sacrifice. My reward, after a life's work like mine: to be butchered. Every success a consequence of suffering; every trace of happiness tainted by dirt; every encouragement a mockery, every good deed punished by crucifixion. But the Ram can also signify Spring, a renewal. Who knows what conclusions to draw?'

Nine months before his birth, on 22 April 1848, the Sun had in fact been in Taurus for two days; Strindberg, however, did not hesitate to amend the workings of the heavens in favour of his personal mythology. An almanac would have provided him with an even more pointed reference to the sacrificial lamb: 22 April 1848 was Easter Saturday—when according to Christian belief, the slain Christ has descended into Limbo; to prepare for his triumphal Resurrection.

On 14 April that year, Stockholm harbour had been opened to steamship traffic. The city's streets still reverberated with echoes of the March riots which had been an extension of the revolutionary wave sweeping across Europe. The newspapers reported the numbers of dead and wounded in the war between Prussia and Denmark. Large advertisements in the same papers indicated that Stockholm was preparing for a number of public masked balls: these were traditionally held on Easter Monday.

The Strindberg family came from Norrland, and August Strindberg was to become attached to the notion that he had Lapp blood in his veins—and, consequently, indigenous magical powers. His grandfather, Zacharias Strindberg (born in 1758), was a clergyman's son from Jämtland who emigrated to Stockholm to become a grocery store owner. He prospered, achieved the rank of major in the Stockholm city militia, received a Pro Patria medal for civic merit, and was one of the founders of the Order of Aurora, an organization dedicated to the edification of youth by means of dance, music, and theatrical events. His grandson would have felt at home in that company: fantasies about his role of sacrificial lamb did not prevent him from enjoying a full social life.

Zacharias married a daughter of the German Naijber family. Strindberg, who liked to incorporate the great men of this earth as well as the bodies of the firmament into the saga of his life, would later connect his grandmother with the Count Nejpperg who became a lover of Napoleon's second Empress, Marie Louise of Austria.

Zacharias Strindberg wrote plays for the Order of Aurora, one of them entitled *The Magnanimous Lover* (a title hardly relevant to his grandson). He had three children, all of whom did well in life. His daughter Lisette married, in 1822, the British inventor and steamship builder Samuel Owen, who had been living in Sweden since 1806. Owen was an influential industrialist. In 1818, the year that one of Napoleon's field marshals, Jean Bernadotte, became Sweden's King Carl XIV Johan, Owen introduced the first steamship to Sweden. The city of Stockholm named a street after him. Lisette Owen appears in Strindberg's childhood memories as an elegant lady wearing a lace bonnet and demanding to be greeted with a kiss on her hand.

Owen's pioneering soon led to a great number of paddle-wheelers plying the waters of Mälaren and Saltsjön. The Strindbergs became specialists in selling steamship tickets and dealing with steamship freight consignments. As early as 1828, Zacharias Strindberg was selling steamship tickets in his grocery store as a result of his daughter's marriage. Zacharias's eldest son, Johan Ludvig Strindberg (born in 1794), became a steamship agent and proceeded to the realms of higher finance—as wholesale merchant, shipowner and stockbroker—and to a life as a member of the *haute bourgeoisie*.

Johan Ludvig's brother Carl Oscar, seventeen years his junior, took over the family ticket agency. Carl Oscar was August Strindberg's father. Royal names were *de rigueur* at that time in middle-class families with ambition: Carl Oscar was named after Carl XIII who inherited the Swedish throne from his nephew Gustav IV Adolf following the catastrophe of 1809 (when Finland was lost to Russia); after the heir-apparent's son who was to become Oscar I; and after the latter's third son, August. As a steamship agent, Carl

Oscar (and his family) became closely involved in the rapid technological progress initiated and powered in the nineteenth century by steam. Carl Oscar Strindberg never omitted to note in his diary the date when the ice started breaking up in the spring, and again when the waters froze in late autumn, thereby bringing navigation to a halt.

The steam vessels on Strömmen and moored by the Riddarholm quay must have been among the first things August Strindberg became aware of outside the walls of his home. According to a description in 'The Romantic Sexton of Rånö' these ships were all the colours of the rainbow: 'sea-green and cinnabar red below the waterline' and resplendent with 'highly polished brass and white steel, black smokestacks and copper-red steampipes'.

A considerable number of these vessels were indeed brand-new. Carl Oscar, who could almost regard them as his own—he dealt with the freight of over 30 per cent of them—entered their names and engine power in a ledger as they were launched: *Hermoder*; *Elfkungen*; *Thor*; *Aros*; *Sten Sture*; *Berzelius*. The *Berzelius*, built in the year of August Strindberg's birth and named after the famous natural scientist who had died the year before, mustered an imposing 120 horsepower.

Carl Oscar Strindberg's social circle consisted mainly of shipping and seafaring people. He was a guest at First Mates' weddings, and godfather to Captains' children. He was elected a member of the Sea Command's Order of Neptune whose members, according to *Old Stockholm*, a work of cultural history edited by August Strindberg with Claes Lundin in the 1880s (see Chapter 5), made summer excursions in the environs of Stockholm to plant the symbol of their order, Neptune's trident, 'on the cliffs of the archipelago'. Strindberg grew up in a world that smelled of the sea. He often used the quays of Stockholm and the waterways leading to them as settings in his literary work. In the Stockholm that he knew, a multitude of small steamboats swarmed through waters that are dull and lifeless now, docking at many different places within the city: Strömparterren, Museum, Skeppsholmen, Logårdstrappan, Grevbron, Nybron, Köttorget. Speed is a constant characteristic of Strindberg's descriptions of nature: he first observed it aboard those vessels. There are innumerable descriptions in his work of the beauty of the shores of Mälaren and of the archipelago as seen through the round porthole windows in a steamer saloon.

Such firm roots in terms of both geographical location and social status brought a sense of security that Strindberg was never to lose completely throughout his life, no matter how many intellectual and emotional experiments he would subject himself to for his art's sake. In his famous analysis of *Huckleberry Finn*, Lionel Trilling sees the Mississippi River and the camaraderie of Huck and Jim on the raft as reflections of America's Golden Age dream of freedom and equality before railroads, robber barons, and human exploitation took over. Stockholm's waters teeming with steamboats became Strindberg's equivalents of Mark Twain's river. They present an image of childhood innocence, of a natural world not yet threatened, of a feeling of boundless optimism under the command of worthy captains. Time and again Strindberg would return to that golden age.

2

Carl Oscar Strindberg spent a relatively long period of his life as a gregarious bachelor. He has been described as a good-looking, if rather overbearing man. At the inn at Liljeholm, on the outskirts of Stockholm, he met a pretty waitress, Ulrika Eleonora Norling—known as Nora—and fell in love with her. In his short story 'The Bird Phoenix', part of the series *Marrying*, Strindberg describes her according to family tradition: full-breasted, with honey-coloured hair and skin 'fresh and soft as a kid glove'. She was doubtless all the more attractive for being twelve years younger than Carl Oscar.

Nora became Carl Oscar's mistress, then the manager of his household, and they married in September 1847, when they already had two sons; this was a fairly normal sequence of events in those days and caused no embarrassment to either partner. Strindberg would later claim that he was born but not sired in wedlock (although as we have seen, he was mistaken in this).

1–2   Strindberg's parents, Carl Oscar Strindberg and Ulrika Eleanora Norling

3 The harbour at Riddarholmen. Detail from a lithograph of Stockholm by O. A. Mankell

When the third child, August, was born, the family was living in an apartment above the steamship agency on the Riddarholm quay, directly opposite the massive Palais Wrangel on the other side of the water. August was followed by another boy, Olof, and three sisters: Anna, Elisabeth, and Eleonora. Strindberg had to stand up for himself among six brothers and sisters, although it went without saying that the sons were privileged in terms of education and opportunity. When Elisabeth, the sister Strindberg was closest to, became mentally ill, she shared that fate with innumerable women who had been denied a chance to develop their inner resources.

Carl Oscar Strindberg ran the household, which included a number of servants, with all the authority of a paterfamilias of his day. As his daughters later observed, there was little genuine intimacy between the members of the family. Obedience, frugality, and first and foremost orderliness, were obligatory. (As Strindberg grew older he became more and more like his father in this respect.) Carl Oscar was competent in his job, had a number of active interests outside the steamship business, and felt a strong sense of social responsibility. He served as a governing member of Sweden's Handicrafts and Horticultural Associations and also belonged to the Order

Par Bricole, whose poet laureate Bellman had been. His son's lifelong hatred of Bellman could be seen as a protest against Par Bricole's sentimental adulation of that poet.

Nora Strindberg's role in the household was a subordinate one. The name Strindberg was what mattered, and August would later bring his creative imagination to bear on the family's fortunes. Nora's father was a master tailor, and her relatives were simple people.

She gave birth to twelve children, of whom five died as infants, and these continuous pregnancies sapped her strength. Her rapid and tragic decline is the theme of 'The Bird Phoenix'. As far as we know, she was a kind and considerate person. 'Mother', Strindberg writes in *Inferno*, 'imprinted in me the conviction that dirty feet are a sign of disgrace.' It is one of the few times he refers to her in his writings, and the memory may be characteristic of her role in the home. Like her husband, she was a devout Christian. Evening prayers were obligatory; the Bible and Wallin's *Observations* were read out loud; Sundays were churchgoing days. From the very beginning, Strindberg had a close grounding in the vocabulary of Christianity.

Secular literature played a less prominent part in his upbringing. At home there was a bookcase containing Franzén's and Tegnér's poems, Emilie Flygare-Carlén's novels, *Don Quixote*, a few history books, Sven Nilsson's *Scandinavian Fauna*, *The Arabian Nights*, and some fairytale collections. The fairytales made a deep impression. Strindberg himself was a 'third son' and thus, in the world of those tales, the one whom everyone despises at first for his stupidity and slovenliness but who triumphs in the end. It did not take him long to adapt himself to that pattern. The ever-popular *Robinson Crusoe* was also available and, according to Strindberg's autobiography, 'of tremendous importance' to him. A sentence from the autobiography tells us: 'On Wednesday and Saturday afternoons one could observe the eleven-year-old in his dressing-gown and nightcap, given to him by his father, with a long tobacco pipe in his mouth and plugging his ears with his fingers, lost in the perusal of some book, most preferably one about Indians.' Tobacco was to be a lifelong habit of Strindberg's, acquired as early as Huckleberry Finn's. Nothing indicates that young August was a particularly precocious devourer of *belles-lettres*: nature and natural sciences successfully vied for his attention. He conducted physics experiments, aided by his father, much in the manner of the time; he collected and pressed flowers, and started collections of insects and minerals.

Music was an interest shared by all the family. Eleonora played the piano, Anna and Oscar the violin, and Axel the cello (he became a professional musician). On Sundays, this quartet performed Haydn, Mendelssohn, Mozart, and, above all, Beethoven. In one of his earliest poems, *Exile*, Strindberg describes one such musical evening. Under lithographs of Tsar Nikolai I and Napoleon, their grandfather's political patron saints, and surrounded by massive oaken bookcases, the children sit and play while their father, puffing on his pipe, beats out the time, and their mother brings in refreshments. Everybody is happy and animated. Such scenes provided pleasant memories: in his adult life, Strindberg regularly invited friends to his home to make music. Brother Axel and his cello participated in those soirées. Strindberg's own households would retain much of the atmosphere of his childhood home; although he was an innovator in thought and language, he was extremely conservative in a number of other spheres of life.

3

The Serving Maid's Son, the autobiographical work Strindberg wrote when he was thirty-seven, has been regarded as a self-evident source book on the author's childhood and youth. Strindberg wrote it in haste: it contains some brilliant episodes as well as many tedious passages. It is useful in terms of the historical background of Strindberg's life, but otherwise it should be read with caution.

During the cholera epidemic of 1854, we are told, the five-year-old August had to wear a copper plate tied round his chest with a blue silk ribbon: superstition and medicine were still closely linked at that time. The Crimean War and the siege of Sebastopol were among his earliest memories. On Sundays—after the Strindbergs moved to an apartment near Klara Church—the bells would ring so loudly that the whole family became highly emotional and it was impossible to hear what anyone was saying. Strindberg describes how on one occasion a policeman appeared at the door and levied a fine because the cook had emptied a bucket of slops into the gutter: the city still had no public sewage system. Gaslight was introduced to Stockholm, but society was hardly enlightened; it remained hierarchical, with marked class distinctions. The resident in the royal palace was Oscar I, who died in 1859; his funeral impressed itself on the ten-year-old's mind. On two other occasions he came even closer to royalty: once when he saw the Crown Prince—later, Karl XV—standing in a field and driving a horse around in circles on a long line by means of a loud rattle and pistol shots; and again that same summer when, out riding with a beautiful cousin, the Prince reined in his horse and graciously enquired the boy's name.

In the apartment building in Klara, the lower floors were inhabited by wealthy and distinguished families who thus avoided the strain of climbing stairs. The higher up you went, the more modest the tenants became; the Strindberg family occupied the fourth floor—a middle-of-the-road position, one might say. Outside lay not so much the great wide world as an obscure corner of it—the small agricultural kingdom of Sweden; a fact which was traditionally a cause for lament among ambitious young men regretting the accident of their birth. Yet Sweden's glorious military past was a frequently cited source of national pride; it would preoccupy Strindberg a great deal. In the Riddarholm Church were the tombs of two kings who had died in battle, Gustaf II Adolf and Karl XII, and of another, Gustaf III, who had been assassinated at a masked ball at the Opera. All three appear in Strindberg's plays.

As for the central content of Strindberg's life, *The Serving Maid's Son* is useless as a source. What we are told about the child August—here called Johan, since the book is formally a novel—is either useless or downright misleading. The qualities Strindberg emphasizes in his child protagonist are common to *all* children: that they are born frightened; that they experience themselves as weak; that they react to pressure; that they have a weak sense of ego; that they feel themselves treated unjustly by older people and playmates, and that they are always anticipating such injustices. Little Johan is Everyman, like the protagonist in Hofmannsthal's great play. He does not serve as a reflection of the childhood of August Strindberg.

That being the case, we shall bypass, in this first chapter, all intricate problems relating to Strindberg's attitudes toward his parents, his brothers and sisters and his social environment: we will not dwell upon any of those opinion-forming, tear-jerking little episodes with which *The Serving Maid's Son* is so liberally seasoned: accounts of wine bottles the child is suspected of 'tapping' or screw-nuts that are believed to have been stolen. From the outset, any biographer of Strindberg must in a sense protect himself from his subject: for every phase of his life, Strindberg decided how he wanted to be understood and deliberately created a persona for himself. A large proportion of his work has been regarded as autobiographical, often without justification. He has an extraordinary talent for making us believe what he wants us to believe. With a kind of instinctive vehemence he would, throughout his life, react against any attempt to peek behind the scenes or to characterize him in any way that differed from his own specifications. Small wonder, then, that anyone who attempts to formulate his own concept of Strindberg's life and character is confronted by extraordinary problems.

4

There was nothing striking about Strindberg as a child that would have attracted other people's attention; consequently testimony is sparse. Of the brothers, Axel, the oldest, was their mother's favourite, and Oscar the father's. Strindberg grew up in the shadow of two taller and stronger brothers whom the parents preferred to him—no doubt this was a stimulant to the ambition that would characterize his life. Yet August Strindberg was spared the torture to which his transatlantic contemporary, Henry James, was subjected—continually to see his brilliant older brother William turn the corner, heading for new triumphs.... In his childhood home Strindberg soon discovered that he could after all be 'the lion', and a firm though continually negated conviction of his own worth remained with him all his life.

His father's diary chronicled not only his steamship business but also the major events of family life. A special column was reserved for the children's height as measured each New Year's Day. August grew normally, finally reaching a height of nearly six feet, which caused contemporaries to describe him as 'a man of stature'. But it took a while before he caught up with his brothers' physical development. There is an echo of that measuring ceremony in one of the first prose pieces Strindberg ever wrote, *The Beginning of Ån Bogsveig's Saga*. Here he offers us a fragment of autobiography in Ancient Norse guise. Ån is the younger of two sons. His older brother is liegeman to the King, while Ån remains at home by the fire, poking the ashes like a kind of Cinderella figure and being chided for his laziness. He has carved a notch in the floorboards, seven feet away from the fireplace, and refuses to budge until he has grown tall enough to reach that mark: the serfs have made him believe that until this point is reached he cannot become a real man.

Contemporary accounts are unanimous about young Strindberg's shyness and reserve. At home or school he was far from being cock-of-the-walk. His brother Axel has claimed that August would creep into a cupboard in order to change his underwear unobserved by his brothers. 'Quiet and shy' is how a schoolmate, Robert Geete, describes him, adding that 'he did not attract any attention whatsoever'. His college friend Carl Oscar Larsson mentions his 'reserved nature'. Shyness and timidity stayed with him all his life and played a decisive role when he chose to communicate with the world by means of writing. He was soft-spoken, and whenever he did raise his voice, it became shrill. All his brothers and sisters spoke quietly—possibly a habit acquired during their mother's serious illness.

One of Strindberg's earliest preserved letters is dated 30 December 1861, not long before his thirteenth birthday, and is addressed to his brother Oscar, then studying in Paris. August relates a remarkable event that took place on Christmas Day:

> In the morning, Uncle and I and Axel were supposed to go to Solna, but when we got there, there was no service, so we just took a walk. In the afternoon I was sitting around and said to Mademoiselle, 'I wonder what I'll be doing tomorrow'. Well, I was going to go skating the next day when Mother walked in and said, 'your friend Flodcrantz is dead'; he had

crashed through the ice on Brunnsviken at 4 pm by the little red gazebo out on the promontory, and I cried. Today he was buried and I saw his corpse; it was very beautiful, he was laid out on the floor above. The room was draped in black with silver stars and there was a black canopy with an eye in the middle and four candelabra.

Most children in August's situation would have either reported the awful event right away or at least prepared the letter's recipient for some horrendous news. Instead, Strindberg chooses to present his brother with a cleverly constructed and precisely detailed drama: after the introductory exchange about skating between him and the governess, his mother enters with the tidings of death. The reader of the letter is compelled to think that August, too, has experienced a brush with death: was he not planning a skating excursion, but was saved by the warning implicit in his friend's death? Thus Flodcrantz is no longer the main character: the narrator is. The letter concludes on a conventionally Christian note of beautiful reconciliation—the dead boy lies resting under God's wakeful eye.

With hindsight, it is not hard to see the future dramatist and wrestler with the angel in that letter.

5

Far from being a 'serving maid's son', Strindberg was raised in a secure and comparatively well-to-do home. True, his mother had been in service with a family for a short time in her teens, but this was only for a short spell and was no more than a temporary visit to a class well below her own. Strindberg's portrayal of her as a drudge is a political act (see p. 40) but has little to do with reality.

As Allan Hagsten has demonstrated in his excellent study of the young Strindberg, everyday life in the Strindberg home was a comfortable one. Food was wholesome and plentiful: according to surviving detailed accounts for 1862, each member of the household consumed half a pound of beef or pork per day—a fact which has to be set against the autobiography's first chapter title, 'Afraid and Hungry'. A bankruptcy in 1853, in the wake of the spectacular crash of Johan Ludvig Strindberg's business the year before, seems to have caused little hardship. During August's childhood and adolescence a state of reasonable prosperity was steadily improved upon, and this family progress can be documented by their choice of residence. In 1856, when Strindberg was seven, the family moved away from Klara to live in a series of so-called 'stone mansions' along Norrtullsgatan, almost rural with their gardens, stables, and barns. From there, it was not far to Brunnsviken.

Strindberg grew up in this idyllic suburb dominated by the Observatory, a scene which recurs in his writings. As in Joyce's Dublin, the view included windmills, called 'Great Adam' and 'Little Eve'. Strindberg used them as 'life station number one' in his last play, *The Great Highway*, written in his old age. His father was an accomplished gardener, although according to August, pelargoniums were his exclusive interest. Yet the son paid attention and acquired an early familiarity with gardening and animal husbandry. In 1860, a horse named Bruno was purchased so that the steamboat commissioner could ride in style to his office, which was still located at Riddarholm. In his autobiography, Strindberg makes much of having been obliged to drive the vehicle pulled by Bruno—he regarded it as socially degrading. Nevertheless it enabled him to become familiar with the species *equus*, and riding was one of the things he enjoyed all his life.

What with the number of children and servants, and the governess, and relatives who came to stay for a while, actual space in the home was at a premium. In those days people lived in far greater propinquity than they do now, and the world outside was equally well populated. All his life Strindberg retained a strong need to have people in his immediate vicinity. 'In order to develop a rich, free life, the psyche needs a great deal of human company. The more people one meets and converses with, the greater the number of points of view and experiences one gains,' he writes in his autobiography, momentarily oblivious to his intended emphasis on the subject's essential loneliness. In his childhood, life and death crowded in on him, and solitude was an impossibility. A neighbour, a butcher called Falk, kept fierce dogs the children were afraid of, and these serve to justify Strindberg's lifelong hatred of canines: people who preferred to spend their time in the company of animals rather than with other people he regarded as monsters.

The first school Strindberg was sent to was in Klara. He was seven years old, and it was a long way from Norrtull. On dark winter mornings, the streets not yet cleared of snow, it was a sombre walk; he would pass the Observatory and proceed down Kungsbacken, at that time part of Drottninggatan, and there he would stop at a bakery to buy his breakfast bun. The Klara school was reputable but strict. Strindberg's classmate Robert Geete approvingly quoted him as saying that the school provided an 'apprenticeship for hell, not for life'; nor were the opinions of other pupils any milder. Facts were crammed in by means of the cane and by fear of it; this would doubtless prove a useful training for later life, provided the memory was not blocked by psychological trauma.

In 1860, Strindberg moved from Klara for a short while to Jakob School, whose pupils came from lower-class homes, and from there, in the autumn

of 1861, to the Stockholm Lyceum, a private institution where more liberal
and modern teaching methods prevailed and the students were even allowed
to think for themselves. Many of them were sons of the city's most
prominent families. Strindberg graduated from the Lyceum on 25 May
1867. Of his brothers and sisters, he was the only one thus privileged: the
others were given a more practically oriented education.

Nora Strindberg's illness and death caused a major upheaval in the
family's life: she died on 20 March 1862, of tuberculosis of the lungs, two
months after August's thirteenth birthday. To his brother Oscar who was
still in Paris (a good indication of the family's solvency) he reported on the
event on 22 March, giving details of the shrouding of the deceased, of the
governess who was sewing mourning clothes for the little ones; of the fact
that the butcher Falk had died, too; he says that Oscar should not weep too
much 'because it was God's will', and he concludes by quoting the following
hopeful stanza of a hymn that had been inscribed on the coffin:

> My day of joy, I await thee,
> I am ready, I put on the white
> marriage vestment. Come, Jesus!
> 'Yes, I'll come soon,' is thy answer:
> clearly I hear thy voice
> cutting through the dawn.

The mother left a kind of testament to her sons, in which they were
warned against the 'vice of drunkenness' and 'visits to whorehouses', two
sins that deprive a young man of his 'true virility'.

The governess referred to in August's letter was Emilia Charlotta
Pettersson, not yet quite of age at the time of the death of her mistress.
Within the year, the sorrowing widower, though thirty years her senior,
had married her. She was only four years older than her eldest stepson. It is
easy to see that tensions would develop within that family structure, and
Strindberg makes much of them in his autobiography. He was soon to
discover that his situation was a classical one, that of Hamlet, although the
stepfather-king had been replaced by a stepmother-queen. That simply
increased the possibilities of interesting complications. All his life Strindberg was to exist in the most intimate visceral contact with the great
mythical and literary figures, and it was just as well to get an early start.

He was not a particularly distinguished student; his childhood and
adolescence were a time of preparation, providing the observer with little of
note. The summer sojourns in the country proved important: the family had
access to free steamship travel, and took frequent trips. In the interests of
their health and of preparatory school reading the older boys spent several
subsequent summers in various parish clerks' homes along the shores of
Mälaren, where Strindberg was able to glean an invaluable hoard of

impressions. In the happiest poem he ever wrote, *The Trip to the City*, the hero is one of those parish clerks who travels to Stockholm one Midsummer's Eve, on the steamer, in order to purchase a grand piano to replace the worn-out old upright, and observes the most magnificent scenery on the way. The poem was written in the early 1900s, arising out of memories dating back forty years. It is proof of the vigorous way in which life impressed itself on the boy.

4 Strindberg aged thirteen or fourteen

In the autobiographical novel *Legends* (1898) Strindberg claims that it was at one of these 'sexton's farms' that sin first became a reality in his life. An older friend seduced him into masturbation, and he succumbed, according to the text, to this temptation 'unknowingly, a child who receives a pleasure cordially and generously proffered by nature, but one punished with death according to divine law'. As Nils Norman tells us in his brilliant treatise *Young Strindberg and the Revival Movement*, the thirteen-year-old Strindberg read a universally known book by the prominent German Pietist Karl von Kapff which dealt with the dangers and degradations of self-abuse. Among other theses, von Kapff presented the astonishing one that the revolutionaries of the era most likely practised masturbation which, according to von Kapff, was a ravaging plague, a deadly poison, one that impoverished the blood and threatened the vitality of its victims. A great number of contemporaries shared these views which established a strong connection between sin and sex. Later, Strindberg would struggle to free humanity from the terror which revivalists like von Kapff had spread, and which he had experienced himself. Yet it is difficult to establish how deep his childhood pangs of conscience and fear really were, because he left varying reports on them, according to where he found himself on his life's voyage. Probably in most adolescents, and adults too, a commonsense attitude to these matters prevailed, counteracting von Kapff's fire and brimstone preaching.

In his mid-teens, Strindberg became a tutor. In the summer of 1866 he moved into exalted circles as tutor to the children on the Hammersta estate in the Södertörn Archipelago. His employer was Carl Otto Trotz, whose wife was a lady of the baronial family Löwen: Strindberg addressed her as Baroness. There was sailing, riding and hunting. One Sunday, he was asked to deliver the sermon in church—an episode he gives some importance to in his autobiography. In July 1866, he wrote to his brother Oscar in a mocking manner about being dressed up in a dog-collar and smock ('that cursed article of clothing, I think it makes one look like a hypocrite'), and about how he was tempted, while waiting in the vestry, by the communion wine labelled 'Piccardon'. Eighteen years later, mention of that same wine almost landed him in gaol: it occurred in a provocative context in one of the stories contained in the book *Marrying*. As for the sermon, he claims he made it so vehement that he moved himself to tears and was afterwards addressed as 'pastor Strindberg'. Sunday afternoons, however, where whiled away with games or dancing to the strains of *La Belle Hélène*: this was Offenbach's heyday in Europe, and his operettas introduced a note of levity into the atmosphere of solemn domestic piety.

Strindberg returned to Hammersta for Christmas and the New Year and also visited Häringe Castle where Baron Löwen, a brother of Hammersta's mistress, 'talked with me about Father's steamboats', according to a letter to his brother. He was 'having a wonderful time' and even paid a return visit to the pulpit, this time a little 'woozy' after beers at the local inn. 'I wanted to mount the steps to the pulpit', the letter continues, 'wearing a large fur coat I had borrowed, but the pastor claimed this would have been unsuitable—I was angry but kept my mouth shut while thinking, what was Jesus of Nazareth wearing when he preached his doctrine that would sweep the world?' This is the first time on record that he compared himself to Jesus and also touched upon the notion that his own words would reach the world at large: this was to become one of his most cherished lifelong preoccupations.

During one of these early years Strindberg had a decisive formative experience. He participated in a paramilitary 'sharpshooters' exercise' at Tyresö in the Stockholm Archipelago. The sharpshooters crawled around in the blueberry and juniper bushes and emerged on to the top of a steep cliff by the shore, to a view of the sea, its bays and islands. Strindberg writes, in *The Serving Maid's Son*:

> That picture impressed him like the rediscovery of a country seen in beautiful dreams or in a preceding existence, one he believed in but did not know anything about. The chain of riflemen wound its way to one side, into the woods, but Johan remained sitting by the precipice and, yes, worshipping: that is the word. The adversaries had drawn closer and opened fire; bullets whined by; he simply hid, he was unable to leave. This was his ideal landscape, the true environment of his own nature; craggy granite islands overgrown with spruce trees, scattered across wide and stormy bays, with the boundless sea as their background, seen from a proper distance. And he remained true to his love, not simply because it was the first; neither the Swiss Alps, nor the olive hills of the Mediterranean, nor the cliffs of Normandy were able to oust it.

In his book, Strindberg interprets this experience in terms of a landscape he had discovered, and the Stockholm Archipelago did indeed become the central natural domain of his work. Yet the revelation of Tyresö was not simply one of ravishing natural beauty: more importantly, it involved a feeling of recognition and psychic expansion. It was not so much a question of a landscape artist stumbling upon his subject during a military exercise, as of a visionary and mystic experiencing a premonition of his future life. He remembered it often, and in the entry of 15 August 1899, in his *Occult Diary* he himself used the phrase 'moved as if by a revelation'. The archipelago is only an image behind which another reality can be glimpsed. Strindberg would later use his experiences in such glowing moments in works of apparent realism: yet from the very beginning they point towards another, invisible, realm.

Chapter Two

A LITERARY APPRENTICESHIP

I

DURING THE FIRST two years after his graduation from the Lyceum, there were many changes of scene for Strindberg: he attended the university at Uppsala for his first term, then started working as a primary school teacher (at an annual salary of 900 riksdaler) in the spring of 1868; he prepared himself for medical studies by taking chemistry courses at the Technological Institute, and started a job as a supernumerary at the Royal Theatre in 1869. He also worked as a tutor in the homes of two well-known Stockholm physicians; in his autobiography he describes the dramatic contrast between the primary school with its smell of poverty and the upper-class homes where he tutored the privileged children.

It all seems like a fairly volatile entry into adult working life—typical for any young man who is aware of extraordinary inner resources but does not yet know how to use them. He is gaining the advantage of experience which he will make use of later.

One of the physicians, Axel Lamm, of wealthy Jewish origins, had a number of artists among his friends, and adopted a paternal attitude towards Strindberg. The shy, reserved, taciturn young man naturally attracted such a response, and he was to have many patrons in the future. Lamm offered Strindberg a room in his house on the distinguished Västra Trädgårdsgatan, in the middle of the city. Strindberg lived there for more than a year, from the autumn of 1868 to January 1870, when he went back to study at Uppsala. Lamm simply wanted him to be a general companion to his sons, and to give them some help with their homework. One of the sons, Per Aron, who was five years younger than Strindberg, became a bookseller in Paris and a useful aide to his former tutor when the latter embarked on his long European odyssey.

Dr Lamm surgically removed three disfiguring birthmarks from Strindberg's neck. Their constellation resembled that of Orion, but we do not know whether surgeon or patient made any comment on this concordance between Strindberg and the celestial map. Strindberg referred to the operation much later, in his *Occult Diary*, at a time when he had begun the search for strange connections. That diary—mentioned in the previous chapter—will be frequently quoted: Strindberg kept it between 1896 and 1908, recording primary data relating to the occult, poetic world view he was constructing during that time.

The room on Trädgårdsgatan was memorable, at least if one believes Strindberg who says that it was the place where he discovered what he called the artist's generative faculty. That discovery determined his fate: in *The Serving Maid's Son* he tells us how it occurred. He had auditioned at the theatre, hoping to be hired as an actor; he was not accepted but was advised to enrol in the theatre school. Shattered by this humiliation he rushed home in tears. In his room, he swallowed a long-hoarded pellet of opium, wishing to leave this hateful life. The poison, however, did not have the desired effect. A friend arrived and took him on a consoling tour of the city's bars, which resulted in massive intoxication. The following day, 'shattered, wounded, torn', 'drunkenness and shame' still fiery in his body, he stayed in his room thinking that even 'honour' was now lost, since he had made both his patron Lamm and his father believe that his salvation lay in the theatre.

In that state, he read Zachris Topelius's popular historical romance *Tales of an Army Surgeon* and came across a passage in which a stepson and a stepmother are reconciled. He recognized his own situation and fell into reverie. In a couple of hours a comedy in two acts had taken shape in his head. As he tells us in his autobiography, this work was both painful and pleasurable, and took place in a feverish state, 'without any exercise of my own will'. It took him four days to finish the play, and when it was done 'he gave a great sigh, as if years of pain were now over, as if a boil had been lanced. He felt happy, as though he were singing inside.'

Until he had that experience, Strindberg had been trying out at random things which had never led anywhere. From then on, he would invest all his ambition in writing. There were to be a number of jobs and professions, but these were merely to provide a livelihood. In his day, no beginner could openly declare himself a 'professional' literary artist.

Can we trust his description of his awakening to his vocation? Yes and no: each part of *The Serving Maid's Son* bears the subtitle 'The History of the Development of a Soul', which emphasizes Strindberg's intention to offer us the story of his inner life. Renaming himself Johan, August also gives himself permission to dramatize and to concentrate; we cannot, and should not, make him responsible for any inaccuracies in details.

Early on, he developed a very special relationship with language, which needs to be considered if one is to understand him at all. Around the time of his realization that he was chosen to be a writer he also began a voluminous correspondence and became one of the most industrious and extraordinary letter-writers of world literature. His letters allow us to follow his life closely, sometimes on an hourly basis. He wrote letters of every kind, from love letters to missives of extortion, but in addition, during most of his life—between, roughly, the ages of twenty-one and fifty—he always had a favourite correspondent (invariably a man), to whom he wrote about matters great and small, before whom he wept, boasted and fantasized, not unlike a small boy who runs to tell his mother about everything. It is this correspondence that has given him the reputation of a confessor and unique revealer of intimacies.

The first one of these favourite correspondents was his cousin Johan Oscar, the son of the great merchant Johan Ludvig Strindberg who loomed like a colossus in Strindberg's childhood and who probably served as a model for the merchant Carl Nicolaus Falk in *The Red Room*. After a sequence of merely informative letters to his cousin in 1870, Strindberg burst out with a great howl of anguish on 8 October. To indicate his state of mind, he referred to that month by its old Swedish name, 'butchering moon'.

What was it all about? After the completion of his first play (which he burned) his creative streak continued and he wrote a number of others: a tragedy, set in antiquity, called *The Decline of Hellas*; a play in a contemporary setting, *The Freethinker*, whose protagonist, the student Karl, devotes himself to teaching in a primary school in order to spread 'enlightened and practical knowledge' among the common people; a grand verse drama about Erik XIV, the unfortunate Swedish Renaissance prince who ended his life half-mad in a prison tower and in whom Strindberg sees a Swedish Hamlet; and, finally, a play about the Danish sculptor Thorvaldsen.

His efforts met with modest yet, considering his youth, respectable acclaim. His cousin financed the printing of *The Freethinker*, and the Thorvaldsen play was accepted for a double bill at the Royal Theatre where Strindberg himself had played bit parts and where he had a gracious patron in Frans Hedberg, reader, playwright, and head of the drama school. At this time, Hedberg was one of the two major figures—the director, Royal Marshal Erik af Edholm, was the other—of the national theatre, and thus a most imposing figure in a young playwright's universe. Strindberg tried to get through to him by means of flattery, humility, and rage, succeeding at first but later running into stubborn rejection; we will hear more of this in a later chapter.

The Thorvaldsen play had its first night on 13 September 1870, a great event in the 21-year-old author's life, and got a sympathetic reception from the press. *The Freethinker* did not fare so well. *Nya Dagligt Allehanda*, among other newspapers, demolished the play: according to the reviewer, it was 'remarkable only for its inferiority in every respect, and thus hardly deserving of further scrutiny'. This was Strindberg's first encounter with public malice, and prompted his 'butchering moon' letter, in which he claims to have fallen into the deepest pit of hell and says that he now doubts his vocation, that he has wasted his life. His mood—that of any sensitive young man after his first major setback—seems only natural; it must have been a relief to pour out his suffering to his friend. The sentences in the letter are in hot pursuit of each other, their intensity heightened by the fact that Strindberg at this time favours the dash to comma and full stop, to keep things moving at full tilt. Nevertheless, he transcends the limits of reason and credibility when he goes on to say:

> The night before last—I had got to the second act of *BlotSven* and found it miserable on rereading—the night before last—don't judge me too harshly I had arrived at the conviction that my life was wasted and there was no future for me—the poison flask stood on the table—I was no longer master of my senses—death would have been a joy—only a few moments and the world would have been rid of a failed poet—a restless heart put to rest—maybe a few friends would have shed a tear before forgetting me—but then a friend showed up and realized my state— wanted to console me—as he did not want to leave me I had to go with him to the tavern—that's where he thought life's joy was to be found— well not really but he wanted to calm down my madness—I had no will of my own—the two of us finished a bottle of brandy . . .

The letter goes on to describe the night-long drinking bout in a concise phrase Strindberg was to use frequently: 'I was an animal'—which probably indicates total inebriation. But on the next day, according to the same letter, Strindberg's spirits revived considerably in the company of a charming cousin, Maria, who had come to stay in Uppsala, and the letter concludes with a cascade of questions and greetings to 'all our friends'.

That bottle of poison would reappear in a great number of Strindberg's letters and autobiographical writings. He claimed to have obtained it in the course of his laboratory work.

He was to declare his readiness for suicide hundreds of times. Towards the end of his life he assures us that he first considered this desperate way out when he was only eight years old. However, apart from his own testimony there is no record of one actual suicide attempt, and the incredible frequency of his suicide threats gives cause for reflection.

Like Strindberg's letters to his best friends, his love letters are pleadings for sympathy and understanding; furthermore, they are literary exercises, much given to hyperbole, whose recipient becomes an experimental audience. Thus anyone who wants to use the letters as biographical material needs to read between the lines and interpret the words themselves closely: to do this, the serious scholar needs to compile and constantly refer to his own 'dictionary' of Strindberg vocabulary and terminology, which will enable him to get at their true meaning: Strindberg research has failed to do this, to a regrettable degree. The same principle naturally applies to his autobiographical writings as well. For example, Martin Lamm, justifiably regarded as the grand master of Strindberg scholars, takes the opium pellet seriously (the one that Strindberg claimed to have taken after the disastrous audition in *The Serving Maid's Son*) and so does Erik Hedén, Strindberg's first perceptive biographer. They have gained numerous followers.

With Strindberg, expressions like suicide or the threat to commit suicide are used frequently as mere figures of speech and slip by so fast that one needs to pay close attention to become aware of them. They occur in material written in a consistently beautiful and calm hand and expressed in clear and always controlled language.

By the time Strindberg wrote *The Serving Maid's Son* in 1886, his hyperbolic style had long been quite familiar to close friends from his letters. In the Strindberg dictionary, the word suicide finds its closest approximation in 'state of great distress'. Suicide is a symbol, not a hard fact. Year by year, Strindberg became to an ever-increasing degree a creature of his own imagination, living in a world of his own invention. It was, perhaps, enough for him to take a grain of opium to feel the approach of death, and possibly he experienced the mere thought of suicide as a genuine attempt to kill himself. We, however, have to keep remembering that talking about suicide is not the same as the act itself.

2

Strindberg's characteristic mood after his 'discovery' was one of ebullience rather than of despair and sadness. Most of his letters indicate this, and he describes his (considerable) state of poverty as picturesque.

In the spring of 1870 he participated in the foundation of a literary association, Runa, whose members all adopted names from ancient Norse mythology. The association belonged to a distinguished tradition, with the Gothic Alliance of the turn of the century as an inspiring precedent. Strindberg chose the name Frö (Seed), god of fertility. He always claimed that this principle of the productive and potent was his particular strength.

'The work proceeds—to write—yet not to neglect my studies that is the problem I have decided to solve—and I'll do it,' Strindberg writes to his cousin Johan Oscar on 2 March 1870. Yet this seems to have been wishful thinking. He comes closer to the truth in a September letter to the same recipient, in which he admits that the studies are merely a form of camouflage. 'You mustn't believe that I can put up with such a soul-killing life—no, books are my only consolation! By which I mean, not the kind of books that lead to the desk and the exam, but the ones which inspire me to future works in the field I have chosen!'

A student friend, P. G. Lyth, has provided a lively description of what Strindberg was like during these years. One evening, after a seminar in art history in Uppsala, he took offence at some imaginary slight and tossed a glass to the floor, 'I can't stand being sneered at!' A moment later, he and Lyth were reconciled, and went together to his room.

> He talked about the events in his life [Lyth relates]. And how he talked! I'll never forget how fascinating he was. I found myself truly bewitched, and all his words were poetry. How it roared and seethed and stormed, within that breast. Injustices, pains, sufferings and renunciations. And amongst it all one caught glimpses of such a tender soul, always ready to submit to the hand which would be able to tame such a restless heart with loving kindness.

Strindberg found it easy to evoke the kind of warm, enthusiastic response that is evident in Lyth's description and, even though he kept on stressing his loneliness and dwelling on the hatred which he encountered, he was in fact surrounded all his life by people who reacted like Lyth and testified accordingly.

Strindberg spent almost six terms at Uppsala, although he lived in Stockholm for part of the time. He passed the Latin examination, which at that time was required of all students. He also took a number of minor examinations in Nordic and modern languages, and aesthetics, and wrote a paper on the Danish poet Oehlenschläger's verse drama *Hakon Jarl*. His grades were consistently lower than anticipated, which is not surprising: he was listening to other voices, not those of his professors.

He consigned both *Erik XIV* and *BlotSven* to the flames, yet they were flames from which new plays were to rise like phoenixes. *BlotSven* gave rise to *The Outlaw*, written in the spring of 1871. The play takes place in Iceland during the time of the sagas, and in it a Christian daughter, proud and stubborn, confronts her savage, heathen father. The play was accepted by the Royal Theatre and had its first night on 16 October 1871. Not a hand was moved to applause when the curtain fell, as *Aftonbladet* described in its review, but Karl XV, himself an enthusiast for ancient Nordic matters, saw the play and rewarded Strindberg with a stipend of 200 kronor—which was worth more than the actual money involved. Strindberg came down from Uppsala to thank the King at a special audience, and was ushered into the presence of the sovereign who by that time was mortally ill, probably with syphilis. In *The Serving Maid's Son*, Strindberg remembers his smile and friendliness, standing there 'with his long tobacco pipe'. The stipend was intended not so much as an encouragement to further literary work as to help with the expenses of Strindberg's studies. The King, like an exalted father-figure, advised the young poet to find a place in society and to cultivate literature simply as a hobby, as he did himself.

The Outlaw is not a strong play, yet it contains a scene in which creative force is matched by ability. The hero, Thorfinn Jarl, the pagan father, has to choose between exile or death at the hands of overwhelming adversaries. He is a strong man, a man of action. Strindberg was already familiar with Kierkegaard, who was such a strong influence on his generation, and it is Kierkegaard's ethics that we hear expressed by the Jarl when he chooses death. His counterpart is Orm, the skald, for whom fine words are enough. In a long soliloquy Thornfinn relates how he was once shipwrecked on a small island. Fear and thirst soon constricted his throat. One morning the wind dies down, and in the silence he can hear his own heartbeat. He loses consciousness, and when he wakes up again, he hears someone panting, close by: with renewed hope, he jumps to his feet, only to find that it is a seal which had lain down to rest next to him. He thinks that it is looking at him with eyes moistened by compassion, and he reaches out to touch it, another living creature—but the animal flees, and he finds himself doubly alone. When Strindberg wrote this passage he may have had in mind the passage from Homer where Menelaus finds the sleeping Proteus surrounded by seals keeping him warm with their rank breath.

3

'On 3 March, August left Uppsala,' says the entry in Carl Oscar Strindberg's diary for 1872. Strindberg left in the middle of a term, and without having taken any examinations. We cannot be sure whether the decision was voluntary or due to economic pressure. Strindberg never became an active member of the student body, but he gained many life-long friends at university. Two of these, the actor Georg Törnquist and the natural scientist Gustaf Eisen, tried to keep him at Uppsala by means of a grant, which was initially offered anonymously. In March, Strindberg wrote to Eisen from Stockholm, confidently discussing his literary plans. 'People are complaining about my madness, but that does not bother me—and the streets here aren't so narrow that one has to run into one's dead every time one steps outside.'

A few years later, Strindberg wrote a collection of short stories dealing with the Uppsala milieu. Characteristically, the students depicted do not seem to have any academic problems but are eccentrics, outsiders from the regular course of education. The masterpiece of the collection takes us to a young medical student's funeral. Friends, dressed in black, assemble round their banner in the Uppsala cemetery. It is a winter's day with hoarfrost on the trees and 'blue shadows' on the snow. A ravaged-looking clergyman conducts a half-hearted service. After the ceremony, the dead man's friends congregate at the pathological institute where the recently dissected corpse of a middle-aged man lies on a table, the surgical knife still beside him. The students drink and make cynical jokes about the deceased, yet find themselves unable to escape the horror of death. As they proceed homeward, late at night, their footsteps suddenly stop crunching in the snow: the ground is dark and soft. Without knowing it, they have just passed the dead man's home, where spruce branches have been spread on the sidewalk, according to custom. The silence that engulfs them when they no longer hear their own footsteps is extraordinarily effective. Strindberg certainly kept his eyes and ears open in Uppsala—but not in the direction of the professors, upon whom he would soon be heaping scorn.

Strindberg rented a room in a police constable's home, no. 7 Grev Magnigatan, on the eastern outskirts of Stockholm. Across the street were the barracks of the 2nd Life Guards, whence energetic drumming and bugling could be heard in the mornings and evenings. Beyond the barracks lay Ladugårdsgärde and Djurgården. The painter Carl Larsson, who lived in the same building at the same time, but did not yet know Strindberg, described the place with revulsion in his autobiography, calling it an inferno of poverty, disease and vice. In his novel *Alone*, many years later, Strindberg recounts a gruesome memory of this, his first private dwelling. One night he lies listening to a neighbour who is tossing, turning and groaning on his bed. He falls asleep but wakes up to a cry—not knowing whether it was his own or someone else's. The other room is quiet, with a freezing silence that seems to penetrate the wall. The neighbour, a labourer, has died during the night, and Strindberg reflects upon the fact that all this time he has been lying only a foot away from a dead man. The following day he listens to the preparations for burial, hearing the sounds of the coffin clattering up and down the stairs, and the slow talk of the old women.

Despite the misery and poverty of his surroundings, Strindberg settled into the place in a 'festive mood', according to *The Serving Maid's Son*. 'For the first time, he felt free . . . and discovered a resilience of mind he had never known about, as it had not been called upon until then': these words are taken from a deleted section of *The Red Room* which refers to the novel's hero Arvid Falk—surely an *alter ego* of Strindberg's—who resides in the house on Grev Magnigatan.

5 Korsö Lighthouse. Painting by Strindberg, 1901

He became explosively active: in March, he wrote a long short story about an old eccentric music lover, entitled *For Art's Sake*; in April, the story *The Beginning of Ån Bogsvein's Saga*, in which the measuring ceremony of Strindberg's childhood is described (see p. 21); and in May he started an autobiographical novel with an island setting, appearing in it under the name Örn (eagle). It was round about this time that he started using Örnen (*the* eagle) as a pseudonym. He had chosen Frö (seed), symbolizing the god of fertility, as his name in Runa: now he complemented it with the name of the most regal of birds, symbol of Jupiter.

He established contact with the radical, or neo-liberal, newspaper *Stockholms Aftonpost* and wrote a number of articles on social and artistic matters while also contributing to a new ladies' magazine, *Svalan*. Yet, as he wrote to Eisen, all this was merely 'rubbish that gives me bread for the time being'. His main ambition was engaged in the writing of a major play which he had been drafting since the autumn of 1871 and which he hoped would make him world-famous.

Early in the summer, he and three friends from Uppsala, Eugène Fahlstedt, Algot Lange, and Hugo Philp, moved out to Kymmendö in the Stockholm Archipelago, where they lodged with the island's farmer-fisherman Jonas Eriksson, a former servant who had married the lady of the manor, many years his senior, Susanna Elisabeth Berg. This couple later became the models for the hired hand Carlsson and Madame Flod in the novel *The People of Hemsö*. Strindberg had visited Kymmendö the year before, and during one of these summers he had an experience resembling that on Tyresö. He described it in the *Occult Diary* on 21 November 1900: he and his friends were cruising out of Sandhamn when

> I woke up and went up on deck; didn't know where we were; saw the lighthouse at Korsö in the light of sunrise. Felt ecstatic and saw some perspective on the future, connected with the lighthouse! Many times in my life I have remembered that moment, one of the most wonderful in my life; and I have often wanted to paint the lighthouse as it was at that moment.

On Kymmendö, surrounded by congenial friends and great natural beauty, Strindberg wrote *Master Olof* in one great rush between 8 June and 8 August. It is his play about Luther's disciple Olaus Petri, the father of Sweden's Reformation. King Gustaf Vasa was his powerful patron, but later they came into conflict, and Olaus almost lost his head on the executioner's block.

Most literary works of a stature that makes them milestones in the pages of literary history and spontaneously gains new readers for them in later generations (and only these, one assumes, should be counted among the 'classics') have been written by mature authors. In such works the fictional

characters are of course often young, but not those who create them. But
there is a small number of works—Goethe's *Werther* being perhaps the most
obvious example—in which the young write about the young, and this
makes those works special. Through them we gain an understanding of what
it feels like to be young, not only of what it felt like to have been so in
retrospect. *Master Olof*, the work of a 23-year-old, belongs to this category.

A great number of ideas, impulses, and emotions come into conflict in this
dramatic work, to collapse in a kind of swoon at the end. Reading it, one
finds it hard to decide where the main emphasis lies: in each scene one is
made aware of the author's determination to succeed, to create something
particularly splendid, to compete with the best. At times, this yearning for
glory becomes so obtrusive that the play's characters disappear and only
young Strindberg remains on stage.

In Act I, scene 1, we encounter Olaus Petri, 'Master Olof', in the grounds
of the monastery church at Strängnäs. He is a young Catholic priest, busy
instructing his young confirmands who are to perform the play *Tobiae
Comoedia* which deals with the captivity in Babylon of the children of Israel.
Laurentius Andrée enters and expresses his surprise at Olof's 'playing with
children' at this moment when the great work of liberation, the
Reformation, is about to begin. Olof replies that he is too young, but
Laurentius is quick to quote scripture to him: when Jeremiah tried to excuse
himself by his youth, the Lord declared that he already had been chosen in
his mother's womb to be 'a prophet among many nations'. The imposing
parallel excites Olof, yet he remains hesitant.

But Laurentius does not give up. When Olof expresses his anxiety about
the disgrace which will befall if he rebels against the church, Laurentius tells
him: 'Olof! You were born to vexation; you were born to strike. The Lord
shall heal all wounds.' Olof is won over and has a youthfully ecstatic vision:
he sees an angel coming toward him, bearing a chalice in one hand, a cross in
the other—the emblems of suffering. Now both Jeremiah and Christ stand
by his side.

This is undoubtedly a self-portrait, if an idealized one. Perhaps
Strindberg saw the very same cross and angel related to his own future
during that 'ecstasy' by Korsö lighthouse. But by putting Olof into this
mighty context, the most central in our culture—that of Israel's liberation
which symbolizes that of all mankind; of the prophets who represent
willingness to suffer for truth; and of Christ who shows the way through
suffering—Strindberg, from the very beginning, gives the play a universal
significance.

A little later in the play, Gert Bookprinter tries to persuade Olof to go
beyond spiritual freedom and to strive for political and economic liberation
as well. Again, Olof complains that Gert is trying to drag him into
'misfortune'. And Gert applies exactly the same method of persuasion that

6 Title page of the Kymmendö manuscript of *Master Olof*. University Library of Göteborg

Laurentius found so successful. He tempts Olof with great parallels of other suffering:

> 'Well, if it is misfortune' [he says] 'to be bereft of all earthly happiness, to be dragged to prison, to suffer from poverty, to be scorned and maligned for the sake of truth—then you are not worthy of such great misfortune. I thought that you would understand me; I counted on your help, because you still have the fire, but I can now see that you are tempted by the world; so, swim downstream and be happy!'

These words cause Olof to make up his mind: it is the same siren song of suffering that Strindberg will listen to throughout his life.

In the final scene, Olof makes a speech of apology: he has conspired against the King, he has been imprisoned and condemned to death. Gert, too, condemns him with the play's last line: 'Apostate!' The reader-viewer cannot disregard the possibility that such an ending means bliss for Olof: he concludes the drama of his life condemned by one and all, and thus attains the cross and the bitter cup he has been longing for.

It is, however, possible to give *Master Olof* another reading. Until about 1870 there is no evidence of any political consciousness in Strindberg. 30 November 1868 was a day of great commotion in Stockholm: it was the day of the official unveiling of Karl XII's statue in Kungsträdgarden. Special seating had been erected, but as the general populace was unable to witness the actual ceremony, this led to rioting, stone-throwing and counter-attacks by the police. The day reached a further dramatic climax when the poet and 'people's hero' August Blanche dropped dead in the street after introducing the Uppsala singers who mourned the dead King. In *The Serving Maid's Son* Strindberg gives a lively account of these events and claims that his mother's lower-class origins compelled him to side with the protesters. A few years later he adds that he was one of the stone-throwers, but this definitely seems like a later reconstruction of the truth. There is no reason to believe that he attached any deeper significance to these events at the time.

The trip to Copenhagen in the following year, commemorated in a sonnet sequence, was in fact undertaken by Strindberg as a member of a tour arranged for Royalist Stockholmers to witness the entry of Karl XV into the Danish capital as the Father of the new Crown Princess, Louisa. During that spring, the royal marriage had been the excuse for magnificent festivities in Stockholm, in marked contrast to the poverty and famine that plagued the land in these years: crops failed in Scandinavia in both 1868 and 1869, and more and more people were forced to emigrate. That spring, Stockholmers would wake up to posters distributed during the night with slogans like 'Down with Karl XV!', 'Long live the Republic!', '50,000 riksdaler on Karl XV's head!'

Since then, world history had taken a decisive turn. The Franco-German War of 1870–1 led to the fall of the Napoleonic empire and the birth of the German one. The Paris Commune was created in March 1871. We have no detailed knowledge of Strindberg's reactions to these events, but he sided with France, which was an obvious result of his family's Francophile orientation. In the Runa circle, as his student comrade Axel Jäderin has told us, Strindberg was the only defender of the Commune.

7 The Paris Commune, from *L'Illustration*, 1871

The Outlaw (see p. 34) was written in January 1871, and on 2 February Strindberg read it to his fellow members in Runa. 'The whole world is trembling in these days', the poet Orm says in the play to Thorfinn Jarl, 'because she is about to give birth—in tremendous pain, she will give birth to a glorious hero . . . who will be the ruler of all nations . . . and whose name is the new age!' Orm is prophesying Christianity's approaching conquest of Iceland; yet it must have been hard for the Runa comrades not to relate these words to the tidal wave of revolution that had been rising in France since the autumn of 1870.

In Sweden as elsewhere in Europe the Communards were described as murderers and arsonists, and Socialism was a contagion, a spiritual plague, the rotten fruit of the First International founded by Marx in 1864. It was dangerous to engage in any open opposition to this powerful wave of hate and indignation. Even Victor Hugo—by then one of Strindberg's idols—who had triumphantly returned from his long exile after Napoleon's overthrow could not afford to side with the Commune·in 1872, *l'année terrible*: an excited mob attacked him, and he was forced to leave the country again. But there were more moderate voices: *Stockholms Aftonpost* (and perhaps this was a reason for Strindberg's choosing to write for this paper) and *Dagens Nyheter* pointed out the underlying causes of the rebellion, connecting it with France's revolutionary traditions. *Dagens Nyheter*, to which Strindberg made advances shortly after *Master Olof*'s completion, disapproved of the Commune but was courageous enough to point out that the world had to thank 'the Parisian rabble' for the preservation of the ideals of freedom, and that the Commune's principles belonged to the future.

8 *Erik XIV and Karin Mansdotter*, the painting by Georg von Rosen discussed by Strindberg. National Museum of Sweden

In the spring of 1872 Strindberg adopted the same line. One of his articles in *Stockholms Aftonpost* consists of a review of Georg von Rosen's famous painting of Erik XIV and Göran Persson. In it we see how the King, hesitant and anxious, finds himself compelled to sign a fatal document by his popular advisor Göran Persson, who is presented as a dark, demonic figure.

Persson, Strindberg writes, is a representative of the people, and the hatred expressed in his face has been generated by oppression. The document in his hand is directed against the abuse of power and those who engage in it, and dictated by a sense of justice. If Persson is a criminal, his crime is only one link in a justified chain of retribution.

With *Master Olof*, a few months later, Strindberg took a further step. During the summer of the play's composition, the people of Stockholm were treated to balloon trips by visiting Frenchmen who had, according to *Dagens Nyheter*, 'made aerial sorties from Paris during the siege of that city'. One July day, a M. Pascal was blown across Saltsjön, and perhaps his balloon could be seen from Kymmendö. But Strindberg did not need such obvious reminders. The Commune was an active presence in his mind, and its violent eruption joined his own youthful will to effect change in the world. Gert Bookprinter's lines express the nineteenth century's longing for a more equitable society, and Strindberg demonstrates for the first time that he speaks not just for himself but for many. By now, he was familiar with Stockholm's social miseries. His duties as an elementary schoolteacher included visits to students' homes, and the descriptions of the Södern slums in *The Red Room* reflect what he saw on those visits.

A number of distinguished scholars have analysed how ideas from George Brandes, whose *Main Currents Part One* Strindberg read with passionate agreement in the spring of 1872; from Thomas Buckle's *History of Civilization* and its vision of society which is not too far removed from that of Marx; from Edvard von Hartmann, Kierkegaard, and several other influential thinkers of the time, were cast into the bubbling cauldron of Strindberg's mind and transformed in it. Nevertheless, what makes *Master Olof* original and great is Strindberg's fidelity to his own experiences, his attention to life, not books.

In the play, Olof first proceeds along religiously reformist lines, until Gert teaches him that spiritual freedom cannot be gained unless secular power is seized as well (this is reminiscent of Buckle). Thus, he joins the conspiracy against the King. When Gert shows Olof the book he himself, the bookprinter, is writing, it comes to represent the later literature of social indignation. About its contents, Gert says:

> 'On every page you will read a cry of complaint, a sigh of thousands who have been blind enough to believe that God's will obliged them to suffer from oppression; who believed that it was their duty not to *dare* to believe in their liberation. . . . The eyes of the people have been opened, there is heat and ferment, soon the oppressors will be crushed, and the people will be free!'

Gert dies indomitably defiant, his hope for the future intact, thus imitating the Communards who reportedly had died in that spirit. Allan

Hagsten is probably right in his claim that Gert's penultimate lines—those preceding 'Apostate'—are not of religious but of political significance. 'Farewell, Olof!' he says. 'Take care of my daughter, and never forget the great Whit Sunday!' In 1871, Whit Sunday was on 28 May. That same day General McMahon, commander of the Bordeaux Government's forces, issued a famous order announcing that the Commune had been crushed for ever. Thus Gert was not alluding to the dispensation of the Holy Spirit but to the rebels' death and hope of resurrection.

4

After the play's completion, *Master Olof* was submitted to the Royal Theatre. But September was to be a month of mourning, for both Strindberg and his country. On the 18th, Karl XV passed away after ceremoniously bidding farewell to his people, these being represented at his deathbed by grief-stricken courtiers. At approximately the same time, Strindberg's play was rejected. According to Gustaf Uddgren, Strindberg first heard rumours of this rejection at La Croix's café on Norrbro. He became suddenly indisposed and had to leave.

This marked the end of royal favours, from both throne and theatre. Later, Strindberg would often describe the Sweden of Karl XV's reign as an era of pomp and festivity, and the King himself as an enlightened sceptic who knew that the people wanted to be presented with spectacles. In a letter of late September 1872, Strindberg reveals his disappointment at the refusal together with his dislike for the new regime. 'Pietism will be the new state religion,' he writes after having met the new King, Oscar II, in the street, accompanied by a representative of the upper-class pietism that became one of the characteristics of the late nineteenth century—a piously gilt-edged foil to the dreams of secular revolution among the people. Strindberg was not mistaken in perceiving Oscar II as an enemy. His letter is the first round of a feud between king and poet that lasted thirty-five years.

According to the painter Per Ekström, who had also been favoured by Karl XV, he and Strindberg fled to Djurgården on 9 October, the day of the King's funeral. There they sat down to sketch pine trees, turning their backs on the city where cannon were booming and churchbells ringing out over the royal benefactor's dead body.

After the summer they had spent together, Strindberg had chosen Eugène Fahlstedt as his favourite correspondent. In a letter to him dated 26 September, Strindberg describes himself as mentally torn to shreds, close to madness, and tired of all of humanity. He writes that only the stupid, selfish, violent, and rich succeed in this world, and that he refuses to be their buffoon. In its heat and passion this letter far exceeds the suicidal one to his cousin; here, too, he bids farewell to life, reassuring his friend that he is being driven to his death by nothing so ignoble as ruined finances and an empty stomach, but rather by the insight that he is 'irretrievably lost'. The official reason given for *Master Olof*'s rejection was that the play lacked respect for the sanctity of history. The era regarded reverence for 'historical truth' as one of its main virtues. It is, however, quite likely that the readers suspected that there was a political wolf lurking in the religious wings. Then as now it was regarded as reprehensible to censor literary works on the grounds of opinions expressed in them. It was safer to camouflage such censorship with historical and aesthetic objections.

A few years later Strindberg wrote to the theatre director Ludvig Josephson that Frans Hedberg 'must have been ordained by Providence to be my particular nemesis!' A few more years passed, and in 1886 he used even stronger language. Talking about *Master Olof* and Hedberg in a letter to Albert Bonnier he wrote that Hedberg had committed a crime by using his position of power, which he had gained 'without commensurate ability', to 'hold back an entire era'.

5

Although Strindberg had come up against a wall of steel, the shock of the impact had not dulled his senses. He instantly proceeded to take effective measures for survival. Far below the higher literary echelons patronized by the King and rewarded by the academy, there were those of the freelance journalists and littérateurs who made a living from all kinds of hackwork. The latter had an especially low social status: they translated serial novels, wrote daily 'occasional' verse, and composed broadsides and texts for cliché plates purchased by publishers and newspapers. Many of them were willing tools of the yellow press, notably the tabloid *Fäderneslandet* (*The Father-land*), and not infrequently practised a little blackmail on the side.

In eighteenth-century England the collective designation for such pen-pushers was Grub Street, since that is where many of them lived under miserable conditions. As his brilliant biographer W. Jackson Bate tells us, Samuel Johnson received a large part of his intellectual and moral up-bringing on Grub Street, gaining psychological and linguistic insights for life. The same can be said about Strindberg, although conditions were considerably more pleasant in the Stockholm of his day than they had been in the London of the preceding century. But he did describe the two years after *Master Olof* as a period of debasement, and it is possible that he actually felt that way at the time. In a letter written in 1870 he equates the hack writer with the dockland ruffian and promises that he will never sink to such depths. In actual fact, these years were an apprenticeship of great significance for his further development. He took in real life as it was lived on the streets and in bars, and this sense of reality would become an antidote to sentimentality and flights of romantic fancy.

Before the rejection of his play, Strindberg had written his article 'Life in the Stockholm Archipelago', his first exploration of the Aladdin's cave that island life and nature was to become for him. He sent the article to *Dagens Nyheter*, whose proprietor and editor-in-chief Rudolf Wall printed it on 4 September 1872.

At about the same time, Strindberg met a certain Otto Samson who had started an insurance company, Nordstjärnan (The North Star), the preceding year. Through Bonnier's publishing company, Samson commissioned an article extolling the value of life insurance, and Strindberg accepted the commission, writing a brisk short story about young Mia who is visiting Stockholm and writing home to her fiancé Axel in the provinces. As it happens, right across the street from her uncle's apartment on Drottninggatan shines the name 'Nordstjärnan' in large golden letters. Her uncle, who is a commercial dignitary, starts holding forth about the usefulness of life insurance policies; Mia listens and gains additional respect for the Nordstjärna emblem as she witnesses how a maternal uncle, who was uninsured, departs this life, leaving behind a wife and six children unprovided for. Samson liked the piece and offered Strindberg a job as editor of an insurance magazine which was intended to function in the same way as the short story about Mia. Strindberg accepted and spent a considerable part of 1873 working for this concern.

During the two 'years of degradation' Strindberg passed through various phases and laid the foundation for a knowledge of society that he would use to the utmost in the satirical part of his work. The insurance magazine, *Svenska Försäkringstidning*, folded after six months. Small wonder: clever as Strindberg had been to get the job, he quickly perceived what he had to do to get rid of it again. Not only did he direct harsh and sometimes unfair criticism against certain named insurance companies, but he questioned the legitimacy of the entire business; maritime insurance became his favourite target, later exploited in *The Red Room*. The British MP Plimsoll had launched a virulent attack against this branch of the business, and following his lead Strindberg wrote in his magazine about British and German shipowners' disregard for their sailors' lives. He wrote that these magnates, in order to collect, had no scruples about arranging to rid themselves of a worn-out vessel, with total disregard for the crew's fate.

In the autumn of 1873, Strindberg undertook a veritable cross-country odyssey, pursued by creditors. He had left Grev Magnigatan in the summer. For a few weeks, he worked in Göteborg as a bit-part player in a theatre. On 12 October he arrived in Sandhamn, where he was accepted as an apprentice at the telegraph station. Sharp-eyed as ever, he used this time to write a remarkable article about a shipwreck, with an appended captain's protest.

Dagens Nyheter responded enthusiastically to the shipwreck story, which was not surprising, as it was fast-moving, amusing and full of authentic dialogue. In December 1873, Strindberg became a permanent staff writer.

As was the custom then, he wrote about a wide range of subjects for the newspaper. As a drama critic, he got his revenge in digs against the Royal Theatre, but he also covered debates in the Diet, reviewed art exhibitions, made pronouncements on Iceland's Constitution, gave a positive review to Anders Fryxell's anti-royalist *History of Sweden*, which became one of his main sources for his dramatic work, and urged readers to purchase good copies of classical works of art—a new method of colour reproduction, chromography, had just been invented—rather than mediocre Swedish originals that would cost ten times as much. This met with some strong reactions: a humorous magazine depicted Strindberg as a donkey wearing a dunce's cap with the letters DN on it, engaged in kicking over a painter's easel.

His excessive wilfulness made him enemies within the paper as well. In May 1874, he retorted sharply to a remark made by Wall and walked out, never to return. According to an eyewitness he did this after flinging his pen away with such force that it pierced a Norwegian, a Danish, and a French newspaper and lodged itself firmly in the tabletop underneath. The steel pens of that time were solid instruments.

During the winter with *Dagens Nyheter* he lived in Djurgården with his brother Axel who had first rented Villa Diorama on Djurgårdsslätten and then moved to a house at Oakhill.

A casual piece, entitled 'Spring in Djurgården', is an internal and external 'situation report' of this period. In it, he describes himself as a lonely wanderer, tense, sensitive and poor, trying to cure his self-pity by means of jokes and cynicism. As he walks home from work in the evenings, two dogs attack him regularly, by the sixth lamp-post on the pontoon bridge leading to Djurgården. Because of them, he carries a stone in his pocket, all the way from Skeppsholmen.

Spring marks the beginning of a series of humiliations. The spring sun reveals his overcoat to be green with age, the buttonholes turning white, ancient stains reappearing in the fabric. One night he walks into his customary pub only to find that no one greets him, and that there is nowhere to sit except at the cab drivers' table.

This is his first draft of a self-portrait as an outcast—one whom everybody despises, yet who is the object of everybody's attention.

Chapter Three

SIRI VON ESSEN

I

IN THE SPRING of 1874 Strindberg moved from Djurgården into town, renting a room at no. 18 Kaptensgatan. He lived there for three and a half years: a long time for someone who was constantly on the move. His room was on the top floor and had two mansard windows from which he could see the sailing vessels teeming in Nybro harbour: Strandvägen's magnificent row of buildings did not yet exist to obstruct the view. As Strindberg told Gustaf af Geijerstam many years later, he could even see a building going up on Blasieholmen that was to play a prominent part in his life: a new theatre, which was in fact called 'Nya teatern', with three rows of boxes and capacity for an audience of 1,050. It was nearing completion in the autumn of 1874, and Strindberg hoped that *Master Olof* would be its inaugural play.

From 1872 to 1877, Strindberg's life is intertwined with this play: he and Master Olof are twin brothers, one of flesh and blood, the other a creature of the imagination, a shadow. Yet while observing them one finds that they sometimes fuse or exchange roles. In the room on Kaptensgatan, the new theatre building going up before his very eyes, Strindberg proceeded to subject his manuscript to thorough revision. It is difficult to decide how much of the transformation is due to opportunistic concessions, how much to a genuine change in Strindberg's view of life. Master Olof had been a man who after initial doubts and hesitations dedicated himself to a cause, then betrayed it, and was condemned. Now, in the revised version, he became a reformer who learned that one cannot bend the bow too hard; that it is the right-minded man's duty to become an apostate, if he wants to effect any change in this world. Gert, the noble revolutionary, now became a blinkered sectarian whom no one could take seriously. No longer did he cry 'Apostate!' at the end—that exclamation was assigned to one of Olof's confirmands, and Olof replies, calmly, that such ideas belong to youth, but that age brings maturity and compromise.

Thus Strindberg and Master Olof joined forces in order to gain social acceptance—but in vain. In December 1874 Strindberg submitted the play to the director of the new theatre, the famous sixty-year-old actor Edvard Stjernström. In February, the play was returned to Strindberg having been turned down. Stjernström wrote that he felt 'the great world-renowned names were not done proper justice' but acknowledged 'the play's beautiful message', a compliment that must have sounded like mockery to Strindberg. A few days later Strindberg wrote to Frans Hedberg that he had considered destroying the manuscript but had decided against it. 'My play', he wrote, 'had mutated into an obsession, for which, for two years, I sacrificed everything and ruined my economic position.' He declared himself willing to undertake yet another revision if the Royal Theatre would give him a chance.

> But if I should undertake such a task without any hope of success, I would grow weary, and if I grew weary, my career as an author would be absolutely finished. Perhaps there are many who would regard this as a gain for the art, and welcome it as a laudable enterprise. I do not know what you, Herr Hedberg, feel about the matter these days. That is, indeed, what I hope to hear from you at your convenience.

2

In December 1874 Strindberg was given an appointment to Stockholm's Royal Library, with the title 'Royal e.o. secretary'. Like Master Olof, he compromises, gives in to society's demands.

Earlier that year, in *Svenska Medborgaren* (*The Swedish Citizen*), he had published two articles full of praise for the Library, calling it 'the foremost educational institution of the people'. He also stressed the library's need for more staff and funds. The articles demonstrated an astonishing range of knowledge, gleaned from his former teacher at Klara School, Richard Bergström, who had become a librarian. The Royal Library's director, Gustav Edward Klemming, clearly remembered the articles when he approved Strindberg's application with special permission, which was necessary because Strindberg did not have any academic degrees. One good turn deserves another. In the autumn Strindberg travelled to Uppsala to obtain private certifications from his professors, and this also proved helpful.

In the revised play, Master Olof had become a 'pastor primarius', without any pangs of conscience, and August Strindberg became a civil servant at the same time. He had visiting cards printed, with the legend 'August Strindberg, e.o. amanuensis of the Royal Library'. In his autobiography, he makes much of the social standing the appointment gave him, contrasting it with the miserable existence he had been leading until then which, with typical hyperbole, he equated with that of 'the lowliest proletarian'.

Nevertheless, being an 'extraordinary amanuensis' meant little more than holding the title. The appointment involved few duties and equally few rights. At that time, it was the custom for young men to secure appointments to a number of government offices and then visit their desks very infrequently: later, in *The Red Room*, Strindberg would satirize this practice with considerable relish. Salaries were entirely nominal. In 1875, Strindberg's combined income from the library was 180 kronor, of which 130 was his salary and 50 a bonus. During the following two years his annual salary increased to 140 and 150 kronor; the rent for the room on Kaptensgatan was 200 kronor a year.

In reality, Strindberg went on living the insecure life of a hack writer, taking on whatever jobs and commissions there were, and also working as a part-time teacher at Hilda Widell's private school for girls. One of his students, Gurli Linder, remembered him as a slim, elegant man in a dark blue serge suit; his voice was soft and melodious, and he was a demanding and engaging teacher, especially in the subjects of history and natural sciences; students adored him but found him humourless, incapable of 'looking at himself, and at life, with any degree of detachment'. He wrote captions for reproductions of famous works of art for the illustrated monthly *Förr och Nu* (*Then and Now*). He translated *Dagens Nyheter*'s serial novel for a fee of 40 kronor a month. He was caught up in a vicious circle of loans and repayments that would become part of his everyday life—a cause for continuous complaint, yet at times, it seems, adding a kind of spice to his life as well. To Eugène Fahlstedt, one of his creditors, he writes on 18 April 1875: 'My financial situation is desperate, to say the least. A tailor's final statement and a bail bond with a threat of a summons as well as six demand notes have been causing me anxiety during this part of April.'

He assures Fahlstedt that the need to work all day long just in order to eat has made him into a 'decided Communard'.

> I feel capable of writing verses for the coronation for a half-dozen oysters my anaemic body craves; I'll go and take communion for a steak. All the dinners I've missed cry out for revenge, all postponed pleasures roar like lions, all good intentions have decayed from lack of air and light and have turned into sheer ambition. I am currently reading *La Terreur*, Paris 1853, st. 8:0 2.v. I have decided to create a stir in the world, at any cost, except that of physical discomfort!

One of the intentions of the letter's emphasis on Strindberg's penury was to invoke Fahlstedt's patience in regard to the money Strindberg owed him. Strindberg was to use these tactics frequently, and would develop the art of startling the world without resorting to physical suffering.

At this time, the Royal Library was housed in the north-east wing of the Royal Palace. Uno Willers, Royal Librarian from 1949 to 1977, speaks in his book *Strindberg as a Library Man* of the wretchedness of the place: the Library was filthy, inadequately heated, and conditions were very cramped. A new building was under construction in Humlegården.

Looking north from the north-east wing, one could see out over Norrbro with its row of low houses, its bookshops and cafés. At noon, the Royal Guard would come marching to the accompaniment of a band, to relieve the watch around the Palace. Strindberg could see its progress across the bridge from a window 'directly opposite the left lion', to quote a direction given by himself.

Despite such touches of royal glamour, day-to-day life at the Library was tough. In the big room overlooking the bridge winter temperatures approximated those outdoors: a fur coat—'the Library fur'—hung on the wall for the use of those employees who dared go there. The caretakers had the worst of it. In December 1877 Strindberg drafted a petition to the King for a pension for the widow and five children of a caretaker who had died at the age of forty-five. His premature demise, Strindberg wrote, had been caused by 'continuous and diligent work in the Library's cold, draughty and damp rooms'.

3

Most of the documentary material on Strindberg's life from the spring of 1875 has a surface appearance of gloom and penury, with an undercurrent of vigour and happiness. Strindberg renders his adversities with such brilliance that they no longer seem painful. In a photograph taken in April 1875, he is looking directly past the viewer, with an expression which combines youthful voracity and arrogance: something of a wolf ready to attack the sheep. The lips are closed; above them is a moustache that is still downy and not too well groomed. His hair does not have its later leonine quality: it is softly waved and grows down low on the neck. An artfully tied cravat adorns the starched white collar. His girls' school student considered him elegant (see p. 50): all his life he would take great care of his clothes, buying new ones as often as he could, and complaining vociferously if anything was wrong with them. He reacted with positive revulsion to the least indication of decay or dilapidation, in himself as well as others.

9 Portrait of Strindberg, April 1875

Our information on this virile young man's relationships with the opposite sex is incomplete because Strindberg himself worked hard to keep them secret. He provided intimate reports on his marriages: about other liaisons he was as discreet as was customary in his day and age. In *The Red Room* and elsewhere he wrote about times with male friends during the 1870s; about young men supporting one another, borrowing clothes for festive occasions, drinking, gossiping. Only when the evening was well underway did they go to visit girls. Whenever this is mentioned, Strindberg adopts the kind of casual tone he might use to order a late sandwich and a beer at a tavern. This is entirely in keeping with the spirit of the times.

However, we do have some details about one relationship. In December 1873, just after getting his job with *Dagens Nyheter*, Strindberg met a woman at an informal party with friends. She was a waitress, her name was Ida Charlotta Olsson, and she became his lover. By all accounts, she belonged to a circle of women who were available to 'better-class' gentlemen without any obligation of marriage.

Strindberg's association with her lasted until April 1875. Sometime during 1874 he tried to persuade a friend to take her off his hands: there is a somewhat cryptic letter concerning that transaction. In March 1875, Ida Charlotta became pregnant, and on 19 December she gave birth to a son, Johan. *The Serving Maid's Son* discreetly relates this episode: Strindberg's paternity is denied and Ida Charlotta—not of course mentioned by name—appears as a married woman, gone astray, who takes the active part in the liaison. Strindberg claimed that she even followed him to the editorial offices of *Dagens Nyheter* after he had tried to break with her. When he gained the appointment at the Royal Library, she became even more afraid of losing him. She tried to gain the upper hand by being unfaithful to him: this gave him cause to send her packing, and to transfer his affections to a young woman of good family.

Strindberg's relationship had elements of unreality; in a fragment from the *Inferno* period the woman is described as a whore; but as they cannot be verified, we have to pass them by. We do not know with any certainty whether or not Strindberg was the father of the child who was given his middle name: no doubt he suspected this to be the case. His accusation of infidelity is exactly of the kind to which many men in similar situations tend to resort. Nevertheless, it was possibly true. Strindberg's conception of a man's responsibilities was unquestionably frivolous, even brutal in modern terms. When, a few years later, his friend Carl Larsson was suspected of having got a maid pregnant, Strindberg provided him with cynical advice and regarded the whole thing as a joke: not a word about the tragedy it was for the mother. In a letter to Larsson he says he has heard that all that is required is to give the girl 'a fifty' which will 'be enough for a year, if you want to avoid the expensive orphanage, as it's always possible that the child will die!' He concludes with a postscript: 'Next time you fuck those girls, don't forget to put something in between!'—a revealing example of that group's sense of bawdy camaraderie.

It seems likely that it was actually a painful decision to part ways with Ida Charlotta just as she became pregnant. The attachment to the girl of good family—her name was Elisabeth Cervin, and she was a friend of Strindberg's sisters—did not last long, and perhaps its main function was to block out Strindberg's feelings of guilt. What letters remain from it— indeed, Strindberg was so proud of them that he incorporated them in *The Serving Maid's Son*—are literary exercises in the vein of Heine and Byron. A typical witticism: considering the general misery of the world, God should have created butterflies so that they would hatch with insecticide on their wings instead of 'that oft-praised powder'.

Later, Strindberg would dedicate himself to vigorous attacks against the kind of affected wooing that these letters express. He had practised the art himself, and pondered, early on, the abyss that existed between erotic practice and erotic lyricism: more material in this respect was coming his way.

4

The infatuation with Elisabeth was no more than a prelude: she merely paved the way for what was to come.

One of Strindberg's friends from his student days, Algot Lange, was a singer-actor employed by the Swedish Theatre in Helsinki. In May 1875 he asked Strindberg to look after his fiancée, the pianist Ina Forstén, who was coming to visit Stockholm. Strindberg did so with a certain thoroughness.

Ina Forstén had a friend, Siri von Essen, a Finland Swede like herself, who was married to a Swedish captain, Baron Carl Gustaf Wrangel. As the Wrangels were passionately fond of the theatre, Ina Forstén decided to introduce Strindberg to them and arranged for the young author and Baroness Wrangel to meet.

This meeting took place in late May or early June 1875—Strindberg himself was uncertain about the date, but other details imprinted themselves on his memory with great force. He returned many times to this moment that became a decisive one in his life: the first time in a poem, 'Sailing'.

Det var på Drottninggatan	*It was on Drottninggatan*
en brinnande junidag	*one fiery day in June*
på trånga trottoaren	*on the crowded sidewalk*
vi möttes du och jag.	*that we met, you and I.*

In the poem, the primary memory is of a blue veil that floats above the lady's blonde hair. In *The Serving Maid's Son* Strindberg adds that she was wearing 'a small Japanese hat' under that veil, and in *A Fool's Apology*, the novel about his relationship with Siri von Essen which he wrote in 1887, he expands the description to include her 'shoulders like those of a princess', her figure 'slender as a switch', and 'a way of inclining her head toward one that was at once relaxed, respectful, and distinguished'.

Sigrid Sofia Mathilda Elisabeth von Essen was born on 17 August 1850, and was thus a little over a year younger than Strindberg. Her grandfather, General Odert Reinhold von Essen, had been a hero of the Swedish–Russian War of 1808–9 which separated Finland from Sweden. Runeberg dedicates one of the poems in *Ensign Stål's Legends* to Essen, making him out to have been a corpulent figure, both courageous and irascible. Siri's father, Carl Reinhold von Essen, had also been an officer but resigned his commission to take care of Jackarby, the family estate. He married a Swede, Elisabeth In de Betou. A combination of mismanagement and hard times forced him to sell the estate and to move to Sweden with what modest capital remained. Siri had grown up at Jackarby, where her grandfather's glorious memory was the family's primary heirloom. She loved the outdoor life, especially riding, and according to her daughter Karin Smirnoff who wrote an excellent book about her, her nickname was 'Careless Siri'. She had light blonde hair, dark eyes, a beautiful forehead and a determined chin. As befitted her station in life, she had gone to a convent school in Paris and spoke French well; otherwise, her education had been sketchy, and she was apt to spell the word *kjol* (skirt) as *tjol*—something which Strindberg would later point out as one of her shortcomings. She was an only child, spoiled and accustomed to being the centre of attention. Strindberg's start in life had been different: rivalry for attention with six brothers and sisters. When, at the beginning of their love affair, he acted as her humble servant, that was a game both of them were well equipped to play. In *A Fool's Apology* he compares Siri to the goddesses of antiquity: she does not resemble Venus with her firm breasts and strong hips; nor is she like Juno, the mother, the woman with child who exhibits her body proudly; even less like Minerva, flat-chested under male armour. Strindberg decides that Siri has her counterpart in Diana, goddess of the hunt and the night, cruel in her chastity which nature imposes on her—too much the boy, not enough the girl, roused to anger when she is surprised at her ablutions. What we know about Siri does confirm that image: she was not obtrusively femine, but rather *gamine*; not remote, but immediate and active.

Siri as Diana is the prototype of the women Strindberg fell in love with and described in his work. One is aware of the presence of the goddess of the hunt even in his most famous female character, Miss Julie: the description of Siri applies to her as well.

Siri's parents worked hard to arrange a suitable marriage for her. She became one of the beauties of Stockholm. The Crown Prince himself, later Oscar II, whom Strindberg had already chosen as an adversary, danced the *française* with her at a palace ball in 1872. It was her dream to become an actress, but her parents resisted that: as a consolation, they allowed her to study at the Musical Academy. One of her many attractive features was her pretty soprano voice, although after a couple of years she had to give up her musical studies, due to an inflammation of her vocal chords. In the course of her social life she met the then Lieutenant Baron Carl Gustaf Wrangel, and without showing any signs of passion she married him on 17 August 1872— her own birthday. On 16 June 1873, their daughter Sigrid was born.

Wrangel's commission was with the Svea Guard, the most distinguished of the infantry regiments, whose commander was the King himself. Wrangel came from a family that could trace its origins back to the thirteenth century. Its most famous member was his namesake Field Marshal Count Carl Gustaf Wrangel, one of the greatest Swedish heroes of the Thirty Years' War, who later built the Palais Wrangel that towered with its turrets and mighty façade above the house on Riddarholmen where Strindberg was born.

At the meeting on Drottninggatan Siri invited Strindberg to visit her at home. The Wrangels lived at no. 12, Norrtullsgatan, in the same apartment rented by the Strindberg family between October 1864 and April 1867, a coincidence that neither Strindberg himself nor a subsequent series of psychological interpreters failed to exploit. It fits almost too well into the Oedipal pattern that Sigmund Freud was yet to describe: Strindberg enters his parental home in order to kill his father, represented by Wrangel, and to marry his mother or, alternatively, stepmother, in the form of the charming Baroness.

During the summer and autumn of 1875 Strindberg was a daily visitor to the Wrangel home. When he assures us in his autobiography that he was unable to fall in love with a woman of robust shape, who had ugly fingernails and large feet, this may well be an echo of his thoughts during that period, when the waitress Ida Charlotta had to compete with the aristocratic Siri in his consciousness.

Three-cornered friendships tend not to stand much of a chance in this world, and this one was potentially explosive from the very beginning. The surviving letters allow us to follow the progress of the triangle drama, day by day. At first, Strindberg conceals his passion behind various masks. He makes his entrance as the young Baroness's disinterested adviser. She still dreams of the theatre, but for the wife of an officer in a distinguished regiment those have to remain dreams. Strindberg tries to persuade her to take up a literary career instead, and even compiles a handbook in the art of writing for her.

Next came a routine in which he described his own situation as 'an admittedly failed author' and claimed to feel unworthy of the Wrangels' friendship. Now that he had become a civil servant, he continued, he had to

> hear how those who hate me find themselves in the right, and what is worst, how even those who secretly love me but can never admit it lose their illusions, and in the privacy of their hearts weep over him who they had hoped one day would be their spokesman, and the spokesman of all the oppressed, in front of those who inherit or steal power; I feel like a deaf-mute, as I cannot speak and am not permitted to write; sometimes I stand in the middle of my room that seems like a prison cell, and then I want to scream so that walls and ceilings would fly apart, and I have so much to scream about, and therefore I remain silent.

This feeling of frustration, muteness, imprisonment in a cell would seem to be a truer characteristic of Strindberg at this point than his labours to transform *Master Olof* into a champion of resignation.

Not content with concealing his true emotions behind literary advice, Strindberg also pretended to have lost his heart to Ina Forstén. In a letter dated 3 August and addressed to both Wrangels he claimed that he had placed a rose in front of Ina Forstén's portrait and lit a candle as well, as upon an altar. He then proceeded to concoct a drama of jealousy in which Algot Lange threatened him with a revolver, while he himself was weighed down with pangs of conscience over the seduction of a friend's betrothed.

It did not take Strindberg long to discover that his presence in Siri's home found a piquant complication in a pretty nineteen-year-old cousin of hers, Sofia In de Betou, with whom Wrangel had fallen in love. It was possible that Wrangel even welcomed a young man in the house, to generate permission and opportunity for him in regard to the young lady. Strindberg, concerned for his manly honour, found himself in an embarrassing dilemma. He had to choose between being a St George who wins the virgin-countess, imprisoned in the tower of marriage, or an assistant gardener who has been enticed into the salon to service what the count himself has rejected.

In his biblical sequence of novels, Thomas Mann has analysed the temptation Potiphar's wife presented to Joseph. She stood not only for extravagant erotic pleasure but also for Egypt's opulent culture, its treasures, insights, and aesthetic values. To possess her was to take a short cut, to conquer the alien empire by means of direct physical contact. In *The Serving Maid's Son* Strindberg claimed that a man could fall in love only with a woman of his own or a higher station in life. Siri was a symbol for his own rise in the world. Her husband was not only the scion of an illustrious family; he also wore the uniform which in the authoritarian Sweden of those days was a mark of power. To win Siri was to share those vestments of authority.

Strindberg was extremely familiar with both biblical Josephs: the one whom Potiphar's wife tried to seduce, and the one who had to bear the stigma of the immaculate conception. Yet, as the American scholar Harry G. Carlson has demonstrated, his particular interest lay in Joseph's innocence and the Egyptian seductress's guilt. In his copy of Dante's *Divine Comedy*, Strindberg inscribed an apparently approving 'NB' in the margin of the passage in Canto XXX where Dante assigns one of the most severe infernal punishments to Potiphar's wife. This does not mean that he would have been unable to comprehend the interpretation Thomas Mann was to present many years later: we will return to this matter in the chapter on *Miss Julie*.

Siri was in a difficult position. Strindberg was in love with her, her husband rejected her. But if she admitted the Baron's rejection, she ran the danger of devaluating herself. On the other hand, a new marriage could give her the freedom to become an actress. The Wrangel home began to resemble nothing so much as the set of a farce with a strong love interest. During their excursions *à quatre*, Wrangel fondled Sofia and let Strindberg court his wife. How far was it possible to go before an officer's honour had to assert itself? In the Wrangels' case, pretty far.

That autumn, Strindberg made an attempt to extricate himself from the situation. He wrote to Rudolf Wall, asking to be sent to Paris for a month.

> Buy me—alive; I am quite cheap. I believe that the debauching influence of a sojourn in Paris would improve my style, lend colour to the narrative, and make the tone of it appropriately callous—I believe I could be an excellent writer if I were allowed to live, because I am no longer embarrassed by any kind of conviction, and I believe that the French way of looking at things would liberate me completely from that morbidity that generates unhealthy notions of living, that is to say, dying, starving to death for ideas, which is just a prettier name for stubborn fixations, no matter how crazy.

He did leave Stockholm: on 6 October, he embarked on the steamship *Motala*, destination Le Havre. The evening before he invited his friends to supper at his apartment on Kaptensgatan. The description of that party is one of the best passages in *A Fool's Apology*: Strindberg gives a detailed description of his smartened-up room—the derelict wicker sofa covered with an imitation tiger skin, the cracks in the light fixture artfully concealed with a garland of inorganic ivy. Karin Smirnoff says in her book that it was during this farewell party that Siri realized what she had long feared subconsciously: she was saying goodbye not to a friend but to a lover.

Strindberg's trip did not take him very far. He got off the boat in Dalarö and sent the Wrangels a telegram saying that he had fallen ill. The same evening he wrote an excited letter to Carl Gustaf Wrangel, in which he described himself as madly in love with Ina Forstén, continuing to use his well-practised double talk. He writes that his soul has grown to be as one with hers; 'every little thing in my room stood in its right place, for her sake.' Now he is bedridden, his fever is rising, he is like unto Saul, persecuted by the Lord. He mentions that he has sent for a clergyman and assures Wrangel that he has found his Saviour.

A Fool's Apology contains an extended description of Strindberg's trip to Dalarö. The protagonist, Axel, finds his senses numbed by a deadly love potion. He rushes out into the woods, searching through the fallen leaves for tracks of his beloved's enchanting feet—in the summer, the Wrangels and Strindberg had made a joint excursion to Dalarö. Strindberg lets Axel howl with despair, decide to die, take off his clothes and dive into the ice-cold water, only to get out, climb a tree and sit there naked.

Strindberg scholars have drawn far-reaching conclusions from the Dalarö episode, regarding it as proof that Strindberg experienced a serious psychic crisis or even manifested signs of mental illness at that time. They reach that conclusion by considering the passage in *A Fool's Apology* as strictly autobiographical, filling in details with the letter of 7 October. But the *Apology* is a novel, and it seems to me that the letter, like the letters to Elisabeth and the cries of distress to friends, is a literary product, as Gunnar Brandell also has pointed out. It was written in a state of creative intoxication similar to the one Strindberg first experienced in the room at Dr Lamm's house on Västra Trädgårdsgatan.

It is possible that Strindberg went for a swim. It is possible that he roamed the woods. We do know that he really did send for a man of the cloth; yet all these actions seem more symbolic than anything else, and his alleged state of extreme agitation is described with remarkable linguistic control. Do phrases like the following really sound as if they had been written by someone who has just tried to take his life?

> What are all of Antwerp's cathedrals and the artistic rubbish of the Louvre compared to injury to a human soul—I have rebelled against God—I have blasphemed [the blasphemy consisting of his having called his beloved his 'Christ and saviour']—I have wrestled with him like Jacob—Saul! Saul! no one cried that though—but now my hip-tendon is lame—Pity me and forget me—the most noble of human beings— because that is who you are—because you have always recognized the likeness of God that I have tried to besmirch within myself—I shall never forget you—you have saved me from the belief that *all* human beings are wretches—God once promised to spare a city if there were two—Should he ever decide to punish your city I'll say to him: halt! there are two here and what's more they have a friend whom they will make as good and who will teach people that they do not need to be vile if they do not want to!

Perturbed by the telegram, the Wrangels rushed to Delarö. They found Strindberg in bed, and the Baroness fussed over him. In *A Fool's Apology*

Strindberg says that he felt like the wolf 'who has devoured grandmother
and now lies in her bed preparing to gulp down Little Red Riding Hood as
well'. He may get closer to the truth in that sentence than he did in his
biblical guise in the letter.

Alone again on 10 October, Strindberg wrote a long and carefully
composed letter to the Wrangels. It includes two bad poems as well as an
inadvertent passage he would come to regret:

> Oh, if Carl only knew what a good turn he has done me by demonstrating
> to my old beloved, prejudiced, disillusioned father that there was
> someone who believed in me and that I had not merely 'attached myself'
> to an acquaintance flattering to myself which would dissolve again on the
> first occasion!

Evidently there had been hints that Strindberg was a social fortune hunter.
Wrangel had obviously reassured Strindberg's perturbed father, who had
heard about his son's precipitated debarkation at Dalarö from the *Motala*'s
captain, who was a friend of his. When, some years later, Strindberg edited
his and Siri's correspondence for publication, he took care to cross out the
cited passage with energetic strokes of the pen.

5

After a few more days, Strindberg returned to Kaptensgatan, despite his
protestations of 7 October that he never wanted to see his room again. The
winter passed with new developments in the love drama and without the
slightest trace of madness in the recently distressed lover.

According to a letter from Siri to Ina Forstén, Strindberg visited the
Wrangels on Christmas Eve 1875, on his way to his parental home, bearing
'a profusion of the sweetest presents' for little Sigrid, for whom he is 'Uncle
Augis', as well as a 'charming bouquet' for little Sigrid's mother. In January
1876 Siri read, on Strindberg's recommendation, Flaubert's *Madame
Bovary* and found her to be 'a bit of a monster'. The judgement may reflect
her own self-defence against adultery. In February, she asked Strindberg to
forget 'that I am a woman', which naturally inflamed his passion further.

The preceding month had brought a significant change in Strindberg's
life. On 8 January 1876, his father noted in his diary: 'Attacked in my own
rooms by my son-in-law H. v. Philp and my son August with the coarsest
insults. End to my knowing these fellows.' And the following day: 'Another
visit to Philp and August, and they literally laid hands on my wife.' On 10
January, Strindberg sent the Wrangels his visiting card with this note: 'I

come to you tomorrow at noon, twenty years older—outlawed—disinherited—mother-and-*father*less—alone in the whole wide world—but faithful to my promise in sound health—Bear with me! For God's sake be friendly even though you have your worries too. You are two—I am *alone*!'

The conflict had to do with the elder Strindberg's decision to leave his firm to Oscar. Strindberg's sister Anna had married Strindberg's friend Hugo von Philp in 1875, on 5 October, the day before Strindberg's departure. The quarrel resulted in a total severance of association between Strindberg and his father: they never saw each other again.

Strindberg was never able to incorporate this event in his autobiography, important as it must have been to his subsequent view of life. 'He had taken an active part in a dramatic family confrontation,' is all he had to say about it in *The Serving Maid's Son*. Later in life he often returned to the question of his father and the guilt he incurred by breaking with him. 'The Unknown' in *To Damascus*, his autobiographical play dealing with a wanderer, counts among his sins the fact that he did not attend his father's funeral.

It was Siri who set in motion the process that led the lovers into each other's arms. As late as March she still loved him 'with a sister's affection'. On 11 March, however, after the two secret loving couples—Sofia was living with the Wrangels—apparently had given each other certain permissions, Siri wrote to Strindberg in the evening and told him that after he left, her husband had asked her if he could go to Sofia. 'My first reaction was anger,' Siri explained, 'the second, amusement, and the third, contentment.' Her husband's request, she felt, had brought her closer to Strindberg.

The letter took immediate effect. Enraged, or pretending to be, Strindberg wrote that Wrangel had insulted them both. Wrangel, he said, was throwing away his wife like 'a wilted flower' and dragging her through the dirt. His shamelessness allowed Strindberg to declare himself her lover. He inundated Siri with terms of endearment, but still followed the Platonic rules she had decreed. It was her soul that he loved, and her bedroom was a temple whose mysteries had been desecrated by the 'beast', her husband.

Line by line, Strindberg's letter rises towards ever more dizzying heights. In his imagination, Siri and he fuse into a single character, just as later in life, and on innumerable occasions, he would enter into blood relationships with his fictional characters, becoming unable to distinguish what was his and what theirs. He calls Siri a genius, imprisoned, insulted and maltreated like himself. 'Rise, young lioness,' he exclaims, 'shake your golden mane and let your wonderful eyes blaze to make all fools shake with fear, tear yourself away from that disgusting menagerie—out into the forests, to wholesome, free nature, where a heart, a head, and an embrace await you.'

It is her duty, he goes on, to abandon this home that has been sullied by adultery, and to join him. Together they will become king and queen 'in the eternal non-sensual world'.

10 (*top left*) Carl Gustaf Wrangel as a young officer
11 (*top right*) Sofia Elisabet In de Betou
12 (*bottom left*) Siri von Essen
13 (*bottom right*) August Strindberg

Beloved human being, you don't believe you have the genius—you believe that genius consists of a good, sharp head—not so—my head is not one of the sharpest—but the fire; my fire is the greatest in Sweden, and *if you want me to*, I'll set fire to the entire miserable hole! You have the fire, and it is this dark flame that perturbs you, pains you, glowing as embers for so many years while so many damned fools tried to extinguish it—Come! Fulfil your high goal! You can be an actress—I'll create a theatre for you—together with Edvard B and Frippe—I'll act with you and write and—love you—you have a great crime on your conscience! You have desired the rewards of genius but haven't dared the martyrdom—oh, it is a blissful martyrdom! Realize your destiny, become the greatest actress or authoress in this country! ... Are you afraid to become my wife—afraid of the prosaic—Oh, don't you know that I have a magic wand that makes water spring from rock—that I can extract poetry from dirt if need be.

The words 'my fire is the greatest in Sweden' have been quoted frequently; the next sentence in which he declares himself ready to set fire to their society for her sake, less often. The exalted tone and feeling of strength and inextricably part of Strindberg in his youth. They are given an accompaniment of blasphemies and cynical, insolent remarks, for correction and balance. Strindberg never gets so lost in the more elevated regions that he forgets the lower, cruder ones. While not differing from others in kind, he has a wider register than most.

Strindberg and Siri proceeded to live through a springtime of love with equal measures of happiness and suffering. They met in secret—in tea shops, in the National Museum, in the von Philps' home. Siri even dared to visit the room on Kaptensgatan, leaving imprints of her boots on the bachelor couch.

After much hesitation it was decided that Siri should obtain a divorce. This was set in motion according to a plan that demonstrates, only too well, the hypocrisy of society in the reign of Oscar. Siri was to travel abroad, Wrangel would accuse her of being a 'runaway wife' and demand a divorce. That way, the honour of the Guard would remain intact, and every trace of Wrangel's infidelities with Sofia In de Betou would be eradicated.

Strindberg, however, had revealed the Baron's affair with Sofia to his beloved's mother, the Baroness Betty von Essen, hoping to gain her as an ally in a divorce case that would leave Wrangel in the pillory. Siri persuaded Strindberg to retract this accusation. Exposed, Wrangel would have lost his commission and with it his only source of income. Strindberg gave in and wrote Betty von Essen a tearful letter of recantation, saying that Wrangel's nobility was of an order 'high above my lowly comprehension', and further:

Again: I herewith retract all of my abominable accusations against Carl and Miss Sofi and beg you to consider that you no longer have a right to avail yourself of information which has now been proven and openly admitted to be unfounded, and was merely dictated by the unhappy state of mind jealousy generates, which in easily excited natures resembles something like complete absence of mind! I can never expect you to forgive me; I already have the forgiveness of my faithful friends, and live in hopes of God's charity! Your desperate Aug. Sbg.

There is a comical element in the fact that Strindberg was forced to accuse himself of the kind of jealousy verging on insanity that he really would be regarded as a victim of, only a few years later. Siri herself drove him to a false confession whose reality she would soon let him taste in full.

After Strindberg had written these monstrous lies in order to prevent Betty von Essen from taking up arms in defence of her daughter's honour, the way seemed clear. Siri thanked him in ecstatic tones: 'It is *thus* I want you to be, great enough to sacrifice yourself—that is to say, to make concessions to the world for another's sake, and to help others. Now you are my great, my strong, my proud August—how I love you.'

It was not this kind of self-negating greatness that Strindberg was going to strive for. Siri's enthusiasm appears strange, but it was probably at least partially due to her exertions to get him to this point. In her letter, she represents the public lie as the highest virtue: it is one's duty to submit to convention. She followed that line throughout their marriage, blatantly contradicting Strindberg's personality and objectives. A firm foundation for an unhappy marriage had been laid from the very beginning.

During the spring, Siri wavered again, under pressure from her family to be magnanimous and effect a reconciliation with her husband. In letters to Strindberg she intimated that she was able to envisage a future in which Strindberg would continue as an intimate friend of the family while Wrangel had permission to enjoy Sofia. Behind the strict façades of the upper classes during this era there was more freedom than outsiders could dream of. But Strindberg rejected such proposals with indignation.

As late as the summer of 1876, Siri still claimed that Strindberg was not her lover. Yet on 3 May—the day when Siri's flight abroad began— Strindberg wrote her a letter in which the winter's affected and hyperbolic exchanges of tenderness are replaced by something fresh and immediate. There are human beings of angelic form who do not lose their wings 'even when they touch the earth', and 'the earth' obviously stands for a delicious secret shared by the couple. He called her 'my young little one' and fantasized about the moment when he would be able to lift her in his arms and set her down 'behind our own locked doors' and with his words dispel her 'artificial conscience'.

Four days later, the lover is full of jokes and pleasantries. He returns to his command of everyday language, temporarily lost during the first intoxication of love. He boasts about finding golden strands of hair in his hairbrush and exclaims: 'Shall we get married in the autumn? Tell me! Do you want to be my little wife? You won't say No, will you?'

Strindberg's letter can be compared with the description of Axel's and Maria's meeting in the attic room, two days before Maria's departure. All necessary actions have been agreed upon. Maria is tense and hysterical, switching from one mood to another. In the evening, they share a meal and then convert the couch into a bed. Now Maria has the courage to give herself completely. She is radiantly beautiful, and bliss is reflected in her eyes.

'My poor cubbyhole in the attic [Strindberg lets Axel say], has become a temple, a glorious palace, and I light the cracked ceiling fixture, the desk lamp, and the candles to celebrate this feast of happiness, this visit by the Joy of Life, by this one and only joy that makes our miserable lives worth living. On the thorn-strewn road, the memory of these golden minutes of satisfied love is our companion; this fleeting bliss, scorned only by the jealous, gives us strength to live and surpass ourselves! That is pure love!—Do not speak ill of love, I tell her. Let us respect the forces of nature; may we honour the god who compels us to be happy in spite of ourselves.'

According to the initial plan, Siri was to travel to Paris, but she went to Copenhagen instead, where she could stay with her maternal aunt Augusta Möller, thus becoming a 'runaway wife' only in the legal sense. Another play was staged for the benefit of relatives, friends and the general public, in which she was a woman consumed by a burning and irresistible yearning to become an actress. This passion could be requited only if she were to obtain a divorce from Wrangel. Thus it was necessary to cover up all traces of her attachment to Strindberg—a hopeless undertaking in a city as provincial as Stockholm. Nevertheless, the three main actors threw themselves into their parts with supreme enthusiasm and defiance.

Wrangel went to see his colonel and enquired if it would be compatible with his position to have an actress for a wife. He received the expected negative reply. Wrangel and Strindberg agreed to go and see Siri off at the train in each other's company, and to visit public places together during her absence. In this way, rumours about a love affair between Siri and Strindberg with subsequent animosity between him and Wrangel would be nipped in the bud. To clinch the matter, Strindberg asked Rudolf Wall to publish his articles in *Dagens Nyheter* during Siri's absence, as proof of his remaining in Stockholm and working. On 13 May, the newspaper published Strindberg's long review of Egron Lundgren's paintings. The reviewer's enthusiasm was perhaps not exclusively due to all the exotic subjects— young girls, carefree beggars, old men discussing politics, female lute players, orange vendors, snake charmers, diamond merchants, elephants, pomegranate blossoms and bird-cages—that Egron Lundgren conjured up in southern European and Indian settings.

> The eye becomes intoxicated by these strong Spanish and Italian wines, and there is a pinch of opium in the Turkish tobacco; the viewer feels giddy and gets the urge to dash away from the campfire on an elephant's back, to climb a city wall, scale a balcony, break windows and do crazy things, while the well-trained elephant quietly grazes in a rose-garden, waiting for the sun to rise on the mosque-fringed horizon. It is like flower poisoning, or an opium dream.

During those tumultuous days, Strindberg did more than just provide multiple proof of his presence in the Swedish capital. He completed yet another revision of *Master Olof*, begun in May 1875, in which the reformer continued to be a sceptic on his way to spiritual death but was endowed with great new lyrical powers—a consequence of his creator's new phase of life. Olof's mother was given a more prominent part in the play. On a midsummer's night, Olof sits by her deathbed and bursts into a great soliloquy on peace in which he invokes all nature around Stockholm to come to her aid with healing sounds and fragrances.

The meticulously planned divorce drama did not proceed without a hitch: Wrangel, for some reason, failed to appear at the railway station. The clandestine lovers found themselves standing on the platform in precisely that compromising situation they had tried to avoid. Nor was that all. Siri's nerve failed, and she implored Strindberg to come with her for at least part of the way; he was unable to resist. When the train pulled out to cross the bridge, then still fairly new, between Vasagatan and Söder, Strindberg was in her compartment, and there he remained all the way to Katrineholm, where the two ate a late supper in the station restaurant: 'Jesus Christ, it was hard to leave the train,' Strindberg wrote a few days later.

Small wonder, then, that Stockholm was buzzing with rumours the next day. Elof Tegnér, a colleague of Strindberg's at the Library, heard that an official of his institution had eloped with a baroness. Considering their status as civil servants, Tegnér called the statement absurd, if amusing; when he entered the reading room the following day, he started to say: 'Have you heard...? To his surprise, he was greeted by an embarrassed silence, during which some of those present made mute gestures in the direction of Strindberg, who sat by the window, silent and morose.

Even the main action had its setbacks. Wrangel submitted his petition for divorce on 4 May as follows:

> To the Magistrates' Court, Stockholm. As my wife, Sigrid Sofia Mathilda Elisabeth von Essen, has left me, out of malice and antipathy, and has travelled abroad with the intention no longer to remain and live with me, I herewith petition for a lawful summons to be issued to my said wife and urge the court to rule that our marriage be dissolved.

For such a summons to become legal, it had to be delivered to Siri, to be acknowledged by her. She, however, was now in Copenhagen, surrounded by aunts who were trying to persuade her to return to her husband. Thus the writ was retained for a few days: Siri received it only on 11 May, and the magistrates' court discussed it on 16 May.

Siri wrote desperate letters to Strindberg, imploring him to come to Copenhagen. Strindberg tried to calm her down, pointing out that their entire plan would be destroyed if he appeared there openly as her lover. It would also invalidate her sacrifice of her position in society for art's sake.

Suspecting that Wrangel had opted out of the plan—his non-appearance at the railway station indicating this—Strindberg wrote a coarse letter to him in which he also took the opportunity to release his feelings of anger about having had to rescind his accusations against Wrangel. The letter begins:

The very moment when you abandoned your wife for a younger and prettier woman, you yourself gave all and sundry the right to act as her defender, and at the same moment you were unchivalrous enough to deny the main reason for the whole unhappy affair and to accuse your wife in front of her mother, and thus you do not deserve any sympathy in the matter.

The entire letter proceeds in this ranting tone, speaking of 'brutal outbursts of marital tyranny', complimenting Wrangel on 'the excellent manner' in which he performs the part of a martyr 'in this play'—'although the performance hasn't been as smooth as one would have expected, and the make-up left things to be desired'—and exclaims pathetically about the fact that Siri had recently begged him to lie, for her sake: 'And this woman whose pure brow never has had to blush over a lie, I'll teach her to lie, yes, to lie to make the whole world blush!'

Such a letter was not the best way to demonstrate the unbroken friendship that was part of the plan. Nevertheless, the comedy continued. Strindberg used his contacts in the newspaper world to try to keep malicious rumours in check and told Siri on 14 May that only her mother's 'maid and her friends' were talking about 'any scandal'. He offered to crush Siri's enemies, adding: 'I have pens to pierce donkey-hides, if need be—But it has to be for your sake, I do not like squabbles—if there is to be a fight—give me a country—a city—a commune to fight with—but with women and those under age? Never!'

Siri's reply was very affected. She used oaths without any apparent motive and informed her lover that she had made 'the acquaintance of a charming Danish gentleman whom I encourage to be as charming as can be. I have to play the coquette, even if just a little. But it may not work, ha! ha!

Still, one has to console oneself as best one can.' She did not know what kind
of fire she was playing with: that Danish admirer was to become a bone of
contention between the lovers during the following summer, and, even-
tually, he became a character in *A Fool's Apology*, unquestionably an
effective one.

On 19 May, Siri was able to return to Stockholm. At first, she lived with
her mother on Drottninggatan: 'Now I'm home! Living with mamma.—
Just knock on the door across the hall. Are you coming to see me?'

Chapter Four

'THE RED ROOM'

I

AUGUST STRINDBERG and Sigrid von Essen were married on 30 December 1877. 'It was a winter Sunday, strangely quiet and uncannily solemn for me as I made ready to leave my untidy bachelor's existence and to take my place at the marriage hearth with the woman I loved,' Strindberg wrote many years later, in *Legends*. There, he also tells us that on his marriage morning he felt the need to breakfast alone and did so in a basement café in an obscure alley. In that cellar room, lit by gas lamps, he sat among men whose faces were ghostly pale from sleeplessness and drinking. He recognized a couple of them; one of the company approached to greet him, but was suddenly uncertain of Strindberg's identity. The author congratulated himself: in this mysterious way, he has been spared a confrontation with a representative of a dismal past.

It is impossible to be sure of the authenticity of this description of the morning of his wedding day. Strindberg rewrote his life continuously, in order to adjust it to its successive phases. Yet the pattern of events in the subterranean café is a characteristic one. Strindberg had a readiness for new departures—it was an intrinsic part of his nature—and a corresponding need to describe the past as appalling and horrible. It is hard to think of one period in his life on which he did not, at a later date, pass the worst possible judgement.

It seems likely that he did feel unusually solemn on that 30th day of December. Seven years before, he had written a letter from Uppsala to his cousin Johan Oscar Strindberg (one of the wedding guests), in which he described a sunny family scene he had witnessed on the way to the place where he was dining. Looking into a window he had seen a father and mother with their children assembled around an appetizing table. 'I felt an emptiness in my chest,' he wrote. 'I missed the family—regrettably, not *my* family—but family life in general.'

That was what his dream of a happy life on this earth looked like: father, mother and children gathered around a well-appointed table. The fact that he was singularly ill-equipped to play his part in such an idyll did not prevent him from remaining faithful to it all his life. Perhaps that was the very reason it had such a strong appeal for him, and perhaps there was indeed a moment when friends of bachelor days appeared macabre and threatening. But not for long. In his 'breakthrough' novel, *The Red Room*, completed in a little more than a year after his marriage, Strindberg builds a memorial to the happy male camaraderie of the 1870s.

The wedding day found Siri seven months pregnant, a condition that could not be concealed, and thus the ceremony took place in the apartment at no. 17 Norrmalmsgatan (later renamed Biblioteksgatan) which Strindberg had rented and furnished that month. The service was conducted by the Reverend L. M. Fischier, and the guests were, in addition to Johan Oscar, Anna and Hugo von Philp, Algot Lange and Ina Forstén, the initiators of the love story, and Carl Gustaf Wrangel. It also happened to be Wrangel's birthday, one of those coincidences Strindberg would later invest with uncanny significance.

The past year had been a trying one for both bride and groom. In her book, Karin Smirnoff describes her mother's situation as 'repulsive', which was, evidently, the very word used to describe it at the time. On 20 June 1876, the Royal Court Consistory (Siri had been admitted to court) declared that her marriage was dissolved, and she was free to remarry, but she still had to live up to the legend of the well-born lady who had left her husband for the sake of art. Therefore, she and Strindberg had then lived secretly as lovers, having to resort to all kinds of humiliating subterfuge, and in constant fear of pregnancy. In *A Fool's Apology*, Strindberg claims that he tried to reassure Siri by inventing an obstruction of his urinary tract that he said would make him less likely to become a father. According to the same unreliable source of information on Strindberg's relationship with Siri, she then inundated him with recriminations for that lie and urged him to marry her to 'save her from disgrace'.

For Siri, the pregnancy certainly was a setback, for her reason in going through with the divorce had been in order to become an actress—at any rate, this had been as powerful a motive as her love for Strindberg. From the very beginning, he had treated her as an artist of equal stature, and initiated her, with a modicum of bathos, into the mysteries of the artist's life. 'Welcome to the company of those who suffer and struggle to succeed, in the Name of the Eternal! Thus greets you one of the unworthy, as we always have to remain here on earth!!!' This, in his letter to her the day she departed for Copenhagen. During the 'free' year of love Siri had prepared herself for the stage, studying dramatic roles and working on her provincial Finland-Swedish accent. And her lover had helped her with pertinent, sensible advice. Among other things, he suggested that she memorize Runeberg's poem about her grandfather, in order to appeal to Sweden's ever-latent colonial patriotism in regard to Finland. True to the old hack strategies, he also slipped into his newspaper articles many a good word for persons with influence at the Royal Theatre: for that was the stage Siri, like himself, was aiming for.

In December 1876, Siri auditioned with Frans Hedberg, who was still the head of the theatre school, and her public début audition was to take place on 27 January. According to Karin Smirnoff, Siri's four-year-old daughter Sigrid had been ailing, pale and quiet, since the previous summer, and on 13 January 1877 she died of tuberculosis of the brain, according to the autopsy. Siri's grief was heightened by self-reproach: for the sake of rehearsals, she had failed to give the little girl the care and attention she had needed. Siri's mother, Betty von Essen, who was still hostile towards the new liaison, hinted that the child's death was a punishment for Siri's leaving her husband. Nemesis Divina, God's punitive retribution, would become one of Strindberg's imaginative obsessions: it was not an eccentric one—he was surrounded by others who believed in it.

Siri's début went well. The newspapers responded to it with encouraging reviews; the circumstances of her divorce doubtless helped the publicity. In June 1877, she was engaged for the coming theatre season by the 'Directorate of His Royal Majesty's Court Ensemble and Theatres', for a salary of 2,100 kronor a year plus 3 kronor per performance. There is hardly another episode in Strindberg's oeuvre as well known and well liked as the one in *A Dream Play* which deals with the officer waiting for his bride outside the Opera House: young, radiant and expectant, he appears with a bunch of fresh-cut roses in his hand, to sing out his 'Victoria!' in front of that imposing façade. . . . But the years pass, and every time he returns, he has grown more grey, and the bouquet of roses has turned into a bunch of dry twigs—yet he never abandons hope: the beloved will come. In the autumn of 1877, Strindberg started collecting material for this particular life of a character, as he stood waiting for Siri in front of the Royal Theatre building in Kungsträdgården.

During that year of waiting, Strindberg had, at long last, let *Master Olof* go. In May 1876, when his love affair with Siri was in its most tumultuous phase, he had written the final act, and on 19 May he reported to Siri: 'Now Master Olof is done! Hooray! He'll do it! Now I'm not afraid of anything any more!' The same month, Strindberg revived the proud *nom de guerre* of his earliest youth, The Eagle, and playfully combined it with the bird that symbolizes love above all others—the dove. 'Your sorrowing turtle dove The Eagle', is the signature of a letter dated 9 May.

Exuberance soon had to give way to defeat and shame. The Royal Theatre rejected *Master Olof*, and so did the New Theatre, where Edvard

Stjernström (whom Strindberg called 'an animal') still wielded power.

This meant a definitive end to all theatrical projects for the time being. Strindberg saw himself forced to reorient his literary ambition, especially as he now had a family to provide for. He made plans for his own cultural review, a weekly, entitled *The Gazette*. After a single issue in September 1876, the project collapsed; later, Strindberg would accuse Siri of being the cause of failure. He decided to flee to France, as there was an opportunity for him to complete the journey he had started the previous year which had ended in the amorous drama of Dalarö.

In October, after travelling via Kristiania and across the North Sea—to his disappointment, 'calm enough to be crossed in a rowboat'—he arrived in Paris. If credence can be given to a satirical poem, probably written a few years later, he was impressed neither by the Venus of Milo in the Louvre nor by Madame Judic as La Belle Hélène at the Variétés, and longed for home, 'the far dear brandy land'. These may have been defensive thoughts, mustered against the 'great world' which for him was the centre of the cultural universe, just as Rome had been for Augustine, or New York City for Auden.

Only five years before his arrival in France, the Communards had been vanquished. It seems probable that Strindberg was already planning a great sequence of travel poems, in the manner of Heinrich Heine: a fragment of this can still be found in his collection of poems, published in 1883, under the title *Exile*. According to a preserved list of titles, several parts of the sequence were to be dedicated to the Commune, with the sack and burning of the Tuileries as a climax. A line in the Paris poem indicates the spirit he intended to work in: 'My Republican fervour felt encouraged by the sight of the burnt-down Tuileries.'

Nevertheless, Notre Dame became Strindberg's main focus of attention in Paris, which is not surprising in a contemporary of Victor Hugo. In a brilliant article, published in *Dagens Nyheter* in December 1876, Strindberg described a visit to the cathedral: under the dark vault, he notices two women, one of them has just lit six large wax candles in the great gilded candelabrum and has made her confession to Monseigneur himself in the richly carved walnut-wood confessional. The other woman is old and poor, and the candle she is lighting is about the size of a pencil. 'What is this old woman praying for', the author asks himself, 'in the middle of a bright Wednesday afternoon, alone, worshipping in this overwhelmingly vast and splendid Notre Dame? For a sick child? For an absent son whom perhaps she considers lost for ever? For a husband, shot like a dog in 1871, against some wall in the *buttes* of Montmartre?'

All three alternatives for the old woman's prayer present a connection with Strindberg himself. At home in Sweden, a woman with a sick child was waiting for him. He himself was a traveller, whom his father considered lost:

the following Christmas, his father would write in his diary: 'All children home except for the two lost ones, August and Anna.' The man shot like a dog on the hills of Montmartre stood for Gert Bookprinter, the revolutionary, from whom Strindberg had tried to escape.

When he returned to Sweden, Strindberg engaged himself seriously in the writing of narrative prose, an endeavour which would continue through most of the 1880s. He wrote the Uppsala stories 'From the Firlot' and 'The Black Creek'. In Paris, he had first seen the Impressionists' paintings at the Galerie Durand-Ruel, and in a *Dagens Nyheter* article he discussed the paradox inherent in the attempt made by these artists to render what ought to be impossible in a stationary image—that is, motion. It was motion he was after, himself, and in 'A Promising Youth', the short story about a young medical student's funeral discussed in Chapter 2, it is possible to perceive some influence by the French masters in the quick transitions within each paragraph. As an artist, Strindberg was well and truly launched.

The book was published in December 1877 by Albert Bonnier and received well-disposed if rather shallow notices. *Ny Illustrerad Tidning* thought that it considered student life from 'a high-spirited jester's point of view'. Yet even that was a pertinent comment: there is a friskiness of tone and a delight in expression for its own sake that was to remain typical of Strindberg's work.

2

The apartment in which the newlyweds settled was 'to the right in the courtyard and down below', to quote one of Strindberg's letters of invitation. The quarter was called Pumpstocken (The Pump Log), and the house was situated in the still relatively undeveloped area between Norrmalmstorg and Humlegården.

They regarded themselves as a progressive couple: they were to be equals, two modern professionals. They had separate bedrooms, and they had made a legal agreement to keep the property of both partners separate. It was Strindberg who had suggested this, according to his own words in *A Fool's Apology* in order to 'prevent the unpleasantness of ever being suspected of having devoured my wife's property'.

According to the marriage protocol established at the magistrates' court in Stockholm on 7 January 1878, the bride's share of the estate consisted of three couches, one chiffonier, three armchairs, eighteen chairs, two large mirrors, bronze candelabra, tableware (including three silver-plated stoppers for wine bottles), two gold-plated clocks, and so on—all of it valued at a total of 2,697 kronor. Furthermore, the bride's assets amounted to a small fortune—twelve 100 per cent and two 50 per cent capital stock certificates of the firm Guillemot & Weilandt, to a total nominal value of 13,000 kronor.

The groom's property was more modest: a convertible couch, an 'Athenian' (a small table for knick-knacks), a silver-plated clock, and a few modest paintings that could not match the glamour of the family portraits included in Siri's list. All of it amounted to 900 kronor.

As Strindberg looked around his new home, he found himself in an upper-class milieu: he had definitely risen on the ladder of the extraordinarily class-conscious society of his day. When, a few years later, his feelings for Siri turned to hatred, he attempted to erase the memory of their first home completely, as though it had never existed. In a letter to Gustaf af Geijerstam in 1890 he related how, after an evening at the bar, he had gone to visit whores in 'the same house where my marriage took place!' and that it had been 'an exquisite pleasure to be able to soil the sweetest memory one should have retained for life'. A few more years passed, and he let Falkenström, his *alter ego* in the novel *Black Flags*, have the same experience and exclaim:

> 'Newly married! Home! Wife, child! Garbage, all of it! And is it not better to tell people that, right away, so they know what they have to deal with? Just think: the same apartment, and now it is a brothel. I cannot deny that it was a wild pleasure to be able to go and spit on that past that I once believed in and which turned out to be nothing at all. I was living in a dung-heap without knowing it; just went along with it, carefree, faithful, and simple-minded. . . .'

It was the very same symbolic drama Marcel Proust was to enact a few years later, when he moved his parents' marital bed into a brothel.

Nevertheless, neither of those outbursts could be anticipated in 1878. Strindberg and Siri von Essen lived together in Stockholm for five years in a far from serene but often bright and happy marriage. In *A Fool's Apology* Strindberg gives a King Charles spaniel, loved by Maria and hated by Axel, a prominent part in the introductory description of their marriage: the animal, repulsive to Axel, becomes a bad omen, a symbol for all the impurity and beastliness of what is to follow. The dog had a counterpart in reality, by the name of Mutte, which Siri adored. In a letter to a friend in Finland, Emelie Björksten (Runeberg's last love), dated September 1878, Siri referred to herself as Mutte's 'mamma' and claimed that from the armchair where he was reclining he was sending the friend a greeting with his 'asparagus tail', longing to kiss her hand. This love for canines was typical of Siri's circles: Strindberg himself, in the heat of infatuation, sent maudlin regards to dear Mutte. At that time, he obviously had not yet discovered the unique possibilities in the tragi-comic genre that 'beast' would provide.

The couple moved house frequently—a characteristic trait of the Strindberg family. As early as October 1878 they found a new apartment on the same street, and in November 1879 they moved to Stora Humlegårdsgatan. They stayed close to Humlegården, where the Royal Library had moved in 1877/8—a gigantic operation, observed by all Stockholmers with great excitement. On New Year's Day, the move was completed, according to E. W. Dahlgren, by the spectacle of Klemming striding across Norrbro toward Humlegården, a folio under his arm, preceded by a library caretaker 'pulling the enormous "Devil's Bible" on a sledge'—one of those spoils of war Sweden was still proud of, as a one-time great military power in Europe.

In January, Strindberg reported to *Finsk Tidskrift* (the Finnish Magazine), whose correspondent he was, on the Library's new quarters, proudly describing how the scholars, who 'in the bad old days' had to work elbow to elbow, now had a room the size of a church at their disposal. Despite his newly married status, he himself celebrated the move by a glorious spree in the company of Richard Bergström. Late at night, the two gentlemen, for the duration of that day quite able to cope with 'the squalor of bachelor life', decided to take a final look at the now empty rooms in the Royal Palace. They were carrying a bottle of champagne, and Strindberg proceeded to make a sacrifice to the *manes*, the spirits of the past. A few old chairs were smashed, and the 'pyre' was soaked with champagne.

We know this from the memoirs of one of Strindberg's colleagues, Elof Tegnér, who has also told us that the Head Librarian held an interrogation a few days later to establish the identity of the culprit. Terrified, Strindberg exclaimed under his breath: 'Now my future is ruined!' The reprimand, however, consisted only of the comment: 'What a pointless prank that was!'

But the marriage began with a tragic episode as well: on 21 January, according to Strindberg a couple of months too early, Siri gave birth to their child. It had been conceived out of wedlock but born within it—just like Strindberg himself, as he pointed out. Nevertheless, the couple felt that it would jeopardize their social standing to recognize the child: it was entered in the church register of the Jakob Congregation as born of parents unknown. On the very day of its birth it was left in the care of a midwife, and two days later it was dead, having been privately baptized (again, according to the church register).

Strindberg's father had two sons before he married their mother, and he never concealed his paternity. Had public hypocrisy risen to new heights since then, or was it Strindberg's advancement to more elevated social status, where bigotry had a stronger grip on people, that caused him to act so differently? On 11 April 1888, when his marriage was falling apart and he had just finished *A Fool's Apology*, he wrote to his early confidant and cousin Johan Oscar Strindberg about the child.

14 (*top left*) The Royal
Library, completed in
1877
15 (*top right*)
Strindberg's drawing
of G. E. Klemming,
the Head Librarian

16 (*left*) The new
Library's reading
room. Drawing by
Vicke Andrén
17 (*bottom*) Strind-
berg's visiting card as
an amanuensis at the
Library (handwritten:
'has been indisposed')

The purpose of the decision to give the child to the midwife was to protect the mother's and the father's delicate positions as royal civil servants, and they intended to adopt the child later. Then life was taken up with other events, work and quarrels, and the whole story was forgotten. Yet, time and again, I heard Siri accuse herself of having been a coward when she gave the child away. Well, from an idealist's point of view it was cowardly, but it was prudent to save the parents first, as the child would not have had any future at all without them; being born prematurely, it died, and that put an end to all further discussion of the matter.

For himself, Strindberg refused to admit any pangs of conscience—which is of course no proof that he did not have them. He raised the subject in 1888 because he had begun to suspect that the child was, in fact, alive, and that Siri was secretly sending sums of money for its upkeep. In his letter, he asked his cousin to investigate the matter on his behalf and provides clues which cast a sombre light on the era's secretive mores. 'Now, to find out if it's all a mystification' (in other words, whether the child is alive) 'the simplest thing to do would be to look for the midwife Johansson. In 1877, she was living on Smålandsgatan, and later moved to Regeringsgatan. She was small, pale, had lost her teeth, and had a terribly emaciated face.' It was to this unknown creature that the Strindbergs gave their love-child, in order to 'protect' and 'save' themselves. It is difficult to imagine an act farther removed from that natural instinct which Strindberg would soon extol as the only true guiding principle of human existence.

3

The marriage had provided some temporary economic relief, and, as of 1878, Strindberg's position at the Library became more lucrative. That year, his earnings from it were 915 kronor, and the year after that, 1,010 kronor. As before, he supplemented that income by writing articles, translating, editing, and proofreading. In his capacity as a civil servant he seems to have taken things relatively easy, and his colleagues' descriptions of him are far from kind. Elof Tegnér speaks of him with hatred, calling him 'repulsive', referring to his 'gloomy and suspicious stare', his 'perennially cloudy' brow.

Nevertheless, Strindberg enjoyed the protection of the Head Librarian, Klemming, even if that protection was not, perhaps, given quite voluntarily. On several occasions Strindberg dropped dark hints about having something on Klemming: he fantasized that the Head Librarian had had a child

with the institution's cloakroom attendant. To quote one of Strindberg's
many descriptions of Klemming, he was a man 'built like a warrior, with
eagle eyes under colossal brows, and a huge German moustache'.
Strindberg goes on to compare Klemming with the Zeus of Otricoli—
amusingly enough, the same classical sculpture Georg Brandes refers to in
his description of Strindberg's own head. Klemming was a spiritualist and
Swedenborgian—he edited Swedenborg's journals—and this was one of the
reasons for Strindberg's lifelong preoccupation with the man. One night,
long after Klemming's death, Strindberg thought that he could feel his
ghost approaching in the dark: he called out, 'Is that Klemming?' but
received no answer.

Klemming's greatest fear was that of being buried alive—a phobia which
was very common in the nineteenth century and has since been replaced by
the fear of being technically 'dead' while still actually alive. As a precaution,
Klemming kept a coffin woven out of willow twigs in the basement of the
library: he had given instructions that his corpse was to be placed there, and
only after unmistakable symptoms of decay had manifested themselves, was
it to be cremated.

During the 1870s, Sweden went through an economic boom which
provided the base for its future wealth. However, at the end of the decade
this was followed by a crisis (which affected all of Europe) and a series of
spectacular crashes. Strindberg did not escape the consequences.

His permanent state of indigence had made him into an expert in loans
and IOUs. *The Red Room*, which he was to begin shortly, is a real textbook
in the art of borrowing and scraping by. Several of the book's comic
highlights—Olle Montanus who gets arrested on his way to the pawnbroker
with his landlady's sheets; the successful pawning of Arvid Falk's gold
watch and the subsequent celebration—describe economic transactions of
the kind Strindberg and his comrades engaged in.

As a married man, Strindberg continued these practices, driven to them
by a tendency to be extremely extravagant whenever possible. Siri shared
his tastes: as soon as there was money, good wines, delicacies and new
clothes flowed into their home. Strindberg sold some of Siri's stock in
Guillemot & Weilandt, using others as collateral for loans. At the end of
1878, however, that firm, which had seemed so solid, suddenly collapsed:
the stocks became worthless overnight. Thus these debts as well as those
resulting from other loans became due immediately, and a critical situation
ensued. On 14 December, Strindberg wrote to his classmate from the
Stockholm Lyceum, Isidor Bonnier, of having 'lost my entire base of
operations and become insolvent and willing to relinquish my and my wife's
property, which is even more painful considering that I only contributed
debts to our marriage'.

Isidor Bonnier was the guarantor of one of Strindberg's bank loans. Other friends and patrons had underwritten other transactions or given him cash loans, among them Rudolf Wall, Edvard Bäckström, his successful competitor for performance space at the Royal Theatre, Gustaf Meyer, his cousin Johan Oscar, August Strömbäck, an old friend from school and university days, and others. There was hardly a bank in Stockholm where Strindberg's name would not appear in some series of loan transactions. Siri's jewellery and silver had also been pawned, and their creditors included small shopkeepers and artisans. On 9 January 1879, Strindberg was forced to file for bankruptcy. According to his own calculations, his total debt amounted to 9,252 kronor; the assets, to 5,591 kronor. Following the magistrate's decision in July, the creditors accepted Strindberg's offer of 60 per cent. He does not seem to have lost any of his furniture or valuables, nor was his social standing affected by the bankruptcy any more than his father's had been twenty-five years earlier.

4

On 15 February 1879, while the bankruptcy proceedings were in full swing, Strindberg started working on his novel *The Red Room*, firmly determined to achieve literary prominence with one bold stroke and, at the same time, repair his finances. Voltaire's dictum: 'Rien n'est si désagréable que d'être pendu obscurément' ('Nothing is so painful as to be hanged in silence') became the book's epigraph on the title page. Reading it, one gains a strong sense of the author's determination to attract attention.

He wrote in the mornings, when his 'brain was at its clearest'. The day began with a cold rub-down with a wet towel, coffee, and a long walk to charge the batteries. Then he worked at his desk for two to three hours, and left for the Library at noon. He was particular about his paper and steel-nibbed pens. His favourite paper was Lessebo, folio or half-folio size. For reasons of economy, he wrote on both sides of the paper; later, after his first success, he would use only one side.

Arvid Falk, the novel's main character, re-enacts Master Olof's drama in a different key. Falk is an idealist who wants to expose society's injustices and frauds: in order to do so, he resigns from his civil service post and takes up journalism. Like Olof, he is driven in a radical and revolutionary direction.

When Strindberg had just about reached the halfway mark in his book, Sweden experienced its first large-scale strike, in the town of Sundsvall: 5,000 sawmill workers walked out in protest against their employers' decision to cut wages in response to the depression. The local governor,

Curry Treffenberg, notorious for his violent resistance against the Representation Reform of 1865 (which put paid to the supreme powers of the aristocracy), called out the military and brutally put down the strike—by all accounts, a popular, spontaneous one. These were momentous events. The ruling class saw the Paris Commune and World Revolution rearing their dragon's heads in the Norrland woods. As Carl Reinhold Smedmark points out in his erudite study of *The Red Room*, Strindberg demonstrated his solidarity with the workers by letting Falk start writing for the newspaper *Arbetarfanan* (the *Workers' Flag*). The former labourer Olle Montanus becomes his 'Gert', and Falk swears allegiance to the cause of the oppressed. Nevertheless, he betrays it just like Olof, and in the final chapter we see him standing at the foot of the royal throne, acting as a herald at the ceremonial opening of the national parliament. He is vested in the purple cloak of power, wearing a plumed hat on his head and carrying a staff in his hand. He has made a compromise and sold his soul. Yet, according to his friend Dr Borg, the eyes of a fanatic are still burning behind the stony mask of his face, and a day of explosive rebellion will come.

Arvid Falk does not, however, dominate the novel to the extent that Olof dominates the play. Strindberg kept his interest in Falk in check, investing him with some fire now and again but then passing him over in favour of characters with greater public appeal. A villainous merchant surrounded by fawning parasites; hypocritical charity ladies visiting the slums; artists with hearts of gold gathered round the smörgasbord and bottles in Bern's restaurant (where one of the rooms is the Red Room); erotic scenes from the prostitute Marie's professional life; the tear-jerking funeral of a child; a society clergyman doing a brisk trade in God and the sacraments; and poor Bohemians trying to assuage their hunger on a winter's night by reading out loud to each other from a cookbook—what more could one ask for! Through twenty-nine brilliant chapters, the author demonstrates his knowledge of the entire tapestry of his society, in language that is taut, concrete, yet incredibly supple.

Swedish connoisseurs of Strindberg tend to know the beginning of the novel by heart. The first sentence, 'It was an evening in the beginning of May', has become almost proverbial. We find ourselves high above Stockholm, in the park on Mosebacke in Söder, the city's expanse stretching out panoramically below. Falk appears, and the reader's attention becomes equally divided between the grand perspective and a series of sharply focused details in the foreground—snowdrops, about to fade; chaffinches, building their nests out of the love-philters contained in the still dormant buds of lime trees; tufts of hair left from the coats of dogs who were fighting here on 'Josefina's Day last year'.

Like a classical landscape painter, Strindberg sets off the closely observed idyll by the larger, wider view. Sight and feeling oscillate between these two planes, expanding and contracting, giving full rein to the imagination; it is a masterpiece.

The Strindberg scholar, Göran Lindblad, has pointed out that Strindberg can be seen as a student and competitor of Victor Hugo in his composition of the beginning of *The Red Room*. In *Notre Dame de Paris*, Hugo describes Paris in the light of evening, seen from the spire of that church. This explains why Strindberg, too, sets his scene in the evening, although many details seem to belong to the city's morning life. Why should a maidservant start removing the storm windows at 7 pm, and work be in full swing at Bergsund at that time? Reading the sentence: 'Far down below him [Falk] the newly awakened city was rumbling' it is, of course, possible to interpret the phrase 'newly awakened' as a significant slip of the pen; on the other hand, it is also possible that Strindberg is referring to an awakening from winter, not from night. But, as a matter of fact, Strindberg presents events from around the clock, in order to overwhelm us from the start with the wealth and depth of his descriptive powers.

The ambiguity resulting from that simultaneity of morning and evening is, indeed, characteristic of the entire novel and forms part of its charm. Falk resigns, in the same way as Master Olof did, and so does Rehnhjelm who wanted to play Hamlet but becomes a *petit bourgeois*. Falander burns himself out with cynicism and absinthe. Olle Montanus commits suicide. Reactionaries rule the land, swindlers like the wholesaler Falk and his charitable spouse and pastor Skåre, the religious wheeler-dealer, emerge victorious. The artists and writers in the Red Room are forced to lead a twilit existence. The flames of rebellion are extinguished, political passion driven underground. Olle Montanus hopes that he will look happy as a corpse.

Nevertheless, there is at the same time a radiance of morning in this novel. Its language is youthful, fast-moving and versatile. The newspaper *Gråkappan* (*Grey Coat*: the target is *Aftonbladet*) is to change course and become reactionary, since its owners have realized that Liberalism no longer pays. It is looking for a new editor:

He was to be incapable of working independently, even a little stupid, as the company knew that true stupidity is always accompanied by conservatism of thought and a certain shrewdness which perceives the bosses' wishes before they are uttered and never forgets that the public interest is, in fact and when properly understood, the private one; furthermore, he had to be middle-aged, thus more obedient, and married: the company, good businessmen all, had seen that married hired hands behaved better than the unmarried ones.

And the reader tells himself that victory, after all, belongs to the man who, in spite of *Gråkappan*'s spiritual disarmament, is able to formulate these sentences, applicable to every era.

18 Letter of 6 April 1880 to Anton Stuxberg about *The Red Room*

5

On 14 November 1879, *The Red Room* became available in bookshops. Strindberg had devised a strategy he felt would lead to certain victory. In a letter to his publisher Joseph Seligmann, one of his associates from his days as a literary jack of all trades, he provided advice as to the order in which review copies should be sent out. Negatively predisposed newspapers were to get their copies last. 'In regard to *Aftonbladet* [*Gråkappan*] I think we should wait eight days until *Dagbl.* and *Allehanda* have published comments—and then, so as not to ruin all future chances, write a small apology to go with the copy of the book, or else just forget about it altogether.'

To stimulate interest even further, Strindberg spread the rumour that *The Red Room* was a *roman-à-clef*, and that the Triton insurance company lambasted in it was, in fact, the Neptune Company in real life; likewise, the book's civil service department was 'completely true to life'.

The book was instantly a wild success: the first edition sold out quickly, and by the spring it had gone into its fourth printing. A report in *Lunds Weckoblad*, dated 24 November, stated that *The Red Room* had been 'the main topic of conversation among members of the educated public in Stockholm during this past week'. This was no exaggeration, and from that moment Strindberg would remain in the limelight for the rest of his life without having to resort to efforts of his own to generate publicity. Henceforth, the self-image he created would be a public one.

Almost all the reviewers considered the novel a gloomy and deeply pessimistic book. 'Wicked, sometimes downright repulsive' was one opinion: another found it vitiated by 'the biased bitterness of the author's entire view of life'. *Aftonbladet* stated that the author defiled everything he touched. Professor Nyblom, who had been Strindberg's mentor in Uppsala, could not find 'the least bit of poetry' in the novel—'only darkness and poisonous satire'.

Nevertheless, the majority of newspapers admitted the book's merits, referred to the 'great talents' of its author, spoke of 'masterpieces of satire', and, like *Dagens Nyheter*, started calling Strindberg 'a man of genius'. From then on, that phrase became an adjunct to his name.

It is ironic to consider that a novel which now reads like a spirited call to arms, full of hope for the future, seemed so dark and rebellious to its contemporaries. The explanation has to do with the fact that this was the first time in many years that a Swedish author had spoken out directly—and it shocked those who had become accustomed to the artifices of 'serious literature'. Strindberg came in off the street, from newspaper offices, taverns and studios, and brought with him some of the language spoken in those places. Small wonder that he seemed sinister and dangerous to readers who had been living in a world of affectation and pretence.

As Smedmark has demonstrated, Strindberg's satire was not, generally speaking, any more savage than that practised in the liberal press of the day. However, Strindberg was expressing himself in another medium, that of *belles-lettres*, in which readers did not expect to find that type of attack. Nevertheless, there are a few icy blasts blowing through the novel that remind one of Gert and the revolutionary movements of the day. It is, first and foremost, Olle Montanus who provides that quality, being a curious hybrid of buffoon and guiding spirit. After he has drowned himself, friends find a thick and slimy wallet in his breast pocket, covered with seaweed: echoes of Ophelia. The wallet contains a bundle of closely written papers, inscribed 'to him who wants to read'. It is a message from 'the bottom of the ocean', to quote Ibsen's *The Wild Duck*, and it can be seen as an expression of the novel's subconscious level.

Olle's friends take the manuscript and proceed to the restaurant Piperska muren (Piper's Wall). While they have drinks by an open fire—for the proximity of death has chilled them—Dr Borg starts reading. It is a bitter text—about the curse of manual labour; about the artistic impulse as selfish yearning for freedom from responsibility; about the impossibility of living without suffering damage to one's soul; and about death as the only possible and dignified way out. Perhaps the critics were not, after all, so far off the mark when they sensed something wild and unusual in this book. The feeling of insufferable pressure caused by life in a hypocritical society finds an outlet in Olle Montanus's symbolic suicide.

Chapter Five

'THE SWEDISH PEOPLE' AND 'THE NEW KINGDOM'

I

F OR A SHORT period during the years after *The Red Room*—'the happy days of my life', as he called them—Strindberg was tempted by the bourgeois existence his father and grandfather had led, and tried to find happiness in 'the little life'. He was making money: *The Red Room* alone earned him 2,200 kronor. On 26 February, Strindberg was married 'to the earth and eternal life and duties and society and bourgeois law', to quote words he himself used when congratulating a friend on the birth of a child: for on that day, his daughter Karin was born. She was his favourite child, and inherited flashes of his genius. As Strindberg pointed out, playfully but he had a point, she was born with a dowry: only a day or two after her birth, the Royal Theatre—that long-besieged citadel—accepted a play he had written in the course of the preceding weeks while his home, through Siri's pregnancy, had been filled with creative forces.

The play was called *The Secret of the Guild*. Written in a triumphant mood, it deals with two master masons, Jacques and Sten, who vie with one another for the task of the rebuilding and completion of Uppsala Cathedral. It is a transparent allegory in fifteenth-century guise: an excellent demonstration of Strindberg's ability to invent for his own consolation tales about heroes who emerge victorious, after afflictions and humiliations.

The strong, joyful, productive Sten is Strindberg's *alter ego*, and behind the sombre and scheming Jacques and his accomplices and benefactors we glimpse Strindberg's competitors: Henrik Ibsen, Björnstjerne Björnson, Edvard Bäckström, and the Royal Theatre's custodians, Frans Hedberg and Erik af Edholm. The cathedral to be rebuilt stands for *The Art of Drama* whose forgotten Shakespearean secrets Strindberg had revealed in *Master Olof*. Sten, the master mason, is the first in a long series of self-portraits by the adult Strindberg, showing him as he wished to be seen now that his youth was over: a vigorous Renaissance man, often clad in the travelling garb of a pilgrim.

It is Jacques who gets the commission: Ibsen was still the dominant figure in the theatre, and a play of Björnson's had been chosen for the inauguration of the New Theatre which Strindberg had so wistfully contemplated from his window on Kaptensgatan. But the tower Jacques has built collapses; Sten is forced into exile and considers suicide, although he soon regains his self-respect. We are told that his rival envies him in the way a barren woman envies those who have children. Interestingly enough, Strindberg does not entirely abandon Jacques to the spectators' hatred but is able to identify with him as well. Jacques is an evil man and ready to commit the most gruesome crimes in order to achieve his goal—he even uses rat poison to rid himself of an adversary—but he is also a suffering man, shaken to his very foundations, shattered by his own passions, of which the most dangerous is his ambition, his willingness to go to any lengths. If Sten is Strindberg as fairy-tale hero, Jacques is the wicked brother, driven by similar ambition but lacking scruples. If one combines the two, one may catch a glimpse of Strindberg himself.

The play's first night was on 3 May. Siri played a minor part, that of Jacques' wife Margaretha who tries to console her conscience-stricken husband. According to her daughter, Siri liked the play for its certainty of belief: the villian gets his just deserts. There is no record of any positive reaction on her part to *The Red Room*.

2

In the summer of 1880 Strindberg wrote a prose poem entitled *Haze* (for which the Swedish word is *solrök*—'sunsmoke'). It reflects, with charm and precision, his psychological and physiological state during the first years after his breakthrough. The poem begins by describing the family's springtime move to their summer dwelling on Kymmendö, the island where *Master Olof* was written. The poet is seen standing on the deck of the steamer, a dutiful *petit bourgeois* paterfamilias, keeping an eye on the family belongings: armchairs, a drawing-room sofa, a bathtub containing potted plants, and the baby's perambulator, which was white with a blue folding top stained with milk. Had the poem been written during one of the subsequent summers on Kymmendö, the objects on deck would have certainly included a number of soapboxes, obtained from the grocery store and filled with seedlings of cucumber, melon, purple gillyflower, mignon-ette, etc., which Strindberg used to plant as early as March in the bay windows of his city apartment, and which were then transferred to the garden on Kymmendö, which he cultivated with passion.

Haze goes on to describe the island itself, in a series of fresh and lively tableaux: all his life, Strindberg smothered it in endearments—'my flower-basket in the sea', 'island of bliss'. But the most interesting passage of the poem deals with an excursion the author makes to a nearby, uninhabited island. On it he discovers an abandoned felspar mine and waxes indignant over the violation of nature caused by the mining operation. The ground is 'broken as if by unclean, rooting animals', and 'the intestines of the earth' have been exposed. He launches into curses against man who defiles and destroys what was once innocent and peaceful. In the grass, he finds the sole of a rough working man's boot: it belonged to one of the men who were forced to do slave labour in the mine, and indicates a deformation of the foot. Then the author flees from the scene of devastation, back to his boat: on the way, he is surprised to see footprints in the sand. An unexpected footprint on an uninhabited island is one of the archetypal scenes of our culture. Strindberg does not mention *Robinson Crusoe*, one of his favourite books; nevertheless, the dramatic effect stems from it. Does it belong to the miner with the deformed foot, come back to exact revenge? The next instant, Strindberg discovers that he has merely crossed his own tracks. He takes out his telescope, points it across the bay, and sees his wife's white dress and the blue hood of the perambulator. He gets into the boat, has a drink and a sandwich, hoists the sail and asks himself, as he takes the tiller: 'You have received everything you wished for, the very best things in life—so what are you complaining about?'

In *The Red Room*, Arvid Falk swears that he will not abandon the working man's cause. In *Haze*, the memory of the deformed foot is swept away by the sight of the wife's dress and the perambulator. In Arvid Falk's name, Strindberg had pledged himself to political causes, and the prose version of *Master Olof* contains the implicit declaration that he would stake everything on his poetry and refuse any form of compromise. Understandably, the wind of success that was blowing at this time made him a little reluctant to redeem his pledges.

In August 1880, Alexander Kielland, one of Norway's leading authors, wrote a letter of praise to Strindberg, saying that he had found compassion for the world, a 'secret sob', which came through the seemingly 'heartless tone' of *The Red Room*. Strindberg had every reason to regard Kielland as an empowered emissary of Norway's young radicals, but he replied to the letter in a spirit Kielland can hardly have expected. He did not mention the 'sob'—instead, he talked about his love of the sea and his happy marriage, and urged Kielland to read *The Secret of the Guild*. He adopted the same dismissive attitude towards Edvard Brandes, Georg Brandes's brother, who wrote to him in July. Edvard Brandes praised the virile tone of *The Red*

Room, as well as its attacks on reaction and hypocrisy, and invited Strindberg to collaborate with him. Strindberg replied that there were other things besides social criticism in the book—in particular, he pointed to the great drinking party at Falk's house, which is one of the comic bravura pieces in the novel. Furthermore, Strindberg was hesitant about the possibility of collaboration:

> I dare not predict what use I might be to any party! I am afraid it would be minimal, as I am still busy picking up the pieces, am not entirely lucid, and seem to myself merely a conglomerate of discarded convictions, having fought myself into a state of exhaustion; unfortunately, too, I possess 'talent' to such a degree that the ethical never gains clear expression, or else I have become so sceptical, having seen how most of what I enthused about was, in the end, sheer vanity, that I hardly have anything left but my noble hatred of all oppression and all attempts to gild wretchedness!

3

Kymmendö became the scene of happy summers; a particular highlight was the christening of the Strindberg's second daughter, Greta, in the summer of 1881. The family had been accompanied to the island by a midwife, 'the earth woman' as Strindberg called her, and the baby was born on 9 June, when the lilies of the valley were blooming. The christening became a major event. Carl Larsson, who drew the beautifully coloured invitation—with Siri and August in the centre—later described the festivities in his autobiography. The male guests wore tails, and when one of them, Anton Stuxberg, appeared without his decorations, Strindberg took that as a slight and flared up: happily, Stuxberg had packed his decorations in his luggage.

In *The Occult Diary*, Strindberg writes that Kymmendö was always an occult experience for him, one of supernatural beauty. It was, possibly, his orientation towards absolutes that doomed him to perennial disappointment and continual separations, from both people and places. He had an insatiable appetite for company, festivities, and pageants, and he described the joy of sitting around a table with friends better than any other Scandinavian author; yet there was always something missing, some small detail that marred and destroyed everything. Strindberg's accounts of happiness gain an almost ecstatic quality from the fact that this happiness is constantly threatened.

19 Invitation to Greta Strindberg's christening on Kymmendö, 20 July 1881. Drawing by
Carl Larsson

Like many other basically shy people, Strindberg wanted his social life to be organized, and to accomplish this he founded in the autumn of 1880 The Club, a society of friends in a long-established but at that time still thriving Stockholm tradition. His grandfather Zacharias would have approved. The Club's members entertained themselves with theatricals, excursions and dinners. Strindberg devised a parodistic 'ceremonial of reception' and arranged for the printing of huge brightly coloured posters which gave exact details of the agenda of festive meetings. Thus, for example, in April 1881 the Club's puppet theatre performed a carnival play by Hans Sachs, translated by August Strindberg and titled *Ulenspiegel's Entanglements with the Priest's Housekeeper and His Horse*; in it, 'Mr August Strindberg' made 'his first stage appearance, as The Horse'.

Not content with literary achievement, Strindberg's ambition extended itself into the realms of scholarship, and those pursuits were to attain formidable dimensions as the years went by. Strindberg had taken advantage of his library post in order to conduct research of his own, mainly in the field of cultural history. One of his projects concerned the ladybird: he drew a map indicating the geographical distribution of various names for that insect in different parts of Sweden. According to his own statement, he had conducted interviews with travelling salesmen about this matter. He then used the results of the inquiry to demonstrate that the population of Sweden was not of unified ethnic origin.

Strindberg devoted himself with particular enthusiasm to the study of Swedish achievements in foreign lands. This was an ambition typical of the expansionist, empire-building nineteenth century, but Strindberg had an additional, personal incentive. His closest friend, Anton Stuxberg, a zoologist, was chosen to be a member of Adolf Erik Nordenskjöld's expedition aboard the *Vega* which was to navigate around Asia by the northern route. The success of that expedition made it the greatest exploit in nineteenth-century Swedish history, and it became firmly imprinted in Strindberg's consciousness. King Oscar II himself was one of its sponsors. 'You have to see to it, *without fail* and no matter what the cost, that I get back my dress suit which you borrowed last year in March or April. Tomorrow, Friday, I have to go to dinner at the Palace, and *must* have my dress suit,' Stuxberg wrote to Strindberg on 25 January 1877, immediately after receiving the notification.

The voyage of the *Vega* lasted from July 1878 to April 1880. During the winter of *The Red Room*'s composition, the *Vega* lay frozen in the Arctic Sea, unable to communicate with the rest of the world, in a womb of ice out of which either triumph or death would be born. Strindberg and Stuxberg (both their initials, incidentally, were AS) had parallel destinies, and they supported and inspired one another. 'Stux', as Strindberg called him, financed the printing of *Master Olof* (the verse version). 'Strix'—

Strindberg—for his part provided his friend with data from his research into Swedish travellers in the Far East and Siberia.

Strindberg had become especially interested in the fates of Karolingian prisoners of war in Siberia after the disastrous battle of Poltava in 1709 in which a large part of the Swedish army was surrounded and taken prisoner, while Karl XII managed to escape and flee to Turkey. One of those prisoners, Johan Gustaf Renat, had drawn a map of Lop-nor and the Tarim Basin. It had been forgotten until Strindberg came across it in 1879 in the library in Linköping. That discovery was to play a strange part in his life: it became his main weapon when, in 1910, he launched his full-scale attack on Sven Hedin, the purpose of which was to prove that Hedin's Asian discoveries were nothing but humbug and bragging. Renat's map was the main piece of evidence. In March 1880, the Geographic Society of Russia awarded Strindberg its Silver Medal for his discovery, an international honour that to some extent matched the one accorded to Stuxberg. Had Strindberg known that a distinguished member of the Russian society, Prince Kropotkin, had just been expelled for opinions that were close to his own, he might not have accepted the decoration.

On 22 April 1880, the *Vega* returned to Stockholm and became the object of the greatest celebration the city had seen that century. 'It is going to be amazing. They'll ring the church-bells, and Skeppsholmen will be blown to smithereens with dynamite!' Strindberg told Stuxberg on 6 April. As it turned out, the celebration was, indeed, almost as spectacular as Strindberg had anticipated: bonfires were burning on the Palace roof, buildings were festooned with garlands, and on the Logård steps stood the King himself, 'a God the Father wearing plumes and the Seraphim ribbon, to hand Nordenkjöld a diamond-studded decoration', in the words of Hjalmar Söderberg, who attended the event as a ten-year-old.

It may have occurred to Strindberg that the festivities of that spring coincided appropriately with the powerful upswing of his own career. The *Vega* expedition provided him with a concrete connection with the nineteenth century's triumphs in the natural sciences and voyages of discovery—at the Royal Library he worked on the expedition's collection of Japanese material, being relieved of his regular duties to do so—and also with a direction in which to channel his future ambition.

4

His research into cultural and historical subjects provided Strindberg with material for a great deal of discursive writing which became his bread-and-butter during the following years—a more elevated version of the hackwork he had engaged in during the 1870s. The reading public of the time was eager to know more about the hidden life of 'the people', and Strindberg knew how to take advantage of that enthusiasm. As was pointed out by Buckle in England, Taine in France, and Georg Brandes in Denmark— three great stars in Strindberg's literary firmament—the development of cultures and nations is determined by time, nature, and environment, and not by great personalities and the ideas proposed by them. In Sweden and all over Europe it was a time of intensive folklore studies, and a phalanx of liberal historians proceeded to undermine the monarchy and the aristocracy, using historical examples as ammunition against contemporary rulers.

One of the founders of the association Hantverkets Vänner (The Friends of Handicraft), Jakob Kulle, was also a member of The Club. Strindberg was an early publicist of his activities. In the 1870s, Artur Hazelius began his lifework, founding the Nordic Museum in 1880; in the same year, he also proposed the creation of an outdoor museum in Stockholm which would present Sweden's past in the form of authentic peasant dwellings, workshops, church steeples, even country manors, surrounded by all the indigenous fauna in an environment that would be as natural as possible. The result was Skansen, and it assumed a place of importance in Strindberg's life; later on, he described the zoo's caged wolves as symbols of a revolutionary working class.

Strindberg became an early associate of Hazelius and provided him with various suggestions, being a talented browser and scavenger, turning things up during his early morning walks through Stockholm, often in the company of Richard Bergström. One day he wrote to Hazelius about some gilded leather wall-coverings he had discovered in an attic in Solna parsonage, and later about an 'invaluable collection of old tiles' on Strandvägen, 'this side of the Djurgård bridge'. He donated a Tarot deck to the Nordic Museum—an example of the cards used by gypsies since time immemorial, full of occult significance.

Strindberg's first major work in the field was *Old Stockholm*, which appeared between 1880 and 1882 in serial form, which was popular in the nineteenth century: Dickens had been its acknowledged master. A shrewd author knew how to create 'cliffhanger' endings for each instalment, in order to hold his readers' interest. Strindberg went to work with boyish enthusiasm, descending into cellars in Stockholm's Old Town with a miner's lantern, mountaineer's rope, and a ball of twine like Theseus in the labyrinth. He investigated the attic of Storkyrkan (the 'Great Church') which contained old pillory benches, stretchers and discarded certificates of burial, and described his adventures in that bleak place and elsewhere in a series of articles in 1881.

Old Stockholm is a lively description of everyday life in the city through the centuries, with its celebrations of Christmas and Easter, and the heyday of its associations—the Order of Aurora included; it tells us how the cane was used in schools, how the fire departments operated, how people stared at eccentrics in the street. Not unexpectedly, we meet the cartographer Renat, just returned from Siberia, on an imaginary walk through eighteenth-century Stockholm.

Strindberg managed to create the illusion that he had access to a collective memory which included the city's entire history of 600 years. In his autobiography, he states that this work made him feel ancient, to the degree that he 'had drawings made of objects from his childhood as if they were antiques; while reading the proofs, I had to discard them, since they were too new'. Dublin made Joyce feel the same way.

Old Stockholm was merely a prelude. In April 1881, Strindberg signed a contract with Fritzes, the publishers, for a comprehensive cultural history of Sweden, for the considerable sum of 10,000 kronor. Its complete title was *The Swedish People at Work and Play, in War and Peace, at Home and Abroad, Or, One Thousand Years of the History of Swedish Education and Customs*. The work, almost 1,000 pages in its original edition, with Carl Larsson as its main illustrator (which was the reason for his stay on Kymmendö in 1881), became one of the decade's most lavish book productions.

Strindberg wrote rapidly and impetuously, examining one epoch after another from the people's point of view, as he had learned to do in his days as a journalist. It was, of course, an impossible task to write an entire cultural history of Sweden in eighteen months. It took Troels-Lund, who had started work on his monumental *Daily Life in the North in the Sixteenth Century*, a lifetime to complete it. Strindberg had to stretch his narrative canvas over a framework consisting of far too few facts. Like *Old Stockholm*, the book was published in instalments; reading it, one becomes keenly aware of the moments in which the author finds himself in acute difficulty and starts gearing himself up for the next instalment. A wooden fifteenth century is followed by a lively sixteenth; after barren stretches about medieval merchants and artisans we get exuberant ones about the lives of peasants and, certainly, fishermen.

The Swedish People can be regarded as a work in the spirit of Artur Hazelius, a cleverly arranged outdoor museum, where, as in most museums, a wealth of objects compensates for a lack of living spirit and imagination. Food is a favourite subject, as it always was in Strindberg's personal life. We are given ample data on soups, roasts, and pâtés as well as on the condiments these required. The joint of beef in the manorial kitchen, marinaded for twenty-four hours before being coated with lard, is noted with as much relish as the broth prepared from partridges, capons, mutton and veal 'which are hermetically sealed in a copper vessel and cooked for twelve hours'.

One of the prerequisites for Strindberg's prodigious output was his ability to deal with such large amounts of data, his insatiable appetite for facts. *The Swedish People* became a huge warehouse on which he could rely later whenever he needed details for his historical plays and stories.

5

The drawing of Strindberg by Carl Larsson for the cover of his collected juvenilia which Adolf Bonnier published in 1880 gives a good impression of Strindberg's appearance during these honeymoon years with Swedish society, but it does not afford much insight into his personality. In the drawing, Strindberg looks calmly straight ahead; his forehead is smooth and clear, as if the thundercloud Elof Tegnér saw on it had never existed. His hair is unruly, but looks soft. To the left of his head is a drawing of a coltsfoot, to the right, a flowering hawthorn branch. The collection was titled *In Early Spring*, and the book cover is green. It seems inconceivable that the hawthorn would ever sting.

But soon afterwards Strindberg's life became stormy. It is not easy to establish exactly why, although Strindberg himself has given us a whole series of interpretations. In a letter to Verner von Heidenstam in 1885 he claimed that he bade farewell to the social establishment in order to follow his vocation as a spokesman for the oppressed. One year later, on the other hand, in *The Serving Maid's Son*, he played down that motive and, instead, pointed to his 'passion for discovering errors' and to his desire to take revenge for the injustices suffered by his class. One thing remains certain: he contributed actively to his own adversity.

He wrote a provocative back-cover blurb for the first instalment of *The Swedish People*: in it, he said that Erik Gustaf Geijer, revered as the country's foremost historian, counted only 'the King's lackeys as members of the Swedish people', and that he, Strindberg, intended to atone for Geijer's failure by describing people 'in the small circumstances of their quiet lives'.

He was instantly made to feel the consequences of such provocation. Once again, wrote *Aftonbladet*, Strindberg had demonstrated his 'colossal lack of understanding for what is elevated and noble', by attacking the 'great late historian'. In *Stockholms Dagblad*, Strindberg's colleague at the Royal Library, Christoffer Eichhorn, compared him to a barker at a fair who by his shouts and fanfares tries to attract the public to the 'wonderful curiosities' to be found inside the tent. Worse still: a number of Sweden's leading professional historians, Hans Hildebrand and Oscar Montelius among them, became irritated by Strindberg's presumptuousness and published extremely negative, sometimes, admittedly, even petty, reviews and comments. A bronze razor which, according to the critics, Strindberg had wrongly dated, was just one of the many examples of his research errors, which were discussed in the newspaper columns during the autumn of 1881.

Strindberg defended himself vigorously, calling for support from Denmark and Norway: now, he found, the formerly rebutted allies could be of use. In October, Alexander Kielland was told that Strindberg stood 'so infernally alone in the midst of this conflagration I have caused ... I have knocked down an old idol [Geijer], and now the people want to stone me to death.' And, in June 1882, Strindberg wrote to Edvard Brandes that he was 'utterly friendless and hounded by one pack after another'.

In reality, all that this isolation and loneliness consisted of (much as he makes of it even in *The Serving Maid's Son*), was that a large faction of the liberal persuasion closed ranks around him. Typically, an editorial in *Dagens Nyheter* of 1 November 1881, praised Strindberg's readiness to speak 'for the people's cause' and compared him to Germany's Professor Mommsen who was not afraid to tell Bismarck the truth. Swedish servility resulted in accusations of sacrilege as soon as anyone 'who is not rooted in the soil of the universities dares to publish his independent historical theories'.

Even more encouraging was the fact that Strindberg began to acquire ideological allies: sparks from *Master Olof* and *The Red Room* kindled the imagination of the young. Strindberg had cause to remember the Gert of the prose version whom he had defused in later versions of *Master Olof*, and the play re-emerged from the dungeon to which it had been confined: it was the leading feature in the collection of youthful works. Thus the original version had now become universally available: moreover, Edvard Stjernström was dead, and the New Theatre's director since 1879 had been Ludvig Josephson, uncle of Ernst Josephson, modern Sweden's most prominent painter, whose career Strindberg had followed closely down the years. Ludvig Josephson was an extremely erudite and enthusiastic theatrical administrator who had a passion for drama in the grand manner, that of Shakespeare above all. In January 1881, Strindberg sent the prose version of *Master Olof* to Josephson, who immediately decided to put it on the stage, angrily chastising the directorate who had refused it as lazy and lacking artistic acumen. The first night was on 30 December 1881, Strindberg's wedding anniversary. He could not muster the nerve to attend the performance but remained at home on Östermalmsgatan, where the family had moved on 1 October, contemplating the nine years he had been forced to wait—the greatest injustice life ever inflicted upon him, as he was to claim repeatedly in later years.

The critics received the play well. Strindberg was a celebrity now, and was treated with respect. Nevertheless, it did not attract audiences, any more than *The Secret of the Guild* had done. It was too long—six hours—

and the theatregoers missed their customary drinks after the play. Yet it was of decisive importance that this revolutionary work of his youth had made its existence known.

The economic depression of the 1870s continued into the eighties. While the strike in Sundsvall was still a subject for discussion, strikes in general became more common: Stockholm experienced two of them in 1881. Strike meetings were held at Lilljans, where the rooster had crowed so idyllically in *The Red Room*.

In March 1881, Russia's Emperor Alexander was murdered; to the terror of Klemming, who went into hiding, the Tsar had not long before that time inspected the Royal Library during a state visit to Sweden. In the fall of that year, August Palm began his agitator's activity on behalf of Socialism, receiving a great deal of abuse in the press and threats from incensed landowners. The carpenter's bitter words in *The Red Room*, addressed to society ladies engaged in charitable works, became increasingly pertinent every day:

'And a day will come when things get even worse, but that is when we'll come down from Vita Bergen, from Skinnarviksbergen, from Tyskbagar- bergen, we'll come with a thunderous din like a waterfall, and we'll ask to have our beds back again. Ask? No, take them! And you'll have to lie on carpenter's benches as I had to, and you'll get nothing to eat but potatoes until your bellies get taut as drums, as if you'd had to go through the 'ordeal by water', just as we've had to. . . .'

In the autobiography, Strindberg writes that the young men who approached him in 1881 seemed to him to be representatives of a developing climate of opinion that one day would become the one shared by the majority. 'Symptoms of an awakening youth have become visible, and you'll see that both of us, before long, will stand at the head of our own armies,' Strindberg told Kielland on 2 December 1881, adding: 'And that is not possible without sympathy! Alone, we wither! Isn't that so?'

One member of that awakening youth, which Strindberg called Young Sweden (following the Danish example), was 21-year-old Hjalmar Branting who would become the founder of Social Democracy in Sweden, as were Pehr Staaff, Erik Thyselius, Isidor Kjellberg—who had done time in prison for violations of then current press laws—and several others; all of whom joined Strindberg and Knut Wicksell, the economist and proponent of birth control who was to achieve international fame, in planning a newspaper to present their views.

Strindberg claimed later that from the very beginning he was afraid of becoming a pawn in other people's games. In January 1882, he wrote to Carl Rupert Nyblom and his wife—who has extended their sympathies from *The Secret of the Guild* to *Master Olof*—that he felt like an old idealist among these young friends and feared that they would tear him to pieces as soon as he refused to go along with them. At the same time, he predicted 'a time of wolves' and social 'eruptions', and stated that he would side with those who came, weapon in hand, from below. His friends had impressed upon him that he had to take a stand in the class struggle, and he was taking the first step in the direction of 'the serving maid's son'. In 1882, he read Georg Brandes's book on Ferdinand Lassalle and criticized Brandes for not stressing the man's message sufficiently, and for failing to suppress all negative aspects that might do that message harm.

Strindberg was, ideologically, more radical than any of his friends, and they soon realized that he might be a dangerous ally. With increasing frequency he referred to the era's favourite terrorist's weapon—dynamite— and in a poem paid homage to its inventor, Alfred Nobel, little knowing what miseries that name would cause him later. He wrote that Nobel had, with 'his white ointment, healed many wounds made by cane and knout'. Berthold Swartz, the inventor of gunpowder, had given kings the power to train their cannon on the common people: now dynamite gave those people a chance to retaliate. The poem ends:

> Du Swartz, en liten edition lät taga
> för de förnäma och för furstehusen!
> Nobel! Du gav en väldig folkupplaga,
> som ständigt lägges upp i hundratusen!

> *You, Swartz, had a small edition published*
> *for the nobles and the princely houses!*
> *Nobel! You published a huge popular edition,*
> *constantly reissued in a hundred thousand copies!*

Strindberg's friends hoped that he would act as a kind of battering ram in their attack on the status quo. In the spring of 1882, Strindberg did, indeed, make promises in that direction. He arrived on Kymmendö earlier than customary. Siri was on tour in Finland and received reports from him containing the suggestion that he should henceforth take care of house-keeping in order to keep expenses down. It was not well received.

On 13 April he had finished *The Swedish People*—an amazing feat, especially considering that during January and February he had written the fairytale play *Lucky Per's Journey*, a commission from Josephson, experi-enced the illness of his youngest daughter, Greta, and experienced endless difficulties with the illustrations for *The Swedish People*; in addition, Siri had lost her job with the Royal Theatre in the spring of 1881, and he had busied himself appealing to friends in the theatrical world to provide her with work.

At this point, Strindberg was more relaxed than ever, in an intellectual sense: he was seized by a mood of irrepressible levity, and his love of exaggeration became very evident. 'Reaction here in Sweden is growing by leaps and bounds, and it is remarkable how I myself call it forth by my own excesses,' he wrote to Edvard Brandes on 13 December 1881, making it clear that he was conscious of the effects of his provocative writings. His friends received letters that were more light-hearted than usual. Carl Larsson, who had been attacked during the polemics around *The Swedish People*, for historically imprecise illustrations, received directions that were followed to the letter. Thus, Strindberg on 2 March 1882: '*The Factory Worker*. The yard of a glass factory; blazing furnace; a sweaty, breathless worker (the future Communard!) throws his head back and breathes in fresh air (Michael Angelo's slave!).' Or: '*The Forest Guerrilla*. Hey! Society's enemy (Aug. Strindberg!) stands at the edge of the woods, shaking his fist at a burning village to which he has just set fire; his other arm embraces his mistress.'

In a letter in May to Pehr Staaff Strindberg renamed Kymmendö 'the den of Nihilists', and it was there that he sat down to write his reply to the attacks on *The Swedish People*, also hoping to meet his friends' expectations. On 16 May, he wrote to Staaff:

> I have been outside, greeted all old friends, trees, rocks, picked morels, carried horse manure to the cucumber beds, turned the soil, sowed spinach, radishes, etc. Drank evening toddies with the fishermen, talking nonsense about sea-birds and different kinds of fish, while not forgetting to use the opportunity to refresh their hatred of royalty and institutions, and I think that those little seeds fell on to a well-fertilized, clayey soil.

By the end of the month, he was in full swing: 'Now I'll plug up my ears and get going on my work for the summer, you'd be able to shoot me down like a blackcock at his mating song, I won't say a word.' The mating woodcock, or as it is known in Scotland, capercaillie, becomes so engrossed in its love rites that it does not notice the hunter: the image is exact, in regard to the combination of intense concentration with clarity and fluency which characterizes Strindberg's creative intoxication at that time. The work in question was *The New Kingdom*, and it proceeded apace. On 2 August the finished book was sent to Claes Looström, Strindberg's new publisher, an easygoing and imaginative person with whom Strindberg corresponded in a manner that was far more self-indulgent than any affected by him towards other publishers.

6

The New Kingdom consists of ten chapters of contemporary Swedish manners, chronicled at a tremendous pace—to the accompaniment, as it were, of cracking whips and rolling drums in a circus tent. For almost a century, the book has been, for Swedish readers, what Voltaire's *Candide* represents for an international audience. Its main satirical theme is straightforward and unequivocally expressed in the epigraph of the title page—the scene in Dickens's *Pickwick Papers* in which Mr Pickwick solemnly addresses Mr Winkle with the famous words: 'You are a humbug, sir!'

Swedish society, as seen in *The New Kingdom*, is ruled by crooks who support and protect one another. They speak of the common good but think only of what is good for them. The public lies about God, the homeland and the obligations of power and prosperity merely conceal greedy self-interest and materialism of the most crass kind. 'You are a humbug, sir,' is what Strindberg wanted to shout from every public building, in every congregation, on every street, in order to evoke liberating and mocking laughter.

It is a satirical tradition with popular roots, still practised in the daily press at that time. Strindberg's inspiration derived not only from Dickens but to an even greater degree from the young American nation where Mark Twain, Artemus Ward, and Bret Harte—whose work Strindberg had translated in his Grub Street days—cultivated precisely that slightly frenzied irreverence towards everything and everyone.

As we have seen, Strindberg had long practised ways of looking at society from above or below: in *The New Kingdom* he descends even further, scrutinizing the homeland from a perspective of gutters and basement windows. In the chapter 'Claris majorum exemplis' ('After the shining example of the forefathers'—part of the inscription on Stockholm's House of Nobility), the target is pretentious nobility. The narrator of the chapter is an old bedbug who has lived in the great hall of the House of Nobility for a hundred years: in the company of her 99-year-old daughter, old Madame Bedbug makes a laborious excursion from one end of the hall to the other, passing, on the way, a row of brightly painted coats of arms. The bugs crawl over serpents, griffins, dragons, towers, castles, spires, stars, and suns—the trademarks and insignia of the aristocracy—and finally reach a blue fold in the recently restored painting of Mother Svea, where the old bedbug tells her daughter about the noble family of Hund af Hutlösa (The Hounds of Shameless). One member of this 'infamous' family is Strindberg's enemy Hugo Nisbeth, editor of the journal *Figaro*: anyone interested in the matter could easily verify this by looking up Nisbeth's coat of arms—as in the book, it consisted of three identical dog's heads, each one bearing a bone in its jaws.

The book's satirical tableaux are all viewed from a similarly low perspective. Each one of them is aimed at some social weakness—fawning upon royalty, the lies of speechmakers, hereditary snobbery; the academies and their pretence of being the spiritual leaders of the oppressed; the mercantile system which knew how to exclude troublesome outsiders. At the same time, each one is a personal settling of accounts with an adversary or competitor. When Strindberg was taken to task for this, he replied that every idea is represented by a person, and that it was impossible to criticize matters without naming names. He even cited Dante as the great example of satire which is both general and specific.

Indeed, it is questionable whether it is possible to create effective satire without personal targets. Anyone who scourges vice in general will be greeted by universal applause, and no one will feel personally affected. Strindberg is matter-of-fact and direct: his work gains life and impact from the fires of personal anger, from the way it homes in on specific individuals.

He took this impetus a long way. The bedbugs travelling across those coats of arms do not seem to pass the turreted wall of the Wrangels or the helmet of the von Essens, yet Siri must have thought of the possibility. . . . But when personal matters have been forgotten, and no one any longer remembers either the coats of arms or the journal *Figaro*, the chapter nevertheless remains a lively diatribe against hereditary privilege and the power it wielded at one time.

The critic Wirsén became the subject of one of the book's most overt attacks, disguised very thinly by the initials 'WCD' instead of the 'CDW' he used to sign his work with. He is described as a 'literary bailiff', the keeper of the great seal of 'idealism'; the characterization of his criticism, which specialized in searching out what he called 'filth', is really brilliant, and applies to a certain type that can be found in every era.

7

On 28 September 1882, *The New Kingdom* appeared, with the subtitle: *Satirical narratives from the era of assassinations and jubilees.* It was a bomb that exploded right in the middle of Sweden's establishment; it was read by everybody and became the talk of the day. The serious right-wing newspapers observed a haughty silence—always the most reliable method of repression. Secretly, many rejoiced in the liberating word. The poet Count Snoilsky who had been forced into exile by a divorce, yet cultivated a stance of silent opposition, did not dare to express his sympathies directly to Strindberg, far less to the public, because of the attack on his colleague in the academy, Wirsén: then as now, it was important to remain united on the surface of things. Nevertheless, he conveyed a message of encouragement, via Klemming.

In the newspaper *Nya Dagligt Allehanda*, two days after the book's publication, it was compared to the obscure scandal sheets which were peddled in the streets 'in a more or less secretive manner'. This initiated a favourite and oft-repeated theme: the word 'repulsive' featured in the columns of various publications, and *Figaro* announced on 1 October that Strindberg had decided to move abroad 'due to an attack of insanity'. One cannot, wrote the paper, 'but congratulate him most enthusiastically on such a wise decision, which must have been determined by a most urgent necessity'. Strindberg still remembered that notice when he wrote *A Fool's Apology* and, in that book, connected it with his wife's machinations.

Even the liberal papers were hesitant. In *Handelstidningen*, Karl Warburg made a lame attempt to defend the book. *Dagens Nyheter* exercised great diplomatic skills, praising Strindberg for his 'disgust with the hypocrisy in all social situations and among all social classes', but finding it 'embarrassing' that he took revenge for personal slights and transgressed against 'good taste'. Strindberg's intentions were described as 'noble and ambitious', and the notice ended in explaining the author's errors by his having 'led a life of the soul into which little sun has fallen, causing him to look at the world from its dark side, from the very beginning'. It was hoped that 'soon a mild ray of the sunshine of hope and philanthropy would penetrate the presently dark night of his world view'.

It was—and still is—a persistent notion that anyone who criticizes and points out lies and inequities must be of a sombre disposition, while anyone who praises things must be of a bright and positive cast of mind. In addition, the article in *Dagens Nyheter* was one of the first indications of a myth that regarded Strindberg as having been exceptionally oppressed and damaged by injustice: with his own enthusiastic assistance, that myth was to thrive and become impossible to eradicate.

During the autumn, Strindberg spent much energy in composing crushing rejoinders to his detractors, and he encouraged his friends to assist him. Work began on a collaborative pamphlet—tentatively entitled *The Old Kingdom*—which was designed to wipe out the opposition. The enterprise never really got off the ground. Strindberg invented all kinds of witticisms, lethal one-liners, episodes that would embarrass his adversaries: a form of infamous gossip that thrives in small societies and nourishes its frequently energetic life by doses of envy, overcrowding, and love-hate feelings. Aristophanes of Athens, Dante of Florence, Joyce of Dublin are specialists of this, and Strindberg aimed to join their ranks. But he soon grew tired of petty polemics, and in October 1882, diverted his energies to a sequence of short stories, *Swedish Fates and Adventures*: in these, the battle was transferred to a more elevated artistic level.

He rented a studio room to work in, far out in Djurgården. A scrap found among his posthumous papers states that he had to do this in order to escape from the beggars who invaded his house after the publication of *The New Kingdom*. While furious rejoinders kept on appearing in the papers, and hardly a day went by without the public's being reminded of Strindberg's existence, he, with incredible ease and speed, wrote a number of stories that have since become among the most popular of his entire production. He was writing about himself, and at the same time gaining freedom of movement by means of historical costume. He also boosted his self-esteem by a number of artistic innovations.

The most memorable of the stories is entitled 'For Better and for Worse'. It is an extraordinary example of Strindberg's ability to incorporate the emotional turmoil of the moment in truly well-balanced works of art. At the beginning of December, Stockholm saw the publication of an unusually unpleasant pamphlet, *The Newest Kingdom, Characteristic Narratives from the Era of Thoughtlessness and Impudence*, authored by a pseudonymous Michel Perrin. In it, Strindberg's bankruptcy was discussed; *The New Kingdom* was described as a 'lucrative speculation on the book market'; and invidious insinuations were made about Strindberg's marriage to a divorcee. 'When fortune denies the realist his own marital hearth, he shares that of his friends and acquaintances'—a sentence that gives a clear indication of the pamphlet's level of discourse.

Pehr Staaff published a simultaneous counter-attack, but it did not console Strindberg; after reading the Perrin pamphlet, he wrote to Looström and asked him for an immediate advance for travel—2,000 francs—'so that I can travel and get out of here'. At this time, he also wrote his short story, delivering it to the publisher on 11 January 1883.

Its protagonist, Hans Brevmålare (Hans Letter-Painter), lives in medieval Stockholm. His passion for the truth drives him to expose corruption among the clergy. The culprits take action against him, and he becomes the subject of a damaging libellous pamphlet. The populace becomes inflamed by the accusations contained in it, and we witness a grandiose speech in which Hans defends himself, stressing the fact that his actions were punishments, not acts of revenge. 'Did you believe Jesus Christ', he shouts, 'when he stepped forward and exposed the Pharisees and those versed in the scriptures? No, you hanged him on a cross, after getting The Lie to sit in judgement upon him! So do you believe that Hans Brevmålare asks for a better fate than his?'

Hans is condemned to be burnt at the stake. Against a magnificent background, and with a master's brush—Victor Hugo by his side, as Göran Lindblad has pointed out—Strindberg paints the death of his hero on Järntorget, attended by fanatical black-robed monks and flames sweeping through adjoining houses. But after this terrifying spectacle people gather in the taverns, and a voice is heard in the crowd putting in a good word for Hans: 'Oh, the playing cards he made! You'll see, you'll miss him yet.'

Invention and fact are matched here, down to the smallest detail, and yet it has all been transformed in an amazing way. Hans Brevmålare, the Christlike innocent sacrificial victim, is a new, dreamlike self-portrait. Strindberg had sketched it several times before, and now he was beginning to get a firm grip on it. When Hans dies, when the traitor Nigels, like Judas Iscariot, perishes due to his own malice, and when the entire city is about to go up in flames, we find ourselves close to the curtain that is rent and the ground that shakes in the Gospels when the Redeemer dies on the Cross.

8

In the spring of 1883 Strindberg decided to extend his literary repertoire by publishing a collection of poems in the autumn. Traditionally, poetry was accorded the highest social esteem in Sweden. Both Karl XV and Oscar II wrote verses and published them in expensive editions. As Strindberg says in *The Serving Maid's Son*: 'By Christmas, he was going to be a bard and thus climb up again after his friends the hack-writers had dragged him down, not to their level but, as usual, below it.'

It was significant that in the summer of 1883, which the Strindbergs naturally spent on Kymmendö, they were paid a visit by young Karl Otto Bonnier who was to play such an important part in Strindberg's life. With his father's permission, young Bonnier had come to persuade Strindberg to become one of the authors of their publishing house. Strindberg signed a very generous contract for a book of poems to appear in the autumn. The Bonnier company also took on all of Strindberg's debts to Looström, who remained the publisher of *Swedish Fates and Adventures*.

Strindberg's first book of poems is a charming hotchpotch of verses dating back as far as the 1860s; what gives it strength and backbone is the section entitled 'Wound-fever' in which Strindberg expresses his political stance and continues to upbraid his enemies. Some of the poems are quite obscure and call for elucidation. Strindberg's scars have taught him caution; thus, for instance, he expresses a novel passion for the fox-hunt—with hounds, gun, and strychnine! The reason for this? The old Swedish nickname for the fox, Mickel Räv (Mike Fox) echoed the pseudonym Michel Perrin. Similar lyrical exercises in the slaughter of other equally repulsive beasts are directed against Wirsén, Bäckström, and others.

The two main poems are *For the Freedom of Thought* and *Loki's Revelations. Freedom of Thought* is closely related to the polemics of *The Swedish People*. In 1879, the liberal politician and military historian Julius Mankell had published an essay in which the traditional image of King

Gustav II Adolf was described as a falsely glorified one. Contrary to the claims of official Swedish history, Sweden was not under any military threat in 1630, when the King became a participant in the Thirty Years' War. He was not motivated by the demands of religion or concern for the welfare of his subjects, but driven by egotism and a lust for war. Mankell's thesis caused a violent debate: its main contention became the question of whether or not Gustavus had been a protector of the 'high ideal' of freedom of religion. Mankell came under heavy fire. He was called a traitor, and even Oscar II jeered at him in public. When, in 1882, the 250th anniversary of the Battle of Lützen (in which the King died) approached, the controversy flared up again, with Strindberg ready to side with Mankell.

In seven stately, rather poorly rhymed sections, the poem describes the festivities of 6 November 1882: Oscar II's stilted peroration, the celebration in Riddarholm Church among the shades of the heroic kings, the banquet in the palace with its menu that included a dish called 'Boeuf à la Lützen'. Thus we are made to observe this celebration of the freedom of thought, while the true freethinker, uninvited, is seen sitting in a tavern, alone with his 'wound and ridicule'. At the end of the poem, Strindberg himself appears, pushing Mankell aside, and compares himself with the celebrated king-hero who perished on the battlefield:

> Jag vet en man som for en annan tro
> fick ge sin ära men behålla livet
> och hopen ger sig ingen ro
> förrän hans liv är sönderrivet.

> Vad är för konst att smakfullt dö
> och på en katafalk få krona bära.
> Nej, då är svårare att slita spö
> och dras med livet utan ära.

> *I know a man who for another faith*
> *had to sacrifice his honour to remain alive*
> *and the mob will not rest*
> *until his life has been torn apart.*

> *It is not much of a trick to die tastefully*
> *and wear a crown atop a catafalque.*
> *No, it is harder to run the gauntlet*
> *and suffer life without honour.*

But what really makes Strindberg's *Poems 1883* a revolutionary work is the long poem *Loki's Revelations*. Yet, due to the fact that it is verse, and is thus not to be taken 'seriously', not all that many readers were aware of its message, swathed as it was in mythology. Strindberg assumes the shape of the Nordic deity, Loki, and sees him as a Promethean figure; thus his poem competes with one written by Viktor Rydberg two or three years earlier, in which Prometheus appears as suffering mankind's defiant representative, within a grandiose framework of ideas. Like Strindberg himself after the success of *The Red Room*, Loki had sat at the tables of the great, but had soon become nauseated by the 'brimming dishes', and had left and proceeded to reveal the selfishness and power-lust of the great. His punishment: the dungeon—and the designation 'blasphemer'. But—and this is the poem's message—the day Loki breaks his shackles, the present world will come to an end. He calls for his son, the Midgard Serpent, whose tail churns the Volga, whose chest and head hover above Poland, the Pyrenees, and the Seine. The world revolution's fire sweeps the globe, and the old gods are overthrown.

By the time this revolutionary vision of the future was published, its author had gone into exile.

Chapter Six

AN UNACKNOWLEDGED
FIRE-FIGHTER

I

ON 12 SEPTEMBER 1883, the Strindbergs left Stockholm for France. Strindberg was carrying a substantial letter of credit, to the sum of 3,500 francs, the result of his negotiations with the Bonniers. He had conducted these shrewdly. Karl Otto Bonnier recalled later that Strindberg took him on a tour of his garden and demonstrated more concern for his melons than for his poems, which was a good tactical pose.

Strindberg was thirty-four years old. approaching middle age, a dangerous time according to ancient authorities—Dante among them—but also one of great potential. If one is to give credence to a drawing Strindberg made of himself in 1882, he had grown slightly slack around the middle. His moustache was silky and a little curly, and his chin bore the traces of a goatee beard. During the summer, he had complained vociferously about the state of his health, but other indications point to extraordinary physical fitness and a sense of increasing intellectual prowess. Growing self-esteem, even arrogance, were typical of Strindberg in the year that followed.

Siri, his wife, was thirty-three, of regal posture and elegance; on the voyage she may have been wearing the coat tailored out of checked trouser cloth which her husband had designed for her the previous year. According to her daughter, Siri's mood differed from Strindberg's. She had packed their numerous suitcases in a mood of 'heavy resignation'. She had not approved of the 'acts of revenge' in *The New Kingdom*, and she was afraid of being alone with her unpredictable husband in a foreign country. As a freelance actress, her success had been no more than moderate, consisting of only two guest roles at the New Theatre in the preceding season; but this journey abroad meant that she could not even hope for further engagements. Furthermore, she was expecting her third child, without any enthusiasm. In the autumn, Strindberg had been graciously pleased to declare that it was going to be a boy this time.

Karin was at this time three years old, Greta, two. The travelling party also included the nanny and maid, 36-year-old Eva Carlsson. Eva had a son, Albin, who remained in Sweden, being one of those children who could be taken care of with '50 kronor' as Strindberg had written to Carl Larsson (see p. 53). Typically, Siri told her children, as they grew up, never to reveal the secret of the illegitimate child, since it was a disgrace. Eva Carlsson kept a journal, written in a staccato style, and containing gross spelling mistakes that demonstrate the failure of compulsory primary education (introduced in 1842) to make all that much impact on her generation.

The journey proceeded slowly, train travel being anything but smooth at that time, and according to Eva, stops were made at 'hortels' almost every night. Despite stomach pains in Germany, which were cured by means of 'oysters (excellent) and Rhine wine in the Rathskeller in Lübeck, ditto in the good Rathskeller in Bremen', Strindberg was in truly high spirits and reported to Pehr Staaff on 18 September:

> Being the filthy-minded writer I am, I have made a special study of the water-closets in the hotels. The most dazzling invention was the one I found in Hamburg. There, one excreted into something that looked like a soup tureen, and on looking around, there was nothing to be seen, despite the fact that one could have sworn to the deposition of a couple of metres; the bowl was still shiny enough to serve genuine turtle soup in; however, no splashing of water was heard, as in Stralsund, where the seat activated a stream of water as soon as one sat down. It was quite magical.

Thus Strindberg's powers of expression would transform even visits to the toilet into a treat for those friends he honoured with his letters.

The Strindbergs intended to stay abroad only for the winter: Siri was to give birth to her child at home. Strindberg had arranged to rent out Kymmendö, for five periods at 150 kronor each, and reassured Siri that they would soon return there. But in fact the family was never to return to the island. Strindberg had embarked on fifteen years in exile, living out of a suitcase. It liberated him, particularly as an artist, but for this he had to pay a steep price; so did Siri—apart from a small theatrical venture in Denmark in 1888, her career as an actress was over.

2

The Strindbergs first stayed in Grez par Nemours, a small town a few miles south of Paris, which harboured a Scandinavian artists' colony, with Carl Larsson at its centre. During the following years, the Strindbergs returned a number of times to Grez, but their first visit was a brief one. Strindberg just had time to note that his own vegetables at Kymmendö were superior to those grown in the garden of the Hôtel Beau Séjour, and that there were perch in the creek running through the garden. Then, as the cold autumn weather set in, it was time to move to Paris.

After a few temporary lodgings the family settled in a furnished apartment on avenue Neuilly. There was a white, iron-girt tile stove for Eva to prepare meals on; contrary to the habits of women of her class, Siri herself had to go shopping for lamp oil and other household purchases, as Eva was unable to acquire the necessary command of French. Nevertheless, Eva noted in her journal that 'prete' (*prêter*) was the word for 'borrow'. Strindberg, contemplating the fortunes of his poems back in Sweden, saw a calf's heart displayed in a paper ruff in the window of one of the avenue's butcher shops and wrote a poem in which he portrayed his collection, displayed in the bookstore window on Norrbro in Stockholm, as precisely such a disembodied heart, shivering in the cold:

> Där hänger på boklådsfönstret
> en tunnklädd liten bok.
> Det är ett urtaget hjärta
> som dinglar där på sin krok.

> *There hangs in the bookshop window*
> *a thinly clad little book.*
> *It is an extracted heart*
> *which dangles there on its hook.*

Björnstjerne Björnson and Jonas Lie were living in Paris. They visited Strindberg who became wildly enthusiastic about both of them. He wrote to Albert Bonnier that he 'loved' Björnson:

> He is the man I have been looking for so long; mostly, perhaps, because I am so unmanly myself. It is not the blows I receive that hurt me most, but the blows I give—believe me! Which is why I am no good at fighting. When the right man appears, I'll salute him, and, like David, anoint Saul and fade into the background.

The notion that it was more painful to be the executioner than his victim was one which Strindberg would often express, not least during the great feud of 1910. Jonas Lie was accorded even warmer praise. In the autobiography, Lie is called 'the gospel' as opposed to Björnson's 'law', and a conversation with him was a delight. 'We left one another breathless, not knowing what was mine or thine among these children of the imagination that had been created, among these thoughts that had two fathers.'

At the same time, Strindberg was afraid of these friends. As he says in the chapter of *The Serving Maid's Son* that describes his meeting with them: 'Friendship, life's most delectable spice, is something the public man has to renounce, as it weakens the free action of his thought and distorts the fated path of his will.' Strindberg had traits of softness and tenderness in him that made him an ideal companion. Presented with new friends, he was always ready to take them into his confidence and frequently used sexual metaphors in his descriptions of a good conversation with them. Nevertheless, he realized the danger of such openness. In the short novel *Alone* (1903) he says that he particularly enjoyed communicating with friends who were strong personalities. Life shared with others crowded his psyche with alien elements, prevented him from choosing his own spiritual diet and arrested his inner growth. As Strindberg grew older, he acquired an ever stronger sense of near-reverence for that inner growth and felt that the preservation of his integrity was an absolute condition of life. He was irresistibly attracted to brilliant and productive people, but soon found himself on the defensive and was forced to leave them.

In a newspaper article, Strindberg described Björnson in Paris, relating how the author sat at his desk by an open window, wearing a wolfskin coat and a Scottish tam-o'-shanter. He went on to claim that the Norwegian lion no longer felt homesick for his native forests and mountains—that his homeland was, now, the whole world. Strindberg himself, however, as Björnson quite accurately pointed out, had an innate love of his own country—its landscapes, its air, its customs and above all, its food. He addressed positively heart-rending letters to his friends concerning the difficulties he encountered in trying to procure the victuals to which he was accustomed, and was ecstatic when Claes Looström sent him a bag of yellow peas, instantly arranging a celebration.

Another exile in Paris was the Finland-Swede Ville Vallgren, the sculptor, whose naked sea-goddess Havis Amanda greets all travellers who arrive in Helsinki by sea. Vallgren sculpted a bust of Strindberg, the first of a long series: as time passed, Strindberg became one of the most popular subjects of his day for both painters and sculptors. He was always willing to sit for them. His shyness and tongue-tiedness made him a difficult subject for interviews, but he was at his ease with artists, who worked with their hands and their eyes. He felt comfortable as a model, striking dignified poses, in full control of his expression and posture. Having himself photographed was one of his favourite pastimes, but no one ever caught him unawares. In Paris, he frequented a studio called 'Otto', and in a picture taken there in January 1884, his expression is an excellent illustration of what Vilhelm Ekelund calls 'The deer-like, skittish, alert quality of his features. The pained coquetry.' It is, indeed, amazing to consider how humorously and irreverently the same man was able to express himself in his letters.

Christmas was celebrated with a Norwegian fir, surrounded by the fragrance of candles and sealing wax, evoking—at least in the light-hearted piece *Martha's Cares*—expectations of snow and the sound of sleigh-bells, even in the drab grey weather of Paris. The holidays brought news of a triumph on the home front: *Lucky Per's Journey*, which had its first night on 22 December, had become an instant hit, providing Strindberg with an additional income of 2,000 kronor. This enabled the family to escape the pollution of Paris and to move to Switzerland.

They settled in Ouchy on Lake Geneva, near Lausanne. At the Pension Famille Le Chalet Strindberg paid 360 francs for room and board for three adults and two children, acquiring a pleasant corner room to work in. The Alps made an overwhelming impression: when he first saw them from the train 'they caused such turmoil in our brains', he wrote to Björnson and Lie, 'that my wife cried and I scurried back and forth in the compartment like a squirrel in order to look out of both windows at once.'

'My stay in Switzerland', Strindberg wrote twelve years later to Torsten Hedlund, 'was like a Sunday that lasted a year. A quiet, carefree time, festive as Whitsuntide, and the great bell in Lausanne had a sound that seemed to emanate from another world.' He felt stimulated by his proximity to the cultural centre of Europe. Rousseau's spirit hovered above the region, and Strindberg remembered that it was, indeed, at Ouchy that Lord Byron wrote *The Prisoner of Chillon*. He started to take unusual care of his body and claimed that all spring he had imbibed nothing stronger than red wine. He hired riding horses for exercise, paying three francs for the first hour, two for the second.

> Such air! [he wrote to Looström]. Breathe deeply! Well, I'm breathing all the way down to my balls. Believe me, here one doesn't just jog along—in these parts, one rides so that the horse stretches out parallel to the highway, shaking up your liver and your lungs. Cold baths in the morning—so I expect some of these worn nerves will mend again.

He even took fencing lessons.

3

During his first year abroad, Strindberg developed phenomenally, both as a man and as an artist. He had been earning his living as a freelance writer for the previous four years: after a number of more or less discretionary leaves of absence, he had formally resigned from the Royal Library on 31 August 1882. The commissioned historical works had used up much of his energy. Now he was having to rely entirely on his creative work, both for income and for social status. He had actually taken the step Master Olof and Arvid Falk in *The Red Room* only dreamed of. He had put all his eggs in one basket, and now began to appreciate exactly what his situation comprised.

In *Lucky Per*, the protagonist grew up in a church tower, in the company of his cantankerous old father. Per could see the city down below—'that multi-coloured painting people call life'—and became strongly aware of his alienation from it. A fairy godmother appeared to give him a wishing ring, and with the aid of this ring he found himself able to travel from one character-forming situation to the next: he was a Caliph in an Oriental Kingdom, getting a taste of power; then he became a reformer and philosopher, a 'great man' in a city that is a caricature of Stockholm; he experienced nature, love and so on. He travelled through a world cast in a mould reminiscent of Ibsen's *Peer Gynt*—his name indicates that kinship. The play is an amusing and charming fairytale, full of humour and theatrically most inventive. Per, who with the help of imagination—the wishing ring—gains a magical *entrée* to many worlds, is a good symbolic representation of his creator.

Strindberg proceeded to take a less light-hearted look at the problems confronting the creative writer. He wrote a cycle of four poems, giving it the title *Somnambulist Nights*. In each poem, he undertook, in the shape of a bird, a journey from exile back to Sweden, landing on some high point of the city in each dream. On the first night, his landing-place is the Adolf Fredrik church in which he had been confirmed. He rests on the cross on top of its dome, thus enjoying a vista similar to Lucky Per's. On the second night, his destination is the National Museum; on the third, the Royal Library, and on the fourth, the Observatory dome up by Norrtullsgatan. From that vantage-point, he is able to see Norra Kyrkogården (the Northern Cemetery) where his mother rests, with, as from the beginning of 1883, his father.

Carl Larsson designed the book's cover, following a detailed sketch provided by Strindberg. On the left, we see the shadowy façade of a house, possibly Strindberg's house in Paris, and in front of it a meadow, strewn with a variety of objects: books, a microscope, a candlestick, an antique marble statue, and a large crucifix: a human skull grinning among the debris seems to indicate that all this is doomed to annihilation. Above this meadow hangs a large painting depicting an American Indian on horseback galloping across the prairie and swinging his lasso above a herd of buffalo.

That image is an excellent resumé of the content of the poetic cycle. 'High' culture, as sought for in church, museum and observatory, has been found wanting, and salvation is possible only through a return to nature, here represented by the Indian. And that is Strindberg's cultural-political doctrine for the years to come.

The fourth somnambulist night is of particular interest. Below the Observatory, the poet sees Johannes Fire Station (which is still there). He explains that the intention of his work has been to warn the city of

20 Strindberg as the woodsman
in Carl Larsson's illustration to
The Swedish People, 1881–2

21 Carl Larsson's cover for *Somnambulist
Nights*, 1884

impending danger and conflagration—the revolution that must follow parasitism and luxury. However, the body politic does not want any guardians apart from those it has employed as its watchdogs. 'You have a fire brigade,' he addresses the anthopomorphized city, and you ask the firemen to 'save your house from fire':

> om ej, så lär du på ansvar yrka.
> Men jag, som kommer så oombedd
> och ej är i uniformen klädd,
> mig tar du helt enkelt i håren
> och frågar av vem jag blev sänd;
> du önskar hellre bli innebränd
> än väckas av en som är utom kåren.

> *If they do not do it, you'll surely hold them responsible.*
> *But me, who arrive so uninvited*
> *and do not wear the uniform,*
> *me you simply grab by the hair*
> *and ask who sent me;*
> *you prefer to die in your burning house*
> *to being roused by one who does not belong to the brigade.*

It is an extremely clear formulation of the writer's new role. As Arne Melberg's penetrating study has shown, earlier generations of authors had criticized society in their capacity as representatives of institutions and particular movements. Few were able to act as one-man fire brigades: Carl Jonas Almqvist, Strindberg's greatest predecessor, had made the attempt and perished in it. Anyone who appointed himself a critic, and relied on his conscience as his only arbiter, had to struggle to establish his legitimacy—a struggle complicated by the fact that the audience who was to be informed also wanted to be entertained. Writers have had to struggle with that insoluble dilemma before as well as since.

4

It would seem to be a natural consequence of the 'fire brigade' line of reasoning that the author dedicated his *work* to the service of progressive ideas. This was the doctrine instituted by Georg Brandes, whose star disciple was Ibsen: during these years, Ibsen's plays took on one great social question after another.

Strindberg, however, split himself into two quite separate figures—the artist and the prophet. In May 1884, he wrote to Björnson, who for a short while was his favourite correspondent, that he was compelled to write novels in order to make a living, but that his conscience told him that he ought to offer 'the pure naked truth' instead. He continued: 'But here comes the crux! To be of use, I have to be read! To be read, I have to write "art", but I consider "art" immoral. So: either die, with a pure soul, or continue with an activity I see as immoral!'

Strindberg imagined the work of art as, at best, a pretty little box containing good thoughts. He wanted to throw away the box, since it represented sinful pleasure. In action, he would negate that aesthetic philosophy a thousand times: his ideas became active in society precisely when they had been given artistic form. Nevertheless, he was to remain an adherent to this primitive way of thinking for a long time, perhaps just because he found the act of artistic creation so delightful; although the moralist inside him condemned it.

In Ouchy, with a view of the Alps, and with the new child growing in Siri's womb, Strindberg wrote a series of articles on political and social subjects. In them, he compiled what he called 'the horoscope of the times', uttered warnings, and gave advice as if the world's fate depended on his words.

When he sent the first one of these essays to his publisher on 12 February 1884, he said in the accompanying letter: 'This is the key to my entire oeuvre, and it has been germinating and growing within me since 1872.' This was an accurate assessment: the foundations of his social views were, indeed, apparent in the articles he had published in *Stockholms Aftonpost* in the spring of 1872. For a man who had the reputation of being a faithless turncoat, Strindberg demonstrated a curious constancy.

In his book *The Age of Capital*, the British historian E. J. Hobsbawm claims that the 1870s were a period of transition from one era to another. The time of individualism comes to an end, the time of collectivism begins. The thesis is illustrated with three examples: the isolated entrepreneurs, manufacturers, wholesalers, factory bosses—all heroes of liberalism—begin to join one another in monopolies and cartels that will soon encompass the globe. The working man who used to dream of clearing and cultivating his own piece of land now seeks out his fellows, to start unions and socialist parties. Finally, the State, which according to early liberalism would guarantee liberty and happiness for all by interfering with society as little as possible, begins to extend its regulating governing influence to an increasing number of areas.

Seen from that perspective, Strindberg belongs entirely to the pre-1870 era. His view of society is based on an extreme brand of individualism, mistrustful or hostile towards every kind of organization and bureaucracy. In a small pamphlet he compiled during the 1870s, entitled *Notes of a Sceptic*, he declared that modern society's ills were due to its division of

22 Portrait of Strindberg, 1884

labour. We are ruled by princes, generals, priests and geniuses who demand our submission. In the creation of a true democracy, every citizen would have to become a warrior, statesman, priest or poet. Strindberg then draws a picture of this ideal figure, with traits and professions chosen from his own ancestry. He describes a future grocer who paints pictures and writes verse in his spare time. The results may not be all that marvellous—if they were, the store might suffer from neglect; we have to sacrifice quality to democracy. On Sunday mornings, the very same grocer stands on the field at Ladugården in his sharpshooter's uniform, preaching to a congregation of 2,000. He is a city councillor, soon to become a member of parliament, and he attends lectures at the university. '*Voilà un homme!*' Strindberg exclaims, adding, as further corroboration of his vision, that 'Sophocles was an author, dancer, actor, public speaker.'

Just as in *Notes of a Sceptic*, the division of labour is singled out as the main evil in the articles Strindberg wrote that spring in Ouchy. He demanded a return to a form of society in which one person is capable of doing everything. The grocer was replaced by the independent farmer, who was to become the foundation stone of a new and better society. At the present time, Strindberg claimed, people remain incarcerated in their specialization, thus becoming blind to their society's true shortcomings and needs. Only the creative author, who is an outsider, is able to see clearly: therefore, it is his duty to stand guard, and to wake people up.

Strindberg entitled the most voluminous of these pieces—it runs to 100 pages in the *Collected Works*—'On the General Discontent, its Causes and Remedies'. Did he remember that he had given an equally, and ironically, grandiose and presumptuous title to a lecture given by Olle Montanus in *The Red Room*: 'On Sweden: Some Points of View'? In the book, Olle does not do too well with it. He delivers the lecture at a workers' association, Nordstjärnan (The North Star). His main thesis: everything that is any good in Sweden has been imported, only the bad things are indigenous—one of Strindberg's provocative bravura pieces. But as the listeners, false representatives of the working class, are extremely patriotic fellows and start heckling him, the incensed Olle begins to intensify his argument. He tries to get the audience to join him in a fourfold 'Hurrah!' for Karl XII, pointing out that this was the King who devastated his wretched country with his wars. When he finally reaches the subject of poetry and Stiernhielm, the originator of typically Swedish poetry, he utters the demented cry: 'Down with that stupid dog Georg Stiernhielm!' and that is when the audience throws him out. Outside, in the street, he then explains to Arvid Falk that he cannot understand what came over him.

Strindberg at the political lectern is Olle Montanus's brother, propelled by his sense of calling and sympathy for the underdog, while suffering from a built-in mechanism that causes him to lose all proportion. In these articles, he introduces sudden paradoxes. Thus he proclaims that the railways are unnecessary luxuries; questions the usefulness of steamboats and telephones; doubts the advantages of literacy, pointing to a tenant farmer of his acquaintance who, although illiterate, was a worthy member of society. He even finds disparaging words for the compass, regarding it as an unnecessary and unnatural invention. He claims to have been in danger of running aground in the company of ten crown pilots with four compasses. The entire century is condemned as useless because it bases its progress on 'boiled water'—that is, steam power.

It is possible to gain the impression that these social polemics were no more than a game, something to pass the time while waiting for the 'real' task. But there is evidence to suggest that such a conclusion would be both risky and wrong. For Utopians like Strindberg the gap between reality and dream becomes insanely wide, and it is only natural that they react with desperate sarcasm when confronted with such absurd contradictions. That may well be the psychological reason for the absurdities that so depressed his allies and frightened his publishers.

Nevertheless, there are passages in Strindberg's socio-critical work that have withstood the passage of time. He exploited the glamour of his name and the power of his pen, forging a number of verbal swords that are as serviceable now as they were then. Thus, for instance, what he says in his pamphlet *Small Catechism for the Lower Class* (paraphrasing Luther) is no less subtle than Herbert Marcuse's analyses of the means of persuasion which the governing use on the governed.

Ideologically, Strindberg was fifty years behind or a hundred years ahead—whichever way one chooses to look at it. To deny progress, to question modern technology in the era of triumphant industrial exhibitions, was a blasphemy that could not go unpunished. While the workers' movement regarded as sacred the certainty that victory would be achieved in the sign of solidarity and collectivity, Strindberg continued to see the self-sufficient farmer as the man of the future. As Allan Hagsten has demonstrated, he also parted ways with his young radical friends around the same time that the Social Democrat Party was founded (1889) and the unions started growing stronger.

5

The spring of 1884 was the first supercharged period in Strindberg's life. Gripped by a manic urge for action, he resembled some electrical device overloaded beyond its capacity so that it sends sparks in all directions. At the same time, his control centre still operated with strange certainty, and he was able to assimilate all the psychic energy that was streaming in. Perhaps the paradoxes evident in his work reflected a subconscious attempt to check himself.

He found time to engage in innumerable other projects besides the large socio-critical articles. He took French lessons, with the intention of becoming an author in that language. To Carl Larsson he suggested that the two of them should journey on a barge from Le Havre to Marseilles and 'show the French what their country looks like. All the wretches know at the moment is Paris!' It was a viable plan: French high culture was, indeed, focused on its capital. Henry James had the same idea, and realized it. Strindberg also considered taking a bicycle tour through Europe, in search of the 'aborigines'—still quite unknown, in his opinion. No doubt he had in mind the ideal peasants, those who had not yet become aware of the curse of the division of labour. 'I have a tremendous urge to travel! These are our best years, Lars; soon our sailing days will be over.' It was, of course, his intention to persuade Carl Larsson to illustrate his texts.

The idea of putting the peasantry of Europe on the map became a mighty project, one that preoccupied him for several years. Its main attraction was the pioneering angle: 'I intend to spend a few summers of my life discovering Europe the way Stanley discovered Africa,' he told Carl Larsson. He wanted to call this new work *Through the Continent of the Whites*, by analogy with *Through the Dark Continent*.

The forging of these plans did not prevent Strindberg from taking the entire family on a trip to Italy on 1 March. It was a short one, yet not without its adventurous aspect, as Siri was in her eighth month of pregnancy. During the trip, Strindberg wrote seven long articles for *Dagens Nyheter*, in which the much-described Mecca of tourism was considered in its aspect of an 'unknown continent'—unknown until August Stanley Livingstone Strindberg sets foot upon it.

Immediately upon the family's return, Strindberg's third child was born, on 3 April: a boy. 'While the birds were singing and the sun rising above the Alps—hurrah!!!' he wrote to Carl Larsson.

He told his brother Axel that he was about to make his entry into French literature: 'That's the only way I can show those laggard Swedish pigskins! Soon you'll see them trotting toward me, tail between their legs, to be kicked in the a—e by yours truly! They thought they would kill me by silence or swinishness, but I can't die, because I was born to live and to—win!'

During the spring, he was preoccupied by the thought that his immortality was guaranteed by his children—that they were to realize his human ideal—and it gave him impetus to make his peace with society. He returned to *belles-lettres*: the week after his son's birth he began the short story 'Pangs of Conscience', in which he demonstrated that the power he had felt within himself did, indeed, exist.

23 'Pangs of Conscience' in the Peace Association's series, 1884, and in an edition of 1908, with a cover by Carl Larsson. The story was later included in *Utopias in Reality*. During the First World War, it was translated into numerous languages; here, a translation into Romanian, printed in Bucharest in 1916

6

'Pangs of Conscience' deals with the German geologist von Bleichroden (Strindberg is about to conquer Europe, hence his German protagonist), who, as a lieutenant of the reserve, has been called up for service during the Franco-Prussian War of 1870–1. The story begins a fortnight after the battle of Sedan on 2 September, in which one of the French armies was surrounded and Napoleon III taken prisoner. Von Bleichroden's company is stationed in the French village of Marlotte, near Grez. In the story, we hear a church-bell tolling in the village.

Von Bleichroden is put to an appalling test. French irregulars—*franc-tireurs*—are operating behind the enemy's back. The Prussian government does not recognize them as soldiers and orders them to be executed wherever they are found. Three of these *franc-tireurs* have been captured by von Bleichroden's company and are at this moment awaiting their execution in the billiards room of the village inn, the company headquarters. It should be noted that Hans Lindström has discovered that the idea for the story stems from a publication entitled *The coercive acts, robberies, and cruelties committed by the German armies in France*, which Strindberg had read, and which contains an episode in which an officer becomes insane after executing irregulars.

From the beginning, the story employs innovative, daring imagery. We first meet von Bleichroden as he is sitting down to write a letter to his young wife. He has thrown his stiff-collared officer's tunic over the back of a chair, where it hangs, slack and limp as a corpse 'with the empty sleeves looking as if they were spasmodically gripping the chair-legs to prevent a headlong fall'. This is the first time Strindberg uses the uniform as symbolic of the male role in life. In von Bleichroden we may also see something of Strindberg himself: he, too, had been called up to serve, with the pen as his sabre, in the 'war' against social injustice, but found the uniform of opinion and party discipline difficult to bear.

When a French priest arrives to plead for clemency for the prisoners, von Bleichroden reaches for his tunic. 'But when he had buttoned the tight-fitting tunic,' Strindberg writes, 'and felt the vice-like grip of its tight collar around his neck, it was as if the nobler organs had been constricted and the blood stopped in its secret channels to the heart.'

Lieutenant von Bleichroden cannot escape the constraints of martial law. To kill the prisoners seems like murder, but it is his duty to obey. He gives the orders for execution but is unable to witness the act and leaves for a long walk. When he returns to the village, he passes the place of execution in the garden, staining his boots with blood. Back at the inn, he takes them off, but he has worn a hole through one of the soles: his sock is bloody, and he leaves tracks on the floor of the room. That is the beginning of von Bleichroden's breakdown, both psychological and physical. His terrible hunger as he sits down to eat; his nausea as he lifts the lid off the stew-pot and the smell of meat strikes his nostrils; his fury as he sees the red radish that sits on top of the little mound of butter, and the wine bottle, which both remind him of blood; his discovery upon going to bed that there is a body lying beside him—his own; the hollow voice from underneath the bedsheet—these are details among a hundred others designed to create an hallucinatory impression. When von Bleichroden is finally taken away, completely demented, the reader has witnessed the entire sequence of events leading to the breakdown, and thus cannot doubt its verity.

In *The Serving Maid's Son*, Strindberg claimed that the story reflected his pangs of conscience over his ill-treatment of his adversaries: it is their murdered corpses that accuse him. But in the essay 'What is the Battle About?', written shortly before 'Pangs', he compares himself to the *franc-tireurs*. Just as they had fought a hopeless battle against overwhelming odds and had been killed unjustly, Strindberg had found himself at the mercy of Sweden's reactionary literary establishment. In the short story, Strindberg is present in both executioner and victim, in von Bleichroden and in the murdered Frenchmen whose bodies are laid out on the billiard table. It is this double presence that gives the story its strength: the author identifies with both sides, and that is an advance for him, in human and artistic terms. Previously, Strindberg had found it only too easy to take sides: Arvid Falk, Hans Brevmålare, Sten Ulvfot, and Loki appear in too shining a light in their battles against the gods of the day, and their adversaries are left in too great a darkness. This results in a certain superficiality and woodenness of characterization. Von Bleichroden's conflict in 'Pangs of Conscience' gains depth from the story's flexible perspective.

That depth gives the story its effectiveness as a plea for peace. Strindberg himself felt that it was the best he had written to date, and it has since become one of his most popular works, thus proving to its author that it was possible for an accomplished work of art to have social relevance. The story soon gained wide dissemination in Europe, and it is still one of the standard pacifist works.

7

Strindberg's brain remained overheated all spring, and his sense of creative power grew stronger. Yet there was a strain of suffering in his tumultuous thoughts and feelings, and he felt close to exploding. In letters to friends, his language grew more violent, more strongly charged with sexual innuendo.

He called Wirsén and his associates back home 'those old whores of idealism'; Geijerstam was told that he would 'pee in his boots' at the sight of Alpine nature, and also that he would be able, in the mountains, to 'see heaven all the way to the clitoris'. In rapid alternation, Strindberg was writing short stories, articles, essays and letters: the last-mentioned in such quantity that the period from 1 April to 1 August that year takes up almost 200 pages in Torsten Eklund's edition of his correspondence.

In a single month he wrote twelve stories dealing with married life, all of them inspired by the notion that all that arises out of nature is good, all that is against nature, sinful. Among these we find the extraordinary 'The Reward of Virtue'—soon to cause him a great deal of trouble. The stories were to appear in the autumn as the collection *Marrying*.

Strindberg was worrying about the state of mind he found himself in: how seriously, it is hard to say, as he always kept up a mocking tone. On 27 May he wrote to Jonas Lie: 'Sometimes I suspect that I'll end up in a madhouse, myself, because I can get quite wild sometimes, thinking about the insanity of the world!' And a few days later, to Carl Larsson: 'At the moment, I'm engaged in such a revolution against myself, and the scales are falling from my eyes, but I'll need a long time to get my vision back again.' 'My poor brain', he wrote another day, 'is once again subject to changes of weather. It goes round and round, and cannot stop.'

Yet the boost in output boosted his ego as well. In May, he wrote to Björnson that he would achieve such fame 'that my compatriots will listen to every rustle of my shirt-sleeves and send telegrams when I sneeze!' He told Bonnier that he was writing like a somnambulist who must not be woken up: (here we see the mating woodcock again). On 10 June, he sent an insulting letter to Claes Looström, based on an accusation, unjustified by all accounts, that the latter had cheated him of royalties—as if he could have afforded to lose friends on a whim.

The weather was getting warmer in Ouchy, and the Strindbergs were planning to move up into the mountains. Surrounded by packed trunks, he wrote to Carl Larsson on 20 June: 'Now I have to go up to Mount Olive like Jesus, elevation 2,000 feet, to contemplate the world and its craziness.' He ended the letter with his name and new address, as follows:

> August Strindberg
> Address: Hotel Victoria
> Chexbres–Vevey
> Vaud
> Suisse.
> Europe
> The Old World
> The Earth
> The Universe.

Every child, at some point, signs a letter according to this pattern. In *A Portrait of the Artist as a Young Man*, Joyce makes his hero do it, as a little boy. Strindberg's joke was a belated one, a step back to an age when one is not ashamed to occupy the centre of the universe, not even in front of others.

In Chexbres, the Strindberg family inhabited a small house, consisting of two rooms and a large kitchen with an open hearth, which belonged to the Hotel Victoria. They stayed all summer. The owner of the hotel was a physician who prescribed calcium bromide for Strindberg, 'for stress'. The hotel owner's sister, Hélène Welinder, who was married to a Swede, was a lady with keen powers of observation; she spent some time with Strindberg during those months and wrote, after his death, an article which is by all accounts based on her diaries of that time.

She relates that she had shared her contemporaries' suspicions about Strindberg but changed her opinion as soon as she met him face to face.

> I was seized [she writes] by an enormous and, as it seemed to me then, completely unmotivated feeling of compassion. I could not understand it: animated by his walk, he looked neither unhealthy nor depressed. Nor did I know anything about his unhappy childhood and tumultuous adolescence; all I knew was that he was the author of a number of disagreeable books.

Mme Welinder goes on to ask herself what the cause of her first impression might have been. She describes Strindberg's manners as full of delicacy and consideration; the incredibly sensitive expression around the finely drawn lips, the wistful smile, and something indefinable about his entire person, all gave her the spontaneous impression that 'he belonged to those who are, as it were, predestined to a measure of suffering that is greater than normal. This is not a conclusion I arrived at later—it was a totally immediate, intuitive feeling.'

Theoretically, it is possible that Mme Welinder, who did not publish her memoir until 1912, had read the play *To Damascus* and had been impressed by The Lady's words to The Unknown One in Act 1, Scene 1. When The Unknown One asks her if she has come to undo him, The Lady replies: 'I harbour no such thoughts, and you mainly appeal to my compassion— indeed, I have never seen a person, never in my life, whose mere appearance makes me want to weep. . . . Tell me, what is on your conscience? Have you committed some reprehensible act that has not been discovered or punished?' But it seems more reasonable to suppose that Mme Welinder's impressions and words are her own. It is possible that Strindberg often heard such expressions of empathy: perhaps he exuded the kind of anguish that was the price he had to pay for his creative work.

Hélène Welinder also remembers a carriage excursion with her brother and Strindberg in the driver's seat. Strindberg kept turning back to the passengers to point out details in the landscape, but on the way home he complained that his limbs were getting stiff; he jumped down from the carriage and told the doctor-hotel owner to keep going at a full clip: he would try to keep up with them.

To this day [writes Mme Welinder], I can see him running after our carriage, covered with dust, his curly hair sticking to his temples. 'Aren't you getting tired, my beloved piggie?' his wife called out, but he only shook his head and kept on running, keeping up with us all the way. We stopped at a crossroads, and he swung himself, breathless but proud and contented, up on to the driver's seat again.

Chapter Seven

AN INVOLUNTARY PEOPLE'S HERO

I

THE TWELVE SHORT stories, collectively entitled *Marrying*, were to appear in the autumn of 1884. 'If I may say so, I think they're damned good!' Strindberg wrote to Karl Otto Bonnier on 31 May. One week later, writing to Bonnier again, he went further: the book was 'the most amazing I have ever written'. He needed money, and it was important to convince the Bonniers of the excellence of his new work.

Marrying exploits experiences from Strindberg's own marriage—although in a rather playful vein. Once in a while we catch a glimpse of a bare claw, but marital happiness is never in question. The newborn son was a shield against that, and Strindberg presented only the comedy of marriage and the interaction of types. 'Nature' is the name of the ruling deity, its preferred incarnation being a child whose birth redeems all that has gone askew between a man and a woman. At this time, Strindberg was working in the full knowledge of the artistic advances he had made in 'Pangs of Conscience'.

The strongest of the stories, the first in the book, bears the title 'Virtue's Reward'. Its main character is Theodor Wennerström whose parental home, like his creator's, was on Norrtullsgatan, 'to the left of the Observatory Square'. It was surrounded by a large garden in which there was a green swing—on this young Theodor, one Whitsun afternoon, engages a girl in erotic play, their youthful urges harmonizing with the movement of the swing.

Theodor's sexual awakening coincides with the beginning of spring, yet the contrast is heart-rending: while narcissi and lilies freely disseminate their pollen and the neighbour's black tomcat, after dispatching a rival, is received by the house cat with 'frenetic embraces', Theodor, whose blood is

just as hot, remains a captive of his culture and can only look forward to
decades of martyrdom—more games on swings, masturbation, and 'bad
girls'.

Strindberg's target in this story is the 'edifying' reading matter of his
childhood, von Kapff in particular. Theodor is doomed because a perverted
upbringing has forced him off the path nature intended him to follow. The
story gives stylish artistic expression to what had been the main theme of
Strindberg's cultural polemics the previous spring.

Bonniers had not been doing all that well with their newly acquired
author. *Poems, Like and Unlike,* and *Somnambulist Nights* had not been
selling well, but *Marrying*'s prospects looked good, and the publishers
printed a first edition of 4,000 copies. No one expected it to become the
subject of a blasphemy trial.

The book was in the shops on 27 September. Three days later, just as he
was leaving Chexbres for Geneva, Strindberg received his copies and wrote
to Carl Larsson:

> Against my usual custom, I have just read my book in print. I find it
> 'seminal': it is like good honest copulation, as opposed to Ibsen's
> hysterical jerking-off. I believe without reservation that my notions are
> right. True, the human animal's powers of discernment are beclouded,
> but if one has a guideline—nature—it would seem possible, to me, to
> arrive at some degree of understanding. To my mind, all those who have
> dealt with the woman's question before me were decidedly abnormal.

The Swedish authorities found this 'honest copulation' too powerful. On
3 October at 3 pm, the city bailiff, whose name was Wäsell, appeared at
Bonniers and confiscated *Marrying.* He was acting on orders from the
minister of justice, Nils von Steyern, who that day had told the chancellor of
justice to prosecute as the book was in violation of paragraph three, section
one of the press law: 'blasphemy against God or mockery of God's word or
the sacraments'.

Wäsell found only 320 copies at the publisher's; perhaps word of the
impending prosecution had leaked out. In Stockholm's bookshops, a total of
141 copies were confiscated, while the shops in the provinces managed to sell
out before the police arrived.

'Virtue's Reward' was the main cause. The passage to which the minister
of justice referred concerned Theodor's confirmation, and the following
three sentences in particular:

> In the spring, he was confirmed. He would long remember the upsetting
> spectacle in which the upper classes made the lower classes swear on
> Christ's body and blood that they would never concern themselves with
> what their betters did. The shameless fraud that was perpetrated with
> Högstedt's Piccadon wine at 65 öre a jug and Lettström's maize wafers at

1 krona a bag, which the minister claimed to be the flesh and blood of the agitator Jesus of Nazareth, executed over 1,800 years ago, did not give him any cause for reflection; there was no such thing as reflection in those days, only 'moods'.

The provocative formulations bear witness to Strindberg's exuberant mood in May when he composed 'Virtue's Reward'. By mentioning brand-names and prices he points to the concrete connection between religion and business, in the spirit of Buckle and Marx. He was aware that he was taking a risk. 'Do you think there'll be a prosecution about the Piccadon?' he wrote to Bonniers on 13 September. The thought was no doubt rather exciting. In the spring of 1884, while 'Virtue's Reward' was being written, Björnstjerne Björnson had been prosecuted in Norway, and when he was acquitted, Strindberg wrote to Karl Otto Bonnier: 'Too bad he didn't get locked up! That would have felt so good, so good!' The 'Piccadon' was a titillating rapier's point, with which the reckless author tested his enemy, Society.

The bailiff and his assistant had scarcely left the publishers when Albert Bonnier sat down and wrote to Strindberg. In his initial state of shock, he did not offer a single word of commiseration or indignation about the matter. His attention was taken up entirely by his own situation. 'The worst thing is', he explained, 'that I, myself, am quite unable to speak on your behalf in court.' The following day he had recovered somewhat, as public opinion in Stockholm did not seem hostile to Strindberg—according to the newspaper *Budkavlen*, people in the capital were 'splitting their sides' over the prosecution and congratulating Strindberg as the foregone winner—and Bonnier wrote to his author that the prosecution was 'an incredible piece of stupidity that will serve you well'. However, he asked Strindberg to send a signed note to the effect that he, Bonnier, would not have to appear in court. 'I take it for granted that you want to come home and reply to the charges.'

At first, Strindberg had no intention of appearing in person. He felt that he had the right to select weapons, and he had chosen the pen. In a letter to Bonniers on 4 October he said that he wanted to have his reply to the prosecution printed as a pamphlet and that he expected to stand alone in his fight 'against judges, newspapers plus hermaphrodites and pederasts plus Ibsenites equals the radicals (friends!)'. By way of explanation he added that he had been told at the Royal Library, when he was working there, that 'half the Supreme Court consists of pederasts'.

Albert Bonnier was a cautious man, concerned about his position as a solid and loyal citizen; since 1881, he had been the president of the Swedish Book Publishers' Association. His Jewish family background made his situation even more precarious. His publishing house could be accused of having favoured that attack on Jesus, that 'murder victim of the Jews' according to a 1,000-year-old yet constantly revived tradition. When it became clear to him that Strindberg did not intend to come home, and when his legal advisers told him that he would, in that case, have to face prosecution, signed note or not, he nervously resorted to all available means of persuasion, including rather insulting appeals to Strindberg's courage and sense of honour. He wrote to a number of Strindberg's friends, imploring them to exert their influence. Thus, to Björnson: 'Please use your influence to encourage him to act in a manly and dignified way.' To Strindberg himself, on 9 October: 'No, this is no time for further negotiation, but a time for a courageous decision—let it be determined by the demands of honour.' On 10 October he even sent his son Karl Otto to Geneva, with orders to bring home the recalcitrant author.

Albert Bonnier's actions were triggered by Strindberg's letter of 4 October, in which he said he had 'no intention whatsoever' to return home; however, there was no indication in that letter that Strindberg would have remained abroad if Bonnier had been prosecuted. In reply to Bonnier's first letter he stated: 'Will come home, of course, if you're about to be thrown in gaol.' His actions were determined by his conviction that the signed note would suffice. In an open letter of 10 October, sent to the journal *Tiden*, he polemicized against friends who had claimed that his cause would be in great danger, should he fail to appear in person.

'My cause is so great', he wrote, 'that it cannot rest on my puny shoulders alone—because it is the cause of the future, and it can stand up in its own right.' Indeed, were he to submit to some 'simple-minded punishment', he would be the loser, because that would be an admission of his guilt.

On the contrary, my cause demands that I create a precedent and by staying away lodge my protest against an absurd law. I am being offered a candidacy for martyrdom. I cannot accept such an honour, as I do not believe in martyrs and have no hankering for popularity. I have expressed my distaste for big words and for the idolization of persons so frequently that I want to try to be as small and simply human as possible. Thus I shall abstain from all scenes on gangways and all speeches on railroad platforms, abstain from all gatherings around food and drink where vast platitudes are spoken, inane promises made, sanguine [the words 'wine-sodden' are deleted in the manuscript] expectations pronounced.

Physical courage results from certain personality traits that Strindberg did not possess to any great degree. He easily fell victim to his own nervous sensitivity and his readily inflamed imagination. There are a number of more or less maliciously related anecdotes about his running away from bulls and dogs. One of his lifelong nightmares was about being locked up, and he was afraid of imprisonment. He was married to a woman who had formerly been the wife of an officer and was herself a descendant of war heroes, and it is possible that he found himself under more or less subtle attack at home.

Nevertheless, that letter to *Tiden* was consistent with a line he had held for some time. His publishers and friends were offering him von Bleichroden's uniform, and he did not want it. Feminists should not forget, when settling accounts with Strindberg 'the hater of women', that he was also an impassioned opponent of the traditional male role.

The differences between Strindberg and his publisher soon became public knowledge. There were rumours about Strindberg's lack of courage. On 14 October an anonymous letter to the editor appeared in *Nya Dagligt Allehanda* in which it was hinted that the faint-hearted poet had been offered a large sum of money by his publisher to entice him back home. Later, Albert Bonnier 'under obligation of oath' publicly denied that malicious claim in *Dagens Nyheter* and other newspapers. *Göteborgs Handelstidning* continued in the anonymous writer's vein: in that newspaper's description of Strindberg's return and reception on 21 October we read that there was a halo around the author's head and that he appeared as 'a courageous man, whether he really is one or not'. Such poisoned arrows were favoured missiles in the Sweden of the day.

Karl Otto Bonnier arrived in Geneva on 14 October and found Strindberg staying in a pension in the suburb of Plainpalais, at no. 3, rue Dancet. The family had moved there from Chexbres on 1 October. Strindberg was in good spirits; although he was reluctant to travel at first, he changed his mind the next day after receiving telegrams from friends in Stockholm. Karin Smirnoff relates that Siri's 'prayers' also brought him to that decision.

The two men—the 35-year-old writer with his dark brown mane under a tall black hat, and the 28-year-old red-headed publisher—travelled homeward in a leisurely fashion. They stopped overnight in Basle, then took a night train to Frankfurt. In Hamburg the next morning, they had to wait for the train to Kiel. They sat down, says Bonnier, at the far end of the outside platform at Klosterthor station. Strindberg was silent. 'Suddenly, I saw him pull out his handkerchief and burst into tears: "Forgive me, it's just my nerves, I can't control them," he said.' In Kiel, the train took the two men to the harbour and the German steamer which was to convey them to Denmark. The boat was named after Kaiser Wilhelm II's spouse. 'But don't you see what it says!' exclaimed Strindberg. '*Auguste Victoria*. Victory! August!' All nervousness gone, Strindberg was in excellent spirits during the long sea voyage.

2

There had been considerable publicity in the Swedish press. When, on 19 October, Strindberg boarded the train in Malmö, a large crowd had gathered to see him. *Skånska Aftonbladet*'s reporter found his figure and posture youthful, his face as stern as ever, 'perhaps a little paler'. The report continued: 'Rarely does a smile illuminate Strindberg's face, never a smile, yet there was a twinkle in his eye when he was told that his book *Marrying* is in such demand that there are many who pay twice its cover price just to borrow it for a day.'

The day before, *Dagens Nyheter* had informed its .readers that 'the intrepid warrior against the hypocrisy of modern society' could be expected in Stockholm 'on the express train which arrives at 8.15 on Monday morning'. Two days later, the paper urged the public to gather at the station. The train arrived on time, and there were over 1,000 people on the platform. All newspapers reported the event except for *Post- och Inrikes* which remained silent and thus earned the contempt of *Söndags-Nisse*, which claimed that its representatives had been almost as active at the station as when Sarah Bernhardt honoured the city by her visit a few years before. *Aftonbladet*, under new editorship, struck a sympathetic, almost warm note:

As the train rolled in under the vaulted glass roof, all conversation suddenly ceased, all eyes hastened to scrutinize the carriage windows while the train kept coming. But the blinds were drawn or the windows empty, and when the train came to a halt, an agitated murmur swept the crowd, until suddenly, at a point right in the middle of the tightly packed heads, all hats were lifted and vigorous cheers were heard which proceeded to spread throughout the crowd. The applause was so strong, so vigorous, unanimous and spontaneous that we have not heard the like at many public occasions of homage.

According to Budkavlen, someone shouted: 'Long live the new August Blanche!' referring to a popular hero of earlier days. The paper itself was equally excited: 'It is possible that this day will never be forgotten in Sweden's history, which has only just begun.'

On the station platform, Strindberg was surrounded by his friends— Branting, Thyselius, Pehr Staaff, Atterling of *Dagens Nyheter*, Knut Wicksell, Ludvig Josephson of the New Theatre, Geijerstam, Jörgen, and Albert Bonnier. Strindberg made a short speech, as follows, according to *Aftonbladet*: 'It makes me happy that we can now begin to get some air into our lungs. When I left Sweden, it was barely possible to breathe here. I thank you for your welcome and assure you that, come what may, I shall do my duty.'

Dagens Nyheter, considering its own as well as Strindberg's sympathies for the working man, wrote: 'Despite the fact that the eminent author's perhaps greatest friends, the working people, could not be present in significant numbers for obvious reasons, it being Monday, a working day, at least a thousand joined in the exultant reception for Strindberg who looked "tired and strained".'

All agreed that Strindberg had been welcomed like a prince and that nothing comparable had occurred in Stockholm for a long time. We do not know who exactly was in the crowd. The paper *Tiden* wrote that all walks of life were represented, and that even 'the odd civil servant had come out to compromise himself'. Undoubtedly there were some present who remembered the great press law case of 1838 against King Karl XIV Johan's adversary, Magnus Jakob Crusenstolpe, whose conviction to three years' hard labour for *lèse-majesté* resulted in vicious riots in Stockholm.

That evening, the New Theatre put on a gala performance of *Lucky Per*. Outside, the gas torches were lit, and a strong police contingent was present to control the curious crowd. Inside, there were veritable orgies of acclamation—time and again the play was interrupted by waves of applause. 'Rarely if ever in a Swedish theatre have we heard such frequent and sustained applause during the play' noted *Stockholms Dagblad*. *Dagens Nyheter* mentioned that the audience, in which there were a great number of women, 'turned, in the orchestra stalls, towards Strindberg's box while applauding, or leaned over the sides of their boxes or balcony seats and cheered the slight, pale man as an occasional flicker of pleasure lit up his careworn, melancholy features, called forth by the festive event and a triumph the like of which few people have ever experienced.'

Lucky Per was an ideal play for such a demonstration. In Act 4, Per appears as a Caliph in an oriental kingdom that is a caricature of Sweden, with many venomous allusions to the royal family and the controversy about Gustavus Adolphus. *Dagens Nyheter* wrote that its respect for the press law prevented it from quoting certain instances of anti-royalist opinion that were uttered during the performance. When the curtain fell, Strindberg was called on stage and presented with a laurel wreath tied with a red silk ribbon while the audience shouted 'Bravo!' and people in the upper tiers even took off their coats and waved them, a homage that became a pet topic for Stockholm's columnists during the following weeks.

It is difficult to say exactly what that flicker was that *Dagens Nyheter* observed on Strindberg's face; perhaps it was not due to any very positive emotion. When, a couple of months later, he described the reception at the station and the gala performance in his novel *The Journey to Kvarstad*,* he directed as much sarcasm and ridicule towards himself as towards his admirers. He observed himself, up there on the stage, from the same viewpoint he had adopted to observe society in general in *The Red Room*—from a

---

* Translator's note: The title of this book is a pun: *Kvarstad* sounds like the name of a town, *stad* being "town, borough" in Swedish. The word *kvarstad*, however, means "impoundment" or "confiscation", which refers to the fact that the edition of *Marrying* was at one point impounded by the authorities.

"Jag kommer hem!"

(Illustration till August Strindbergs mottagande i Stockholm.)

Så helsas han, en sanningstolk,
    af tusenstämmig röst.
Och hyllningen utaf vårt folk
    går djupt utur dess bröst.
Det vet, att han är öppet *sann*,
det känner, tänker, tror som han.

På tankens stora, fria fält
    ej kommenderas man,
som nummerkarlen i sitt tält,
    ej anden bindas kan.
han tål ej väld och barbari,
han sväfvar ljus och glad och fri.

Så helsas »gudsförsmädaren»,
    så helsas han i dag,
den sakramentets »hädaren»,
    som dömas skall af lag.
En stark och mäktig opinion,
som tränger genom vår nation!

Skall man mot denna sätta lag
    och tunga samvetsband?
Nej, fritt man andas vill i dag
    uti vårt fosterland.
Ej våldets makt ger samvetsro,
men fritt man tänka vill och tro!

position down by the door. He mentioned the gas torches, saying they were lit for the police so that they could defend themselves better against possible attacks by the lower classes, and he referred to the cheering as 'shrieking'. Of the 'gala spectacle' he wrote:

> Josephson had been so kind as to let the author see his own play, which he had not seen before! Great shrieking! He is demonstrating! And so I sat there! Alone! Gazed at, cheered! Oh, for my dressing gown and my slippers! Oh, no. 3 rue Dancet, Plainpalais, Geneva! No, I'm just not cut out to be a 'great man'! Can never bring myself to believe in those cheers. They cheer today and give you the bird tomorrow.

3

Strindberg was at the beginning of a strenuous month. He had taken lodgings at the Grand Hotel, on the other side of the water from the Royal Palace, which he regarded as the enemy's headquarters. He believed that Queen Sofia, daughter of Duke Wilhelm of Nassau, was the true originator of the prosecution, and the radical press took up the rumour, alluding to it in the most transparently veiled terms. The King himself, according to Geijerstam's report to Siri in Geneva, was startled and frightened.

On the stage of world history—or at least, of what the ruling white man regarded as the world—that autumn brought the tragedy of Gordon. General Gordon had been surrounded in Khartoum, and after a siege met his death there. Strindberg had the opportunity to draw parallels, but refrained from all pathos with both friends and public and was as daringly outspoken as ever. To Carl Larsson, who was in an ecstasy of admiration, he wrote on 22 October:

> Dear Calle, Greatest of Draughtsmen! Now good old Strix is sitting in a pile of nettles. Goddamn, it's wonderful! Well, would my little piggies be oinking if they knew what the old Boar suffered when they put a ring through his snout! Fling me some silly old Kymmendö word so I can feel my youth in my spinal marrow!. . . It is simmering under leaf and bark in old Stockholm, simmering and sizzling, let me tell you! Hey! The Swedes have roused themselves out of their brandy stupor! Forty thousand sober people are more dangerous than 40 million drunkards! My desk is covered by petitions, proclamations, verses, manifestos, flowers and laurel wreaths (well, one!); I'm being cheered and tossed in the air! Now, if I were an idealist, I'd be taken in by all that, but I have never felt less ambitious—never smaller, than now! But my soft iron is turning into steel!

From the beginning of that year, Strindberg had been boasting about his sobriety. He had had a love-hate relationship with alcohol since his early youth. He drank both on working days and at social occasions and often got drunk. Like all heavy drinkers he preferred to discuss the matter in veiled terms. In *The Occult Diary* of 1908 he wrote, in a disgruntled moment, that all happiness life had given him had been illusory or false. 'The only thing that gave me an illusion of happiness', he continued, 'was the grape! That's why I drank! It even eased the pain of life itself. It made my sluggish mind alert and intelligent. Sometimes it quelled hunger pangs, when I was young!' When he received the telegram with the news of prosecution, he decided to abstain completely and applied for membership in a temperance lodge. He was afraid of losing control while under the influence of drink, and he also thought that he might be able to use the temperance movement for his own purposes.

He discovered, however, that abstinence sapped his strength. In his autobiography he claims to have collapsed like a wet rag, and he was compelled to start drinking again. Alcohol did in its way fuel his life. One pledge would follow another: the *Occult Diary* is littered with more or less pathetic resolutions to quit, promises well within the Christian tradition, solemn pledges to God to do penance and become a better man. As the bar of soap in Leopold Bloom's trouser pocket in *Ulysses* has its own history, a 'soapiad' contained within the large epic, one could also trace an alcoholiad in Strindberg's life, the history of his battle with drink with its many farcical and perhaps even some tragic episodes. His heavy smoking and drinking must surely have played their part in his relatively early death at the age of sixty-three.

A similar tragi-comic parallel occurred in Strindberg's relationship with Björnson. The latter had complied with Albert Bonnier's exhortation and written a somewhat condescending letter in which he likewise exhorted Strindberg to return home. An act he was to regret: on 14 October, still in Geneva, Strindberg replied:

Your Majesty! Am in receipt of your imperial edict and will be honoured to disregard it utterly. Dear brother! Your impudence makes you small. If you need me for some political humbuggery, well, I have other and greater tasks in life. My subtlety, that's my sharper intelligence, and you'll have to learn to respect it! And you'll also have great respect for my knowledge, you who never read a book, according to your own words. If you babbled less and read more, you might be as far ahead as I am! . . . Be truthful! Björnson! You're as false as a banquet speaker. . . . Put away strong drink and drink water like me, and you'll think clearly, and understand my book! There, that's the answer you deserve! . . . Now I shall stand alone in my fight, which is something neither you nor Ibsen ever did while nevertheless bragging about it, surrounded by female worshippers. I am as alone as anyone can be, since even my wife is against me.

On the day of Strindberg's return to Sweden, however, Björnson, who had not yet received Strindberg's punitive letter, published a fiery article in his defence in *Dagens Nyheter*. Strindberg regretted his missive and cabled an apology, blaming everything on his children's distressing illness.

Only a few days later, when Strindberg read the report of his arrival in *Handelstidning*, with its insidious allusion to his lack of courage, he again became convinced that this was Björnson's doing. 'So it is you, cowardly Wolf, who slander me out of envy by means of that editor of *Handelstidning* you esteem so little, but who is of course your friend,' he wrote to Björnson, and in November he increased the dosage: 'For shame! You practise secretive slander via Göteborgs Handelstidning! Don't do it! I am warning you! Keep very quiet and still, or else. . . . This is a threat!'

That was the end of their friendship, one of the prices Strindberg had to pay for his case. On Christmas Eve that year he wrote to Jonas Lie: 'I regret the way Björnson behaved. But, believing in providence as I do, I see a meaning in this! He was an obstacle to my development. At last, I can go it alone!' If he ever felt any guilt about the affair, he was never able to admit it.

4

The publicity Strindberg was receiving—the journal *Söndags-Nisse* predicted that Strindberg cigars and Strindberg punch would soon appear on the market—also attracted madmen and people out of touch with reality, who projected their own obsessions on to him. When the legal action was over, Strindberg wrote to Jonas Lie about meetings he had had in Stockholm with 'young, educated fanatics' who were planning the assassination of the Bernadotte family. 'A national government had been chosen, the constitution rewritten, everything was ready, including blueprints of the palace, investigations of the terrain, placement of mines, etc.' Strindberg illustrated his words with a drawing, in which the King is seen seated on his throne, holding a goblet, while Strindberg, with his hair standing on end, is lighting an infernal device placed under His Majesty. In a note accompanying the sketch the recipient was informed that the King's goblet was filled with Piccadon wine, that the explosive charge consisted of dynamite, and that the assassin Strindberg was none other than Satan. Lie, a mild man, took the conspiracy seriously and reacted with horror. Horever, it seems that (as Carl Gustaf Edqvist has shown) all this savage satire had for its origin nothing more than some dinner jokes in the Branting circle.

The devil played the major role in another episode. In *The Journey to Kvarstad* Strindberg relates how a man, one day, steals into his room at the Grand Hotel and sits down on the edge of his bed. The stranger, who has a round, greasy face, addresses Strindberg as Lucifer, 'you who can undo

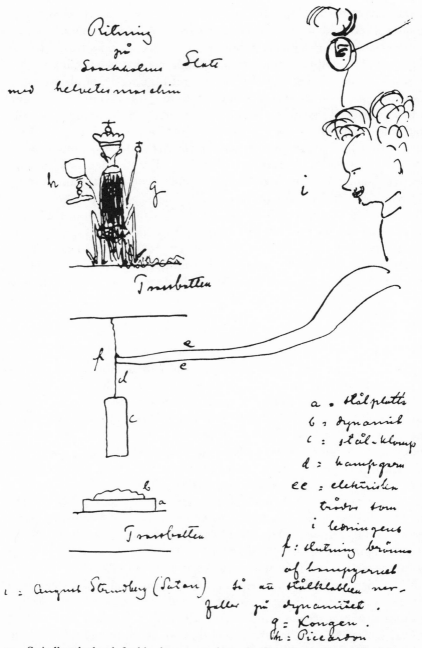

25 Strindberg's sketch for his plan to assassinate the King, in a letter to Jonas Lie, 2 December 1884

your enemy so that he no longer raises his head!' Strindberg, in the novel, treats his visitor with scorn and pokes fun at him. The stranger replies by reciting a list of persons who have been undone, indeed, have either died or contracted diseases because they had opposed Strindberg. The latter protests and shouts that he is not a murderer, and the stranger raises his hands and calls out, 'Undo them, undo them!' Alarmed, Strindberg explains that it is only natural that those who oppose his cause, which is that of the future, have no vital strength—thus acknowledging, in fact, that his enemies have indeed perished.

The episode reads like a dream. Even as a child, Strindberg had always enjoyed dressing up as a devil. Siri and he had even argued about it. In one of Siri's letters, which Strindberg took care not to incorporate in *He and She*, she says that she found it hard to tolerate Strindberg's desire to 'pretend to be the devil' and appear as an assistant to 'the evil one'. She continues: 'I do not believe you when you want to play the devil, and I do believe you in what you call your weak moments, because then I see that you also have a soul and a heart and not only the head of a genius.'

Siri misunderstood her husband. His devil was a relative of the angel of light, Lucifer, who was punished because he rebelled against a tyrant God. Strindberg had written about him in an Epilogue to the poetic version of *Master Olof*, and later returned to him during his journey through the *Inferno*.

On the day after Strindberg's return to Stockholm, the sixth division of the magistrates' court convened under the chairmanship of one of its members, Hjortzberg, to consider the case. Strindberg appeared and spoke with due deference, but firmly. He allowed himself to borrow the occasional ironic note from his poem *For the Freedom of Thought*, whose protagonist was another man accused of 'blasphemy'. Strindberg denied that he had blasphemed against God.

> If God refers to Christ [he said] I feel compelled to point out that until now a negation of Christ's divinity has not been regarded as blasphemy against God. At least, that was not the view held by the municipality which instituted this court, nor by the Professor of Cultural History whose highest achievement was the famous publication *The Bible's Doctrine on Christ*.

This was a shrewd move. That year, Viktor Rydberg had been appointed professor at the University of Stockholm. Twenty-two years earlier, his negation of Christ's divinity had caused a tremendous stir and violent counter-attacks from the ever-watchful church orthodoxy. However, Rydberg was no longer regarded as controversial, but as Sweden's leading cultural figure; he could be likened to keeper of the great seal of the poet's sacred calling, and was adept at concealing his wrath, only occasionally allowing it to explode in huge protest poems. He was not amused to hear his youthful work described as his highest achievement, nor did he appreciate the parallels Strindberg attempted to draw between their respective fates. When the Bonniers tried to enlist him for Strindberg's cause, he responded by evasion.

Strindberg went on to claim that he had not even mocked God or the sacraments, but had merely stuck to the truth, and that his words about communion were to be regarded as informative, not derisive. That line of defence cannot have seemed too convincing, in view of the way things had been put in the short story.

The prosecutor, who got the chance to speak only a week later, on 28 October, upheld the charge of mockery, 'a transgression committed, in my view, under aggravating circumstances, partly because it was committed in the printed word, and partly because Mr Strindberg has also uttered remarkably irreverent words about the founder of the sacrament, in whose memory it has been instituted'. He went on to refute Strindberg's claim to be a purveyor of information. 'Those few lines contain,' he said, 'like the preceding or the subsequent ones, not the slightest attempt to provide an informative discussion of the subject in question.' One phrase in the prosecutor's oration must have caused listeners versed in law to prick up their ears. In his statement before the court, the prosecutor said, Strindberg had demonstrated 'thoughtlessness and frivolity in his view of this matter'. The paragraph under which Strindberg had been charged read as follows: 'Who blasphemes against God or mocks God's sacred words or the sacraments, shall be sentenced to a maximum of two years' hard labour. Should this occur out of thoughtlessness or frivolity, the maximum sentence shall be six months or a fine.' By picking out the 'thoughtlessness' and 'frivolity' the prosecutor indicated that he felt the short term of imprisonment or the fine to be the appropriate sentence in this case. Perhaps he was in his heart, as *Söndags-Nisse* claimed, 'a passionate admirer of Strindberg'.

On 4 November, Strindberg returned to court, and standing by his claim that his intention had been to 'inform', said that *belles-lettres* could be used for such a purpose just as well as scholarly dissertations. He pointed out that the word 'incendiary' came from the Gospels, and referred to Matthew 27:63 in which Pilate calls Jesus a 'deceiver'. He finished by putting himself at the mercy of 'an enlightened court'.*

That ended the preliminary hearing, and the selection of the jurors began. The defendant, the court, and the prosecutor each had the right to choose three. Intense machinations had preceded this procedure. It is quite probable that both court and prosecutor found themselves under heavy pressure from above. Public feeling was running high, which made a conviction undesirable. Perhaps those in authority remembered the events

---

* Translator's note: the Swedish word *upplyst* bears connotations of both 'informed' and 'enlightened'.

following Crusenstolpe's conviction. In Strindberg's easily inflamed imagination, Stockholm was facing revolution for his sake. Later, on 2 December, he wrote to Jonas Lie: 'Had I been sent to prison, there would have been riots. Ammunition had been distributed, and the cavalry had been given standing orders.' Similar hysteria probably prevailed in the Royal Palace. But even the newspapers, as for instance *Tiden* on 18 November, claimed during the trial that a conviction would certainly cause 'serious outbursts of the people's embittered mood'.

Three important men spoke up for Strindberg: Sven Adolf Hedin, a leading political figure, who was often acclaimed as 'legal ombudsman for all of the people', and had been an idol of Strindberg's from his youth; the educational reformer Rector Sixten von Friesen; and Lector Jäderin. The jury's chairman was Pastor Primarius Fredrik Fehr.

On 17 November, the jury assembled in court at 10 am, was sworn in and retired. Its deliberations lasted four hours. Suspense mounted in the packed courtroom. On Riddarhustorget, outside, 10,000 people stood waiting, according to the newspaper *Budkavlen*. After four and a half hours, several knocks against the door indicated that the jury had made its decision. The newspaper *Tiden* related: 'A guard was dispatched to open the door, and out filed the jurors, wearing serious and inscrutable expressions. They had agreed not to reveal the verdict before it was time. and people's attempts at telepathy, which were practised especially on Strindberg's chosen jurors, gave contradictory and uncertain results.'

Jörgen, who sat next to Strindberg, tells of an exchange between them that may well have taken place. Hedin looked angry, and some thought that this was a sign of Strindberg's conviction. 'He's angry about all the stupidities in there,' said Jörgen. 'If he hadn't come out on top in the deliberations, he would look angrier.' 'I believe you,' Strindberg replied quietly.

When chairman Hjortzberg announced that the jury had voted for acquittal, congratulatory hands reached for Strindberg who was standing in the dock 'pale but calm as before'. In a flash, the news had spread outside, and thunderous applause greeted Strindberg when he appeared at the top of the stairs. 'Hats were thrown in the air, and the proclaimer of freedom up there on the stairs was accorded a warmer and more cordial homage than any our time bestows on the rapidly fading splendour of justice.'

The crowd was so dense that Strindberg needed a police escort to the hackney cab that waited for him. According to one source, the King himself, who had mingled with the crowd, got jostled in the confusion and lost sight of his adjutant. In front of the Grand Hotel, where a crowd had quickly gathered, Strindberg made a brief speech: 'I thank you for your acclaim, but I do not take it as directed towards myself personally. I see in it an expression of joy over the victory for free thought and free speech.'

In the evening, friends improvised a 'victory dinner' in the small dining-room of the Grand Hotel. Speeches and applause were interspersed with readings of congratulatory telegrams. A young Finnish journalist who was there reported that the orchestra at one point started to play the royal anthem, encouraged to do so by Jörgen 'as a joke'. Strindberg struck the table with his fist and shouted: 'Pereat! Down!'

The following day, Strindberg boarded the night train for the south. A crowd congregated at the station: a number of whistles were heard amidst the cheers—a counter-demonstration by a few schoolboys and young men. With these mixed sounds ringing in his ears, Strindberg travelled away from his only major public appearance. A couple of days later the paper *Tiden* reported from Malmö that on his arrival 'the renowned author' became the centre of attention, not least that of 'society ladies'.

A young, elegant gentleman who had arrived in the same train had a great deal of trouble to persuade his two lady companions to leave with him. They simply had to see Strindberg, and their escort's expressed opinion: 'I don't want to see the man, I despise him,' increased, rather than diminished, their interest.

5

As soon as Strindberg returned to Switzerland, he sat down to write a report on the days he had spent on trial, in the form of fictional letters to a friend: *The Journey to Kvarstad*. A commemorative medal had been issued in Stockholm: one side showed his head in profile, the other was decorated with a laurel wreath and a quotation from *Master Olof*: 'The truth is always audacious.' Strindberg had made fun of this honour: writing to Claes Looström on 14 November, he suggested that the 'inscrypcioun' should have read: 'For *Tiden*, Posterity, and *Budkavlen*'*—an allusion to the zeal of those two newspapers. He also pondered the fact that the engraver of the medal had previously executed commissions for the royal family.

Many years later, according to *Legends*, he visited a French coin collection and suddenly spotted his own medal in one of the glass-covered display cabinets. 'It is my image,' he exclaims in the book, 'a criminal, ambitious type with hollow cheeks, hair standing on end, and a hateful mouth.' He then bursts into contrite lamentations about having 'mocked the sacred communion' and calls the medal a 'godless memorial, erected to the disgrace

* Translator's note: *Tiden* means time; *Budkavlen* means the messenger's staff.

of impiety by scoffing friends'. He claims that, shamed by this glorification of his 'brutality', he threw the medal to his children to use as a plaything. Then he connects his triumph of 1884 with a blasphemous remark made, as an adolescent, to a female friend: 'I'll chuck morality, as long as I can be a great talent, admired by everyone!'

Like the medal, everything that passed through Strindberg's life became an object of revision and transformation. It is not impossible that in some part of his being he already felt a certain guilt as he stood in the courtroom for his blasphemy against communion. The God of the Old Testament with his rigid moral system and clear-cut commandments did, indeed, remain with him his entire life. However, it is interesting to note that he sees ambition in his own features of 1884: the trial period gave him good opportunities to satisfy his hunger for acclaim. But he always wanted more—not just secular acclaim and medals, but also the everlasting kind that never fade.

In *The Journey to Kvarstad* Strindberg appeared, for the first time, publicly in the spirit if the Nyblom letter—not only as a representative of the lower classes, but as if he himself had belonged to them. Referring to the Italian letters of the spring he explained that they aroused disapproval because 'a lower-class person had dared to take the upper-class prerogative to go and see Italy—without dying of admiration!' Describing the trial, Strindberg alternated between making fun of it, and furious diatribes. Near the end, he wrote to the fictive friend, dating the letter with the date of his acquittal:

> Tomorrow I'm leaving Sweden, again! Remarkably, without bitterness. Yet I've been a prisoner for five weeks! Torn away from my surroundings, my thoughts, my studies. Sitting surrounded by a warm shower of filthy water from the Augean stables. Unable to work, unable to think; condemned to discuss antiquarian questions that have been laid to rest elsewhere in the world; condemned to a role that did not suit me; condemned to listen to so-called enlightened people as they defended lies and superstitions. But why, then, am I going home without bitterness, to a home away from Sweden? Because I saw so many good and beautiful things! Opponents were reconciled, enemies laid down their arms, the voice of envy fell silent for a while, small-mindedness was put to shame, all were united in one great public interest: the hatred against the public lie.

The book was, despite its predominantly mocking tone, an admission of Strindberg's social obligations, and a declaration of allegiance to the community he had fled in 1883. He ended with the words: 'And so farewell, Sweden! It has to blow hard out here in Europe for any waves to stir up in the North. But the storm is raging now! The barometer indicates earthquakes!'

Chapter Eight

TOWARDS A TERMINAL

I

AFTER THE NEWS of Strindberg's acquittal, the Bonniers had received a flood of orders for *Marrying*. The publishers were not ready for them, and this meant considerable financial loss and distress for Strindberg. The books were not available because of growing pressure of opinion throughout the country: during the days following the verdict, the conservative press, using threatening terms, had urged publishers and booksellers not to distribute the book.

Albert Bonnier felt trapped and decided to publish a new edition only if 'Virtue's Reward' was omitted. In effect, this meant that the acquittal was nullified: the most important of the twelve stories was to be removed, and the collection irremediably truncated. State censorship was to be succeeded by self-censorship, and Strindberg had reason to ask himself which was the preferable course. On 28 November he replied to Bonnier's demand for the omission, saying that any alteration was out of the question, apart from the odd 'problematic word' here and there.

> I have declared publicly that my book was a seriously considered work, and I'll stand by that [he wrote]. It would be asinine to hand over one's weapons to the enemy when he chooses to ask for them. I won't change my way of writing and opinions just because I've been abused—you ought to know that, and my previous production should have prepared you for everything that has happened.

The Bonniers even refused to bring out *The Journey to Kvarstad*, declaring that it was not worthy of Strindberg's pen. The truth was that the publishers did not want to risk another flare-up of the debate that had surrounded the trial. During the following years, they invariably gave

Strindberg the same advice: to write novels, to repeat the success of *The Red Room*, but to leave politics and polemics alone! These exhortations were reinforced with monetary advances, rejections, commissions, veiled threats and direct praise, a whole network of subtle, devious exertions of pressure.

Strindberg's relationship with the Bonniers was complicated by the Jewish question. Strindberg was not untainted by anti-Semitism—of which there was a great deal in the European culture of his day—and he did, occasionally, adopt a callous tone toward Jews. What is more, he also adhered to a certain view of the Jewish people that has become almost extinct today, after the holocaust and the foundation of Israel.

According to that view, the Jews were chosen to be 'the nobility of the world'—it was Henrik Ibsen who gave them that distinction—with a mission to represent an ideal world citizenry. The Jews, it was said, did not have their own homeland. Thus they had to be free of all chauvinism and national prejudice. Destiny herself had appointed them to be internationalists and rationalists in their Diaspora. Strindberg regarded the Brandes brothers, in particular, as exemplars for this noble company of Jews, who, it was assumed, had liberated themselves from the Mosaic faith. When, in the spring of 1872, he first read the recently published first volume of Georg Brandes's book *Main Currents*, he wrote to his friend Eugène Fahlstedt: 'Brandes is really sensational—only a Jew could reach such heights—because he is not burdened by that accursed baggage of Christianity and other prejudices we are never able to shake off—he has climbed Mount Everest, if that is the world's highest peak—only from there could anyone be able to see as far as he does.'

In Strindberg's own opinion, his satirization of Jews was directed only against those among them who represented ideals differing from those of the Brandes brothers. *The New Kingdom* contains a chapter entitled 'Moses': in it, easily identifiable Jews are sneered at for kowtowing to the royal family, worshipping hereditary titles, studying only Swedish history and literature, and generally acting as humble and enthusiastic servants of the establishment Strindberg is attacking. Yet it cannot be denied that the chapter also presents anti-Semitic jibes of a cruder kind. It goes without saying, moreover, that it is undoubtedly a form of anti-Semitism to assign the Jews a single role, no matter how noble, and then regard them as fair game if they do not choose to play it. Edvard Brandes was so offended by the Jewish passages in *The New Kingdom* that he refused to have anything to do with Strindberg for three years afterwards.

Thus when, during the period of the trial, Albert Bonnier had indicated Strindberg's religious affiliation as a factor contributing to the difficulty of his situation, Strindberg took this as a sign that his publishers did not want to shoulder the mantle of nobility they had been predestined to wear. He wrote to Pehr Staaff on 13 January 1885:

And talk about the persecution of Jews! That's just their tactics! Instantly 'persecuted' just because no one's kissing their arses any more! That aristocratic entourage of Satan! One hates them as reactionaries, not as Jews! But as soon as one takes a swipe at them, it is of course the Jew who's being persecuted. They've come a long way with those tactics!

Strindberg could not afford to start looking for anyone else to publish the majority of his works. He was considerably in debt to the Bonniers, and his unwilling dependency in that direction explains his harsh words—of which there were more to come. As from 1885, he had to expend a great deal of nervous energy in order to find publishers for the books the Bonniers did not accept. The journal *Budkavlen*, which had supported him during the trial, bought *The Journey to Kvarstad* for 1,000 Swiss francs and ran it in instalments, from January to April. It did not appear in book form. After endless complications, a new edition of *Marrying* came out later in the spring, thanks to the intervention of the warm and generous Isidor Bonnier, Strindberg's former classmate. However, out of regard for his relatives, Isidor Bonnier published the book under a pseudonymous imprint.

2

Most of the years of Strindberg's life could be called years of unrest and displacement, but if one were to choose one as particularly worthy of that description, it would have to be 1885. Strindberg was in unusually dire financial straits that year. In the autumn, all his household goods remaining in Sweden were sold by auction, with the exception of Siri's family portraits. They did not raise very much: after payment of loans and rentals, he received only 680 francs. 'The children go barefoot and the mother is howling for food for her little ones,' was one of his more extreme summaries of the situation. With the assistance of his brother Axel he started putting his manuscripts on the market, *Master Olof* and *The Red Room* in particular.

The beginning of the year found the family living in the old pension in Ouchy, from where Strindberg made an excursion to Rome and Venice. 'Expected little, found even less. Came home miserable in body and soul,' he wrote to Isidor Kjellberg in February. The relics of antiquity and the Renaissance which he saw filled him with revulsion, as they represented a dominant culture built on slave labour. Few authors have been as closely connected to the ancient world as Strindberg, yet he did not achieve that connection through ruins and *objets d'art*, but through classical mythology which had remained alive within him.

In May 1885, a month after the family had moved to Paris, Strindberg witnessed the funeral of Victor Hugo, a tremendous manifestation of popular affection. Here, he was able to see with his own eyes the heights of fame a writer could ascend: it was an incentive. According to the journal of Edmond de Goncourt, the obsequies were accompanied by, among other events, fertility orgies on the Champs Elysées, in which all the whores of the city offered themselves free of charge on the grass. Strindberg saw with his own eyes the coffin resting on its unadorned, pauper's hearse—Hugo's own instructions in this respect were observed—under the Arc de Triomphe, surrounded by a guard of honour consisting of young poets. Later, Strindberg compared the Arc de Triomphe to the gate of an enormous building which at that time had not yet been built—the New France. To Verner von Heidenstam, a still unknown young painter and aspiring writer who had contacted Strindberg after the publication of *Marrying*, he wrote on 31 May, the day Hugo's funeral cortège passed through Paris: 'The cross on the Panthéon was taken down yesterday! Wonderful! The priests were kicked out and the Communion service thrown after those cadavers!' The letter concludes: '(Am about to become an atheist)!'

It is not possible to know exactly what happened to the cross on top of the Panthéon where Hugo was laid to rest. The Communards had sawed off its arms, but in the 1890s it was returned to the place it now occupies, and acted as a reminder to Strindberg as he wandered around Montparnasse Cemetery during his *Inferno* period. Perhaps it was just a temporary removal, as short-lived as Strindberg's atheism.

June found the Strindbergs in Luc-sur-Mer, a small fishing and bathing village in Normandy. Strindberg wrote to Heidenstam that he found the Channel 'a stupid thing to gaze at', as it contained no inspiriting islands or boats. Every summer he spent abroad he came down with feverish homesickness, and then nothing could replace Kymmendö. 'I'm thinking so much about the Stockholm Archipelago that my legs start itching,' was one of his complaints that spring.

He had found it hard to write, all year, which explains a curious venture he got involved in. Mme Juliette Adam, Gambetta's erstwhile friend, was a famous figure of that period: she presided over a celebrated salon in Paris and was the publisher of the highly regarded journal *La Nouvelle Revue*. Her activities included editing a series of intimate descriptions of *mores* prevailing in the European capitals, published under the collective pseudonym 'Count Paul Vasili'. These compilations—*La Société de Berlin*, *La Société de Vienne*, etc.—enjoyed great success and were translated into numerous languages. In fact they were little more than tawdry gossip. In the autumn of 1883 the Bonniers had published the 'Count's' book on Berlin, which was announced in the same catalogue as Strindberg's *Poems*.

Mme Adam had noticed Strindberg and she asked him to write the

Swedish instalment in the series. He immediately saw this as a chance to lay his hostile homeland at the feet of the French public and indulged in the most exaggerated notions of the impression his words would make and the amounts of money he would earn. He was prepared to don a fake coronet and dress himself in skirts, since any glory that might accrue would descend on Mme Adam.

In Normandy, then, facing the 'stupid' sea, Strindberg sat down to work and sent out reports on its progress to both left and right, even though the enterprise was supposed to be a secret one. He was particularly self-congratulatory about his mischievous idea of describing Oscar II as a Prussian in order to make him truly unpopular in France. The king would not be 'too pleased with his portrait, but then he has to learn that one cannot with impunity permit reptiles to slander one's enemies to death,' Strindberg wrote to Albert Bonnier who was appalled at the prospect of the new conflicts the project might bring. Not surprisingly, nothing came of it. When Strindberg sent in his manuscript, it was politely rejected, on the grounds that it did not meet French expectations of piquant detail.

Strindberg did have some pleasant memories of Normandy—for example of fresh-caught fish sold at auction on a stone table at the beach, the event announced by the tolling of bells—and it was with these that he left Normandy with his family in July to return to Grez and a landscape he had described so vividly in *Pangs of Conscience*. The family stayed here for a year, feeling quite at home. The artists' community had grown. A new member of the circle was the painter Karl Nordström; he became a close and faithful friend.

Hoping to entice Heidenstam to move to Grez, Strindberg wrote to him in November:

> We're leading a sociable life here. Old friends from Paris come out on Saturdays, and last Saturday we conducted a well-behaved orgy that went on round the clock for forty-eight hours with singing, guitar, tambourine, pipe and wild *joie-de-vivre*; variety shows, dancing, billiards, midnight snacks, herring for breakfast with the girls (the Danes!), dinner with our own *café chantant*, and a dance at Chevillons. It was almost like the Decameron, and everyone who could contributed songs (a French chansonnette from me!).

The 'Danes' mentioned in the letter were the painter Sofie Holten who painted a romantically idealized portrait of Strindberg, and a young red-headed Jewess, Marie David, who cultivated the legend that she was Georg Brandes's daughter. Marie David was to play a fatal role in Strindberg's life. Her mother had been the mistress of the Danish critic, a notorious philanderer. Strindberg found her and Sofie Holten amusing and considered becoming involved with them.

26 Portrait of Strindberg by Carl Larsson, on the title page of *In Early Spring*, 1881

27 The pension at Grez. Drawing by Carl Larsson for the Svea Calendar, 1884

Nevertheless, there were snakes in the grass in idyllic Grez. During the autumn, Karl Nordström wrote detailed reports of life there to his fiancée, Tekla Lindeström. In these, he denies having spread rumours to the effect that Sofie Holten and Marie David were lovers, but states that he 'cannot stand watching the way David and Siri carry on without feeling nauseous'. He goes on to tell how Strindberg came to him one day and laid his heart bare to him.

> And do you know, it was so damned heart-rending for me to hear and see that I was ready to weep with him—as he revealed to me all the bottomless misery and wretchedness of his married existence. The poor man, joined forever to a creature he despises, who is his bitterest enemy and yet—strange to behold—clutches him so strongly and confidently in her talons.

In *A Fool's Apology*, one of the main charges against Maria (who stands for Siri) is that she had a lesbian relationship with Marie David. Nordström's letter indicates that there were rumours to that effect, but naturally this does not qualify as evidence. It is possible that it was just that rumour which Strindberg later found useful to exploit for artistic reasons. Despite his complaints to Nordström, he came to Marie David's defence on that occasion. Among other things he wrote to Carl Larsson that Nordström's hostility towards the Danish girls was due to their risqué talk about his relationship with his fiancée.

In early October, Strindberg took a journalist's trip to the familistère in Guise. This formed part of his work on a 'new humanity'. Siri accompanied him, leaving Eva Carlsson to look after the children. They could afford to retain her services, although the payment of her wages presented difficulties and Strindberg engaged in long and anxious correspondence with trusted friends about the state of her bank savings book. The trip was a successful one: 'happy as newlyweds', Strindberg wrote to Heidenstam.

Their destination was a famous 'socialist' collective, which had been instituted in 1859 by the wealthy manufacturer of iron goods Jean-Baptiste André Godin-Lamaire. Strindberg wrote three articles about the enterprise for Edvard Brandes's newspaper *Politiken* in Copenhagen. They were full of good intentions but did not have much of an edge to them. There is, however, one passage which seems full of observation. The familistère, where a number of welfare systems (at that time, rare) were being tried out, was built around a foundry. On his tour of the place, Strindberg stopped at a workshop where spittoons were being enamelled. In his article he describes the work in terrifying heat as dangerous to human life and compares the young labourers to gladiators who, in their dying moment, salute the visitor/emperor who witnesses the horrifying spectacle from his privileged position in the audience. Unlike the majority of educated people of his century, Strindberg was conscious of what hard physical labour meant. It is significant that his visit took place during the year of publication of the second volume of *Das Kapital* with its horrendous images of English factory workers' lives.

According to various sources, Strindberg was the most cheerful of all those taking part in the Christmas celebrations at Grez in 1885. Ville Vallgren relates that the Swedes feasted on porridge, ham, pastries, brandy and homesickness. Strindberg sang traditional student songs, wearing a paper version of the traditional student's cap and a pair of spectacles. Charades were performed. There is reason to believe that it was Strindberg who suggested Rembrandt's autopsy painting as a charade. Vallgren was the corpse, wrapped in a sheet. Later that night the guests at the pension woke up to the sound of gunfire: an intoxicated American artist had started firing indiscriminately. Strindberg was seen in a hallway, carrying a mattress on his back. According to Ville Vallgren, the American shot himself a few months later, after suffering heavy losses at Monte Carlo, with the same revolver he had been firing at Grez.

Against these exuberant scenes we have to set the emotional turmoil of Strindberg's letters, which does not abate with the advent of 1886. On the contrary: on 11 January, he informs Geijerstam that he believes 'the end of the comedy' is drawing near. In mid-March he writes to Looström that he has taken to carrying a revolver in his trouser pocket at all times and 'is suspicious of everybody'. However, the next day he discovers that he possesses 'an incredible vitality', and says that he is drinking in order to steady his nerves.

Strindberg had never abandoned the idea of the expedition to discover true peasantry which he had planned in the spring of 1884. In Grez, he had the opportunity to study French peasants, and he wrote a series of articles about life in the village and around it. On 19 February, he offered these to Edvard Brandes, and on 5 March declared that he would be 'a dead man' if they were rejected. In the same letter, Brandes was told that Strindberg's sole joy had been the recent workers' riots in London: 'Did you know that it is possible to pump air into gas mains and blow up entire cities that way? If I had been in London, I would have advocated setting fire to the ships in the docks. Wood and tar aren't bad remedies against old monarchy and state religion, etc.' Those murderous thoughts were followed by the words: 'Farewell. The Facteur (that is to say, the postman) is here. Farewell, you, my last hope.'

It is instructive to compare the articles—which today form the first part of *Among French Peasants*—with the letters Strindberg was writing at the same time. While the letters scoff, buzz and complain, the prose of the articles flows along with a quiet charm. To take but one instance, where Strindberg describes an evening at the inn: an itinerant comedian turns up, and when, after one of his routines, he starts passing the plate round, the peasants turn their wide backs on him, as an expression of contempt for someone who does not 'work'. Strindberg shows the same coolly observant empathy for both sides—the carefree artiste with his hatred of the owners of property, and the peasants whose stinginess is only a function of their vital materialism.

Strindberg's drinking may have been behind the absurdities about gas mains and revolvers in his letters. Karin Smirnoff thinks that Strindberg's unbalanced temper during that winter was due to the fact that he had, after a 'period of total sobriety, taken to drinking absinthe'. In the clear light of morning he wrote what was intended for publication. In the afternoons, he drank. Yet it was not only alcohol that caused this schism between his work of the morning and the letters of the evening: the work at the desk itself had a calming effect. When he wrote, his breathing became more regular, his nerves switched off their alarm signals and he underwent a healing process. In judging the state of his psyche, one has to consider the serenity and dignity of his literary output at this time.

3

Economically, things took a turn for the better in February 1886: the Bonnier publishing house cancelled a debt of 8,000 kronor—accumulated from advances Strindberg had received over the years. Strindberg's numerous letters describing his impecunity resulted in various movements to assist him, and in March a collection organized in Stockholm raised 3,680 francs: Strindberg acknowledged this windfall with 'deepest gratitude'. After a substantial debt to the pension had been paid, the family moved on 14 March into a house called '*la nouvelle maison*', as it was the newest building in Grez. According to Karin Smirnoff, Strindberg paid the rent for six months in advance. Siri rented furniture, kitchen utensils, crockery and a portable stove. A boy was hired to assist Strindberg in tending the garden. For 12 francs a month, the family rented a piano, and a girl was engaged to help Eva.

Strindberg's daughters went to the village infant school, run by nuns along strictly traditional lines. One punishment consisted of the old-fashioned dunce's cap, complete with donkey ears, which the culprit had to wear in front of the whole class. As an 'expression of their father's sympathy for the peasants' the girls wore wooden clogs.

In his new home, Strindberg wrote the first part of his autobiography, *The Serving Maid's Son*, at his customary frenetic speed. He had chosen a good moment to embark on an autobiographical work. The previous autumn, he had published a collection of short stories entitled *Utopias*, reiterating his social and political beliefs in a foreword. In the socialist society of the future, he wrote, we must not repeat the errors of the past. Never again will we build a St Peter's Basilica, never again train and educate a Raffaelo Sanzio, as such exclusive results are based only on slave labour. 'Will the world then be a boring place to live in?' he asks rhetorically, and replies: 'Not at all. Those who think so now will never see that world. And the only unadulterated pleasure in life, which consists of a strong body and the certainty of sufficient means to exist, will replace all those fanciful notions about "higher things".'

Ideologically, that is certainly a terminal position. For those who are starving, it is doubtless significant to be healthy and to have enough to eat; but for Strindberg, waited upon every day of his life and specially educated to be a writer, it was a severe way of looking at the world. No more Michelangelo, no more Raphael—so no more Shakespeare, either, nor, for that matter, any Strindberg. If he was going to live according to his own doctrine, he had to give up writing. He had blocked the way for his own authorship: all that was left to do was to provide a summing-up and retire from the literary scene.

In *Utopias* we encounter characters who are trying to change themselves into new human beings—it seems that Strindberg borrowed this concept of a 'new humanity' from the Russian political martyr Tchernyshevskii's Utopian novel *What Must We Do?* which was the talk among the radical Left at the time. In Strindberg's story 'Relapse', Paul Petrovich, a Russian physician in exile, makes a living as a master gardener in Ouchy. In every way imaginable, he tries to free himself from his upper-class culture, going so far as to suffer pangs of conscience whenever he enjoys the scent of roses in the garden, since, in the future world, only what is 'useful' will be permitted. Paul represents a socio-political pietism that has its absurd side. No wonder, then, that he 'relapses' in his struggle, back into established patterns of sin.

However, Strindberg could not make of *The Serving Maid's Son* what he had intended it to be—a farewell to fiction and a straightforward demonstration of what life looked like down there among the sons of serving maids. As soon as Strindberg sat down to write in earnest, all his talent and powers of expression, and the delight he derived from it, took over. Once in a while he recalled his original intention and inserted something about the slave blood of his mother boiling in his veins, yet such passages are remarkably few and far between. Once in a while it also occurred to him that his hero—Johan, as he called himself in the book—appeared to be fairly egotistical and self-centred. To take care of this, he introduced the excuse that it was merely a consequence of his Christian upbringing which had taught him to study and cultivate his own ego. In a foreword which did not appear in the published edition, he explained that he had indeed described himself as 'a vicious, cowardly, envious, self-loving, arrogant, disobedient, amoral, impious hooligan', a characterization that is true only if the enumerated 'bad' qualities are seen in a heroic perspective in which 'amoral' stands for the highest form of morality. In the book, Johan has all the right on his side: as a result he would be an utterly insufferable protagonist if the prose were not so lively, if we did not find, on almost every page, freshly drawn memories from Strindberg's own childhood, and if the suit which Johan presses against life, the family, and God were not as dramatic and frequently entertaining as it is.

As Strindberg wrote, the entire socialist state of the future which he had envisaged began to fade and wither away in his mind. It had served its purpose, and he no longer had any use for it at this time. When, in the late autumn of 1886, he was putting the finishing touches to this 'long and sad journey through the shadow land of memory' as he called it, he felt that nothing of his former beliefs remained. His fickleness perturbed him, but he changed it, instantly, into a virtue, comparing himself to a hound on the track of its prey—truth: 'Seek! Seek!': this was the force that drove him. Not so long ago, he had thought he was on the right track, after the right prey: socialism. This turned out to be a mistake. The hunt went on.

In actual fact, he had found the right prey—his own self. Many years later, in 1909, when he was writing a foreword to the fourth and final part of *The Serving Maid's Son*, he said that he was not ready for this in 1886: 'Perhaps only got started then.' He was correct in his estimate. Now he was really getting started. It was a practical consequence of the withering of the future state that the scent of roses and works of lyric intensity were permissible once again.

4

The Bonniers were delighted with *The Serving Maid's Son*, as it avoided politics altogether, and they immediately sent Strindberg an advance. He used this to leave Grez, despite the advance rent he had paid, and to move to Switzerland. This time, he was drawn to the German-speaking region, and Heidenstam in particular. The Bonniers were told that the environs of Zurich were especially inexpensive and that Mrs Strindberg was to be trained as a midwife there, a profession Strindberg had also chosen for his daughters. To encourage his publishers to further acts of generosity he assured them that he was planning a Christmas volume, *Swedish Idylls*, composed in hexameters: 'these are from the piggybank I filled while writing *Th. S. M. Son*, in which I have consciously neglected all landscape.' This was one of many occasions on which Strindberg talks about savings and 'capital', by which he means fragments of life and experience that he had not yet used for literary purposes.

Strindberg left first, leaving the family in Grez, and arrived in Switzerland on 10 May at Brunegg, where Heidenstam and his wife had rented a château with a 'knights' hall' which both he and Strindberg described in lively terms. The friendship of Strindberg and Heidenstam turned out to be a brief, hectic affair, offering humorous examples of Strindberg's peculiar talent for fruitful misunderstandings. When Heidenstam first introduced himself, by letter, with witty cracks about the 'smorgas people' (the Swedes), Strindberg convinced himself that he had found a representative of the 'new man' and replied with enthusiasm and in good faith.

Heidenstam had already accompanied Strindberg to Rome and Venice and visited him in Grez. Now the two friends treated each other with great courtesy and consideration, initially at any rate. Both of them were extremely fond of fancy dress and pageantry. In May, Strindberg stayed at the castle for a couple of days, trying on suits of medieval armour, playing a game called *platzke*—in which brass pieces were thrown at numbered holes in a board—and discussing literature and politics with Heidenstam. Knut Hamsun once called Strindberg 'a brain on horseback'. Heidenstam was of the same type, although not as intense nor as serious. They competed in the invention of paradoxes, they compared their lives, they understood one another instantly. Later, Heidenstam called their conversations 'spiritual copulation', and Strindberg characterized their time together as a 'daily opening of the safety valves'. In *The Journey to Kvarstad*, Strindberg had written that except for the sexual aspect he would have preferred marriage to a man to that with a woman. Heidenstam, charming, handsome, aristocratic, and, because he had as yet no reputation of his own, weaker and more receptive, conformed to the ideal image of such a 'marriage' partner.

On 20 May, Siri and the children arrived in Switzerland after a long and extremely expensive journey, and the family settled in a boarding-house in Othmarsingen, so close to the Heidenstams' residence that it was possible to signal to one another from the balconies. The families met, and Siri disliked Heidenstam just as much as Emili Heidenstam disliked Strindberg: this was hardly surprising, as the two men so clearly demonstrated that they preferred each other's company to that of the ladies. Yet the intensity of the friendship had its risks. The families made joint excursions which ended in trouble. On 22 June 1886, Heidenstam wrote an irritated letter to Strindberg, speaking of the latter's 'unreasonable pretensions' and of his 'finickiness' (which, by the way, Heidenstam saw extended to Siri and the children as well).

You, 'the servant maid's son', get disgruntled over what delights hundreds of pampered tourists. Your nervous finickiness has become monomaniacal; you brood over your *idée fixe* that almost everything is worthless and unpalatable. You began in dissatisfaction with society, and end in dissatisfaction with steaks, trout, and billiard balls of too vivid a shade of heliotrope.

Strindberg was hurt, yet his reply was not aggressive but sounded rather like that of a man whose mistress has just thrown a tantrum. 'A chronometer is more finicky than a cheap pocket-watch,' he wrote, 'but who cares—as long as the former keeps time to one hundredth of a second.' Hard-working man that he was, did he not have the right to demand relaxation and pleasure, reasonable food, and courteous service? Which was to say—he deliberately alienated himself from the thinking behind *Utopias*. Heidenstam with his aristocratic leanings had helped him get rid of his self-inflicted hair-shirt.

The families parted in August, when the Strindbergs moved to Weggis by Lake Vierwaldstätter, under the Alpine peak known as Pilatus. '*Wunderschön*. Almost as beautiful as Skurusund,' Strindberg wrote to Albert Bonnier on 3 August, adding: 'I can't stand travelling, but as soon as I've sat in one place for three months and my eye registers disgust at everything, I do have to move on. If only they'd invent movable landscapes! I'm sure it is nostalgia at the root of all that. "Dort wo Du nicht bist, dort ist dein Land".'

5

Strindberg had not forgotten his projected research into the peasantry of France: now this was to become reality. Early that year, he had received letters from twenty-year-old Gustaf Steffen, who would later make an important contribution to economics and social science. Strindberg's books had excited him, and he offered their author his services, little knowing that his idol was in an ideological phase of transition. Strindberg had seen Steffen during his time at the Royal Library: he was the son of the cloakroom attendant whose father, according to Strindberg, was Klemming (see p. 77). Steffen's biographer Ake Lilliestam is sceptical about that genealogy, while Hans Lindström tends to agree with Strindberg. The mother's name was Anna Maria von Reis, and Strindberg was fascinated by her. She had talents as a medium, which Klemming exploited, and Strindberg used her as a model in the long story *Shortcuts*, where she is a witch-like creature, governed by powers from the soul's subterranean regions.

Strindberg replied in a friendly and intimate manner and offered Steffen the task of completing the catechism for the lower classes, since he himself had grown tired of it. 'But write calmly; keep the language mild,' he added by way of advice. Strindberg even decided to take Steffen along as assistant and photographer on the trip to France, and the two soon became involved in discussions of travel routes and equipment. Steffen was inundated with advice and commissions, and Strindberg depicted their future together in glowing terms. They were going to collect objects for a future European museum of agriculture; they would photograph ploughs, rakes, 'farm animals, mangy dogs, old horses'; collect seeds, roots, fibres. 'My intelligence', Strindberg assured Steffen on 5 August, 'has evolved from the aesthetic hallucinatory state, and wants to investigate realities.' In Paris, Strindberg reported, one could obtain 'photographic revolvers' which were carried in the pocket and used with maximal speed. He went on to claim that as a precaution such a device would be preferable to an ordinary camera, since the French police were constantly looking for German spies, and a visible camera might cause complications.

Steffen arrived in Weggis at the end of August. Siri and Eva Carlsson assisted in the preparations for the expedition. Plenty of woollen garments and nerve tonics were packed in the luggage. They left on 30 August, and the journey proceeded briskly. Strindberg claimed that he already knew everything, and so it was merely a matter of 'verifying facts'. They travelled third class on the train, in order to be in touch with 'the people'; they got off at small stations and interviewed peasants in the taverns. One can gain some idea of what those peasants were asked by looking at a notebook, now in the Royal Library, in which Strindberg recorded their replies. Here is one of them: 'What do we care if there's a republic or whoever governs; *le blé, voilà notre République.*'

Some days, they spent up to twelve hours on the train, refreshing themselves—according to Steffen—with oysters and English ale. Altogether, they travelled 3,880 kilometres by rail, and an unspecified distance on foot and by horse-drawn coach. They made notes of things as various as 'oxen with cushions on their heads', 'a cariole racing the stagecoach'—and did not omit to record details of food and clothing.

It was an expensive trip—costing a total of 1,900 francs—yet Strindberg returned home to Weggis in the best of spirits and told Bonnier that it had been a remarkable achievement. Proudly, he wrote:

My eyes are as red as those of a roach, and the lining of my coat has rotted away from sweat; the skin of my feet has cracked from all the walking, while solaced by a glass of cognac poured into my socks; gentian kept my stomach working, rosewater helped my eyes. It was a horse-physic, but I feel refreshed. I needed something like this.

But what had happened to his companion? There is an entry under 15 September in one of Strindberg's notebooks: 'Chased off Steffen having found him out to be a thief and con-man.' Steffen told Klemming in an emotional letter that Strindberg's behaviour toward him had completely changed after a couple of days on the journey—inexplicably so. At first, Steffen tried to excuse it by Strindberg's 'stomach catarrh' and 'extra-ordinary nervousness', but, before long, Strindberg's conduct surpassed any reasonable limit. Steffen was in charge of their funds. In Toulouse, Strindberg accused him of being a spendthrift, and soon thereafter, of 'cheating and theft'. The unhappy young man wrote:

> Finally, at the railroad station in Nimes, Mr Strindberg threw 100 francs at me for my journey back to Berlin, said we would now go our separate ways, and launched a barrage of insults at me: I had 'exploited' him or 'even worse', I was a Jew with an inborn urge to cheat him, the Aryan, I had the physiognomy of a criminal, etc., etc. What was I to do in a foreign country, with my imperfect command of its language? Declare that his words were those of a madman, turn my back and go?

The archives contain a letter from Strindberg to Steffen, written in Clermont-Ferrand on 16 September, which corroborates Steffen's letter to Klemming: in it, Strindberg accused Steffen of having stolen 100 francs from his wallet, and threatened to turn him over to the arm of the law.

In his letter to the Bonniers, dated 20 September, Strindberg enthused about his collaboration with the thief and con-man he had sent packing four days earlier: 'Weighted down with baggage, we ran to catch trains; photographed and described landscapes and buildings from the compart-ment window. Whenever we spotted a new type of house, my comrade instantly sketched the left half, I did the right, and then we put them together.' It is difficult to reconcile this description with Steffen's.

Strindberg's brutality toward Steffen is not unique in Strindberg's life, but on the other hand it is not common either. Intoxication or the experience of finding himself in a tight spot could destroy the consideration for others to which so many of his contemporaries testified; perhaps he found himself in one of these tight spots with Steffen.

Maybe. The following year, he wrote a short story, 'Battle of the Brains', which is a transparently disguised account of that journey. In the story, the trip turns into a battle of nerves and thoughts between the two travelling companions. The younger man represents Strindberg's socialist views before 1886, the older one stands for the new way of thinking. Strindberg found that he was travelling with himself as a younger man. His past was chasing him in more than one sense: he was pursued from one French railway station to the next by the proofs of the second part of *The Serving Maid's Son*, in which he relates how he discovered that he was going to be a writer. Was it a side of himself that he sent packing in Nîmes? It may be noted as a curiosity that the short story describes Schilf (the name Steffen has been given) with a wealth of details and incidents in which his two upper front teeth play a particular part. Schilf, we are told, had 'two large, wide chisels in his upper jaw, just like a gorilla. A predator, I thought [the older traveller is narrating this], who even has a taste for fruit. An unsociable, ill-tempered beast who walks by himself in the forest, and amuses himself in the company of his own malicious thoughts.' On 27 May 1898, eleven years after the writing of that story, Strindberg noted in his journal: 'The last front tooth in my upper jaw (excepting the two right in front which remain) fell out. NB! My front teeth consisted of a bunch of small, stunted, predatory teeth. The two right in front, however, were chisel-shaped.' Were Schilf-Steffen's 'chisels' a hint as to where the solution to these enigmatic events should be sought?

The short story has another interesting aspect: in it, Strindberg experiments, for the first time, with a narrative mode he would soon master to perfection. The older traveller, the narrator, believes that he has been able to demolish completely and annihilate not only his younger companion's arguments but his entire intellectual apparatus. It is, however, obvious that the narrator is deceiving himself. In fact, he is an ingenuous braggart, locked into his own arrogance, and his superiority is only in his own imagination. Thus we observe two equals, travelling together through a strange land—as was the case in reality. Steffen represented the radical ideas that Strindberg actually never relinquished, although he was, at this time, entering a period of the cult of superman.

6

After Strindberg returned from the trip to France, the family moved once again, on 30 September 1886: this time, only a few kilometres east along the shore of Lake Vierwaldstätter, to Gersau.

It disgruntled Strindberg that the pictures taken on the journey to France were unsuccessful, and he blamed it on Steffen's 'apathy'. All the more cause for us to rejoice in the fact that he continued to use the camera. In *Le Journal Illustré*, he saw a series of photographs of the famous French chemist Chevreul, taken to celebrate his hundredth birthday. It was one of the first photographic reportages, and Strindberg conceived the idea of creating a similar documentary sequence with himself as the subject. A new invention, involving a wire, enabled him to take pictures of himself. Strindberg suggested to Bonniers that they publish a book of these photographs, with commentaries by himself.

28–30 Three photographs
taken by Strindberg in
Gersau, 1886. Strindberg
with a fencing foil.
Strindberg and Siri
playing backgammon.
Strindberg and his
daughters in the garden

The publishers were not interested, but the pictures were taken and have survived; in them, we see Strindberg for the first time outside a photographer's studio, but he keeps complete control, just as he did in his autobiography. On one of the cards, he is standing foil in hand, incredibly alert: who would dare approach such a swordsman! On another, he is wearing a top hat, looking a little wild-eyed. In a third one it looks as if his head had just been struck by a lightning-bolt; a fourth shows him bent over his desk, his face buried in papers. It looks like an image of despair and resignation, although the original intention was, most probably, to show off his fine, thick head of hair.

One print is unique in that it is the only surviving photograph to show the Strindbergs together. They are playing backgammon. Siri is seen from behind; Strindberg faces her, holding a cigarette in a holder in one hand, moving a piece with the other. There is a bottle on the table, with a glass by it; the cork is adorned by a rooster, perhaps one of those made out of silver that were enumerated among Siri's belongings in the marriage inventory (see p. 158).

Other pictures show Strindberg in the company of his children, who are looking into the camera with serious expressions. There are gardening utensils, a watering can: Strindberg himself, wearing a hat, is holding a spade. When Strindberg sent the pictures to Bonniers he called them 'impressionist photographs', which indicates the direction in which his ambition for them lay. Yet studying the sequence it is easy to perceive that he was primarily interested in his own face and the enigma it presented.

Chapter Nine

MAN AND WOMAN

I

THE NEW PHASE in Strindberg's life began with a change of scene. At the beginning of January, the family moved to Germany, renting the top floor of a villa in Izzigathsbühl by Lake Constance, near Lindau. Their neighbour downstairs was a German bookseller, Wilhelm Ludwig, who spoke Swedish and had children the same age as Strindberg's.

On or around 15 January, Strindberg wrote to Heidenstam:

In Germany! By Lake Constance, in a country house with Pächter. Patriarchy and masculine discipline; chubby-cheeked recruits, three ells tall; France was all absinthe and self-abuse; Switzerland, matriarchal slop. Here we still have male animals with life in their limbs. I admire Bismarck's speech. He is a realist, a man of our times. If we are to have State and Society, well, damn it, let's do it right. If nations are to exist until further notice, let there be guardsmen; if there are to be guardsmen, let them live in barracks and engage in drill practice from 5 in the morning until 8 in the evening! Oh! We are such nostalgic old idealists!

With satisfaction, Strindberg reported that 'here in Germany' women were not allowed to study at universities.

He had been studying those guardsmen ever since Ludwig had introduced him to officers serving in a regiment stationed nearby. The Bismarck speech he admired contained a few threatening remarks towards France, and there were rumours of war. Strindberg considered a career as war correspondent. On 3 February, he wrote to Albert Bonnier that it 'is very probable we'll have a war, in ten days or ten weeks', and that he wanted to describe it 'without any national or pacifist bias'. Which no doubt meant abandoning the pacifism expressed in 'Pangs of Conscience'. War is a suitable occupation for 'male animals with life in their limbs', and for Strindberg himself 'a rousing of my spirits, something I can really use'.

He informed his publishers that he required 2,000 kronor immediately, to buy a horse, as it was his intention to accompany the staff of the Third Bavarian Infantry Regiment into France. It seems that he was assuming that the Germans were going to repeat their exploits of 1870, taking the war into enemy territory. The remainder of the money was required for 'war expenses' and 'maps, uniform charts, distance cards'.

> I am a good horseman [he wrote] and have an idea of the basics of the martial arts. I don't think there could be anything more welcome to me than a war, as a distraction from all my philosophical and social preoccupations with the role of women and the peasant situation. So! A horse, a kingdom for a horse! I'm really determined to see this thing through, even if it costs me some red blood.

While indulging in these warlike plans—in which he already imagined himself spilling his blood on the battlefield—Strindberg wrote his first important naturalistic play, the tragedy *The Father*, which was not much less horrifying than the spectacle he was referring to in the letter to Bonnier. The man who offered his kingdom for a horse was Richard III, whose drama contains equally agonizing torments of the soul and ends in horror just like *The Father*. On 6 February, three days after that letter, the first act had been completed; the entire play, on 15 February.

Strindberg had the habit of creating the right mood for his work by making certain small arrangements in his study. In the winter, a flower would suggest summer; an old book with beautifully wrought initial letters stood for the sixteenth century. Now he had extended this form of stage management to a larger theatre, by taking his family to Bismarck's Germany of 'blood and iron', in order to get the right feeling for his dramatic tale of a cavalry captain who is compelled to exchange his uniform for a straitjacket.

A few days before starting work on the play, Strindberg had told Heidenstam that he had 'discovered a new, higher, evolutionary form of *belles-lettres*', and called it 'vivisections'. He himself was his first object for dissection, cultivating within himself the germs of virility from which the Captain would be engendered.

2

When we meet the Captain, who is the main character in *The Father*, he is wearing his uniform and cloak, and riding boots with spurs. He is not only a military man, but also a highly talented amateur scientist, specializing in mineralogy. His daughter Bertha says that when he enters a room, it is like removing the inner windows on a spring morning—one of Strindberg's favourite metaphors: until quite recently, Scandinavian houses were built with double windows, and the inner ones were removed for the summer, with the result that one was suddenly able to hear sounds from the outside— birdsong, in particular. Strindberg wants to convey an impression of openness and health: we are presented with a man who has 'life in his limbs', a Renaissance figure.

The Captain's wife Laura, his insidious enemy, has few individual traits apart from a strong will. She wants her daughter to become a painter, while the Captain has chosen a teacher's career for her. Seen from Strindberg's socio-critical perspective this means that Laura wants to turn the daughter into a parasitic upper-class woman, while the Captain wants her to follow her nature—when she gets married, she can use her skills to instruct her own children. A battle to the death ensues: the Captain insists on his paternal authority, while Laura uses all the weapons at her disposal. She tries to undermine her husband's mental health and gives him reason to suspect that he is not actually the father of his daughter. That blow against his manhood unhinges him: driven to desperation, he throws a burning kerosene lamp at his wife. For him, that is the end. In the final scene, the Captain, now a certified madman, is forced into a straitjacket with the assistance of a physician and his old wet-nurse (who is still living in the house); it is into her lap that he collapses with a scream, apparently dead.

Theodore Lidz, among others, has attempted to draw a psychoanalytical profile of Strindberg, beginning with the triangle situation Strindberg became involved in with the Wrangels. The couple, living in the same apartment Strindberg had known as a child, represented an idealized version of his parents. Siri became his mother and, in order to avoid incest, Strindberg fantasized her into a maternal madonna, an inaccessible ideal figure. To counteract a latent tendency to homosexuality, Wrangel was translated into a noble father figure.

When, however, the positions were reversed—Strindberg could have an affair with Siri while Wrangel directed his attentions to the cousin—the madonna fell off her pedestal, and Wrangel became a villain. Strindberg felt obliged to tear his degraded wife from his arms. He also felt that the baron despised him and treated him like a child by encouraging his liaison with Siri: at the same time, he believed that Siri regarded him as timid, which forced him to prove his virility.

But when he proved it, he became guilty of incest, and, like Oedipus, racked by tragic guilt; like the Greek king, he had to redeem himself by death or castration, having had sexual relations with a divine queen. The good-natured baron turned into a vengeful father. Siri, only a moment ago his caressing, consoling mother, changed into a vampire sapping his strength. He was unable to live without her, yet to live with her generated an overwhelming feeling of guilt in him: in the marriage, she was his friend as a mother, but his enemy as a wife.

It is an interpretation worth bearing in mind as a basic formula. When Lidz applies his analysis to *The Father*, he finds that the Captain represents Strindberg who is mortally tortured by inner tension between the masculine and the feminine elements in his make-up, between his need to be victorious and the need to be submissive.

Strindberg was a very feminine man—if one considers delicacy, gentleness, anxiety, patience with children, fussiness, love of flowers, a tendency to weep easily and sudden changes of mood 'feminine' traits. Wherever he speaks of women, he appears more like their rival or sister, noting every detail of their dress, coiffure and facial expression.

As a self-portrait, the Captain is of considerable interest: he represents a dream image—hence the window metaphor—but the masculine role becomes his prison. He is another von Bleichroden, only this time no war or corpse smelling of carbolic acid is needed to cause his breakdown: he is undone by the net Laura throws over him. He wants to be a soldier and, at the same time, a gentle, open human being, and that conflict destroys him.

Strindberg had the bizarre idea of introducing Shakespeare's Merchant of Venice into this play. The Captain parodies Shylock's famous soliloquy in which he asks if a man does not bleed when he is stabbed, die when he is poisoned? 'Why should a man not be allowed to complain, a soldier, to weep? Because it is not manly! Why is it not manly?' The despised Shylock is denied the right of being human, of reacting in a human way. The Captain's despair over his imprisonment in the male role could hardly find stronger expression, and he speaks for all men, down the centuries, who have been forced into uniforms.

When, instead of shouting and blustering, the Captain starts pleading with his wife, her love for him reawakens, and she reminds him that he first came to her like a child to its mother—and that this was precisely the way she had loved him, as a child (it is interesting to compare this with Lidz's analysis). She reminds him that she used to feel shame and pangs of conscience when he was her lover, when 'the mother became the mistress, oh!' The mother was his friend, she says, but 'the woman' his enemy.

Thus both the Captain and Laura desire the same thing—that men should be childish, cry and plead; be a human being first and a man second. Why, then, does the Captain perish? Is it really from the tragic guilt he has incurred by entering into a sexual relationship with the woman whose child he had been at the beginning of their love? The Captain explains that he suffered when Laura assumed the maternal role, since that gave her the upper hand. By 'a great act, a heroic deed, a discovery, or an honest suicide' he wants to regain his position. He wants to go to the wars. He cannot live without honour.

In the last act, which is when the lamp is thrown, the Captain appears to be completely mad, yet the spectator remains uncertain whether he really is insane or merely pretending to be so. The wet-nurse has the straitjacket ready for him and entices him into it by means of fairytales and baby talk which take the Captain back to the nursery. Her tactics are the same as Laura's. She disarms him by acting as a mother, with protective tenderness.

When the Captain realizes that he has been caught, when the straitjacket sleeves have been tied behind his back, he asks for his uniform tunic to be put over him, and calls it his 'hard lion's skin'. All along, the play has been full of mythological allusions. The Captain believes himself to be a Hercules, clad in the skin of the animal he had killed when still in possession of his entire strength. But he also remembers, at this moment, another of Hercules' adventures—his captivity in the court of queen Omphale who dressed the hero in women's clothes and employed him in feminine tasks.

In his analysis, Lidz considers that Hercules experienced being the captive of a woman as a pleasure, and that this is the meaning of the myth. In the Captain's case, we have no reason to doubt that he wished to be freed from the lion's skin, the symbol of masculinity, but was not able to achieve this. Nor is the straitjacket they so cunningly trap him in, anything new. He has, in fact, been wearing one all along, only calling it his uniform. It drove him out into the heroic life where he had to die. It was not Laura who forced him into it: it existed within himself. His suffering was far deeper than that caused by suspicions of his paternity. His tragic guilt lies in the dichotomy between the masculine and the feminine, and behind those poles stands the dark will, the need to dominate, as opposed to fertility, frankness and trust.

In the final act, Laura says that she neither planned nor intended the crimes she committed against her husband. 'I have never reflected upon events, they have proceeded along lines you had laid down yourself, and before God and my conscience I feel innocent, even if I am not.' A strange line. Did it refer to Strindberg's own marriage, in which a battle similar to the one between the Captain and Laura raged? If so, the words can be read as at least a half-admission that Siri was not guilty either, as she proceeded along lines that Strindberg himself had laid down.

3

The first part of *Marrying*, in which the question of the relationship between the sexes was taken up on a grand scale, was written in 1884, when 'nature' was Strindberg's guideline in all things and provided him with a populist, primitive view of women. Reading it, one can almost hear the sea captains, his father's friends, joking and guffawing in the background at the steamboat office on Riddarholmen.

The first axiom of that doctrine is that man is the self-elected lord of creation. He is superior to woman in everything except the art of bearing children and a certain refinement of the psyche which enables her to sacrifice herself to the man in self-negating love. Women without men become 'a little . . . cuckoo', to use sea captain Pall's straightforward phrase in the story *A Doll's Home*—which was directed against Ibsen and his play. But they arise rosy and sound as soon as they get a real man into their bed. In *Marrying*, Strindberg claims that marriage has no future as an institution if the woman tries to emancipate herself. Harmony is restored only when husband and wife return to the roles nature has given them, and the happy birth of a child completes that harmony.

Such a division of roles was as remote as can be imagined from the one prevailing in Strindberg's own marriage. Siri von Essen had few of those feminine traits which 'nature', according to Strindberg, was supposed to bestow on women. She had divorced Baron Wrangel because she could not bear living the life of only a wife and mother: now, after a few years of her second marriage, she found herself in the same predicament. Strindberg had offered her the prospect of a free life with him as an artist, and yet here she was now, confined to a boarding-house, with children and a fussy husband her only preoccupations. Strindberg's broken promises must have been a constant strain on his conscience; his daughter may be right in her claim that his entire view of women originated here. In his love stories, a recurrent theme is the infatuated male's promises 'before' and his qualms 'after', when the conquered female reminds him of her overdue claims. The theme is treated in a range of tones: from the comic in *The Red Room*, where Mrs Falk reminds her husband of what he had promised her before marriage, and the wholesale merchant helplessly replies, 'Well but that was then!' to the brutality of Jean's words to Miss Julie: 'We always have to lay it on thick when we want to get a woman!'

There was no shared, common interest in Strindberg's writing. Siri, with her aristocratic, Christian, idealistic background, sided with the Swedish establishment's view of her husband's work, and had no real understanding of the nature of his art or of his personality.

She did not stand up for Strindberg in tight corners (see chapter 7), but proudly defended her own opinions. She praised *Swedish Fates* with its fancy-dress historicism, but deplored the 'acts of revenge' in *The New Kingdom*: according to Karin Smirnoff, the latter caused the first serious rift between her parents.

Then, as now, women's rights were a much-debated social question, and one that could not be excluded from the Strindberg home. At the time, the most resounding contribution to it was Henrik Ibsen's play *A Doll's House*, in which the heroine, Nora, leaves her husband and children because she has been denied her human rights, and has been treated like a doll. Strindberg's marriage was based on equality and on Siri's self-evident right to develop her own personality as an actress. By the time *Marrying* was written, the situation had changed. Strindberg discovered that he had a Nora in his own house, and his short stories became oblique polemics against Siri-Nora-Ibsen. It was on the bed, not some spiritual fellowship, that a true marriage was based; love was not a matter of will and intellect, but of flesh and blood. Strindberg went on to claim that men and women do not love each other in order to achieve a union of souls, but because they are victims of a force of nature. Marriage, which follows naturally, must then be built on sharing everyday life and raising children.

Strindberg saw *Marrying* as a healthy contribution to the pseudo-debate about the problems of upper-class women that Ibsen's play had generated. He would have preferred a prosecution based on women's rights to one based on blasphemy. 'I know that my book is a great outcry from nature's breast,' he wrote to Jonas Lie, 'that I am right, that my words came at the last moment to save us from a wrong path, in the midst of the monstrosities perpetrated by the culture that prevails today.'

The fact that Ibsen was his main rival as a dramatist gave Strindberg a special incentive. Ibsen's fame was a daily thorn in his flesh. Ibsen always seemed to be one step ahead, occupying theatres Strindberg wanted his own plays to be performed in. Strindberg had a healthy ambition and desire to reach the very top, and it seems as if he designed not only his view of women's rights, but his whole life as well, with Ibsen in mind. As the Norwegian grew ever more taciturn and secretive in his buttoned-up, much-decorated coat, Strindberg ever more enthusiastically explained the inner workings of his own creations to anyone who cared to listen, opening up his coat, waistcoat, and shirt, generating the myth about himself as one who gave and gave of himself, and held nothing back. Ibsen, for his part, viewed such antics with an unsympathetic eye. We know that he had Christian Krogh's portrait of Strindberg hanging on his wall and said that he could not get over 'the crazy person's' eyes.

4

Strindberg frequented prostitutes, particularly in his youth, but, like his contemporaries, made no mention of this in either letters or journals. Such things could not be incorporated in any artistic scheme, and he was far from being an all-inclusive Pepys or Boswell. In *Virtue's Reward*, Theodor

Wennerström is driven to insanity and death by sexual deprivation. Strindberg intended the description of his fate to be his contribution to a world-wide debate on the dangers and advantages of sexual abstention.

In 1875, an international organization, The Federation, had been started in England, with the abolition of prostitution as its main goal. In 1878, the movement reached Sweden, where it published the journal *Sedlighets-Vännen* (*The Friend of Morality*). Siri was a subscriber.

Under Christian auspices, The Federation wanted to strike a blow for morality in general, and was well aware that men were the villains of the piece. Prostitutes were the unhappy victims of the animal lusts of the male. Prostitution could be abolished only if men would apply to themselves the same standards that they demanded of women—abstention and purity before marriage: a requirement which Björnson, to Strindberg's fury, presented in his play *A Glove*. It became a subject for debate whether married couples had the right to 'selfish pleasure' in bed, or whether sexuality was, exclusively, a means of procreation.

Strindberg was hostile to The Federation. In *The Red Room*, he presented a whore, Marie of Nygränd, who explicitly stated that she was not a 'victim'. She had chosen her profession entirely voluntarily because it gave her more freedom than the only remaining alternative—maid-equals-slave.

Although Strindberg had harsh things to say about prostitutes, at best he saw them as good Samaritans, coming to the aid of the sexually deprived. They performed their share of the self-sacrificing role which destiny assigned to women.

Theodor Wennerström in *Virtue's Reward* is raised exactly according to the principles embraced by The Federation, and that is his undoing. With a devilish twist to his pen, Strindberg describes Wennerström's battle with masturbation and with the temptations represented by the realms of Stallmästargården. Prevented from following his natural bent, he becomes perverted, withers away and dies.

Ulf Boëthius, in his dissertation 'Strindberg and Women's Rights', demonstrates the strength of opinion Strindberg had on his side when he claimed that sexual abstention was dangerous. The body is there to be used; if it is not—and this includes the reproductive organs—it deteriorates, according to the international authority G. Drysdale, whose books Strindberg had in his library. Sexual need is worse than hunger, and abstention is a sin against nature, added Max Nordau, another of Strindberg's guiding lights during those years.

As from 1884, sexual deprivation appeared as an increasingly common subject in Strindberg's work. That year, the sound sexual basis of his marriage foundered, and at about the same time Strindberg started attacking the women's movement as his particular enemy. As early as 13 September, 1884, before the publication of *Marrying*, he wrote to

Loostrÿm: 'Soon the autumn thunderstorms will come! This year, they'll be worse than ever, because when the women start fighting, all hell is let loose. But I'll just do this.' To illustrate what he would do, Strindberg provided a drawing in which he is depicted standing leaning forward, stark naked, and showing a wide backside to two naked women who are charging him with rocks in their hands. Between the combatants, high up on an Alpine peak (the letter was written in Chexbres), Strindberg drew an enormous penis, adding Luther's words: 'Here I stand, and can do no other!'

After the trial, Strindberg's invective grew even coarser, and it became increasingly evident that behind all those hostile women stood his own wife—that it was ultimately to her that all his obscenities, insults and suspicions were addressed. At the same time, she became the model he used most, after himself, in his writing.

During their exile, the Strindbergs had been forced into closer proximity, and he had discovered that their relationship was a practically inexhaustible source of material for his writing. As he wrote to Heidenstam in March 1885, no one could be a writer if he did not, however repulsive it seemed, suck 'the blood of his friends, his nearest and his own, like a vampire'.

In *The Serving Maid's Son*, Strindberg had wanted to trace the history of his soul. Now it was Siri's turn. She had made brief appearances in his work before, but only discreetly disguised. One senses her behind Kristina in the verse drama *Master Olof*. The heroine of 'Mr Bengt's Wife', a highly strung upper-class girl who enjoys being beaten, was a first attempt at an in-depth portrait; Hélène, the general's daughter, whose mare meets such a terrible fate in the story 'Against Payment', another. The brutal encounter between the peasant stallion and the well-bred mare would be repeated on a human level in *Miss Julie* where the servant beds the Count's daughter.

Yet it is not so much as a model in any conventional sense that Siri von Essen played her most important part in her husband's artistic production, but as a co-actress in a mythical play. *The Father* was the first step: in it, the wife is faceless, and the husband perishes. Now this strange drama was to continue.

The second part of *Marrying* became extraordinarily misogynistic and hostile to Siri in particular. In the final story, 'The Provider of the Family', Siri was delivered to a public hungry for gossip as a painter of no talent, an alcoholic who neglected her children, as crude, heartless, cynical, and lacking in the least trace of affection for the writer who was slaving away to keep the family—her husband. No wonder that Strindberg's and Siri's friends were shaken—Branting expressed amazement at Strindberg's willingness to drag the closest person in his life through the dirt. Other friends regarded the story as a symptom of insanity. Siri herself, according to her daughter, felt humiliated by having to live on the proceeds of books she loathed.

Nevertheless, this was only a mild prelude to what was to follow. During 1886 and 1887, Strindberg's tone grew more strident, finally reaching such a degree of repulsion towards the female sex that one has to turn to Swift's Yahoos to find an equivalent. Women were evil creatures who ensnared man, the noble and the strong, because they were able to wound him in his sexual being. Women were both criminal and insane, with brains like a kitchen clock compared to man's chronometer. In *A Fool's Apology*, Strindberg cried out:

> I want to exhort the lawmakers to carefully consider the consequences of granting civic rights to semi-apes, inferior creatures, sick children, sick and insane thirteen times a year at the time of menstruation, completely out of their minds during pregnancy, and irresponsible during the rest of their life, unconscious criminals, criminal, instinctively malicious animals who do not even know that that is what they are.

Not all of this invective reached Siri—the passage quoted above is from a version of the book recently discovered in Edvard Munch's posthumous papers in Oslo—but she heard enough to be hurt, and she responded with coldness and contempt, becoming an icy doll in Strindberg's home, and, most probably, in his bed as well. From 1886, she was convinced that her husband's mental health was impaired; she consulted psychiatrists, and watched him for signs of impending outbursts of madness. Strindberg retaliated by accusing her of trying to incapacitate him by having him committed to an asylum. And there, indeed, is the subject matter of *The Father*.

It seems difficult to make any statement about the personal background to all this: even to look for such a background appears as a violation, not because any details would be particularly shameful or personally embarrassing, but because of the infinite number of delicate threads of nervous energy and feeling between two people who once loved one another, which no outsider could ever be expected to sort out. Strindberg often spoke of how lovers attune themselves to one another, reflecting expressions, words, and gestures in such a way that a perceptive observer is able to detect those whom she or he has associated with, or even just thought about.

In Siri's case, there are indications of a sexual tragedy. She had medical problems as a result of her third child's birth. In Othmarsingen, in June 1886, she suffered from bleeding or 'haemorrhages' as Karin Smirnoff calls them, which were followed by 'a protracted uterine complaint'. During that time she probably had a miscarriage. She had to consult a specialist in Geneva, which cost her, according to accounts which have been preserved, 120 francs, of which 50 were 'a gift'. During the autumn of that year, she frequently consulted physicians and midwives in town, and purchased haemostatic remedies—alum—at the pharmacy. In the summer, she broke one of her front teeth, and had to visit the dentist a dozen times, to be given partial dentures for half her upper jaw. A molar had to be extracted causing a fracture of the jaw, and she suffered great pain. While all this was happening, her physically robust husband wandered about the Alps, making his way up through the clouds—a sensation he described in an article.

In *A Fool's Apology*, written not long after, Strindberg described how Maria (Siri) showed the first signs of feminine frailty, in Othmarsingen, where else?

> Her fire burns lower, the age of maturity begins! What sorrow, the day she broke her first front tooth! Poor Maria! She weeps, clutches me in her arms, begs me not to stop loving her! She is in her thirty-seventh year! The hair grows pale, the breasts subside like waves after a storm, the stairs grow tiring for her little foot, and the lungs no longer function with the same strength as before.

5

The Captain in *The Father* is an aristocrat, a giant surrounded by dwarfs. He belongs to the nobility of intellect and sensibility of which Strindberg considered himself a member, as from 1886. It did not require any great reorientation to arrive at this belief: socialism had never affected Strindberg's sense of being one of the elect. During 1887, the 'great' personalities grew numerous in his work. The most moving of them is Peter, artist and genius, trapped and killed by envious, small-minded companions: it is Ernst Josephson, the greatest painter of Strindberg's generation, to whom he pays homage and with whom he identifies at the same time in this story. Among the 'dwarfs' in it was Strindberg's closest painter friend, Carl Larsson. As Göran Söderström has demonstrated in his study 'Strindberg and the Art of Painting', Larsson participated in the rejection of Josephson's important piece *The River Man* for an exhibition arranged by The Artists' Alliance.

During the summer of 1887, Strindberg's letters became more bizarre than ever. It is very difficult to decide what in them is to be taken seriously and what is role-playing and sketches for creative work. It seems certain that he frequently appeared in the garb of his invented figures and spoke through their mouths. At this time he was also taking solitary trips in order to get away from the negative tension that now prevailed in his marriage.

In April, he went to Vienna to discuss contributions to Neue Freie Presse, and in May, to Copenhagen. One evening in a hotel room he wrote a sentimental letter to Carl Larsson, whose friendship he tried to retain by declaring him one of 'the great'. 'Do you remember how young I was, during those rosy days on Kymmendö, when Stux and I still thought it great sport to skim stones! Other stones are flying now! Shit on life! But it was damned good fun at times! And it has been good to me, sometimes even wonderful. Those student years, 70–73, and the first years of marriage! Oh God!—Yes!' The letters ends: 'Good night, old boy; I am really tired, I can feel it. Poor Peter needs his rest!' Peter, as Strindberg called himself here, was the name given to Ernst Josephson in the story 'The Great', and there was much talk of the casting of stones in the piece. Among those casting them was the same Carl Larsson, who now received such a warm letter from Peter-Josephson-Strindberg.

'I can feel my mature age approaching (thirty-eight years) with horrifying passions and frightening ambition,' Strindberg wrote to Edvard Brandes in May. It was fair assessment of the situation. Strindberg returned to Germany in June, and the family moved to a farm in Eichbühl near Lindau which had an orchard and a vegetable garden. Strindberg had a study up in the attic, with a view over Lake Constance reflecting, on calm days, the snow-covered tops of Hohe Säntis. Strindberg drank beer from Munich called Salvator Bräu and sent the farm boys to purchase crayfish at the Hotel Helvetia in Lindau. As at one time on Kymmendö, Karin Smirnoff tells us, rockets were fired from 'the lawn behind the arbour' with much cheering, during the crayfish feasts. And here, while his marriage was moving into a catastrophic phase, Strindberg wrote the novel *The People of Hemsö*, his happiest and most popular book.

For several years Strindberg had been suspicious of Siri and had tried to procure proof of her infidelity. He wrote to friends in enquiring terms, camouflaging his interest at first by claiming that he wanted to protect Siri from malicious gossip. Completion of *The Father* with its jealousy motif did not mean that he had rid himself of suspicion: on the contrary, it seemed as though he had not just written about the Captain's torment, but had lived through it himself, and was now thirsting for revenge.

In June 1887, his imagination became fixed on Marie David, whom the family had met in Grez and who had become a friend of Siri's (see p. ooo). On 30 June, he wrote to Edvard Brandes that Marie David and Sofie Holten had seduced a servant girl in Grez, driving her to her death, and that the police were now planning an arrest. A few days later he wrote to Carl Larsson, demanding information about that servant, and stated that all that was needed to send the two ladies to a house of correction was an accusation by the mayor of Grez. He added that Marie David was pursuing his wife with love letters and exhortations to leave him and the children.

On 5 August, Strindberg began a series of letters to Pehr Staaff, his special ally and errand-boy during the 1880s. In these letters, he provided intimate details of his disintegrating marriage, interspersed with cries for assistance in his efforts to prove Siri's infidelity. He discussed, in detail, who Siri's lovers might possibly be, and reported that he had undertaken psychological experiments with her: their eyes had met in a mirror, and hers had betrayed her. He exhorted Staaff to make similar experiments with one of the subjects, a certain Doctor Forssberg, who had given Siri massage on one or two occasions.

On 13 August, he had discovered 'definite indications' after applying 'psychic torture to the delinquent'—Siri—'with exemplary absence of feeling'. Now the suspect was one of Siri's fellow actors, Mauritz Svedberg. Staaff was given a lively scene-by-scene account. Siri had met Svedberg on a visiting engagement in Helsinki in 1882:

> Upon returning from Finland, Siri sang his praises to me. Soon afterwards, he was engaged by the New Theatre in Stockholm. Silent as the grave! No visit to us from him! Simultaneously: increasing coldness on Siri's side, which even turned into hatred and complete paranoia; leading to my conviction that I was insane and I even wrote to Forssberg for advice. Rehearsals for *Mr Bengt's Wife*. During the evening dress rehearsal I go up to Siri's box. Find food and drink for two. Siri is in there. Outside the door, 'psst! Are you there?' Mr Svedberg is received in my presence, offered food and drink—and—I did not kick him out—but back home I ventured a remark on the impropriety of an actress receiving a gentleman in her box. It was unprecedented! I was abused, called prejudiced, illiberal (ah! the liberals!), etc. Mr S never showed up! Was embarrassed when I ran into him. Siri's hatred against me increased! My unabated passion was naturally compromised, and I had to beg for, or buy, coition!

In a letter dated 18 August, from Ouchy—Strindberg made short trips to Gersau and Ouchy to pursue his investigations—Staaff was told that Siri had confessed. On her return journey from Helsinki she had been raped, more or less, by an engineer. Strindberg declared himself 'happy, almost grateful': the confession had saved his honour, and his suspicions had been justified. He regarded a divorce as a foregone conclusion, but, as he explained on 21 August, it would merely be an 'arrangement': after the divorce, Siri was to stay on as wife and mistress 'without benefit of marriage, while retaining a degree of social standing.' Strindberg felt that this would free him from the stigma of being a 'ridiculed husband, and I won't have any dubious offspring'. He would be master in his own house again. Unmarried, he would also be free to write whatever he pleased about the question of women's rights. 'Admit that it is a stroke of genius! And the punishment is no more than just, without being cruel!'

In the same letter, Strindberg admitted that he had struck Siri, an episode that was to be the tragic climax in *A Fool's Apology*. Staaff was told that Siri loved her husband more than ever after that chastisement, since she felt only contempt for his 'existence as an author', while admiring his masculinity. The letter continued:

Inflamed all the way down to my private parts I went to Geneva and visited a brothel in the company of a physician. Performed the test of strength—not for the first time, by the way—which I would like to call the abduction of Proserpine (well, think of it in terms of Bernini's sculpture). Had my semen and organ examined, which were found to be fertile, and the latter in its excited state sixteen by four centimetres.

The phallic measurements taken in Geneva were an extraordinarily typical procedure for Strindberg who took everything literally and never left anything unproven. The reason for the measuring was that his male organ had fallen into disrepute. He returned to the same question in each of his marriages and took pains to explain that a woman's pleasure did not depend on the size of the organ. In the letter quoted above, he goes on to brag about his virility, talks about his hikes through France, claims to have travelled on horseback from Vevey to Lausanne and back in twenty-four hours, and to have swum across Lake Vierwaldstätter and rowed from Kymmendö to Dalarö and back, unassisted. He also told posterity that he had been 'made fun of' in his youth and admitted that his phallus was not large in its calm state but 'normal when excited'. 'In the presence of witnesses (including a whore) at 3 o'clock one summer morning' he had arranged 'a viewing of the prick outside the Fyllan (the Drunk) tavern in Djurgården. The whore (Vita Björn, by the way) gave me her *approbatur*, though *sine laude*.' For his correspondent's further enlightenment, Strindberg appended a note: 'Compare Hyrtel's anatomy: "small but good".'

The letters to Staaff continued for a couple more weeks, expressing a continuously mounting hatred of Siri who is called a 'closet whore' and is compared to a wounded snake. When both Staaff and Axel Strindberg expressed their suspicion that Siri's confession had been obtained under torture, Strindberg immediately retaliated with abuse, accusing his brother of having gone over to 'the skirts'. He found himself in a vortex of inflamed emotions, a crisis that offered not a glimpse of relief. Even a child could see that the material he presented as proof of Siri's guilt was slight; he was wrestling with phantoms, as though he had been performing the Captain's role in *The Father*. Did he believe in his own accusations, did he really act as brutally as he claimed? In *A Fool's Apology*, Axel, at Sunday dinner in the arbour, is suddenly seized by a terrifying hatred of Maria and starts slapping her face: 'And when she tries to defend herself, I force her down to her knees. She utters a horrifying shriek, and the pleasure I suddenly feel

31 Stage portrait of Siri von Essen in *Sir Bengt's Wife*

changes into dismay when the children, beside themselves with fright, start screaming at the top of their voices. It is the hardest moment of my wretched life.'

Karin Smirnoff recalls the scene. According to her, Strindberg knocked Siri over and on to the ground, where she lay with her blonde hair framing her face. 'With one of his knees on her chest, he beat her with his fist. I was sitting right next to them, and her face was below me, but I do not recall that she screamed—only that she stared at him with large, deepening eyes, without saying a word. We started crying and shouting Papa! Papa! in helpless horror.' From that moment—or probably even earlier—Siri was convinced of her husband's insanity and lived in fear of him. Karin Smirnoff shared her conviction.

There was nothing insane about Strindberg's behaviour in the sense that it was not possible to consider his actions as a rational progression. In his very first letter to Staaff Strindberg hinted that his sole purpose for the investigations was to 'rectify my literary material', and that he would use whatever information Staaff was able to provide 'as leniently as possible'. This was possibly just a link in his chain of attempts to break down Staaff's resistance to participation in the hunt. But Strindberg was entering a period in which he was consciously creating sources of infection—illnesses and passions—in his own organism for the sake of his art. *The Father* was a splendid result of that method; why not continue with jealousy? It is impossible to decide what in these actions was conscious volition, and what was due to compulsion. Strindberg did not always recognize that dividing line, yet remained sufficiently alert to refrain from changing reality and to stick to what material he had. There is total agreement that the attack on Siri was an isolated occurrence. It is entirely possible to read his letters to Staaff, that summer and autumn, as preliminary exercises for the book he was planning—*A Fool's Apology*.

6

The People of Hemsö tells the story of an island and its inhabitants in the Stockholm Archipelago. It was the source material provided by Kymmendö, hitherto untouched because he had hoped to return there, that Strindberg was drawing on now. Madame Flod, the owner of an estate, hires a servant, the shrewd Värmlander Carlsson, who proceeds to seduce her into marriage and abdication of power. Gusten, her son from a previous marriage, a hunter and fisherman, assumes a stance of stubborn opposition. The novel concludes with the lady's death and the usurper's decline.

To a certain degree, the book is a popular comedy, written by one of 'the great' about 'the small'. Strindberg claimed that he was influenced by Dutch genre painting. He wrote the book in order to make money and with the explicit intention of regaining his popularity in Sweden. In the summer of 1887, Albert Bonnier reminded him with brutal frankness that he had, indeed, fallen from favour.

> That your work [he wrote] through a multitude of circumstances, such as malicious attacks from your opponents as well as, no doubt, excesses on your own part, is now suffering from a deplorable and entirely unprecedented lack of popularity—this is a fact that you must be aware of, although you cannot, being at a distance from the homeland, even begin to comprehend how terribly intense it is.

In an enraged reply, Strindberg spoke of 'Your false stock market rumours about my lack of popularity'; but to Staaff he wrote that even if the Swedish public hated him as much as 'the old rascal Albert Bonnier' had tried to make him believe, 'all I have to do is to write myself back into popularity'.

Marrying II, published in December 1886, definitively established Strindberg's reputation in Sweden as an immoral and brutal writer. The moralistic and piously backward-looking reaction of 1884 had grown in strength. In March 1887 the respected educator (later, bishop) John Personne published a tract entitled *Strindbergian Literature and Immorality among School-Age Youth*. It sought to establish that the young indulged, to an increasing degree, in masturbation and associating with whores, and were seduced into this by the 'spirit of the times' as generated, primarily, by Strindberg's disgusting productions. Personne demanded a ban on such literature. 'Society upholds the prohibition of the sale of life-endangering poisons,' he wrote, 'while ignoring the poison with which unscrupulous publishers and authors spread moral death within the family and society.' He called upon the entire nation to rise and shake off the yoke of slavery of opinion which had been created by this new literature.

Personne's work attracted attention. Despite its crude demagoguery, it represented a large body of opinion, which manifested itself the same year by a petition, bearing 6,000 signatures, to the minister of justice: it was a demand for more stringent press laws.

A month after the publication of Personne's tract, a schism occurred within the Swedish Publishers' Association, whose chairman was Albert Bonnier. A number of publishers, members of 'the gang for morality and Jesus' (to use Strindbergian terminology), seceded from the Association, as they could not tolerate the leadership of a man who published Strindberg. The cabal also bore certain anti-Semitic traits.

It would have been reasonable to expect Strindberg to have become more conciliatory towards Albert Bonnier, who was suffering for his sake.

However, unprinted manuscripts were cluttering his desk, and he preferred to put all his enemies into one bag. Bonnier was a 'factual censor of my work as an author, and *he has been more severe than Steijern*', he wrote to Carl Larsson, calling Albert Bonnier a Caesar who had been justly removed from his tyrant's throne. Strindberg even went so far as to suggest that it was Albert Bonnier who was behind Personne's tract—a somewhat extravagant notion, considering that Personne had compared his publishing house to a brothel that profited from immoral earnings.

Later in the spring, Strindberg grew even more enraged against the Bonnier publishing house which, by means of its 'possibly partly well-intentioned system of boycott and reptilian behaviour . . . has caused me such suffering that a lifetime devoted to revenge would not suffice to redress the balance' (letter to Karl Otto Bonnier, 31 May 1887).

Personne, and to some extent Bonniers, were in a way natural enemies, whose blows Strindberg found relatively easy to bear. The vacillation of friends' loyalty was a more serious matter. Shrewdly enough, Personne had written about '*Strindbergian* literature', thus condemning all the new writing of the period. In the subsequent public debate, 'young Sweden' was commonly represented as a bunch of cretins, sycophants and dwarfs around the giant Strindberg. It was both humiliating and dangerous for the younger generation to be classified as his fellow-travellers. Geijerstam, for one, tried to distance himself politely, but did not succeed in fooling Strindberg. Strongly encouraged by the latter, he published a pamphlet that summer which was intended as a refutation of Personne, but chose to emphasize the differences between him and his comrades on one hand and Strindberg on the other, rather than the similarities between them. Strindberg took grim note of all this.

In addition to his domestic turmoil Strindberg had financial worries. In June, he sold his life insurance policies. 'Now I have sold everything that can be sold, all that remains is the corpse (and, above all, the cranium) to the Karolinian Institute,' he wrote to his brother Axel on 28 June.

Thus there was a great deal of incentive to write for a broader public, and Strindberg permitted himself moments of low comedy that were not worthy of his pen. While presenting Carlsson as an articulate and inventive, alert person, he proceeded to humiliate him in order to please the crowd. The false, stilted letter with its borrowings from Afzelius's chronicles, revival sermons and graveside speeches, which Carlsson writes in order to woo the summer guests' servant Ida, is out of character. Carlsson becomes, at that point, a puppet manipulated by his master, and Strindberg himself somewhat of a literary imperialist who believes that rent for the summer cottage and payment for milk and fish also buys the right to ridicule the people who provide those services.

Strindberg himself was aware that he had fallen victim to that particular arrogance characteristic of the urban dweller, with its deep roots in 'popular farces' the 'populace' had never seen. In August 1894, he wrote to Littmansson about the dramatization of the novel he produced in 1889: 'It was both crude and trivial. The author was quite obviously booting his heroes in the backside, and shitting on all that rabble.'

Nevertheless, he was too much of a poet to keep up such calculation for long. The tawdry element in the novel—which is more prominent in the play—becomes only a fleeting odour of decay which does not affect the freshness of the whole. The book has devastating stylistic vitality, incorporating words, phrases, and insights that seem to come directly from the speech of the people. Reading it, one gets the feeling, similar to that generated by *The Odyssey*, *The Divine Comedy* or *Ulysses*, that a life which has lain concealed and anonymous for centuries is suddenly revealed and harvested by a skilful master of words. Diseased pigs are cured with grey ointment, tar is bought in barrels, roosters are borrowed, earthenware jars filled with brandy worn by a belt round the neck while travelling, and the piece of mirror in the window Gusten uses while shaving is known as a 'Sunday glass'—these are just a few of the hundreds of pieces of information which, as in a kaleidoscope, give life and substance to the dramatically constructed scenes.

The seventh chapter describes Madame Flod's death. Carlsson, confident of his position as husband and in the possession of old Flod's sealskin coat with its knitted travelling belt of green, yellow, and red wool—symbolic of his authority—starts making overtures to the maid Clara. Madame Flod keeps a watch on him, and when he slinks out after Clara, she follows. She searches for the couple in the cowshed, the sheep-pen, and the chicken coop, and finally walks out into the pasture—it is Christmastime, with snow on the ground and the North wind blowing—to follow the tracks of the amorous couple. The description of her pain, her fright mixed with a kind of pleasure, upon seeing what she had least wanted to see, is one of the most intense passages Strindberg ever wrote. Jealousy seizes her like a madness. Her knees shake, her blood turns to ice, and, at the same time, she is on fire, as though boiling water were running in her veins. The winter landscape complements the unhappy woman's anguish and final panic. She is both Medea and Othello and has sufficient powers of action to organize Carlsson's ultimate downfall, even though she dies of pneumonia as a consequence of her nocturnal search. If Strindberg really was as jealous as his letters to Staaff indicate, it paid dividends in this passage, and there was more to come.

Chapter Ten

AN ENCHANTED SUMMER

I

In the autumn of 1887, Strindberg decided to move to Denmark, which, mostly through the Brandes brothers, he regarded as a country well disposed towards him. An additional reason for the move was the impending world première of *The Father* at the Casino Theatre.

It was, in all likelihood, 6 November when the family arrived in Copenhagen. During their journey, in Roskilde, they met the young Swedish author Axel Lundegård, who noted that Strindberg's overcoat looked worn. When Lundegård asked him if he was divorced, Strindberg replied that Siri would have to be content, henceforth, with being merely his mistress—'I do not intend to introduce her into my social life.'

While the two men were dining together at the hotel, Siri arrived with the children and Eva Carlsson, and the party seated themselves at a nearby table, demonstrating the Strindbergs' new marital lifestyle. Lundegård felt embarrassed, because courtesy towards Strindberg forced him to act against his instincts and to treat Siri as if she had not been there.

Also in Roskilde, Strindberg went to see Doctor Knud Pontoppidan (to become famous a few years later as Professor Hieronimus in Amelie Skram's autobiographical novel) at the town's mental hospital in order to get a clean bill of health. Understandably, Pontoppidan explained that he was unable to provide one without an observation period. Strindberg had no time for that: *The Father* was waiting.

Denmark was well prepared for Strindberg. Everyone in Copenhagen knew what he looked like: since 1885, his wax effigy had been on display in Bernhard Olsen's popular 'Scandinavian Panopticon'. In a room of that establishment, a replica of the literary Café A Portas on Kongens Nytorv, Strindberg was depicted sitting by himself at a corner table. His head had been modelled after Vallgren's bust. His hair stood wildly on end and was, of course, genuine human hair. The face had been painted with accuracy.

This Strindberg-in-wax was frequently commented on in the Copen-hagen press, reinterpreted every time Strindberg's public image changed. When he arrived in Denmark, the demonic misogynist was uppermost. Before the first night of *The Father* there were rumours that Laura was a portrait of Siri, and the newspaper *Social-Demokraten* wrote that 'only a monomaniac blinded by his anger could see such hyper-sophisticated evil in his own wife.' The year before, the paper *Nationaltidende* had commented that Strindberg in his café corner looked like a ghost, staring straight ahead with dark, lost eyes.

As of April 1887, the Casino Theatre's director had been the young actor H. R. Hunderup, a man in the Strindberg mould — vital, brilliant, careless and incorrigible in financial matters. The Casino had previously been a showcase for light-hearted pieces, but now its standards were to be raised, the theatre becoming a part of the naturalistic freedom movement led by Georg Brandes. *The Father* became a rallying point for those young Danes, and Georg Brandes assisted personally in directing the actors.

The dress rehearsal took place on 12 November, with Strindberg in attendance. He was very upset by what he saw. The previous year, in *The Serving Maid's Son*, he had given a violently dramatized description of his reaction the first time he saw one of his own plays on the stage. It had been the performance of the innocent piece *In Rome*, at the Royal Theatre in 1870. He had stood in the back of the third row, totally tense, tears streaming down his face, ears burning with shame. When it was over, he ran out into the street and wanted to drown himself in the Norrström. Seeing *The Father*, he had undeniably greater reasons for reacting violently, considering that he was witnessing scenes and lines from his own marriage.

All his life, Strindberg looked at his own works in a peculiarly ingenuous way. He defended himself, and his friends defended him, time and again with reference to artistic freedom, warning the reader not to equate his creations with his life. During those rumour-filled days in Copenhagen, Edvard Brandes was taking the same line. Nevertheless, Strindberg did not experience his works merely as art, but also as reflections of his life, pure and simple. And watching *The Father* he was overcome by pangs of conscience.

On the day of the dress rehearsal, probably directly after it was over, he sat down to write a bizarre letter to Axel Lundegård. He said that he wanted to take his life, as he had after *In Rome* (in *The Serving Maid's Son*), and elected Lundegård as his literary executor, urging him to take care that Siri, who has been vilified in the piece, was rehabilitated and he himself designated insane; on the other hand, the letter's recipient was not to forget that the writer was 'all there'. After detailed instructions for practical arrangements following his demise, the letter continues:

It seems to me as if I were sleepwalking; as if life and invention had become intermingled. I do not know whether *The Father* is a work of the imagination, or whether my life has been that; yet I feel that at a given moment, soon to occur, all that will be revealed to me, and then I'll collapse either into madness and torments of conscience, or into suicide. Constant work on my writing has made my life a shadow existence; I feel as if I were no longer walking on this earth, but rather floating, weightless, in an atmosphere consisting not of air but of darkness. As soon as light falls into that darkness, I fall down, crushed! Strangely, too, I find myself in a frequently recurring dream, at night, in which I am flying, without gravity, and finding that quite natural, and all notions of right, wrong, true, and false have been dissolved, and no matter how unusual anything is that happens, it appears to me just as it should be.

Strindberg must have known for quite some time that there was a connection between his artistic fertility and his tendency to confuse reality and imagination—a confusion that entailed a sacrifice of his own life, and that of his nearest and dearest, and exiled him from normal relationships. There are reasons to believe that he speaks 'the truth', for once, in this letter—that he really did not know, standing in the stalls of the Casino Theatre, whether he had imagined *The Father* or lived it. Had he himself been trapped by his wife the way the Captain was trapped by Laura, there would have been no reason to feel sorry for Siri because she had been unmasked. On the other hand, if Strindberg had made it all up, that constituted unforgivable behaviour. It is remarkable to see him note, at the very moment when he expresses these thoughts, that his notions of right and wrong have dissolved, and that he feels as though he is floating weightlessly in space. There, at the Casino Theatre, he saw his future life as it was to become.

2

The Father was a critical success, and a breakthrough for Hunderup, who played the Captain, but the public was put off by the 'atrocities' described in the conservative press—the kerosene lamp, the straitjacket—and the play was performed only eleven times. In order to attract audiences, Strindberg offered to introduce a performance in person. This was a disaster. On 2 December, he appeared on stage, wearing an elegant black coat and grey trousers. As the curtain rose, he was seen standing by a small table on which there was a three-armed candlestick. According to a contemporary report, a large group of admirers in the stalls applauded, and Strindberg gave a little bow, attempted a slight smile and started to read. The audience had expected a lecture on the play: instead, it was treated to one of the

Somnambulist Nights. Strindberg read in a quiet monotone, ignoring calls to 'speak up'. While reading, he kept glancing at his watch and turning pages to see how much farther he had to go, and when he had reached the end, he bowed again and disappeared without paying attention to his friends' applause, which was soon silenced by hisses from the more hostile members of the audience. Hardly anyone had heard a word he spoke.

In Denmark, Strindberg proceeded to resume the habits of his youth, frequenting cafés with new friends. Rumours of wild nights on the town reached the press. One December evening, in Rydberg's cellar on Östergade, in the company of Hunderup and after champagne and speeches of mutual admiration, Strindberg pulled a revolver from his pocket and fired a number of shots at the ceiling. In high spirits, he undertook to climb the bronze horse on Kongens Nytorv. He made an attempt, but found himself caught on the railings around the monument. The police arrived and took the gun away from him; due to his reputation as an author, no further action was taken. As the episode gave rise to a series of more or less imaginary adventure stories, it can no longer be restored to its rightful proportions.

On arrival in Copenhagen, Strindberg had taken rooms at the Hotel Leopold on Hovedvogtsgade, but the hotel proved too expensive, and on 18 November the family moved out to Klampenborg, where they rented a summer house from the director of the sea-bathing establishment, a Mr Hohlenberg. The house stood in the midst of empty villas with boarded-up porches. Siri found and adopted a piteously miaowing stray cat.

The People of Hemsö was published in Sweden in December. At first it proved a financial disappointment: Bonniers reported that the author's bad reputation prevented certain booksellers from displaying the volume. This was in spite of the fact that the publishers, frightened by Personne and his followers, had forced Strindberg to tone down a great number of passages, as described by Lars Dahlbäck in his comprehensive monograph on the novel. 'At least it was true in its crudity before the publisher removed that crudity. Now it is tepid, conventional, nix, and not *Dixi et salvavi animam meam,*' Strindberg wrote to Edvard Brandes when he sent him a copy.

The winter cold and the difficulties with his publishers did not keep Strindberg from writing—in fact they seemed to have the opposite effect. He took up *A Fool's Apology* again, which he had begun in Lindau.

I'm writing and writing away on my Oeuvre, writing intelligently and well; rolling up my soul like a marmoset in winter, neither hearing nor seeing; but am suddenly roused by Director Hohlenberg who is asking for his rent; by the stove that belches smoke, and the food that cannot be cooked; and feel, even in my sleep, that the month is coming to an end and the bills are approaching!

he wrote on 6 December to Lundegård who had become his latest favourite correspondent. The letter also contains this sentence: 'Tell me something that's so rotten I can laugh at it!'

After the firewood had been used up—'now we'll have to burn the bookshelves'—after Hohlenberg had sent a servant to evict him, and after the door had locked itself shut—'so I can't go to the outhouse before the locksmith arrives'—and other similar contretemps, the family went back to Copenhagen, spent Christmas at the Hotel Leopold, and then rented lodgings, in January 1888, from a police officer called Harlew in the small fishing village of Taarbaek by Öresund. 'Summery air, Öresund's blue waters with coupling seagulls, open window, chickens in the yard, fresh brisket with horseradish sauce—life is beautiful,' he reported to Lundegård.

Stimulated by the knowledge that *The Father* was being performed in Stockholm, he wrote to him again the next day:

> Now my pot is really boiling; don't know what it'll turn out to be. No one is as unfree as the poet. But next to the desk sits the immortal black cat with yellow eyes, and its name is Need! Unfortunately Need is unable to rearrange my great brain! Unfortunately! Practical considerations, writing for money, nonsense! If only! I could! Just enjoyed three platefuls of yellow peas with half a pound of bacon, and drams and Bavarians.

3

Strindberg wrote *A Fool's Apology* in French. Perhaps it was easier for him to deal with intimate matters in a foreign language which acted as a kind of veil between him and his subject. His own claim was that he had chosen French out of consideration for Siri, and that the book was not to be published during his lifetime; but there are reasons to believe that he was still pursuing the idea of which he had spoken, at the time of his son's birth, to his brother Axel—of becoming famous in France.

He called the narrative *A Fool's Apology*, and characterized it in years to come as a novel or, alternatively, as a truthful account of his marriage. However, he gave the protagonist the name Axel, safeguarding himself by that simple device. Axel is also the book's narrator. The premise is that Axel is writing in order to refute his wife Maria's accusations that he is insane. Axel scrutinizes his marriage from the very beginning—the encounter on Drottninggatan—to the sojourn in Germany. For his part, he seeks to prove Maria's infidelity. His suspicions are driving him to cruel actions, and for Maria these become new proof of his madness.

As the American Strindberg scholar Erik Johannesson points out, the reader of *A Fool's Apology* finds himself in the same situation as the reader of a detective novel. He or she is invited to accompany Axel, the detective, on his investigations, with the aim of trapping Maria, the criminal. The reader's pleasure consists in his evaluation of Axel's labours—he applauds or criticizes, one moment imagines that he is on the right track, and the next suspects that he has been totally wrong about everything.

Yet Axel—Strindberg himself—is overwhelmed time and again, in the course of his tale, by love for the vampire that is the object of his hatred. His former happiness with her and the joy she has given him in the past rises and struggles with his revulsion, and the result is a dual creature—a woman who is both goddess and evil, insidious bitch. When, in the opening chapter, he encounters her playing with her children on her bed, a Venus surrounded by cherubs, he simultaneously introduces the image of a female lynx playing with her kittens, whose claws are always ready to scratch. Thus the novel turns into a novel of love, and while Axel does not consciously acquit Maria, she receives her acquittal from the lover and artist, combined, who exist within him on the far side of hate. He is a slave of reality, who has to use his material exactly as life has given it to him. Although he may change the focus and the emotional content, the underlying reality emerges none the less, and it is different from the one Axel believes in. Did Strindberg realize that the story transformed itself into something else? That is a question that cannot be answered, yet the fact of transformation remains.

The book sustains itself from beginning to end. On 28 January, Strindberg told Lundegård that he was writing 'freely, superbly, without a thought of that governess Albert Bonnier; sparks fly in the brain, when the right word has to be born in the alien language, but that effort gives me a total vision of what has been experienced.'

In March, the worst cold snap in living memory hit Denmark, and a couple of rooms in the police officer's villa had to be closed off because of heating problems. Copenhagen's steam-powered streetcars stopped running. But Strindberg went on writing at top speed while also attending to his voluminous correspondence, in which his plans to conquer France played an increasing part. The vicar of Taarbaek used to see him out on his morning walks and thought that his face expressed defiance and menace, but also a painful restlessness. That was exactly how Strindberg wanted to be now. His hatred of Siri did not diminish: on the contrary, his letters began to sound as if he desired revenge for the way her beauty was conquering him in the novel, as it had done for so long in real life. He wrote to Edvard Brandes in mid-March:

And I have not only been a father to these bitch-children but a mother as well. They would have perished of dirt and vermin if I had not been there, and their mother would have gone to gaol, if my silence and loyalty had not saved her—the vampire! Now I have whipped her into becoming a conscientious mother, and now I dare leave the children with her, after dismissing the maid, with whom she used to booze and whore!

The letter ended: 'I'll go up to Jerusalem, perhaps my Golgotha, to celebrate Easter, alone, without disciples—as you perhaps are a Peter who betrays his master the first time the cock crows, I confide this letter to you, knowing that you will sympathize with and understand my suffering.' Jerusalem stands for Stockholm, where he had intended to return for Easter.

Towards the end of March, *A Fool's Apology* was finished, and the manuscript sent to Johan Oscar Strindberg. In a letter to Johan Oscar, Strindberg bestowed praise upon himself, saying that he was acting like a true gentleman by refraining from publication of the story. He had lived in a fever of creativity all winter, but the completion of the manuscript did not slow him down. On 23 March, he wrote a letter to Rudolf Wall that was as horrendous as the one to Brandes, and in which the emphasis was on his wife's lesbianism, her 'deformity'. He also described himself as a lost human being, lacking all interest in work and life. 'Fame and such no longer interests me, now that my only concern has ceased to exist'—meaning his children. At the same time, this man who had lost all ambition was working like a madman to create a place of honour for *The Father* in France. Two days after the letter to Wall he wrote to his publisher Hans Österling from Skåne, who had brought out *The Father* and was now printing *Père*: 'Do not forget to send the Royal Library all the variant covers to *Père*, and also the second edition of *The Father*.'

4

Winter was over, and it was time to find a summer residence. An old woman, who used to come to Siri's kitchen door in Taarbaek to sell vegetables, suggested a nearby castle, where her son was acting as steward for a Countess Frankenau. Strindberg was interested, and one April day the family went to see the place: Karin Smirnoff describes the visit in her book. The steward himself collected them in a carriage, an 'old miserable rattle-trap four-seater', pulled by two scrawny horses. The steward was a striking man with fiery eyes, a black moustache, and a huge diamond-pin in his red cravat. Next to him on the driver's seat sat his brother who wore a faded livery of sorts.

After driving through newly green beech forests, they turned into a short, tree-lined drive, passed a stagnant pond with an island in the middle—there

32–33 Two pictures from the marriage drama: Strindberg's photograph of Siri von Essen, Gersau, 1886. Siri von Essen's photograph of her husband's fine head of hair

34 Strindberg posing as a guitar player in a self-portrait, 1886

was a pavilion on the island—and came to a halt in front of an imposing entrance. On the steps stood the Countess, curtseying, wearing a light blue crinoline dress with a tight-fitting waist and bare shoulders; her hair was combed close to her head, with a parting from forehead to neck, and spiralled into two tight braid coiled above her ears.

Instead of showing their guests the accommodation offered for rent, the steward and the Countess proceeded to give a conjuring show. The Countess played a barrel-organ while the steward performed a conjuring trick with the assistance of his sister, sixteen-year-old Martha, who was wearing a tight-fitting satin circus costume. The performance took place in a large, sumptuously furnished hall. The unexpected scene was illuminated by the light of a fading spring day, faintly shimmering through the heavy drapes.

This marked the beginning of the most remarkable summer in Strindberg's life. Strangely enough, he signed the prepared lease on the spot, although the family did not have time to inspect the apartment. We do not know if his decision was influenced by the sight of the sixteen-year-old beauty with her blonde hair and blue eyes, floating free in the air during that conjuring act. Four rooms furnished in Empire style and a tower room for a study, all for only 50 kronor a month: this is how Strindberg described the place in a letter in May to Heidenstam, quite certainly remembering that his aristocratic friend, three years previously, had boasted a great medieval hall in a Swiss castle.

The Danish castle was called Skovlyst. Its owner, Louise de Frankenau, was forty years old in 1888. She was a bizarre person, whose main interest in life was animals. In the gardens, there were turkeys, rabbits, peacocks, chickens, twenty-two sheep, a he-goat named Pingles and two she-goats, Caroline and Mathilde; they were named after the Danish queen Caroline Mathilde, who took her private physician Struense as her lover and was gaoled and exiled after his downfall—an eighteenth-century version of the drama of *Miss Julie* which Strindberg was to write during that summer.

The castle was in great disrepair and the animals were neglected; the Countess in her out-dated crinoline used to cradle the huge rooster Himmelsspraet in her lap and was herself as dirty as the rooms and the furniture. There were eight dogs, among them three gigantic Great Danes, against whom a human being is 'almost defenceless', as Strindberg informed Heidenstam, who was a great lover of dogs. He added that one animal had recently 'eaten an entire kitchen maid alive in a backyard'. To Strindberg's annoyance, Heidenstam had included in his first collection of poems, *Years of Pilgrimage and Wandering*, published that spring, a poem dealing with the poet's refusal to hand a dying friend a glass of water, because the latter had 'stricken a defenceless beast'. Strindberg had good reason to believe that that beast was a canine. 'So weep for the maid instead,' he added.

That the dogs of Skovlyst—as distinct from the majority of the species Strindberg warred with—were, indeed, formidable was proved the following autumn, when the local magistrates' court complied with complaints by the Countess's neighbours and ordered her to keep the dogs chained and muzzled. Strindberg would also ascribe a horrendous role to them in *Tschandala*, the novel he wrote the following winter. With the aid of a magic lantern, the novel's hero, Magister Törner, incites the dogs to attack and kill Jensen—the latter being a pseudonym for that black-moustached, diamond-studded person Karin Smirnoff described so eloquently.

The name of Skovlyst's steward was, in reality, Ludvig Hansen. We know something about him thanks to the Danish literary scholar Harry Jacobsen, who has energetically documented the time Strindberg spent in Denmark. Hansen's mother was a former serving-maid, who had a relationship with Countess Frankenau's father: thus he was a step-brother of the lady of the castle, although propriety did not permit any acknowledgement of kinship. Louise de Frankenau, a lonely woman, had decided to employ the young man as her steward, thereby doing further damage to her financial situation, because Hansen was hopelessly feckless, if not worse. He preferred conjuring tricks and fantasies to work, and the estate deteriorated under his stewardship.

When Strindberg noticed the intimacy between the 26-year-old steward and the Countess, he concluded that they were engaged in a secret liaison. That conclusion was to have awkward but interesting consequences.

Ludvig Hansen had artistic leanings. As a farmer he was a joke, but as a conjuror, actor and amateur author he demonstrated some talent. Strindberg worked in the tower room; when it got hot in the summer, he moved down to the pavilion on the island. The bridge leading to the island from the edge of the pond was, in fact, a drawbridge, and thus it was possible to keep the dogs out. He wrote three of his major works at Skovlyst: 'The Romantic Sexton of Rånö', *Miss Julie* and *Creditors*.

The idyll at Skovlyst did not last long. The estate was teetering on the brink of ruin. Renting out the apartment was a hopeless attempt to recoup some of the losses: Hansen drank and dreamed, the animals starved, the gardens became a jungle. Hansen's sister, Martha the circus beauty, was hired to help with the Strindbergs' children. According to claims made by Strindberg in a letter to Siri of September 1888, Martha invented a series of excuses for coming to his bedroom, preferably at the time he got up in the morning or went to bed at night. Later, Strindberg claimed that she had been incited to this activity by her brother, who was, thus, a procurer. When Strindberg, thirty-nine years old, tried to present himself as the victim of the seductive wiles of a sixteen-year-old girl, he chose a line of defence that did not really stand much of a chance of being believed.

Strindberg started a relationship with Martha, with the tower room as the setting for the dramatic love story. His version of it to Siri, in which he appeared as the seduced party, did not prevent him from describing the affair in terms more befitting a Don Juan. 'After six months of horrible celibacy, I mounted a fully grown maid of eighteen years, whose brother was my landlord and a scoundrel. She did not get pregnant because I had preventives'—this was to Heidenstam.

In the course of the summer, the situation developed in ever more fantastic ways. Hansen contemplated blackmail and started spreading the rumour that his sister was expecting a child by his illustrious tenant. About the same time, there were reports of thefts out on the coast, in Taarbaek, and Strindberg suspected Hansen, believing that he now had a most effective counter-weapon against the blackmailer. Tension mounted in the castle. Strindberg had long since replaced the revolver the policeman had confiscated in December 1887. He took to carrying it in his pocket. Hansen, too, was armed. Shots were heard in the night. Terrified, the children lay awake, listening.

On 2 September, after a violent scene, the Strindberg family fled from the castle and took lodgings in Holte. On 5 September, Strindberg wrote to Harlew, his former landlord in Taarbaek, saying that he had 'some clues as to the identity of the thief' to report, and on 9 September, the newspaper *Politiken* contained a notice, written by Strindberg, in which Hansen was named as the thief. In a police action, conducted like a parody of military manoeuvres, the hapless Hansen was arrested, handcuffed, and thrown into gaol. Five days later, the real thieves were arrested and Hansen released. His nocturnal excursions had been due to a love affair he was conducting in the neighbourhood.

Strindberg's nervous system was well adapted to strong doses of the spices of life. He needed them, even went out of his way to obtain them, if they did not occur naturally. Nevertheless, all this had been more than enough. Although Hansen's innocence seemed certain, his case was to come up on 19 September, and Strindberg was summoned as a witness. On the 18th, he fled to Berlin in the company of Pehr Staaff, who had conveniently arrived on a visit to Denmark. The newspapers got hold of the story. In *Københavns-Posten*, Martha's mother, the lady with the vegetables, declared that Strindberg had done 'the most terrible thing on earth' with her daughter. One newspaper called Martha 'a child', which was tantamount to branding Strindberg as a criminal with the prospect of one to four years' hard labour ahead of him. *Social-Demokraten*—the papers instantly took political sides—came to his defence and sent a reporter to see Martha, who explained or was persuaded to explain that she 'liked him a lot'—a statement Strindberg would use many times in his own defence.

That same summer, Jack the Ripper stunned London and the world with his mysterious murders and mutilations, and his name was mentioned in the same breath as Strindberg's and Hansen's. There was a rumour that Hansen had killed Strindberg and hidden the corpse.

The commotion alarmed Strindberg's friends. They were afraid that the radical cause would be damaged if he did not appear in court, where a new date had been set for 28 September. Strindberg was brought back from Berlin and took a room in the illustrious Hôtel Angleterre, which he had last visited on his way home to the trial caused by *Marrying*. He appeared in court, but had nothing much to say; he kept a low profile, as it was evident that he had pressed unfounded charges.

5

Strindberg had begun that summer by writing the short story 'The Romantic Sexton of Rånö'. There were financial reasons for this return to the Archipelago: *The People of Hemsö*'s sales had picked up, and Bonniers were pleased to see that Strindberg was continuing to draw upon the resources of 'folk life'.

The story deals with a musical store clerk, Alrik Lundstedt, who on a summer's day in 1859 travels from Trosa to Stockholm in order to study the organ at the Musical Academy there. He is shy and timid but brave and self-assured in his daydreams—like his creator and Walter Mitty. At first, Strindberg thought of him as merely a comic figure, a variation on Carlsson of *The People of Hemsö*, and described him in humorous, fast-moving narrative paragraphs. His journey to the capital in the steamboat *Hermoder*, one of those Strindberg's father had listed, is described in the hopeful terms of Bellman's 48th 'Epistle of Fredman'; Strindberg's, and Alrik Lundstedt's, inventiveness in the daydreaming genre know no bounds during that trip.

But Strindberg soon discovered that Alrik was more than just a joke. He is a martyr of his imagination, which blends its own life with that of everyday reality, and this has catastrophic consequences. Just as Strindberg, viewing *The Father*, did not know if he had written or lived the play, Alrik, too, becomes confused by his own fantasies. Believing himself to be the mighty lord of his dreams, he persuades his father, a poor fisherman, to come to Stockholm, thereby acquiring a burden that makes it impossible for him to pursue a career in the world of music.

The strangest passage in the story concerns Alrik and the organ in Jakob's Church. He is allowed to assist the famous professor of music who is also the organist of that church. To Alrik, the professor seems like a magician, controlling this sonorous, trembling beast by means of his art. Alrik is gripped by horror, terrified of being torn to pieces.

To regain his composure, he has to learn to control, to comprehend. He does this by searching out images and analogies that translate the incomprehensible and dangerous into something understandable and familiar. He transforms the organ loft, which had seemed to him like a whale's rib-cage, with the pipes as blood vessels and windpipes, and the bellows, which panted like a terrifying giant's lungs, into a basalt cave by the sea, and the man working those bellows becomes Eolus, god of the winds. Six years later, Strindberg wrote to a friend that the 'Sexton' was the 'fastest' thing he had written. Perhaps he was thinking of precisely that analysis of the role metaphor played in his creative work: it was there in order to tame a frightful and incomprehensible reality, in order to humanize the bestial, to exorcize the subterranean world of demons.

The professor has taught Alrik that the organ manual has one stop that must not be pulled in conjunction with certain others: should this happen, the organ might break, and repair work would involve breaking up the floor. Alrik becomes fascinated by that particular stop, the magic one: he calls it 'the voice'. He sits by the organ for hours at a time, staring at it, and when he feels he is sufficiently melancholy, he wants to pull it: then the organ cave will collapse over him with spectacular thunderous sounds effects, and he will be allowed to die in God's house, and before Angelika's eyes. Angelika is an unknown beauty, down there among the congregation, whom he has chosen as the object of his youthful love.

As the story draws to a close, we are surprised, enlightened and informed: Alrik's existence as a dreamer is grounded in a childhood experience. One hard winter, on the lonely little island where he grew up, his mother fell ill, and his father killed her—a form of mercy killing that was, according to Strindberg, quite common in the Archipelago. Alrik did not participate in the deed, but, as a silent witness, feels increasingly guilty about it as the years go by. His dreams are like a barrow of rocks and earth that he has raised above his dead mother. The sole intention of all his inventions and megalomaniac fantasies is to cover up the one who died. Thus he had generated a desire to mix the real and the unreal in order to cheat himself, to avoid all reality as that included the murder he was unable to remember.

When Strindberg submitted the short story to his publishers, Karl Otto Bonnier found the ending unsatisfactory. The murder seemed contrived to him: it did not fit in with the rest of the description of Alrik's character. Strindberg replied that it did not matter what kind of crime had been committed: the main thing was 'that there was a corpse on his mind, no matter whose'. He went on to say: 'I believe that an author, in his creative fever, knows what is right, even though later, when he is sober, he might think that one thing could have been replaced by another. That is why I hardly ever dare change anything: whenever I revise things, I spoil them. *Summa summarum*, whatever I have written, I have written.'

'The Sexton' was written immediately after Strindberg finished *A Fool's Apology*. In that work, he had pulled a stop that was, normally, taboo, unless one wanted to risk the total collapse of the house one lived in. He had exploited his wife, using the entire tonal register, achieving an artistic victory at the cost of human misery. 'A corpse, no matter whose'. At the same time, he declared that the task of the poetic imagination was to anaesthetize the feeling of guilt—and to conceal the corpse of the beloved.

6

In the middle of the summer of 1888 Strindberg wrote his best-known play, *Miss Julie*. Julie is the daughter of a count who owns an estate: Queen Mathilde Caroline, Countess Frankenau, and Baroness Siri von Essen are three of her real-life ancestors.

One Midsummer Night's Eve, Julie is seduced by her father's valet. The play evolves according to the new dramatic principles Strindberg was applying at the time, within the time-span of a few hours and without any changes of scene. The setting is the castle kitchen with its shiny copper pots and pans; in addition to Jean, the valet, and Julie there is only one other character, the cook Kristin, Jean's fiancée. Although the sexes have been transposed, the events of the play closely resemble the drama Strindberg and Martha enacted at Skovlyst. Partners from different social strata get involved with one another, and this has catastrophic consequences.

The play is constructed with a firmness that stands in marked contrast to the chaos surrounding its composition. *Miss Julie* is difficult to categorize: that is its strength. A comparison with Ibsen is instructive: in *The Wild Duck*, for instance, everything seems calculated and masterfully balanced, and the play's symbolism obtrudes as menacingly as a teacher's pointer in the classroom of olden days. Strindberg, on the other hand, keeps his audience suspended in a state of uncertainty as to what has been calculated and what is the result of a moment's inspiration—and the play is, therefore, still tinged with some of the darkness that prevailed on the face of the deep, before the act of Creation.

At the beginning of the play, Julie has the upper hand. She is confident of the power she exerts over men. The traditional midsummer dance is in progress out in the barn, and she has asked Jean to dance with her. Now, in the kitchen, she compliments him, and by her contemptuous initiative starts the sexual contest between them. She persuades Jean to go for a walk in the park with her. By the standards Strindberg applied to women, she acts like a whore, as only the male is permitted to make advances of a sexual nature.

Just as the couple is about to leave, Jean discovers that he has a speck of dust in his eye. We are not told whether this is a trick or not, but Julie accepts it as a fact, explaining that it must have come from the sleeve of her dress which had brushed against his eyes. She takes Jean's arm and makes him sit down on a chair. She takes hold of his head, pushes it back, and attempts to remove the dust with her handkerchief. After a few seconds, during which Julie has time to comment on the strength of Jean's arms—he is trembling with excitement—the operation is over, and Julie asks him to kiss her hand, by way of thanks.

Now Jean believes, or pretends to believe, that she is fair game, particularly as Julie refers to him as 'a Joseph', indicating that she is as willing as Potiphar's wife. He tries to embrace and kiss her, but is rebuffed by a slap in the face and the exclamation 'For shame!' Jean retreats, declares that he is tired of Julie's games, and asks for permission to return to his tasks, viz., cleaning the Count's dusty boots. Yet it is now that he brings his most effective weapon into play.

He tells Julie how, as a child, he once ventured into the castle park. There he discovered a pavilion overgrown with honeysuckle—the Count's privy garden retreat, furnished with red tasselled curtains and comical portraits of kings and emperors. Jean, not knowing the function of the building, slipped in to admire its intriguing contents. Once inside, he heard steps approaching and was forced to escape through one of the apertures provided for excretory functions. Outside, he forced his way—one may imagine in what a state!— through a hedge of raspberry canes and then caught sight of Julie, a small girl in a pink dress and white stockings. He crawled underneath a heap of cut weeds and lay there, staring at Julie like one of the damned gazing upon one of the angels of light.

Jean's tale comes close to being a parody, but Julie does not laugh. Instead, she exclaims: 'It must be a boundless misfortune to be poor!' Jean sees his chance and, in turn, exclaims that a dog is allowed to lie on the Countess's couch, and a horse may be caressed by the hand of a young Miss but a servant . . .!

Now follows the famous scene in which Jean claims that, hopelessly in love with Julie, he once lay down in a storage bin filled with branches of flowering elder, having heard that this could be lethal. While making this appeal to Julie's sympathy, he does not forget to caress her senses by pointing out that oats—the normal content of that bin—are 'soft to the touch, like human skin'. Immediately after this exchange, the midsummer revellers approach and dance their way into the kitchen. Jean entices Julie to his room, so that they will not be discovered tête-à-tête.

Later—after they have made love—Jean confesses that the oat bin story was a lie. He had read it in a newspaper. The spectator is at liberty to assume that even the rest of his narrative—the park, the garden retreat, the angel—

is a fabrication. Jean reveals himself to Julie as a deceiver, and this leads to the horrendous shredding of the masks, in which the two abuse one another with epithets like 'lackey' and 'whore'. Julie realizes the extent of her degradation. Jean is a thief in the house. But as they are shackled together by the embraces they have exchanged, they try to preserve appearances by fantasizing about a life together. Jean dreams of a hotel in Switzerland, with Julie as both financial backer and the main attraction. Yet his words (like Alrik's dreams) are not capable of concealing the horror of reality from her.

In a scene that was edited out of the play—at the publisher's request—Julie says that she had experienced their love-making as an act of bestiality. 'I would like to kill you, like an animal!' she exclaims, beside herself. Jean gets the point immediately—bestiality is a crime—and replies: 'The perpetrator will be sentenced to two years' hard labour, the animal, killed.' Julie: 'That's right!'

Her instincts have driven her into Jean's arms, she has embraced an animal. Doing so, she has defiled herself to such an extent that she cannot go on living. These, surely, are reflections of impulses Strindberg himself must have felt during his liaison with Martha (which, by the way, left a tangible memento in the form of body lice). In *Miss Julie*, however, the trivial story and the cheap comedy are elevated on to a tragic plane. When Jean indicates suicide as a way out for Julie—he has prepared her by killing her greenfinch—she is ready, but she is not driven to her death by him. She is a chimeric creature, both angel and beast, and when it comes to a confrontation between the animal and the divine, she has to die, being unable to accept herself and her instincts.

7

After the stormy summer, the Strindbergs found a haven in October, a villa not far from Holte. 'Living like a prince now . . . in two apartments for 300 kronor,' Strindberg wrote to Bonniers on 24 October.

To amuse himself, and also to make some money, he wrote a collection of *causeries* entitled *Flower Pieces and Animal Stories* which appeared at Christmas with illustrations by G. Åberg and A. Sjöberg. It presented Strindberg's charming and lovable side which no witches' dance of nerves, no magic organ stop, and no razor at Miss Julie's throat were able to extinguish. His children remembered him—the scene at Eichbühl was a ghastly exception—as a quiet father who liked to show them things in nature and in fairytale books. He appears exactly that way in these short prose pieces, talking about the nightingale's song, and about the wisdom of plants—which was often, he claimed, greater than that of animals. In his old, paradoxical manner he attacked lovers of dogs—'who wants company, has human beings to associate with, and who has fallen so low that he prefers the company of animals should not be franchised in communal affairs, least of all in regard to the dog problem'.

He also described, so instructively and simply that one could use his text as a guidebook, his garden on Kymmendö 'as I last saw it five years ago', adding: 'What it looks like now, I do not know and probably won't ever know again, having written *The People of Hemsö* and *Skerry-men's Lives*!' In general, there was not much 'ordinary' life left for Strindberg. His work would absorb everything. As he now talked about the hollyhocks, which he had formerly despised, giving them various Swedish nicknames, and about the white pelargoniums in the crofters' cottages, now superseded by the arrogant red ones, the flowers were bathed in an almost supernatural light by the fact that they were lost forever. He returned to the hollyhocks, in a visionary context, in *A Dream Play*. According to the introductory instructions, the background consists of a forest of gigantic hollyhocks.

After this excursion into the idyllic, Strindberg wrote the novel *Tschandala*, a historic tale from Skåne, set thirty years after the Swedes took the province from the Danes in 1658. Magister Törner, a representative of the Swedish master race, has been stationed in a castle to keep the natives under control. In reality, the book is a detailed description of the Strindberg family's life at Skovlyst. Just like Strindberg, Törner encounters superhuman sexual temptation in the shape of the maid Magelone, and after he has slept with her, he reacts as violently as Julie: 'He felt that everything had been defiled, his room, his body, his soul. He had never believed that anything so boundlessly revolting could be possible. . . . He had embraced an animal, and after the embrace, the animal had kissed him like a cat.'

Törner's love affair is only a detail. The main subject is Törner's relationship with Magelone's brother, the gypsy Jensen. In the spring of 1888, Georg Brandes was lecturing on Nietzsche, whom Strindberg discovered at the same time. Here were 'the great' again, discussed in magnificent artistic language! In May, Strindberg wrote to Heidenstam that in Nietzsche 'you can find *everything*! Don't deny yourself that delight!' Strindberg was on fire, as he always was on first encounters with outstanding people and ideas. In September, he wrote to Edvard Brandes, employing sexual metaphors that indicated the degree of his desire: 'My spiritual being has received in its uterus a tremendous ejaculation by Friedrich Nietzsche, so that I feel as full as a pregnant bitch. That's my man! Give my best to Georg Brandes and thank him for the introduction.'

Georg Brandes was, indeed, responsible for putting Nietzsche, who was approaching insanity, in direct contact with Strindberg. They exchanged books with mutual compliments, and in November 1888 they began a correspondence, on Nietzsche's initiative. He praised *The Father* which he had read in French. Strindberg recognized certain of his own moods in the extreme self-esteem Nietzsche had developed—in his first letter, Nietzsche declared himself to be 'the most independent and perhaps the strongest spirit alive today'. Strindberg sent the letter on to Brandes with the comment:

> I think it is modern to utter these proud but true words, and remind you that in these days of a strong, awakening consciousness of the self it is only to be expected that a great talent like himself will, by comparison with others, find that his spirit is indeed the greatest and most powerful; and once that discovery has been made, there must be an urge to express it.

Those words apply to Strindberg himself: the incredible creativity he had demonstrated during the previous year gave him the right to see himself in those Nietzschean terms. *Tschandala* deals with such pretensions. The novel could be called a laboratory experiment for the development of 'superman'. The word *tschandala* is borrowed from Nietzsche, and designates the lowest caste in India. The gypsy is a pariah; Törner exists on a higher level.

During a hot summer at the castle, these two try to destroy each other. Törner is the superior talent; the gypsy is cowardly, hedonistic and superstitious. Nevertheless, they are evenly matched, because Törner cannot rid himself of the magnanimity that characterizes cultured man, while the gypsy is shrewd and unscrupulous. Furthermore, Törner himself is receptive to popular superstition and to the temptation which the gypsy's irresponsible way of life presents.

Törner is visited by his friend Bureus, who does not hesitate to plead for the right of the stronger. Whoever is on top, he explains, is there because of his moral and intellectual strength. Thus it is their self-evident privilege to dominate, castigate, and ultimately destroy those who are inferior.

Törner opposes such a doctrine. 'A human being is a human being, after all,' he says, and doubts that it is always the best who make it to the top. He represents the democratic view of humanity Strindberg had always adhered to, but he begins to waver, trying to convince himself that the gypsy is such a low type that he does not deserve anything but death. Finally, he converts to the doctrine of the superior race's right to rule and enjoy: at the same time, his entire personality begins to disintegrate, and this is when, driven by bestial lust, he takes Magelone to his bed.

Like Julie and Jean, and Laura and the Captain, Törner and the gypsy are a pair who, while locked in conflict, take on each other's characteristics— like man and serpent in the Canto XXV of Dante's *Inferno*. Strindberg's description of this phenomenon is a *tour de force*, and we witness the horror of it with bated breath. In *The Father* and *Miss Julie* the higher, psychically more differentiated combatants go under while the lower, cunning, brutal ones emerge victorious. *Tschandala* reverses the process. Törner overcomes his scruples and kills his adversary with the help of the terrifying castle dogs and a magic lantern. The destiny of the superman leads him to an inhuman crime. The Captain and Julie perish but attain tragic greatness in their deaths: they are the moral victors. Törner emerges as the superficial winner, but pays for the victory with his own inner destruction. That is the outcome of the experiment with Nietzsche as Strindberg understood him.

Strindberg, like Törner, would soon succumb to Nietzsche's temptation to declare himself greater and stronger than others. The fates sent him a warning which paradoxically increased his sense of being at the centre of the universe. Strindberg had sent Nietzsche a copy of 'Pangs of Conscience'. Nietzsche thanked him for it on 31 December 1888. The story resounded like a shotgun, he wrote, and continued: 'I have called a meeting of the princes in Rome. I shall have the young emperor executed. Till we meet again. Because we will meet again. On one condition: that we part.' The letter was signed 'Nietzsche Caesar'.

When he received this letter, Strindberg did not know if its author, whom he had just called 'master', was joking or if he had lost his mind. He decided to respond in a humorous vein, a mode he always enjoyed. He chose to write in Latin—most of the letter is a quotation from Horace—and dated it 'Holtibus pridie Cal. Jan. MDCCCLXXXIX'. In translation, the letter reads:

> Dearest Doctor! I want, I want to be mad. I have received your letter, not without emotion, and thank you for it. You would live better, Licinius, if you did not always sail out to sea, nor, for fear of storms, stayed too close to the dangerous shore. We, however, are happy to be mad. Farewell and keep me in your affections! Strindberg (God, the best and highest).

At the same time, Strindberg sent Nietzsche's letter to Georg Brandes, asking him whether Nietzsche might not 'compromise' them. What he had witnessed was the beginning of Nietzsche's psychic collapse, and he was aware that his own hubris could lead to similar results. During the following weeks, Nietzsche's fate was much on Strindberg's mind. In the autumn, he had met Ola Hansson, a young Swedish author, whose story 'Pariah' he was dramatizing; to him he wrote on 28 January 1889: 'I think Nietzsche is blinding me, my brain is like a wound! From over-exertion! But he is probably driving me crazy as well! The incredible self-esteem expressed in his books has given me a similar feeling about myself! Which won't prevent my grey matter from cracking, as it probably will!'

The excess of heat from which Strindberg's brain was suffering—in another letter he said he felt like 'an over-charged Leyden Jar, doing nothing but throwing sparks'—was definitely dangerous for him. When, before

Holtibus pridie Cal. Jan.

MDCCCLXXXIX.

Carissime Doctor!

Θέλω, θέλω μανῆναι!
Litteras tuas non sine pertur.
batione accepi et tibi gratias
ago.

Rectius vives, Licini, neque altum
Semper urgendo, neque dum pro.
                                    cellas
Cautus horrescis nimium pre.
                                    mendo
        Litus iniquum.

Interdum juvat insanire!
    Vale et Fave!
        Strindberg (Deus, optimus
                        maximus).

35 Strindberg's letter to Nietzsche, January 1889

long, he was again to grow tired of *belles-lettres* and abandon them for scientific experiments, one of the reasons was that he needed a cooling-off period.

8

Albert Bonnier wrote to Strindberg in October 1888, congratulated him on his superb new lodgings and expressed the hope that he would, in them, 'create sterling works of genius' which it would be a joy for him, Bonnier, to receive. Strindberg replied, justifiably: 'What is the use of writing works of genius for Sweden, when you won't print them?'

Bonniers had rejected *The Father*, created difficulties over *The People of Hemsö*, and only in August had turned down *Miss Julie*, which Strindberg had offered to them as 'the first naturalistic play in Swedish dramatic literature'. 'Now, don't bet on the wrong horse,' Strindberg wrote, 'and don't be deceived, as I have not been. I did take a step backwards in *The People of Hemsö*—yes, but only to make another leap—forward!' Bonniers paid no attention to those Nietzsche-inspired words, found the play 'too risky', and ventured the opinion that it would hardly be possible to perform it. After a great deal of trouble, Strindberg finally persuaded his old publisher Seligmann (who had brought out *The Red Room*) to publish *Miss Julie* for a payment of 300 kronor, but only after he had given in to Seligmann's ultimatum and agreed to delete a number of the most audacious lines. Thus Julie's and Jean's exchange on 'bestiality' disappeared. Not a single theatre dared to produce the play.

Strindberg decided that a theatre of his own was the only solution. In Paris, in March 1887, André Antoine had opened the Théâtre Libre in order to present new, naturalistic plays—by, among others, Zola, Tolstoy and the Brothers Goncourt. Strindberg, who had followed Antoine's activities from the start, wrote to him and obtained a promise for a production of *The Father*. Ibsen achieved the same for *Ghosts*. Now Strindberg's hopes concerned *Miss Julie* and *Creditors*—they, too, had been translated into French.

On the anniversary of the first night of *The Father*, 14 November 1888, Strindberg followed Antoine's example and founded The Scandinavian Experimental Theatre, later renamed Strindberg's Experimental Theatre. It had a brief but stormy existence. In November and December, Strindberg raised money and acquired props, plays and actors. On 17 November, he published a notice in *Politiken* in which he stated his willingness to consider plays of every kind but 'preferably those with a contemporary setting that are not too long and do not require extensive machinery or a large cast'. No one was able to meet those requirements as well as Strindberg himself.

One fantastic fund-raising project followed upon another. Several of Strindberg's former publishers were asked for loans. Lists were to be circulated in Sweden to collect individual contributions, no matter how small. In *Dagens Nyheter*, Strindberg advertised for a reasonably well-to-do person to become the theatre's backer and financial director. Former professional colleagues received requests for donations. Even an 'enemy' like Harald Wieselgren at the Royal Library received a begging letter: 'Dear Wieselgren, do something for me and my cause, no matter how insignificant it may seem, get me at least some funding, even if it is not all I am asking for.' His pleading was to no avail; nevertheless, his imagination was already teeming with profits in five figures, and in a letter he assured an old friend that this venture was 'the over-all solution of all my social, financial, artistic, and familial problems! as well as my wife's'. His talent for celebrating victories before the event had a field-day at this time.

Siri, recently described as a bitch and a snake, was to be his leading lady as Julie. Strindberg stated that she was blossoming at the prospect and was 'enchanted' by it. His hatred of her diminished, perhaps because his guilt-feelings had some relief. Siri had reacted magnanimously to the Martha affair, rejecting a suggestion to use her husband's infidelity to obtain a favourable divorce. She explained that she did not want to make use of something she no longer cared about, and when the more sensational newspapers got on to the case, she defended her husband. He was impressed.

In January, Siri was appointed the theatre's general and artistic director. She moved in with her maternal aunt Augusta Möller in Copenhagen and installed Augusta's sister Mathilde as a temporary house-mother in the villa. It did not take long to assemble a small theatrical group: a young writer, Nathalia Larsen, whom Strindberg had courted during the winter; Johanne Krum; the author Gustav Wied, one of Strindberg's devoted admirers; and two or three others.

While the inner drama of Strindberg's megalomania reached its climax — he finally decided that the theatre would perform only his own plays, which meant a number of broken promises to other dramatists — his troupe worked with great dedication. The first playbill was to consist of the new one-act play *The Stronger One*, the extraordinary love triangle *Creditors* and *Miss Julie*. *Creditors* had also been written at Skovlyst. For the opening night, Siri ordered a white wool dress with insets of white flower-patterned silk and a large puffed bustle. The young actor Viggo Schiwe was entrusted with Jean's part. The copper pots and pans in Nathalia Larsen's kitchen were rented for two nights and carted down to the Theatre Dagmar for use on the set of the castle kitchen. Rehearsals were often stormy because the actors were not always willing to subordinate themselves to Siri Essen-Strindberg, as she now called herself. But by the end of February 1889, things had progressed far enough for a poster to be printed. The first night was to be on 2 March, and advance ticket sales were satisfactory.

Then came the catastrophe. On Friday, 1 March, in the middle of the dress rehearsal, the police raided the Theatre Dagmar, bringing with them the censor's ban on *Miss Julie*—the result of a hate campaign against Strindberg which had been conducted in the press. The script of the play had been available since the autumn, and the critics had savagely attacked it. Karl Warburg, representing prevalent Swedish opinion, found the play disgusting and written in a language 'used hardly anywhere but in dens of drunkenness and vice'. Judgements in Denmark were equally harsh. According to one critic, the dialogue was enough to induce nausea in any decent person. Copenhagen papers published satirical verses on Julie. The censor was acting in conjunction with these bloodhounds of morality.

For Siri, this was a particularly hard blow. She visited the censor and had an audience with the Minister of Justice, but in vain. In the greatest haste, the newly written short play *Pariah* was substituted for *Miss Julie*, and Siri took Helga's part in *The Stronger One*. It was poor consolation. She did not have time to assimilate the part properly and did not do it justice. Nor did she find any comfort in her husband's words, who wrote:

> It could make a good impression *not* to have the director herself on stage. The play appears in a better light, there can be no accusations of egotism! You can be content in the knowledge that you have been a director of the theatre of the future! And you can say to yourself: Hier liege ich und mache Literaturgeschichte ('Here I lie, making literary history')! That is more than to play a role.

On 9 March, the postponed première had a reasonable success in spite of everything, and mostly thanks to Hunderup, who had joined the troupe at the last moment, to act in *Pariah*. But the first night was also the last. The whole enterprise collapsed, financially and psychologically. Strindberg seemed more relieved than anything, as if a real theatre had been a little too real for him, the poet.

However, there was a sequel. It was decided to put on *Miss Julie* in a private performance at the Students' Association. During the preparations, Strindberg got the sudden notion that Viggo Schiwe and Siri were conducting a love affair, under cover of their parts as Jean and Julie. Just as during the *Marrying* trial, he imagined that the censorship intervention had come about through the concerted actions of women: thus Siri became once again the target for his revived misogyny. He waged a regular war of nerves on her, stripping her of her directorship and even considering Nathalia

36 Skovlyst in Denmark, scene of the 'enchanted summer'

37 Poster for *Miss Julie* at the Students' Association in Copenhagen, March 1889

Larsen as her replacement in *Miss Julie*. Despite everything, the play was performed on 14 March at the Students' Association. After another performance, and a repetition of the playbill on 16 March at the Theatre Dagmar in Malmö, Strindberg's theatrical enterprise reached its final conclusion. Strindberg was ready to move on; he had 'used up' all that Denmark had to offer. A Danish newspaper wrote that he should be deported. 'I have received acclaim, the enterprise was accomplished, but there has been no income—rather, a deficit and debts. Where will I raise money now?' Strindberg wrote to his brother Axel on 18 March:

> So much energy expended, this year! Have written *The People of Hemsö*, *Pariah*, *Simoom*, 400 letters, produced the plays, dictated memoranda, written a lecture on Modern Drama, polemicized, encouraged the timid, attended rehearsals, instructed—all this since 1 January! For *nothing*! Now I give up! Well, maybe not! Damn it, isn't there *someone* who could help?

Chapter Eleven

DIVORCE

I

HAVING LEFT SIRI and the children in Denmark, Strindberg arrived in Malmö on 20 April 1889, after almost six years of exile, and took lodgings in the Hotel Kramer. His homeland did not exactly greet him like a long-lost son, but he was received by friends, who organized a grand dinner of welcome on the evening of his arrival.

August Lindberg, a friend since the early 1870s, was in Malmö; he was the foremost interpreter of Hamlet of his generation, an impulsive, lyrical, unpredictable man. He was preoccupied with a dramatization of *The People of Hemsö* which he had commissioned Strindberg to write. Strindberg's initial response to the proposal had been: 'Me, dramatize *The People of Hemsö*? Start grubbing around in my own excrement? Hell, no!' He did, however, find the money tempting, and during that spring he and Lindberg had corresponded about whether it would be feasible to place a chamber-pot under the intoxicated minister's bed in the wedding scene. Perhaps Lindberg remembered that Strindberg had pleaded with him, almost exactly ten years earlier, for a role for his unemployed Siri in the company Lindberg belonged to at the time, praising his wife's 'burning fire' which the 'unscrupulous murderers at the Royal Theatre have not yet managed to quench!'

In Malmö, Strindberg also met two other friends from his past: Algot Lange and Ina Forstén. 'During that night, I recounted much of my misery', Strindberg wrote to Karl Nordström a couple of years later, and claimed that Henrik Ibsen had somehow discovered what he had said at that time and based his *Hedda Gabler* on it. Strindberg later apostrophized Ina Forstén as 'a Finnish witch' whose tricks had led him to his old parental home, where Siri and his fate awaited him. Algot Lange, who had become a celebrated singer in all the great baritone roles from Don Juan to

Mephistopheles in *Faust*, was also one of those whom Strindberg included in his imagination as telepathic companions. Lange appeared in *Black Flags*, and in the tale *Jubal Without a Name*, which deals with the fate of a great singer, there was a full-scale portrait of him, interwoven with parts of Strindberg himself.

A young man, Nils Odahl, attracted to Strindberg's circle at the time, later described him as having appeared youthful and resilient in Malmö; he added, however, that his face looked caved in under the prominent cheekbones, as if molars were missing, and his front teeth were dark and of an ugly shape. Odahl was a dentist, which explains his specific attention.

At the time when Strindberg liked to satirize anniversaries and jubilees, he had declared that his own great celebration would not be held until 1889. That year had arrived. A century had passed since the French Revolution, but Strindberg had taken care to call off his celebration of it by an article in which he claimed that the Bastille, when stormed, was found to hold only seven prisoners, four of whom were forgers of bills of exchange and two others madmen; he also claimed that Louis XVI was a liberal democrat who became the victim of the sins of his predecessors.

Even if Strindberg had held to his erstwhile ideals, that anniversary no longer had the same resonance as in 1883. Literature and politics were changing direction, in Sweden as elsewhere. His friend Heidenstam, until recently unknown, had published his first book in 1888 and been greeted by the public as a genius almost equal to Strindberg but without the latter's shortcomings. This was, no doubt, a blow to his ambition. Soon, a number of authors were to appear—Fröding, Selma Lagerlöf, Karlfeldt—who represented what Swedish literary history calls the Nineties and was long regarded as an incomparably great period.

When Alfred Nobel, once acclaimed by Strindberg, had collected all the money made in Russia through dynamite and oil and entrusted it to a foundation for the award of international prizes, and the Swedish Academy was appointed to give these to authors, the first candidates were three from that same circle: Lagerlöf, Heidenstam, and Karlfeldt. Strindberg remained an outsider.

2

Strindberg arrived in Stockholm, from Malmö, on 24 April. The nation-wide matriculation examinations had been conducted on 23 April and one of the essay subjects given was 'The veil that conceals the future from us has been woven by the hands of mercy'. It was appropriate in Strindberg's case; for him, there were exceptionally painful times ahead.

After a couple of days in Stockholm, Strindberg—predictably—took the steamer to Sandhamn, and at the beginning of May he rented two fishermen's cottages on Runmarö. He told Bonniers that he lived 'in a sober intoxication of rapture'. His hatred of Siri had abated at the memory of the happy summers they had spent together in the Archipelago. 'If I *have* been mentally deranged', he had written on 26 April, 'that has had its causes beyond my own control.' He added, as so often when engaged in pleading, that he felt 'such tremendous inclination to suicide this day that I am afraid'.

On 5 May, he continues his written conversation from Sandhamn:

> Siri, I am dying, piecemeal—yet I cannot hate you!—Why did you not shoot me that time, recently—then I would not be suffering now! Come here, bring the children, and let me get acclimatized to the illusions of happiness one more time. I will provide for your future, and then, at the point of highest bliss, when I have succeeded in making myself believe once again that they really were true, those beautiful years I lived with you, happily die by your hand when I least expect it. I'll arrange proof for my having died by my own hand, and then you, who love life, will be able to go on in the calm knowledge that you have made a human being happy. I cannot envisage another ending. And you can't begrudge me that. I now have two cottages on an island more beautiful than the greening isle of our youth, and one of them is as fine as a castle, that's the one you and Karin and Greta and Putte will live in, and I'll take the other one.

According to Karin Smirnoff, the Strindbergs had really had a scene involving a revolver. In one of his rages, Strindberg had pointed the gun at Siri, who looked him straight in the eye and said 'Shoot!' Strindberg returned the gun to his pocket with the comment: 'No, you're not worth the gunpowder!' In his letter, Strindberg reversed the roles. His suggestion that Siri find happiness as his executioner was one of his most bizarre whims.

The letters Strindberg wrote to Siri in the days to follow were burned by Karin Smirnoff after the death of her parents—she found them too dreadful. She did, however, give an account of them; we do not know how subjective it was, although it is certain that she regarded herself, all her life, as her mother's defender and apologist.

According to her account, Strindberg talks in his letter of 7 May, two days after the revolver letter, about the solemn silence of 'this beautifully stark landscape' and about its naïve inhabitants: then, suddenly, the poisons course in his veins, and a storm starts raging across the paper. Karin Smirnoff wrote: 'One insult followed another. Siri had utterly ruined him. He begs her to liberate him from the one thing that depresses, degrades, disturbs him—herself. He asks her to leave, and at least let his name be unsullied by hers, as he feels as if he were shackled to dirt! He lets her know that her bad reputation is firmly established, her escapades, notorious!' This curious missive, which should have been dreadful, had it not also been such a parody of itself, ended as follows: 'Go away from me, you evil woman, so I can be good again to everyone, even to you.'

The very next day, Strindberg was trying to entice her back again: with the cottages, with a garden for the children to play in, and a shallow, safe beach for them to bathe on. He claimed to have been 'mentally sick for a fortnight', and regretted that he had been torturing her. 'So attach me to yourself with a little kindness,' he pleaded, as if he had forgotten the horrendous accusations he had flung at her.

It was the last time that he ever pleaded with her. The heat of his reactions bore witness to his difficulty in severing his ties with her, and his sudden changes of mood were disconcerting even to himself. Nietzsche's fate was on his mind. Siri had shown his letters to one of his old friends, Ossian Ekbohm, chief supervisor of customs at Sandhamn: Strindberg wrote to him in order to prevent a feared accusation of insanity:

'I have—notandum—written two letters a day to Mrs Sg. In one, I told her to go to hell, in the other, I asked her to come to Runmarö. We-ell! So what! Shifting states of mind, between hate and love, are not madness! Although it may please the foals of she-asses to pretend they believe that! and then to present letters as evidence for harebrains who are only able to cope with one emotion at a time!'

3

Some time soon after his return Strindberg wrote a new *Somnambulist Night*—the fifth. In the first four, written in the autumn of 1883, he had, as we have seen, imagined return journeys to Stockholm in the shape of a bird. Now he was back in body and soul, noting the changes that had occurred during the past years.

Telephone wires were spreading their webs over new palaces and banks. Sweden had 'taken a tonic of blood and iron'. Strindberg sketches one of the first pictures of Sweden as a modern industrial nation. Carl Jonas Love Almqvist had written about the significance of Sweden's poverty, designating the pale briar rose as the symbol of the nation. Sweden had been, and still was, a country of incredible poverty. In Strindberg's childhood, older relatives were able to tell stories about the wretchedness of life in their native Norrland. But now it was time for a prosperous Sweden. Great fortunes were made when iron ore and wood were exploited for industry and export. German influence was growing—as the result of victory from the war 1870–1—and French receding.

Strindberg was critical. His enthusiasm for things German, cultivated during the period of *The Father*, had faded. At this time, Nietzsche was an influence, with his love-hatred of Germany and his passion for France. Sweden was led by conservative governments. In June 1889, the so-called Muzzle Law was passed, which provided penalties for sedition against the law or lawful authority. The government wanted to go even farther and legislate against every kind of sedition that threatened social order. These laws were directed against the Socialists.

In the new *Somnambulist* poem, Strindberg describes himself taking a walk through Stockholm, past hostile eyes. He goes to the house on Norrmalmsgatan where he was married, reminisces about the wedding, the sparkling wine, the affectionate glances. The curtains in the window are darkened by smoke, and sounds of raucous singing are heard from inside. He has a vision of himself in his old study, where the paper is peeling off the walls. He sees himself, writing, with a trembling hand, but the pen does not leave the least trace on the empty sheets 'white as bleaching linen'. He is witnessing a madman, a deranged person who *believes* he is writing, while being totally incapacitated:

> Se, nu lyfter han handen opp
> liksom ville han tanken giva
> ordets levande luftiga kropp.
> I sitt bläckhorn han ivrigt doppar—
> se, nu vänder han ansiktet till—
> dödmans ögon, stora som koppar,
> stirra mörkt som en enda pupill,
> när mot namnen bekant han nickar,
> pekar tankfullt på verket sitt:
> och ur halsens kotor han hickar:
> 'Ser du, jag börjar att skriva vitt!'

> *See, now he raises his hand*
> *as if he wanted to give the thought*
> *the living airy body of the word.*
> *Eagerly dips his pen in the inkwell—*
> *see, now he turns his face—*
> *a deadman's eyes, large as cups,*
> *stare darkly like one single pupil,*
> *as he nods familiarly to the names,*
> *thoughtfully points at his work:*
> *and out of his bony throat he hiccups:*
> *'You see, I'm starting to write in white!'*

There is ample material available proving that Strindberg was insane, at least when he is being compared to the 'ordinary' person. But his works suffer from incurable health. The man behind the windowpane, whose creative powers have been exhausted and who turns a dead man's eyes towards us, is a self-portrait: but the author, too, who guides his pen with such a firm hand as he describes the poor madman, is Strindberg. Reading this, one understands how he could permit himself violent changes of mood and scoff at the 'hare-brain' who can deal with only one emotion at a time. Ultimately, his poetic *oeuvre* was the bill of health that released him from every straitjacket which his wives or others would recommend. The work evolved out of the chaos that was threatening him, and the more turbulent this became, the stronger was his need to escape into an imaginary universe created by his pen. It is not impossible that he, himself, helped to agitate those vortices, knowing that his wild travels through them brought release. When he was writing, he was not only in control of imaginary destinies, but also of his own life, which provided the material for the writing.

4

Hesitantly, and with feelings of chilly contempt for her husband, Siri came to Runmarö after all. Strindberg was now working on a major new project, another novel with an island setting. He told his publishers that it was going to be 'my *Workers of the Sea* on a grand scale'—thus he was competing with Victor Hugo—and that it would rehabilitate him as 'an author and in other respects'.

Most of Strindberg's works were written at one stretch, without interruption. He trusted his intuition and had learned to regard it as a natural gift. The new novel, *In the Offing*, ran into problems right from the start. Its hero Axel Borg is a bizarre caricature of Strindberg himself. Being endowed with a superhuman brain and nervous capacity, he is one of 'the great', yet simultaneously the most pitiful little snob, waxing his black moustache, wearing almost feminine garb and a gold bracelet in the shape of a serpent, which plays a part in his attempts to control his fellow men by suggestion and hypnosis.

When the action begins, Axel Borg, after outstanding achievements in the natural sciences—he has a row of foreign decorations in his suitcase—abandons that career and accepts an appointment as a Supervisor of Fishery in the Stockholm Archipelago, his task being to find a remedy for the shrinking trade.

It feels like the setting of a tragi-comic opera. In the introductory chapter, Borg has a confrontation with the local people during a trip across icy seas in an open yawl. The wind rises, and Borg, who has never sailed before, decides that the situation is critical and puts himself in command—he takes the tiller from the experienced seamen in the boat. He immediately acquires the ability to take bearings and calculate wind and waves and takes the yawl back into port—truly a miracle. When this has been accomplished, he falls down in a faint.

Strindberg was certainly aware that Axel Borg's feat was an absurdity. He had intermingled two different genres, letting Borg perform one of Alrik Lundstedt's daydreams, allowing his superman to win where no victory was possible. The sailing trip should have been a comic routine—Chaplin, who moves us to laughter and tears by maintaining a gentlemanly pattern of behaviour in situations where its absurdity is evident, would have recognized the situation. He would never have fallen into the temptation of letting the 'gentleman' emerge victorious. With such an opening, the novel could do nothing but grind to a halt.

In the course of the summer, Strindberg tried to get it moving again, but in vain. He filled entire chapters with descriptions of the natural life of the islands, lecturing on fish, rocks and birds. He sent for Brehm's *Life of the Animals* and a great number of volumes on fishing and minerals. The novel refused to take root, and Strindberg distracted himself by various schemes which, like the theatre in Denmark, were designed to solve all his problems simultaneously.

One of these was to send the French Academy a study entitled 'Swedish Contributions to French Culture' (he had written an essay with that title), and instantly gain a scholarly reputation, possibly even membership of the Academy. Bonniers was to publish the study in a *de luxe* edition, dedicated to the Alliance Française. Then Bonnier and Strindberg would call on the President of France and present him with a copy, whereafter they would soon receive the red ribbon of the Légion d'Honneur. Strindberg claimed that one of his reasons for this project was to compensate Bonnier for the 'ignominy' he had had to suffer for Strindberg's sake. Quite understandably, the publisher refused Strindberg's offer, which would have cost him a pretty penny.

In late summer, Strindberg abandoned the novel. 'My great poetic udder is running dry', he wrote to the publishers on 18 September.

5

That month, the family moved from Runmarö to Sandhamn, and when, in November, the sound started to freeze over, they went to Stockholm and rented a furnished apartment in an old Crown forester's house, Jakobsberg by Hornskroken—no. 51, Hornsgatan—near the terminal of the steam-powered streetcar line that had been opened in 1887. It was a long way from the Stockholm Strindberg had known: the area, Söder, was probably relatively unfamiliar to him, and it was still a kind of exile. But the rent was low, a mere 40 kronor a month.

The winter was a restless time for Strindberg: he was full of impulsive notions—one of them being the founding of a theatre in Stockholm. The atmosphere made it difficult for him to work at home. He spent much time in the city's taverns, looking up old friends and acquiring new ones. His descriptions of the situation became ever more extravagant. On 16 January 1890, he gave Geijerstam, with whom he had kept in touch, despite the latter's lame support in the Personne affair, this report:

I have impoverished both of my brothers, raided Eva's savings account, am unable to pay for the children's school which has already started, have endless unpaid bills, have been boozing since 2 January and have to associate with people who compromise me, hanging out in alleys and on streetcorners, outside pawn shops and money-lenders' offices, in one word, probably damaged my reputation so gravely that I give up hope for a decade to see a Government position come my way.

That 'Government position' was one of his obsessions: just as the man of genius, Axel Borg, in his novel, takes a job as a Supervisor of Fishery, Strindberg fantasized about various civil service posts that would solve his financial problems.

Nevertheless, his life was not without its joys, his skies not as dark as he wanted others to believe. The Dramatic Theatre was rehearsing *Master Olof* with Gustaf Fredriksson, possibly the greatest character actor of the day, in the title role. In his anxiety before the first night, Strindberg made a number of more or less inebriated trips into the city. It was at that time, 11 March, that he reported his visit to a whore in his first home after his marriage, mentioned in Chapter 4—a symbolic eradication of Siri. 'Came home at 6! Feel like a ghost today, existence disgusts me,' he wrote to Geijerstam the morning after. But he attended the première with great success, and was called on stage six times. Karin and Greta were there, deeply impressed, as Karin Smirnoff put it, when their father 'under loud salvoes of applause appeared on stage and bowed and received the big laurel wreaths that were hoisted up from the orchestra pit'. Strindberg never lost track of those wreaths: time and again, he gave instructions about their storage and forwarding to various addresses. They were his 'decorations' with a mystical aura, and they often appeared in his writing. This became one of his key scenes—to be crowned with a laurel wreath which is immediately snatched away again, or transformed into a crown of thorns.

The play was performed on the royal stage in its de-politicized verse form. Branting, writing about it in *Social-Demokraten*, stressed that the prose version was the better play, and that Gert Bookprinter, the revolutionary, had been tamed and 'made presentable'. After the first night, Strindberg was guest of honour at a banquet at the Hotel Rydberg, where the editor-in-chief of *Dagens Nyheter*, Vult von Steijern, made a speech. Strindberg proposed a toast to Ludvig Josephson who had staged the original *Master Olof* nine years before.

Early in the spring, Strindberg acquired a new young friend, twenty-year-old Birger Mörner. They met one evening in the cellar of the Grand Hotel—a favourite haunt from the early 1880s—and after the gaslight had been extinguished and the tavern closed, the two men walked across the ice of Riddarfjärden to Strindberg's lodgings, where they drank Benedictine and conversed in whispers so as not to wake the children. Mörner came from an old aristocratic family. One of his ancestors had imported Jean Bernadotte to be Sweden's Crown Prince in 1810, and Strindberg often joked about it. Mörner did not possess Heidenstam's genius, but became a more constant friend. He was an exceptionally handsome man.

Strindberg started looking for an apartment of his own, but the ones he examined convinced him, as he told Geijerstam, that in them he 'would commit suicide or die of starvation from fear of the communal dining-room and its menu'. Once again, the islands were the answer. In April, he moved out to Boo on Värmdö, and from there, in May, back to Runmarö. His family joined him there. It was the last summer they would spend together.

2

Strindberg picked up *In the Offing* again and managed to finish it. On 7 June, he sent the final chapters to Bonniers, claiming that this was 'a tremendous book, in my new grand Renaissance style' and drawing attention to the 'grandeur' of the last chapter. He had realized what was wrong with Axel Borg, the superman: he was not a winner—Strindberg had thought of calling the novel *The Master*—but a great, heroic, tragic loser.

In the chapters Strindberg had managed to finish the previous summer, Borg had incurred the enmity of the local population whose life and fishing he was supposed to be reforming. Two summer guests had arrived on the island, the elderly wife of a councillor of the exchequer and her daughter Maria—who thus bears the same name as the wife in *A Fool's Apology*. A love affair ensues between this girl and Borg, in which Strindberg repeats episodes from his own marriage, with the significant variation that Borg is a hypnotist and miracle-worker who controls his beloved with the same panache as he does wind and weather in the opening scene.

Now Strindberg took the action forward. Axel Borg's recommendations on the fishery prove successful. He seduces Maria and then goes to a ball, wearing all his decorations, on a navy vessel anchored offshore—a cannon-studded symbol of masculinity. After Maria leaves, hostility against Borg mounts again, and he gains a dangerous enemy in a Bible-peddler whose fate is intertwined with his own. In his growing isolation, Borg shows signs of psychic dissolution and starts experimenting with drugs, which does not improve his situation. He feels symptoms of persecution mania awakening within him, and his sense of claustrophobia assumes clearly pathological forms. Even the sea seems to constrict him. The 'blue, turpentine green, grey ring' of the horizon changes in his imagination to a prison yard and causes him the pain of the prison cell. He starts yearning for death.

Strindberg provided Axel Borg with a prominent father, a celebrated topographer who had participated in the construction of Göta Canal and the first railways. Poring over the map of Sweden, and destined to change the physiognomy of entire landscapes by the opening of new channels of transportation, he became used to seeing everything from above, which gave him a sense of power and a tendency to overestimate his ego. Everything began to appear as in a bird's-eye view. Countries became maps; people, tin soldiers. He felt as if he had undertaken the remodelling of the entire globe, and his self-esteem grew to incredible proportions.

It is a brilliant description of the sense of power that modern technology gave its managers, generating the nineteenth century's optimistic world view, and also of Strindberg's own development. In the novel, Axel Borg pursues his father's path *ad absurdum*, and becomes an example of the dangers that lie in wait for the arrogant.

Borg indulges in ever wilder fantasies, planning the economic restructuring not only of Sweden, but of all of Europe. He wants to direct trade from Persia and India through Russia and Sweden—Karl XII's old plan; close off Mälaren so that Stockholm becomes a salt water city; and reintroduce Roman Catholicism so that the North is reunited with Rome and Europe and Lutheran sectarianism abolished. Latin is likewise reintroduced as the language of the educated class, and the Swedish peasant—the self-reliant type from Strindberg's Utopian period—becomes a world citizen, once again able to behold the beauty of image and sound that only the Mother Church is able to provide.

Axel Borg retains sufficient clarity of vision to realize that these plans, which he commits to paper, do not stand much of a chance of publication. He stores them in the drawers of his desk, just as his creator stored his plays. He then attempts other escape routes to freedom. By now, he is an insomniac, beset by fears of losing his mind, of being assassinated. He longs to be reunited with his dead mother, but paradoxically the thought of death awakens in him a desire to have a child.

The reader cannot tell whether the following events occur in reality or in a drug-induced vision, but in no time at all Borg constructs an incubator under a microscope, procures a female ovum from a maid on the island and fertilizes it with his own sperm. Through the microscope he sees how the spermatozoa crowd together and struggle to win the fight to begin a new race and thus 'perpetuate his disposition, graft his lively, creative spirit on to a strong, wild base'.

In a state of great excitement, Axel Borg sees how the fertilized ovum begins to divide. A homunculus is about to be generated, the magician's most challenging task—creating a human being—almost accomplished. A few years were to pass before Goethe entered Strindberg's life as a guiding spirit, but it is clear that Borg competes with Faust in this passage. He does not succeed. A slip of the fingers on the alcohol burner's screw extinguishes the already lit spark of life, and the pain in Borg's heart grows to 'a grief, grief over his dead child'.

But Borg's story does not end with the homunculus. On the day before Christmas Eve, a storm starts raging, and a ship is wrecked close to his dwelling. Very weak by now, he leaves the cottage in the morning and sees the vessel's cinnabar-red underside shine like a torn and bloody breast—an image of his own. Seagulls are screeching overhead, and in the shallows float many brightly dressed dolls with rosy cheeks and blue eyes staring up at the black sky: they are the ship's cargo—toys for the Christmas trade. Borg's warped mind perceives the dolls as children, sent by fate to compensate him for the loss of his homunculus. He picks up five of them, clutches them to his breast and carries them indoors. There is no more firewood, but he breaks up a bookcase, makes a fire in the open hearth, pulls up a sofa and places his wards on it. He starts undressing them, then notices that they are all girls, and allows them to keep on their chemises. He washes their feet, combs their hair, and feels that he now has something to live for. He stretches out on the floor and falls asleep, and that is where the maid finds him the next morning.

Realizing that he is almost done for, he decides to go to meet his fate. He launches a boat, hoists sail and heads out to sea. The last thing he glimpses on land is a Christmas candle burning in the customs official's cottage, scene of a recent murder. The thought of Jesus, whose birthday it is, makes Borg spit into the water—'that idol of all criminals and wretches'. He steers the boat out into the dark, towards a star between Lyra and the Corona Borealis.

The thought of Jesus preoccupies him a moment longer, and he thinks about the star above Bethlehem and utters a curse against the 'Christian sorcerers'. Then he realizes that the star he is setting his course by is Beta in the constellation Hercules, and the novel ends with an invocation to that hero of myth, with whom Borg feels he is about to be united:

Moral ideal of Hellas, god of strength and wisdom, who slew the Lernean

hydra with a hundred heads, cleaned the Augean stables, caught the man-
eating mares of Diomedes, tore the girdle off the amazon queen, and
brought Cerberus from the underworld only to be brought down by a
stupid woman who poisoned him out of sheer love, after he had, in his
madness, served the nymph Omphale for three years. . . .

The one who poisoned Hercules 'out of sheer love' was his wife Deianira,
who received from the centaur Nessus the salve that would ensure Hercules'
love for her. When she anointed his shirt with it, it stuck to his skin and
killed him. Axel Borg's story is a major attempt to discover significance in
classical myth. In Strindberg's imagination, Hercules appeared as the pagan
counterpart to Jesus, who never ceased to both entice and threaten
Strindberg. On the very last page of the novel, Strindberg introduced the
term 'self-incendiary': he was not unconscious of the fact that it was he who
had put on the Nessus-shirt and was now writing, burning to death. Like
Törner, Axel Borg tried to realize a superhuman plan, but perished in his
attempt, a madman and a suicide. At the same time, he was a true hero who
did not retreat from an act of daring, although he knew that his experiments
would lead to his death. Therein lies his greatness, and therein he resembles
Strindberg.

7

After the great effort involved in the completion of *In the Offing*, Strindberg
led a more peaceful existence during the rest of that summer. 'Have been
loafing with fishing rod and sailboat, to restore my head,' he told Geijerstam
on 9 July. He was also reading Balzac who became a lifelong friend. '*Voilà un
homme!* who writes for men,' he pronounced, perhaps without remembering
that he had, in his youth, used that French expression about the multi-
talented grocer who was to be the pillar of the future state. He was planning
a long sailing trip with Mörner and asked the latter, on 26 July, to purchase
for him a Småland harrier 'who goes for hare and fowl both, and bring the
animal when you come here'.

He asks Bonniers for 'a good prime artist's album', that is a sketching pad,
and starts drawing—islands and fir trees among other subjects—working
patiently and conscientiously. Göran Söderström calls the surviving sheets
'amazingly technically accomplished, with a restraint in expression that
gives them a serious and refined character'.

Strindberg had long planned a work on the nature of Sweden and its
people, a continuation of his French journey. The idea surfaced again that

summer, as a phase of his flight from the family. Vult von Steijern of *Dagens Nyheter*, who had assumed Rudolf Wall's old role as Strindberg's guardian and supporter, helped him with money for the trip and organized a collection among well-to-do readers of Strindberg; like Bonnier, these were probably interested in redirecting the great dynamo Strindberg towards nationalist and utopian activities. Nationalism was all the rage. Poets were reading Langbehn's 'Rembrandt als Erzieher' ('Rembrandt as Educator') and looking for their lost roots in their fathers' earth. There were gaps in the wall of ice which Strindberg claimed surrounded him: among his supporters were such different persons as the brandy king L. Smith (who contributed 300 kronor), the wholesale merchant J. F. Rossander (200), Rudolf Wall (300), Karl Warburg (400), General Consul Simon Sachs (300).

Strindberg set out on 10 September. Although he did not know it then, it was actually his final leave-taking from his family. The day before he had sent Siri a visiting card, probably from Stockholm, asking her to send 'first thing in the morning my black oilcloth overnight bag with the books in it and woollens and linens, the telescope, the snuff-brown trousers'. That, more or less, was the extent of his personal effects in the years to come.

He was heading north, proud of his 'Eastman's Kodak Hand Camera', a present from *Dagens Nyheter*. It had been put on the market in August 1888; Eastman had chosen Kodak as a name easily pronounced in any language. In Sweden, it had become available that same year, 1890. Strindberg was always quick to adopt technical innovations.

Setting a furious pace, he enjoyed sleeping in a new bed every night. He went down into the mine at Falun, crossed Lake Silja by steamer and reached Mora. By then he had taken sixty photographs and was 'tired, dirty, lonely, clothes rotting from sweat'. He broke the journey there and went back south to visit Birger Mörner in Lund. From here, he wrote to Ola Hansson, who had enquired about his methods of writing, saying that he had nothing to say because his work grew 'freely in his head, like grapes, or mould'. This hastily formed simile put too much emphasis on spontaneity: it was no ingenuous hand that led Axel Borg down to the beach and those dolls! From Lund, he proceeded north again but at a slower pace, reassuring Vult von Steijern, his sponsor, that he was getting the 'incredible material' in hand. In Västergötland he climbed Billingen, as Linnaeus had once done, and gazed across the plain and its flat-topped mountains. In Norrköping, he took a 'Strindberg steamer' home—his brother Oscar was still in charge of their father's business.

From Vänersborg, Strindberg wrote to Siri and told her to look for accommodation for herself and the children. 'I am going to live by myself this winter, wherever that will be. The children need not be told this. In eight days I'll be in Stockholm, and ask to be spared any personal meeting.'

On 6 November, he moved to Brevik on Värmdö, rented a grand piano, and took his meals with the farm foreman. Towards the end of the month, Siri and the children, following Strindberg's wishes, rented a small wooden house on the estate of Lemshaga, just over a kilometre from Gustavsberg. The house was hard to keep warm in the winter; it was where Siri began her life alone. One evening, before lighting the oil lamp—to avoid any telltale expression on her face—she informed her oldest daughter that she and Strindberg were getting a divorce. 'Won't Daddy ever come home again?' the eleven-year-old asked, and received the reply: 'Never again.' Siri thought that Karin had taken the news badly and that her question was proof of this: as a matter of fact, the child suddenly felt safe and secure. Although Strindberg loved his children and treated them very kindly, he had nevertheless struck fear into their souls. It must be dangerous for anyone to live close to such an emotional and intellectual powerhouse as Strindberg was. Had he known of his daughter's reaction, it would have caused him pain, but it is possible that he would have understood.

8

Divorce proceedings, which had been under discussion for more than three years, were now instituted. They proved to be a process that was degrading to both partners. By Swedish law the couple has to call upon their local clergyman to receive a warning and an admonition that it was wrong for them to live apart. On 19 December 1890, they were received by S. J. Kallberg, the rector of Värmdö, but it seems likely that only Strindberg had occasion to expatiate on his side of the matter. Kallberg, an extrovert, energetic man, turned out to be an old friend of Strindberg's father. During the subsequent proceedings, as they are recorded, one gets a definite sense of a well-oiled 'old boy' network; Siri, about to be divorced for a second time, and outspoken as well, had a hard time of it from the very beginning.

The next step was taken on 2 January 1891, when the Strindbergs appeared before the parish church council, whose chairman Kallberg was. Only after that could the judiciary—Värmdö district—begin to consider the matter. According to the record, Strindberg declared that the reasons he and Siri no longer lived together were 'temperamental differences, different approaches and attitudes in religious as well as in the other most important questions of life', which had led to 'increasing antipathy'. Siri admitted that she probably had 'due to her impetuous temper sometimes given reason for discord'. She said that she was ready to be reconciled, but if her husband insisted on divorce, she would accept it only as long as she were given custody of the children.

Such was the innocuous prologue, probably not too accurately reflected by the record. On 24 January the case was first heard in the district court. Strindberg was represented by a registrar from the circuit court of appeal, V. F. Winroth, while Siri appeared in person, accompanied by an attorney. She read a statement (preserved in draft form by Karin Smirnoff) in which she lodged a protest against the record. She explained that the rector had pleaded with her not to reject all guilt on her part, and thus she had admitted that she had sometimes given her husband a vehement reply. 'Whereupon I', Siri continued, 'turned to my husband and explained that I was certainly willing to apologize to him for that—then stretched out my hand as a gesture of reconciliation, but he did not accept it.'

After listening to Siri's protest, the all-male court decided not to include it in the record. In a letter of 30 January to Karl Nordström, Strindberg claimed in his customary hyperbolic way that Siri had been intoxicated on the occasion and 'talked gibberish. Was told to shut up! Offered her hand in reconciliation! I refused to accept. She received a specific warning from the clergyman who called her a whore! She was trying to flirt with him.'

David Norrman's treatise 'Strindberg's Divorce from Siri von Essen' demonstrates that Strindberg started the divorce battle with a gross insult. In 1887, Strindberg had called Marie David a vampire and a criminal. In *A Fool's Apology* he had represented her as an alcoholic, perverse, bisexual snake who seduces Axel's wife and tries to persuade her to have him committed to an asylum for the insane. Strindberg remembered that slander as soon as Marie David quite suddenly reappeared on the scene. She and Siri had not seen each other since 1886. Siri, financially hard-pressed, had written to her and asked for a loan; one day, in a mild blizzard, Marie's sleigh appeared in the courtyard. Karin Smirnoff tells us that she looked like a little 'gentleman' in her beaver hat and with a cigarette glowing somewhere in the depths of her tall fur collar. She came as a rescuing angel, Karin says, and looked like 'the sun itself' after all the dark times. But radiant as she seemed to the Strindberg children, she appeared as black, indeed blacker than ever, in the imagination of their father. Throughout his life, Strindberg reacted to sexual deviations from 'nature' with a horror that bordered on hysteria. It is possible that this was due to a fear of his own latent homosexuality, as Lidz and other psychoanalytically oriented scholars have claimed. At the same time he represented 'popular', 'decent', small-minded and judgemental views, the likes of which exist in every era, no matter how enlightened, lashing out in condemnation against everything that is not seen as *natural* and therefore *right*.

Strindberg convinced himself immediately that Siri and Marie David were conducting a 'tribadic ménage' at Lemshaga; that alcoholic orgies were the order of the day; that the children's physical and psychological health was in danger. Forgetting that *A Fool's Apology* was a novel about Axel's suspicions only, he now regarded its accusations as facts, and launched a campaign to drive out Marie and gain custody of the children. He wrote to friends and asked them to send him statements on Siri's and Marie's state of morals. He tried to persuade Karl Nordström to frighten Marie by means of an anonymous letter to the effect that Strindberg was distributing copies of her letters to Siri—love letters, in other words—and he started using Eva Carlsson, still in service with Siri, as a spy and informer. He had no qualms about blackmailing poor Eva by promising to take care of her son Albin— whose upkeep she had managed to pay, all these years, out of her minimal wages. She did, indeed, put her signature under a statement compiled by Strindberg, an act she was to regret deeply.

Probably quite independently of Strindberg's campaign, Marie David left Lemshaga in February and went back to Paris. On 24 March, the divorce case came up again in the district court, and a judicial separation was granted. Siri was given custody of the children, and Strindberg agreed to a support payment of 100 kronor a month—a disgracefully small amount, considering that his income during the 1880s had averaged about 10,000 kronor a year. However, it does seem more reasonable in view of his finances at the time. During the past year, he had found it difficult to write. The upheavals in his life had been too great. All he had managed was a couple of stories for *Swedish Fates and Adventures*, among them 'The Wake at Tistedalen' about the death of Karl XII, a king who preoccupied Strindberg all his life.

The funds for the journey through Sweden had been exhausted, and he was unable to meet his obligation to the sponsors—to describe what he had experienced. He was alone in Brevik, and on 27 March 1891, three days after the judicial separation, his letter to Birger Mörner in Lund broke all records in terms of a heartbreakingly graphic description of misery. The district police superintendent had visited him to tell him that his contract for room and board was to end on 1 April.

> I have some provisions here, so I'm getting by. But I miss the quilt, which belongs to my landlord! Thus, begging for: one quilt, large, at 8 to 10 kronor—. My library will be auctioned off for 175 kronor. If someone buys it then, I'll be all right. For if the 175 are paid now, the books will be taken anyway, eight days later, to pay for something or the other. Well, I have been holding my breath all winter, unable to complain until recently.

Not quite true: he had kept up his customary complaints all winter, directing at least one of them to Mörner.

Yet it is not surprising that Mörner and his friend Bengt Lidforss, a brilliant young scientist whom Strindberg had befriended the previous autumn, were deeply shocked by the letter, unfamiliar as they still were with

Strindberg's vocabulary. Bengt Lidforss sent 175 kronor to save the books, and Mörner rushed to Brevik where he found (as he told later) Strindberg in a state of 'highly developed persecution mania'. He was also given to understand that Strindberg's diet during the most recent months had consisted of oatmeal, Baltic herring and plain herring. The delicacies Mörner had brought with him did not please the author as they 'were too great a change from what he had grown accustomed to'. It should be pointed out that Strindberg had written to Mörner a few days before the visit that he was afraid he would soon share Axel Borg's fate—that he had perceived in himself 'approaching symptoms of general dissolution, persecution mania, hysterical yearning for the children; attacks of weeping in public!' Small wonder that a young man, being told such things by an older, eminent authority, took them at face value. As for Strindberg's diet during the winter, his hostess at Brevik, Mrs Anna Dahlquist, reported that after his early morning walk, Strindberg took an 8 o'clock breakfast consisting of

> bread, butter, cheese, reindeer meat, 4 boiled eggs, milk, coffee, and zwieback. . . . He often asked me: What are we having for dinner? He was served fish a couple of times a week, and occasionally boiled chicken or roast spring chicken. Otherwise, he ate steaks, escalopes, meatballs, with peas and pancakes and soups, etc. He was fussy about coffee—it was rarely quite right.

Strindberg then accompanied Mörner to Lund and Copenhagen. Lidforss was a particular attraction. During the spring, Strindberg had conducted a correspondence with him that was unrivalled in its frankness and intensity. Strindberg had embarked on a passion for the natural sciences that was to last for several years. Lidforss was an ideal partner: he told Strindberg that his works had 'impressed him for life'. 'Ever since my brain-atoms have started forming phalanxes that generate thought, it has been your *oeuvre* in particular that determines their rate of oscillation', Lidforss wrote to Strindberg on 5 March and received on 1 April a long reply, enthusiastic to the point of incoherence, containing scientific hypotheses and notions just as original and bold as those evolved by Axel Borg.

When Mörner and Strindberg took the steamer from Värmdö to Stockholm, they discovered that Siri was on the same boat. As they were drinking coffee in the saloon, they saw her walk past the deck window. Strindberg immediately sketched a situation for a play: steamer stuck in ice, two people brought together who are no longer permitted to meet. . . . In Stockholm, he asked Mörner to act as a look-out. Both Siri and he stayed below deck, afraid to come across each other. At last, Siri appeared, an elegant, supple figure in her close-fitting black overcoat. Strindberg looked at her receding back, Mörner tells us, and said, under his breath: 'How beautifully—she—walks!'

38 Strindberg at Värmdö-Brevik, 1891

Marie David returned to Lemshaga, and Strindberg, returned from his happy conversations with Lidforss, appealed against the court's decision, demanding custody of the children. As a result, the Strindbergs were called before the church council on 8 May. The day before, Strindberg, full of spiteful glee, informed Karl Nordström that destiny 'which has sometimes kicked me in the arse' was smiling on him now: Marie, who was drunk on the boat to Gustavsberg, had fallen off the couch and been examined by doctors. 'That's a bit of a victory.'

On 8 May, Siri did not appear. She had scornfully rejected Strindberg's accusations and pointed to his failure to provide the maintenance payments set by the court. Strindberg, on the other hand, arrived armed with a voluminous petition, complete with four appendices and affidavits, in which Siri was accused of alcoholism and neglect of her children, and a detailed account was given of Marie David's consumption of alcohol and her 'suspect relations with other women'.

Strindberg was quite clearly resorting to dishonest means, of which Eva Carlsson's affidavit, written by himself, was only one of many. He justified them by saying that he wanted to save his children, but at the same time he was denying them the support he owed them. His actions are out of touch with reality. He was not in the least prepared to assume the care of his children: all these years, they had been Siri's sole responsibility. A measure of his lack of any realistic consideration—typical of all his enthusiasms—can be found in a letter to Leopold Littmansson in Paris, written in February, at a moment when be believed that he would obtain custody of the children. He wrote that he was thinking of moving to Paris, where he would find employment as a tutor, or as a foreign affairs editor of a French newspaper, or, at worst, as doorman of a large hotel. 'Doormen make lots of money,' he added by way of explanation.

Nevertheless, Strindberg's grasp on reality had not grown so weak that he could not realize that his petition of 8 May could lead to a prosecution for libel. Homosexuality was a punishable offence, and a person who wrongly accused someone else of it could be sentenced to six months in gaol. Marie David did actually pick up this new weapon she had been given. Judging by his letters, at least, Strindberg was more disturbed than ever. He claimed that he was sleeping with a loaded shotgun by his bedside and that the islanders hated him (he had moved back to Runmarö). He nursed the idea of 'pacifying' Siri by threatening to remarry: on 24 May, he told Vult von Steijern 'after mentally dictating a great number of farewell letters from this life I would like to end' how he had already chosen a beautiful and graceful dark girl—whom he had met on the steamer to the island—to be his wife and the blonde, fading Siri's dangerous rival. Only an 'endless compassion for my children' was holding him back.

The church council proved receptive to Strindberg's arguments and decided on 22 May that Marie David 'by actions to be taken by the appropriate authorities' should be separated from Mrs Strindberg if the latter wanted to retain custody of the children. Marie David and Siri, however, were preparing a counter-attack. In July, Marie David sued Strindberg for libel, and started a collection of affidavits to match his: among others, Edvard Brandes stated that he had never uttered any pejorative opinions about her 'morals or way of life', contrary to Strindberg's claim. Siri obtained testimonials from Södermalm's secondary girls' school about her daughters, Karin and Greta. Trustworthy local people testified that Siri was a respectable woman. Things did not look too good for Strindberg, and they were to get worse.

In June, Siri and Marie David moved to Sandhamn, and on Mid-summer's Day, Marie David, accompanied by the former Crown pilot Johan August Wickberg and Siri's new domestic helper, Alma Jonsson—Eva Carlsson had, of course, been dismissed—took a trip to Runmarö, arriving at Strindberg's cottage just as he stepped out on to the porch. According to Marie David, Strindberg ordered her to leave his house immediately, and then struck her in the back so that she reeled against the wall of the cottage: then he grabbed her by the shoulders and bodily threw her down the porch steps. The pilot Wickberg testified that this was more or less exactly what had happened, and that after the fall Marie David lay prone in the yard. Alma Jonsson stated—all of this was according to the police report—that Strindberg had struck Miss David in the chest and that she had fallen backwards down four or five steps.

Thus Strindberg had to face a further prosecution—for bodily assault. Following the adage that attack is the best defence, he outwitted his adversary by lodging a complaint against Marie David for 'violation of domicile', on 22 July. He hastened to add that the pilot, on this occasion, was drunk, and that Marie David's insulting language had caused him to 'in my irritation, push her out of my lodgings'.

It is unlikely that we will ever know how much of a 'push' that was; this scene and the one at Eichbühl are the only ones on record in which Strindberg lost control to the extent of striking a woman. The immediate consequence of Marie David's visit was that Strindberg conceded defeat; perhaps he had had enough of marital warfare. As early as 14 July, he had told Vult von Steijern that he was not 'yet enough of a barbarian to commit murder; beginning to prefer the status of victim'—meaning, no doubt, that he preferred Siri to win.

He moved to another island, Dalarö, the haunt of an entire colony of painters, all of them members of Sweden's Artists' Association, among them Anders Zorn, Richard Bergh, Alf and Gerda Wallander, Eva Bonnier, Ernst Josephson, and Robert Thegerström. Strindberg obtained a quantity of clay and took up sculpture in that medium, while participating in an exuberant social life, laced with alcohol and sexual tensions. As always, he found it easy to live among artists. For months, he continued to speak of his feeling of loss in regard to his children, and about his immediately impending suicide—more and more mechanically, as time went by. Whoever has undertaken to write about nis life is bound to wonder whether the wisest course would not be to ignore all mentions of suicide, as they easily distort the picture of his actual situation.

In the late summer of that year, the 'suicides' stood in particularly vivid contrast to his *joie de vivre* and his love affairs. For some time, his cousin Gotthard Strindberg became his confidant and ran messages for him (a common enough combination), and Gotthard's beautiful wife Martha became the object of his interest: he sculptured a portrait of her. In August, Gotthard received one of Strindberg's usual alarmist letters, followed by another the next day in which he was asked to contact Strindberg's tailor about his dress suit and to compliment the man on 'the new suit he sent, it's an excellent fit'. Strindberg dispatched orders for 'Lysholm' aquavit, 'prime Java', swooned at Mrs Thegerström's feet, and became the object of a 'ravishing' neighbour maid's seductive wiles. A few days later, he considered a *redingote* or frock-coat had higher priority than the dress suit, and ordered the tailor to cut it in the French rather than the German fashion, as he was moving to Paris. All this time (on 6 August, he remitted 150 kronor for the dress suit) Siri did not receive a penny. However, it was clear that he had not forgotten his family; in any case, this would have been hard to do, as the next court date, 8 September, was rapidly approaching. On 12 August, he told Gotthard that he was considering giving up the fight and allowing Siri to keep the children. Should he, however, take his life—he told Gotthard—the latter should inform the children that 'their father never abandoned them'. 'Tell them', the letter continued, 'that during the decade I was alive, that is, had an income, I made sacrifices and worked for them, denied myself nice clothes and the usual enjoyments of life, almost ruined my talent by over-work—and when I no longer had anything to offer, I was discarded.'

The author who had discarded his own wife now represented himself as the outcast: an incredible, yet in some ways unmistakably human quirk.

After crayfish feasts during which Strindberg played the mandolin; after returns to the farcical humour of his youth—in a postscript to a letter to Thegerström of 13 August: 'Should you pass the Grand Hotel, look and see if I'm not still sitting there on the verandah'; after a grand supper at which he was the host, and after other similar festive activities which Strindberg himself subsumed in these words to Thegerström on 23 August: 'A resting-point in my hurricane life, which I'll remember like a truly radiant dream of high summer'—Strindberg embarked, on 24 August, on the steamer *Njord*, in fact in a northerly direction. It was his intention to travel via Storlien and

Bergen to London and Paris. Come what may, he had to be out of the islands by 8 September, the date set by the court.

The journey became a continuation of the 'great Swedish journey' the previous year, if even more of a parody of an 'educational tour'. In Östersund, Strindberg was interviewed by the editor of the paper *Jämtlands-Posten*, Viktor Hugo Wickström, an old acquaintance from Uppsala days, who noted that he was 'dressed with great care in brown travelling clothes and a soft felt hat, which was almost artistically arranged to frame his abundant, already grey-speckled hair'. During this interview, which he vehemently rejected later, Strindberg supposedly replied to the question why he was leading the life 'of a hermit':

> I look for solitude because I love people too much. There are so many who have warm feelings for me, and my heart fills up with sympathy for them to a point where my personality almost merges into theirs. I have to pull away from them, otherwise I would be unable to do my own independent work. After enjoying myself with my friends, I hear within myself a reproachful voice that gains strength and finally shouts so loudly that I cannot silence it, 'You aren't working, you don't have time to enjoy life this way. Out, into the wilderness, out and away to places where you can work, undisturbed!'

Strindberg stayed in Östersund until 31 August, and then went on to spend six days with the wholesale merchant and sawmill owner Magnus Forssell, in Sundsvall. There, festivities were held in his honour which he described in a letter to Robert Thegerström as 'Roman *fin-de-siècle* orgies'—'with good wine and bad women, stoked-up steamboats and Arabs (real ones) hanging out in front of the taverns, an orchestra (his own) and hetairae'. This happened at the time of the great boom era for the timber bosses of Norrland. And this was where Curry Treffenberg had put down in 1879 the strike that had been reflected in *The Red Room*. Now Strindberg was welcoming the embraces of Treffenberg's employers, without revealing his thoughts. During one convivial evening he played the bass drum in the above-mentioned orchestra.

On 8 September, Marie David and her attorney appeared in the district court. As Strindberg failed to appear, his action for violation of domicile was void, and he was fined 10 kronor for his absence. Marie David held a strong hand in her libel suit: aided by a number of statements and affidavits, her lawyer was able to prove that Strindberg had slandered his client. To Strindberg's assertion that he had acted out of concern for his children, the lawyer remarked that he had refused to send support payments and thus subjected those children 'to the greatest need'. Miss David's intervention had been a magnanimous one. The lawyer summed it up:

> That Marie David has helped, and is still helping, his wife, and is thus

making her more independent of Mr Strindberg's whims and tyranny, Mr Strindberg is unable to forgive, and therein lies the true cause for the hatred with which he persecutes Miss David, and for the false accusations he has disseminated about her. In addition, he has attacked and beaten her on last Midsummer's Day, and she is filing a separate suit against him for that brutal violence done to a woman.

This, then, was the suit Strindberg had feared. Marie David demanded 1,000 kronor damages and compensation for the cost of the proceedings. The court ordered Strindberg to appear on the next date which was fixed for 27 January 1892.

Strindberg spent the winter of 1891–2 in Djursholm where he rented a furnished apartment and employed Eva Carlsson for some time as his housekeeper. Now and then, he met his children who were living in Stockholm, and gave them valuable presents—a watch, a camera outfit, a microscope, an electric machine 'that buzzes and hums worse than a steam engine'—but still refused to provide support payments.

Djursholm was a rapidly expanding suburb, designed according to the still novel principle that tried to combine the amenities of both city and country. It was fashionable, prosperous and liberal in outlook. Its inhabitants were eager to demonstrate that they stood above the petty image of Strindberg projected by the conservative press, and that they appreciated the genius in their midst. The town's leading figure, Sven Palme, director of the Thule insurance company which Strindberg had attacked during his stint as insurance editor, opened his home to the author, and his beautiful and lively Finnish wife Hanna, née von Born, possibly opened her arms to him as well. He sculpted a bust of her as well as a small statue of her son Gunnar, the future father of Olof Palme.

He did not appear in court in January and was threatened with a heavy fine, should he continue to fail to respond. After further legal manoeuvres, in the course of which Strindberg admitted, by proxy, that he had pushed Miss David, extenuating circumstances being that she had come to his domicile with the intention to aggravate him, and that the stairs down which she fell had only two steps, a lenient verdict was pronounced on 19 July 1892. There is reason to believe that the court was secretly sympathetic towards Strindberg. He was fined 75 kronor for having circulated 'libellous verses' about Miss David, plus 15 kronor for the assault—which, according to the verdict, had been aggravated by the fact that it was committed on a public holiday. Marie David was awarded 50 kronor damages (instead of the 1,000 she had asked for) plus her court costs. All in all, the affair cost Strindberg some 500 kronor.

9

Strindberg expected his life experiences—particularly the painful ones—to pay dividends in terms of his writing. After the divorce, he had considerable 'capital' at his disposal. He started working on this material in November 1891, and during the following seven months he wrote seven plays, each one of which was somehow related to the divorce. Then Nemesis struck him from an unexpected direction. He started a fairytale play, *The Keys of the Kingdom of Heaven*, hoping to repeat the success of *Lucky Per's Journey*. Almost immediately, he reached an impasse, as he had in the case of *In the Offing*. In mid-December 1891 he wrote to Vult von Steijern that he was 'lame and barren', blaming separation from his children who 'constituted my only interest in life'—'the only tie that kept me in touch with reality'.

Probably during the previous summer, in Djursholm, he had written a short story, 'The Silver Marsh', in which he described his life after the divorce. The story deals with a taxidermist who spends two consecutive summers (as Strindberg did in 1890 and 1891) on an island in the Stockholm Archipelago. During the first summer, he is accompanied by his wife and children, but the marriage is in the doldrums, and the locals see the wife wandering around by herself at night near the boathouse. In the story, Strindberg was suddenly able to give some indication of compassion for Siri, but only in that disguise—never openly.

The commissioner explores the island and makes his way to a lake, the Silver Marsh, a mysterious place hedged around with popular superstitions. He starts fishing there, and catches bigger fish than he ever has before. However, various misfortunes then befall him, which he sees as punishments for having intruded on forbidden ground, flouting a popular taboo. One day, he gets lost in the woods, and is afraid that he will not find his way home. Then he remembers a saying from his childhood: turn your clothes inside out, and you'll find the way home. Being a rationalist, he hesitates to give in to this childish impulse, but finally decides to give it a try.

> The first sensation after this change of costume [Strindberg wrote], was one of discomfort, constriction, awkwardness; and the impression his body had made on the lining side of his coat, now became like a wax impression that he carried on his surface. This gave him the illusion of having been duplicated, of carrying himself and being responsible for the one he was now wearing. On the other hand, he had been relieved of something; he had skinned himself and was now carrying the sweat-warm hide, the way one carries one's summer coat over one arm; but in that hide there was also something of the soul's inner bark, and he experienced a sensation of psychic nakedness, lightness, freedom, which increased his ability to feel, think and exercise his will. Thus he felt he was flying forwards, straight through tree-trunks, floating over the swamps, wafting through the juniper bushes, running through the mountain creeks.

In a moment, he finds himself at home, but before the children embrace him on the hillside, he has had time to turn his coat right side out again, and feels calm in the knowledge that he has returned to his normal self.

The story is related to 'The Romantic Sexton of Rånö'. The forbidden fish correspond to the forbidden organ stop, the magic button. Both the sexton and the commissioner incur guilt, and it seems reasonable to assume that this pattern reflects Strindberg's own feelings upon having exploited traditionally taboo matters in *A Fool's Apology* and in the naturalistic plays.

At the same time it is worth noticing that both Alrik Lundstedt and the commissioner are pioneers who enter previously closed domains with extraordinary results as a consequence. Alrik's imagination gains new courage, when he is no longer afraid even of death; the commissioner finds his way home when he taps the wisdom contained in popular superstition. Both of them delineate Strindberg's own artistic progression.

When the commissioner returns the following summer, he is alone. The misfortunes anticipated by the local inhabitants have occurred, and the idyll is over. He engages in occult speculations and fears for his sanity, like Axel Borg in *In the Offing*. 'It was as if, with the children, he had lost his guardian spirits.'

Even here one might, albeit cautiously, draw a parallel between him and Strindberg. For the latter, his separation from Siri and the children meant his expulsion from the only natural community he had experienced since childhood. He had exploited his marriage in his work, and thus sacrificed the happiness he had been dreaming of since early youth. Even if he was aware that this was his destiny, he could not avoid feeling guilty towards Siri, and his incessant, hateful accusations against her were intended to compensate for that guilt and to make it easier to bear.

Yet the divorce proved fatal even for his art. Siri and the children were his 'guardian spirits' in that they represented a connection with society at large. As long as he lived within a family circle, contact with reality was assured. Siri did not really understand his art and his originality, but simply by being there, close by, she represented an alternative. She and the children asked questions, had reservations, spoke up whenever he confused poetry and reality and prevented him from going astray emotionally.

He was to remarry twice, and he continued to make new friends. Ola Hansson once scornfully accused him of never being able to be on his own. But from this point on, his contacts did not entail necessity or obligation, did not demand any accommodation or concession on his part. They were freely chosen, and as soon as they got in the way of his art, he abandoned them. Only those friends remained whom he could meet on neutral ground, or who worshipped him in total submissiveness.

The seven plays written in the years 1891 and 1892 are lacklustre and lifeless, all their characters either black or white. Strindberg always ran that risk: his imagination related so closely to folktale and myth, in which good and evil always appear in their simplest form. But what gives the Captain, Miss Julie and Axel Borg life are the tensions within them, the battles they wage against themselves. In the new plays, we encounter heroes with not the slightest chink in their armour, redolent with self-righteousness. Instead of an inner struggle, we are presented with external, mechanical confrontations.

In *Debit and Credit*, the main character, Axel, is a famous and noble explorer who is surrounded by nothing but human vermin, parasites on his genius and his goodness. In *Mother's Love* we encounter a monstrous mother who stifles, vampirizes and degrades her daughter; in *The Bond*, a married couple in court—the husband being righteous, the wife, errant—and so on in the remaining plays. As complete moral excellence is made to adhere to a single figure, while the presentation proceeds in a naturalistic mode, the result is an incredible discrepancy between what Strindberg wants us to see and what we are, in fact, seeing. A folktale pattern emerges, but lacks the tone of folktales. The author pretends to be using an objective mode of presentation but ends up in the trivial and lifeless. He seems to be on his way to breaking new ground, but he has not yet learned its secrets.

It was the feeling of having suffered an artistic defeat that brought Strindberg back to painting, with far greater seriousness than before, during the spring and summer of 1892, when he returned to Dalarö. He painted the sea, both calm and stormy, in great bold sweeps, often with a low horizon and a wide and lofty sky above—almost a reflection of the artist's own face with its high forehead above the compressed features. Large, visionary spaces, interrupted only by the odd lighthouse or broom-beacon. The paintings point in the direction he was to follow, playing for higher stakes.

Strindberg was hoping to repair his financial situation by selling paintings, since there was not much hope of getting his plays performed. An exhibition was held in Birger Jarl's Bazaar in Stockholm and became a *succès de scandale*, one of many in his life. As expected, *Dagens Nyheter* took up arms in his favour, but the rest of the press made fun of the canvases, one wit suggesting that the painting *Snow-Mist at Sea* really represented a dirty bedsheet hung out to dry. No one perceived the deep originality and strength of these works; it was not until almost a century later that it attracted an attention comparable to that accorded to Ernst Josephson.

This setback became yet another reason for Strindberg to contemplate exile once again. The year before, he had been on his way to Paris in his new frock-coat: now he decided on Berlin instead. He was strongly aware of the necessity of artistic renewal. Ola Hansson in Germany urged him to come and wrote to him in July: 'Your arrival here will be greeted with pride and jubilation, here in Germany you will have more opportunities and win more sympathy than you can probably even imagine.'

Chapter Twelve

NEW HORIZONS

I

O N 30 SEPTEMBER 1892, Strindberg boarded the southbound express train in Stockholm. His choice of Germany as the country of his new exile was to a great extent determined by the interest shown in his work there, whereas his plays were not being performed in Sweden. *In the Offing* sold poorly. A young admirer, Emil Norlander, soon to become the leading impresario in Stockholm, had tried to put on *Miss Julie* in the spring, but the venture failed when the actress who had been offered the title role backed out at the last minute. Strindberg's notoriety for beating his wife and making a public exhibition of the most intimate details of his marriage did not help. The Swedes regarded the play as a 'vile trick', as Strindberg wrote, without much exaggeration, fifteen years later.

Germany was engaged in vigorous military and industrial expansion under the young Wilhelm II, and during these years there was a great deal of interest in cultural impulses from abroad, as well as a romantic yearning for the North and East. A number of artists and writers from Eastern Europe and Scandinavia passed through Germany towards world-wide fame. In 1890, *The Father* was performed at Freie Bühne, a dramatic enterprise which had been started in 1889 along the lines of the Théâtre Libre in Paris, with Dostoevsky, Ibsen, Zola, and Tolstoy, among others, in its repertory. The fact that *The Father* was banned by German official censorship stimulated further interest in its author.

On 3 April 1892, Freie Bühne put on *Miss Julie* with Rosa Bertens as Julie and Rudolf Rittner as Jean. As a result of protests from the audience, particularly from women, the play had to close after one performance, but a congratulatory telegram was sent to Strindberg at a gala held afterwards. Thus his two dramatic masterpieces had been seen in Germany's capital city, even if only within a fairly modest framework. They paved the way for him to come to Germany, gaining him admirers, a whole delegation of whom were there to greet him when he got off the train at Stettiner Bahnhof.

At first, Strindberg settled in the suburb of Friedrichshagen, which he described in his letters, according to his mood, as Friedrichsruhe, Friedrichshölle, and Friedrichshald—after Fredrikshald where Karl XII fell. Ola Hansson and Laura Marholm lived in Friedrichshagen, and Freie Bühne's headquarters were also located there; there were woods where Strindberg could walk in the mornings, and taverns where he could spend his evenings. During the summer on Dalarö he had experimented with colour photography, and one of his schemes at this time concerned the opening of a photographic studio in Berlin.

Ola Hansson and his wife had done more than anyone else to create publicity for Strindberg in Germany, but he immediately suspected them of using him for their own purposes. It did not take long for their friendship to turn sour. Strindberg and Ola Hansson would provide many slanderous caricatures of each other. While Strindberg depicts Hansson as one of a number of sterile parasites on his own burgeoning tree, Ola Hansson in his novel *Mrs Ester Bruce* presents Strindberg as the painter Ödmann who behaves in a rude and presumptuous manner in the taverns, examining every plate, sending back what does not please him, talking incessantly and—as the empty bottles accumulate—ever more incoherently: this was a portrait of Strindberg as a maniac, 'the brainless animal as genius'.

One of the causes of such animosity was that Strindberg had, right at the beginning of his stay in Germany, fallen into one of those traps he was wont to set for himself. On 13 September, he had written to Hansson from Dalarö that he had, 'in order to sustain life', painted pictures and sold them for ridiculously low prices, that the Swedes were 'laughing at my poverty', and that he would commit suicide were it not for the children. In other words, a fairly typical Strindberg letter. . . .

It is hard to know whether Ola Hansson was alarmed or not, as he later talked about how Strindberg on that occasion played 'his well-worn role of one who is persecuted and impecunious, but he was aware that Strindberg's letter could be used as a weapon in his own campaign against Sweden, and he took it to Maximilian Harden, one of the men behind Freie Bühne, who was just starting his journal *Die Zukunft*, soon to become famous, even notorious. Strindberg's letter appeared in its first issue of 1 October 1892, together with a biting commentary by Ola Hansson. Hansson spoke of Sweden's 'soul-destroying constriction', its pietism and suffragettism that were suffocating human rights and free thinking; he followed this with a plea to save Strindberg from the 'iron industry country' in the north, on the assumption that his article would cause an uproar among the inhabitants of Sweden as soon as it became known there. His article did result in a collection of funds for Strindberg, who had expected to arrive in Germany in triumph but now saw himself introduced as a beggar who had appealed to the compassion of his fellow men. Donations arrived at *Die Zukunft*'s editorial offices, making a total of 1,500 marks—not a great sum but Strindberg used it to pay off debts and it was enough to require his gratitude. During the following winter, he quite frequently played on the beggar theme and imagined—half seriously, half playfully—that he might be arrested for vagrancy after being presented publicly as a person who could not take care of himself.

In November, Strindberg moved to the centre of Berlin, first to a boarding-house on Neue Wilhelmstrasse and, a month later, to a two-room flat on Potsdamerstrasse. Winter brought a number of notable successes: the main one was a performance of *Creditors* at Residenz-Theater on 22 January with Rosa Bertens as Tekla, Rudolf Rittner as Adolf, and Josef Jarno as Gustav. This play about a triangular relationship and a psychic murder reminiscent of the one in *The Father* had been written at the same time as *Miss Julie*. The shocking, incredibly tense story of a divorced man who suffers a breakdown and murders his former wife's new husband without any visible weapon made a strong impression on both the German critics and on the public. A young man, Emil Schering, who attended the first night, was so moved that he decided to dedicate his life to translating Strindberg into German.

In the same month that *Creditors* was being performed in Berlin, *Miss Julie* had its première in Paris. Strindberg began to get a taste of international fame, and his letters turned into victory reports. He described Berlin as the city of his second birth and told Mörner that a turning-point in his 'tragi-comic life' was approaching. Naïvely, he added that Germany 'pays homage to foreign talent, honestly, without reservation, and without the least trace of envy'.

The tavern he frequented, in which Heine, Schumann, and E. T. A. Hoffmann had drunk before him, he named Zum Schwarzen Ferkel—At the Sign of the Black Pig. Its sign was three stuffed wine-skins hanging from squeaky and rusty iron chains, which caused Strindberg to remark one day: 'The pig is squealing a welcome to us!' The Ferkel was situated at the corner of Neue Wilhelmstrasse and Unter den Linden, but, like all the Berlin of that era, has disappeared without trace. It played a part comparable to the Red Room in Strindberg's life, being the frame within which he encapsulated his everyday life, as one of his drinking companions aptly put it. The tavern became a substitute for a home; not only did it provide food and drink, but it was possible to write there, send messages and take care of personal business. It was a place in which to talk, gossip and borrow money, and it acted as a kind of publicity office. Strindberg kept his guitar there. The Ferkel was one of many similar establishments in the nineteenth century which served as cultural institutions, along with museums, theatres,

salons and parliaments, and nurtured a great many of the political and
literary movements of the period.

In his novel *The Convent*, which describes his second marriage,
Strindberg portrays the Ferkel as labyrinthine and cosy with its stained-
glass windows, oaken booths, arches and a big hall in the medieval style. Its
official name was G. Türkes Weinhandlung und Probierstube, and Gustav
Türke, the owner, proudly offered 900 different kinds of alcoholic drinks.
His beautiful blonde wife, who served behind the bar, acted as a further
attraction.

The Ferkel was a place where Strindberg could satisfy his need to
associate with other talented people. The circle he joined consisted of
Edvard Munch whose exhibition in December 1892 scandalized Berlin; the
Finland-Swedish author Adolf Paul; a German physician, Carl Ludwig
Schleich, whose remarkable contribution to medical science was the
invention of local anaesthesia; the Polish musician and author Przybyszewski, who in his lively memoirs assures us that deep down all the drinking
friends really hated each other; the impassioned, violent German poet
Richard Dehmel, nicknamed 'Der wilde Dehmel' by Strindberg; and a
number of other men of similar stature, like the Danish poet Holger
Drachmann, the Norwegian painter Christian Krogh, Christian Sinding,
and so on. All were younger than Strindberg and regarded him as their
mentor; he, too, saw himself as the leader of their circle, and behaved
accordingly.

In time, he became involved in a number of dramatic complications with
many of the members of that circle, and his imagination revolved around
them for many years. Munch and Krogh painted portraits of him,
Przybyszewski, Paul, Schleich, and Lidforss wrote about him with both love
and hate. Jean Sibelius, who had studied in Berlin the previous year and
belonged to the same coterie, found it difficult to work in the city because of
the penetrating shrill whistles of the street urchins. There is no sign of any
such sensitivity on Strindberg's part, yet the noise of the tavern, the
consumption of alcohol and the subsequent hangovers, violent scenes,
intrigues and rivalries, kept him from his work as effectively as the street
urchins whistling kept Sibelius from his. The Berlin winter is one of the few
periods in Strindberg's life when his creative powers suffered because his
external existence preoccupied him completely. The failure of the previous
year's plays was also a contributing factor. Considering his normal pace of
production, he was, at this time, successful with works that he had written a
long time before.

2

As Max Nordau had stated, and Strindberg had agreed, sexual deprivation is as hard to endure as hunger for food. Strindberg had made Magister Törner in *Tschandala* a witness of this fact, among many others. According to Adolf Paul, women in Berlin saw Strindberg's misogyny as a sophisticated form of flirtation. Be that as it may, he was a success with them, and found time for several infatuations. One of these was with Gabrielle Tavaststjerna, a beautiful young actress, who was married to the Finland-Swedish poet Karl August Tavaststjerna whom Strindberg knew from his Dalarö days.

Another infatuation took root and led to a new marriage. On 7 January 1893, at a time when he was enjoying his greatest triumphs and was thus at his most attractive, Strindberg met, at a literary reception, twenty-year-old Maria Friedrike Cornelia Uhl (who was known as Frida); by the beginning of February, a passionate affair was under way.

Frida was the daughter of Friedrich Uhl, counsellor to the Court of Austria and publisher of the well-known Viennese newspaper *Wiener Zeitung*. She had received an education similar to Siri's, in convent schools in France, England, and Austria. Once again, affairs of the heart involved social advancement for Strindberg. At the time, Frida was in Berlin as a reporter on cultural affairs, enjoying a degree of freedom that was unheard of among young ladies of her class. Her father worried about her. She wrote for his newspapers—he was also an editor of *Wiener Abendpost*. She enjoyed the patronage of prominent cultural figures, and it was rumoured that she had had a love affair with Hermann Sudermann. Later, Strindberg accused her of having pretended to be a virgin, and claimed that he was too experienced a man to have been taken in by that pretence. The claim is dubious: just like Alrik Lundstedt, Strindberg was capable of making himself believe practically anything.

Frida combined all the traits Strindberg condemned in women. She was emancipated, ambitious and independent, yet her tastes in art were no more advanced than Siri's. Later she wrote a book about Strindberg and about her marriage to him. Its style is florid; there are long passages which are nothing but sheer invention, but then there are sudden flashes of insight: Frida definitely was the most intelligent of Strindberg's wives. In the book, she tried to suppress what her remaining letters clearly demonstrate—that it was she who at the beginning of their acquaintance took all the initiatives, and thus acted like a 'whore' according to Strindberg's moral code. She suggested meetings, walks and visits to museums, and she invited him to supper in her boarding-house room. She courted him as if she had been a young cavalier, giving him roses, tying his shoe-laces in the street, and finally surprising him with the first kiss. Strindberg was captivated by her.

39 Frida Uhl   40 Dagny Juel. Painting by Edvard Munch

41 *Jealousy*. Lithograph by Edvard Munch, 1896

Marcel Reja, the French writer and psychiatrist, who befriended Strindberg a couple of years later, wrote an article after his death in which he discussed Strindberg's attitude towards women. He claimed that Strindberg was doomed to unhappiness in his relationships with women, for two reasons. First, he jealously guarded his own ego, and tried to conceal his inner life from others. Second, his shyness, related to his natural reticence, made it imperative for him not to do the choosing but to be chosen. Reticence combined with a strong sexual urge meant that he was always attracted to women who were sufficiently forward to insist.

This is an acute observation. Strindberg the confessor and self-revealer is a myth. When he feels like confessing, he always disguises himself, while the purported self-portraits are designed to lead us on to false tracks. The maternal woman he claimed was his ideal could never come his way: she was unable to take the initiative that would have pierced his reticence and arrogance. Because of this he remained lonely, and his judgement of people was incredibly poor.

Siri had been an aggressive partner. Frida was even more so. In his novel about his second marriage—*The Convent*—Strindberg, like Frida herself, rewrites the facts to some extent, in order not to look too much like a kidnap victim. Yet the underlying pattern is obvious. One evening, at the beginning of their infatuation, they went to a restaurant, at Frida's suggestion. She chose an establishment where she was well known. She described herself as wearing a leopard-skin coat, with a silk scarf round her head. In the entrance hall of the restaurant, she slipped out of the coat to stand before Strindberg in a dark green dress which clung to her body like a snake-skin, coiling round her feet in a pointed train. According to her version, Strindberg blushed and there was something humble and imploring in his expression. The leopard does not appear in Strindberg's account of the same evening, but the tight-fitting green dress does. He tells us that he was unable to conceal his emotion, and scrutinized her figure as if trying to 'discover a hidden enemy with a spotlight'. 'Eros! now I am lost! he thought, and from that moment on, he was!'

Thus passion and hostility were awakened at the same time, and Strindberg was terrified of being despised as the weaker one, of seeing his protective walls crumble. At the same time, this is probably exactly what he wanted. He found it exciting to assume the feminine role—but really to commit himself to it would have meant abandoning the shelter he had built around himself, and that he was unable to do. This conflict was resolved in a comic way during the evening at the restaurant. Strindberg went outside for a moment, and Frida took the opportunity to settle the bill for their dinner of lobster, chicken and wine. When Strindberg returned and discovered this, he made a scene: he did not wish to assume the feminine role to such a degree. The episode proves how bold Frida's advances were: in her day, it was still an unbroken rule that the man had at least to appear as the dominant partner who paid the bills. During February, Strindberg's and Frida's affair proceeded behind a façade of romantic trappings—Siri would have recognized it all. Frida had a firm grasp of the possibilities of the situation, and started acting as Strindberg's literary agent and impresario. All winter, she had eyes only for him. She has described him attired as a lover in his mustard-yellow frock-coat cut in the English style, with a white gardenia in his buttonhole, and a soft top hat precariously perched on his leonine locks. In March, Frida left Berlin for Munich—summoned by her suspicious father—after the lovers had agreed to consider themselves secretly engaged. Strindberg had promised Frida to avoid the Ferkel tavern during her absence, yet he returned there with renewed eagerness. He acted like Axel in *A Fool's Apology*, who, in the initial phase of his love and tired of the sentimental exchanges he has to engage in while the baroness, looks for relaxation and natural behaviour with drinking companions and prostitutes.

Although the Ferkel was a predominantly male preserve, a female star had appeared in its firmament during the winter; this was Dagny Juel, a Norwegian childhood friend of Edvard Munch's. Munch had been in love with her, and she is a central figure in his paintings; she was a demonic woman, who often found herself in triangle situations similar to the one in *Creditors*. Both she and Munch were proponents and practitioners of free love.

Dagny Juel had a lasting effect on the lives of several men. Within the circle, she was called Aspasia, after Pericles' outspoken and slandered friend. As for notoriety, she achieved it to a remarkable degree—mainly thanks to Strindberg who reviled her with incomparable malice and never relented in his hatred of her.

In one of the *Vivisections*, he described her as tall, thin, ravaged by alcohol and late nights, speaking in a languid voice that sounded as if it had been broken by held-back tears. He claims that she lacked all 'desirable modesty', and threw herself at him at the Ferkel, and that he was physically revolted by her. His picture of her is like a caricature of Frida, the type of woman he was doomed to, the alluring mortal enemy.

We do not know what really occurred between Dagny Juel and Strindberg; according to one Norwegian source she turned him down, saying that he was too old for her, and making fun of his corpulence. Munch not only painted a portrait of Strindberg but also made a lithographic print, on which his name is misspelled as 'Stindberg': this was, possibly, a deliberately unpleasant pun—'stind' in Norwegian means thick, or swollen: an act of revenge by Dagny's gallant supporter Munch.

Strindberg claimed that Dagny Juel was his mistress for three weeks, whereafter he bequeathed her, under brutal and humiliating circumstances, to Schleich or, in other versions, Lidforss. According to Frida, Strindberg threw Dagny out of her own bedroom after their first night together, locking the door in the belief that he was in his own quarters. Strindberg also claimed to have awoken Dagny's sleeping soul, to have freed her from the anxiety of a disordered life and the painful awareness of it, and to have caused her hollow cheeks to bloom—but that she could not endure the debt of gratitude she had thus incurred, and consequently turned against him with furious antagonism.

Dagny Juel was, by all accounts, an interesting and powerful personality, the equal of Strindberg in her personal lifestyle. Yet for several men, Bengt Lidforss among them, she became the incarnation of the *fin de siècle* dream of a voluptuous mingling of the poisonous with the delicious, 'a radiant flower in a swamp', to quote Lidforss. In August 1893, she married Przybyszewski with whom she led a stormy life. In one of Munch's best-known paintings, *Jealousy*, she is portrayed standing between two men— like Tekla between Gustav and Adolf in *Creditors*—and that seems to have been a key situation of her existence.

Strindberg described her as though she was not human, but a dangerous animal. He called her a whore, a reptile, a rotten cadaver. He planned ways of getting her arrested as a prostitute. In his imagination, she appeared as a vulture waiting on the outskirts of battlefields where worthy men are fighting, to suck their blood and poison their souls. She was a vampire, whose embrace killed, and a witch, who had to be burned at the stake.

For Strindberg, Dagny Juel embodied all that he feared in women from a sexual point of view. She represented the extreme opposite of that virginal, maternal image Strindberg tended to project on to the women he loved. The ruthlessness with which Strindberg treated Dagny Juel during the following months arose out of a fear of something within himself that was threatened by her, and it is consequently difficult to take his vile behaviour towards her quite seriously.

Frida returned from Munich, curious about the obscure allusions her secret fiancé had been making in his letters. 'I am afraid of myself,' he wrote on 13 March. 'During recent days, since you left, I have gathered so many transgressions on my conscience that I want to die. And the money keeps running, rolling, walking away.'

Creditors had provided him with some income, although a lot less than he had expected; hence the extravagance. A newspaper announced his betrothal. Frida persuaded him to write to her father, to ask for her hand in marriage: as she was still under age according to Austrian law, her father's consent was necessary. It was given, but her family was understandably anxious. Frida's older sister, Marie Weyr, married to the well-established (in contrast to Strindberg) sculptor and professor Rudolf Weyr, wrote to her husband: 'I am afraid that his—Strindberg's—love for her is mainly of a sensual nature, as Frida is incapable of satisfying him spiritually—not that there is a woman in the world who would be.' She added a few perceptive words apropos the paintings Strindberg was working on: 'It is just as if the talent within him did not quite know how to express itself. But there is no trace of any joyous, healthy creativity: it is more like an urge, the way a criminal is driven to murder. Gruesome, truly gruesome. I do not understand how Frida can put her life into such a person's hands.'

On 11 April, Strindberg and Frida exchanged rings and became officially engaged. Strindberg brought gifts for the occasion, a parcel of Lessebo paper and a huge dark grey eagle quill—the insignia of his own profession, as if to transfer his power to her—as well as a freshly painted canvas of a stormy seascape, entitled *The Night of Jealousy*.

Frida played her protective role with renewed energy. When her father gave her a certain amount of money for the wedding, she wanted to use it to pay off Strindberg's debts. 'Don't suffocate me with your love,' the fiancé exclaimed upon hearing that suggestion. According to Frida, he did, however, agree to acquire elegant new clothes for the occasion. He ordered a 'soft, light beige English suit with matching sailor's hat and silk cravat, wide, black with dark green stripes'.

Later in life, Strindberg was pained by the memory of having used Frida's dowry for his own benefit. He regarded it as an obligation of honour to repay the sum involved or else 'put a bullet through his head', as he declared in 1897, after the divorce.

On 27 April, Strindberg and his bride left Berlin. Paul and Lidforss saw them off with a presentation of roses, purchased with money borrowed from Strindberg (or his bride?). The couple's destination was Helgoland in the North Sea, which had been a British colony until 1814, and where the procedure of posting the banns was less time-consuming than in the rest of Germany. The wedding took place there on 2 May. Two pilots acted as witnesses—something which Strindberg, as a long-established lover of islands, perhaps experienced as reassuring. He wrote later that during the ceremony, the bride was seized by a fit of hysterical laughter which almost brought the proceedings to a halt. According to Frida, this was due to Strindberg's misunderstanding one of the questions the marriage liturgy addressed to her, as concerning him; thus, he pronounced: 'I vow never to bear another man's child under my heart.' If Frida told the truth, which is quite possible, the mistake was well worth a laugh—but also the reflection that it had its roots in the bridegroom's subconscious. Strindberg had played a feminine role in this love story, and regarded women's fertility as something of a threat to himself.

The couple rented a cottage on Helgoland, which was surrounded by lawns and flower-beds. Their sexual life together had begun at an earlier date, as is witnessed by a letter from Strindberg to Frida on 17 April, in which he discusses a favourite subject, the size of his penis. He deals with it in courtly imagery: the vulva becomes a glove, the phallus a hand. Strindberg points out that it is the hand which decides the size of the glove, and asserts that 'a small hand' is the sign of an aristocrat, a big one that of a plebeian. He then quotes an expert in anatomy as testifying that very long 'hands' are frequently found on cretins and masturbators. He encourages Frida to study the statues of antiquity, in which the slaves seem better endowed than the heroes in this respect. The following summer, Strindberg developed the subject in an article, claiming that the male reproductive organ would shrink further in the course of evolution: the élite man is no longer a stud, and sexuality becomes a mere pastime. The article also demonstrated that even in his other aspects the man of the future would be rather like Strindberg himself, with 'abundant growth of hair on the cranium', a small chin, and short, broad hands.

Both Strindberg and Frida described their honeymoon as happy but brief. On 20 May, they travelled to England, hoping to make Strindberg's work better known there. First, they lived for a couple of weeks in Gravesend, not far from the cemetery where Pocahontas was buried, and then moved to London and lived in a boarding-house in Warwick Street, near Eccleston Square. When, many years later, Strindberg wrote about Shakespeare's imagery, he cited a line from *A Midsummer Night's Dream* as an example of how an indication of a certain time can be made concrete and lively: 'When wheat is green and hawthorn buds appear.' He added that these words perfectly described the English countryside such as he saw it for himself one day in May at Gravesend.

Strindberg's command of English was poor, almost non-existent. Frida, who had gone to school in England, had the advantage there. He found the beer pleasantly strong, but the heat, noise, and smell of the busy streets hard to bear. In Gravesend, his past had caught up with him: the first copies of the German translation of *A Fool's Apology* arrived. In Germany the previous winter he had overcome his scruples about publishing it. His constant lack of funds played a part in his decision. Frida had promised that she would not read the book; however, she was no more able than the ladies in the tale of Bluebeard to resist the temptation to open the forbidden door.

'Like a nightmare, the past sat on Strindberg's neck,' Frida wrote in her book. 'And like a nightmare, it now descended on me as well.' She claimed that she became afraid that he would abandon her as he had abandoned Siri. After reading *Miss Julie*, her father had joked: 'First Miss Julchen, and then comes Uhlchen.' It is, however, more likely that Frida felt tempted by such a risk. She pursued celebrities all her life and was too light-hearted a person to care about how they immortalized her, as long as they did so.

While Frida was reading the *Apology* (as she tells us in her book), a thunderstorm swept the countryside, and when she went to Strindberg's

42 Edvard Munch's lithograph of Strindberg, 1896. Strindberg was annoyed by the misspelling of his name and by the nude female figure in the border

room she found that he had sought cover behind bed and table, where he was sleeping on the floor. He was not only a man 'who has killed' but also one who 'tries to kill, time after time'; this was her dramatic commentary.

While reading her husband's book Frida certainly made one important discovery: Siri's powerful hold on his imagination. Between kisses on their wedding night he had exclaimed, with the rancour of tenderness scorned: 'Don't believe she [Siri] would have thought I'd find such a young girl!' That sounds like an authentic quotation. Frida received many reminders of that sort. Strindberg would call her Protean, said that she acted like a woman of the world one day, a cocotte the next, and a schoolgirl the day after that. That impression was probably due to the fact that he was not observing her too closely: in his works, she became a woman without a face.

When, in 1898, he wrote the novel *The Convent* which offers a narrow selection of exact details from his second marriage, he called himself Axel— a name which had long been a favourite with him—and made Frida into Maria, just like the heroine of *A Fool's Apology* and *In the Offing.* In the houses of upper-class families of the past, a recently employed servant was always given the same name as his or her predecessor, to indicate that he was a servant, not a human being. Frida was devoured by Siri. Strindberg was developing a symbolist mode of creation, in which there was no room for individuals—although individuals had always found his work to be rather cramped quarters, next to himself.

3

On 17 June, less than seven weeks after the wedding, Strindberg left London—alone. Frida stayed behind to take care of theatrical and literary business. Strindberg took a coal-freighter to Hamburg on the way to Rügen, where one or two members of the circle from the Ferkel were spending the summer. At sea, he wrote to Frida: 'Everything, past and present, merges in my mind as in a dream. And life makes me sea-sick, if the sea itself doesn't. What pains me most? That I have dragged you, dear child, into my misery. As if you hadn't had enough with your own troubles!'

It is as if, out at sea, he had suddenly seen Frida as she really was, hence his compassion. One night that summer he dreamt that he saw Frida with a black mask on her face: when he tried to embrace her, she had vanished.

Strindberg stayed in Hamburg for a few days, sending out a series of SOS missives—the hotel bill was mounting and he was penniless, starvation threatened, his revolver was loaded, cholera was approaching in the summer heat and was declared to be a welcome visitor. On Rügen, surrounded by

trees, sea and friends, he grew calmer. Later, however, he would describe
the time there as a single prolonged month in hell. The light, fine sand,
burning hot under the midsummer sun, reminded him of the desert in
Dante's hell, he wrote in *The Convent*, forgetting that the rain of fire
punishes homosexuals, among them Dante's teacher Brunetto Latini, and
remembering only that the desert was the place for blasphemers, among
whom he still counted himself.

On Rügen, Strindberg's interest in science revived with increased
strength, and for a while it overshadowed his writing. This passion has
greatly contributed to the image of Strindberg as a madman obsessed with
fixed ideas. Harsh judgements have been pronounced on his scientific
achievements, often coupled with pejorative remarks about his sanity. The
Svedberg, Nobel Prize winner in the field of chemistry, summed up his
thorough study of Strindberg's voluminous chemical writings as follows:
'Strindberg was in his inmost being a stranger to all genuine research.
Therefore, all his efforts and labours in that direction proved vain and like
chasing the wind.'

Nevertheless, Svedberg's opinion has its limitations. All his life,
Strindberg had been working his way towards the natural sciences,
belonging, as he did, to a generation for whom the scientists were the heroes
above all others, totally eclipsing the artists and poets. What were Tolstoy,
Ibsen and Zola compared to Darwin and Pasteur! Strindberg's fictional
heroes had also begun to change professions. The reformer Master Olof and
the writer Arvid Falk gave way to mineralogists and commissioners of
conservation. When Strindberg in the summer of 1889 ran aground with *In
the Offing*, he contemplated the writing of a scientific work instead—'my
future Antibarbarus,' as he called it in a letter to Ola Hansson. On
Helgoland, his first intention was to return to Axel Borg, and he drafted a
sequel to the novel. True, Borg had sailed out to sea to die, but perhaps
someone had rescued him. ... When the sequel proved recalcitrant,
Strindberg took up the Antibarbarus notion again. After fiction had failed,
he continued Axel Borg's existence in his own person.

In 1885, Strindberg had renounced the deism of his youth and declared
himself an atheist. This did not mean that he had given up a belief in a
unified and animated world. Schopenhauer's dictum, 'the world is my
conception', never lost its applicability to him, and that, in itself, was a
guarantee of unity. All existence revolved a central point, the ego.

In his penetrating study 'Strindberg's Inferno Crisis', among other
things, Gunnar Brandell provides, a chart of Strindberg's evolution as a
scientist. In the Germany of this era, 'monism' was the main catchword of
popular philosophy, and its prime exponent was Ernst Haeckel. Haeckel
started out from the doctine of evolution as formulated by Darwin: as all
animals and plants had evolved, step by step, from a primal cell, it was

reasonable to assume that all life in the universe, both organic and inorganic, had to be the product of the same primal material.

In October 1892—just as Strindberg arrived in Germany—Haeckel gave a noted lecture to a scientific congress in which he proposed the theory that the elements were evolutionary products generated by combinations of varying numbers of primal atoms. In this context, Haeckel mentioned that the alchemists' old dream of transmutation of the elements was, perhaps, approaching its realization.

These were thoughts after Strindberg's heart at the time, and they became his guidelines during his first scientific period. He called himself a monist. The previous year, he had come up with the notion that he himself, in his subconscious, was able to perceive how his organism had passed through all the evolutionary stages. In April 1891, he had written to Bengt Lidforss that he believed more in this subconscious contact with animals and the material world than in experiments and laboratories.

> Is there somewhere in my heritage, not from my grandfather, but from the animal, the plant, the mineral or the primal gas, which I have passed through, a dark awareness of pleasure or pain when my consciousness has to review the entire evolution of which I am the last exponent? I frequently find myself in an unselfconscious state, not through intoxication or such, but by means of distractions, play, games, sleeping, and reading novels, and then I let my brain work freely without regard to results or acclaim, and something emerges that I believe in—just because it has emerged out of necessity, like my family tree.

Brisk man of action that he was, Strindberg immediately wanted to take steps to prove in practice that the elements could indeed be transformed. It is hardly necessary to point out that the very premise of his activity misrepresents Haeckel from the start. During his months on Rügen, Strindberg wrote his first scientific work, *Antibarbarus*. Its main subject was sulphur. Strindberg believed that he had proved it could be broken down, and so was not an element—which, according to him, meant the beginning of a new chemistry. As he stated on the opening page, he took as his starting-point 'the prevailing monistic theory of nature's all-pervasiveness and unity, as applied by Darwin and Haeckel to the other natural sciences'. Now he had applied it to chemistry. All the elements were related and had been generated by one another, and it was possible to make them take on each other's manifest forms again.

Strindberg's manner of procedure was at the same time frightening and impressive. He had long been accustomed to appearing in the natural world as though, like Stanley in the jungle, he were the first man to set foot in it, and as if all previous results were null and void. Now he wrote to Dehmel in Berlin, asking him to send both literature and chemicals, the necessary basic elements. He asserted that he would be able to demonstrate the presence of carbon in sulphur within a fortnight—eight days would suffice, as long as he had the technical apparatus.

These experiments with sulphur would occupy him for years. His equipment was primitive, and often the only source of heat was the fire in the hearth. After sulphur he proceeded to iodine, soon convincing himself that he would be able to produce it synthetically, and thus revolutionize the iodine industry. From iodine, he took the leap to the queen of the elements—gold. It is as a 'gold-maker' that he has been subjected to the most devastating ridicule; it was an activity he pursued to the end of his life, believing that he had solved the problem. He claimed to have produced a gold oxide from iron sulphate and ammonia: when it was tested over the glowing tip of a cigar, yellow metallic scales of gold appeared. Triumphantly, he sent samples of the substance to his friends, but it proved unstable, and professional chemists rejected it. Nevertheless, Strindberg remained steadfast in his belief that he had succeeded.

Thus his efforts did indeed 'prove vain and like chasing the wind'. By 'genuine' research the Svedberg means the objective examination of natural phenomena and the ability to draw general conclusions from the information thus gathered. By such a standard, Strindberg was a failure, for his method was diametrically opposed to it: the rule came first, and the research was designed only to prove it. In his studies, he tried to demonstrate the unity of nature, as he had perceived it in his subconscious, and as he had found it confirmed in works of natural philosophy from antiquity onwards, in exactly the same way a believer thinks that he is able to see the traces of God's hand in nature and life. It does not matter, in that context, whether an occasional mistake occurs, since The Unity does not always reveal its secrets, any more than God does. The main thing is that the work is dominated by important connections. As Gunnar Brandell has demonstrated, Strindberg did not take his guidelines from nineteenth-century empirical science but from the classical natural philosophers, especially Francis Bacon. Brandell says that Strindberg imitated Bacon's attitude and style of research. Bacon was filled with the sense of power of the Renaissance, and the conviction that a new pattern was to appear in nature now that the rule of reason had at last begun.

4

While Strindberg was advancing even further into the mysteries of monistic philosophy on Rügen, he conducted a correspondence full of repeated misunderstandings with Frida in England, calling her, by turns, 'my beloved sheep' or 'my mean sheep', and sometimes signing his letters 'your happy badger'. This epithet was borrowed from a poem of homage Richard Dehmel had dedicated to him the previous winter, in which he was compared to a gigantic, misty cave, where an ancient badger lies dreaming about new worlds. Once in a while, the badger extends its heavy paws through the bars of that cave, and with grey, cruelly sad eyes seizes its prey—a human brain. Dehmel completes his Strindberg image by those of a beautiful but deranged woman, clad in a green sack, who weeps over the sad badger at the back of the cave, and a man with a godlike forehead and tremulous, shy, feminine lips, who is dishevelled 'as if he had just stopped flying'. Aubrey Beardsley would have been a suitable illustrator of this highly mannered poem.

It can be complemented by another image of Strindberg, which dates from that time on Rügen. Adolf Paul, the Finland-Swedish author, who often acted as Strindberg's 'butler' in Berlin and learned to see him with hostile lucidity, shared lodgings with him on the island. One day, Paul saw Strindberg dive into the water head first; when he came up again, he had metamorphosed into

> an old hag. His head had lost half its volume, the lion's mane stuck close to the forehead, and his face was angular and wrinkled with a tiny pointed chin and small, petulant mouth, and his arms thin yet muscular. The old hag who was wont to carp about life's little vicissitudes, day in, day out, now stood before us, as large as life. The impression was amazingly strong and impossible to forget.

At the end of July, Strindberg received an invitation from Frida's mother to visit the family's summer villa at Mondsee in Austria. Frau Marie Uhl, *née* Reischl, who was fifty years old at this time, lived mainly with her parents, as her marriage was not happy, but she used to join her husband at Mondsee during the summer. They were naturally curious about their daughter's husband. Frau Uhl, who had occult leanings, had an uneasy relationship with Frida, who was her youngest daughter. Strindberg decided to accept the invitation, even though Frida remained in England.

Early in August he travelled to Mondsee via Berlin. He was nervous about the impending meeting, but regained his courage, as he wrote in *The Convent*, 'as always from the author's point of view: even if it does not work out, I'll always get another chapter for my novel!' He was to meet this totally unknown family alone and penniless. According to *The Convent*, his sister-in-law received him in a manner that was 'chilly and conventional', while the mother embraced him uttering religious incantations.

He received a visible demonstration of the wealth of his wife's family. The summer villa, which still exists and is a national monument, due to its connection with Strindberg, is a huge, three-storeyed house with an army of

servants and drawing-rooms as large as concert halls. Indeed, both Wagner
and Brahms had performed there. The landscape in which it was set was
Arcadian. On the far side of the lake rose Schafberg, 'The Sheep Mountain',
which had given Frida her nickname.

Strindberg stayed at Mondsee for twelve days and never returned there,
which makes the memorials to him—the street now bears his name, and an
iron plaque commemorates his visit—seem a little excessive. He went
fishing on the lake with his father-in-law whom he described as '*ein schöner*,
junger Kerl', listened to the parents' reminiscences of Frida's sweetness as a
child when she took her bath, conversed with her old nanny and was bitten
by her dog. All this is recorded in a letter to Frida, whom he reproached for
not showing sufficient understanding for her mother and her religion. In his
letters, Strindberg appeared unnaturally prim and proper and falsely
moralistic: they convey a strong sense of his efforts to adapt to an absurd
situation. The ground was burning under his feet just as hotly as on Rügen.

Frida refused to come to Mondsee, and as early as 4 August Strindberg
was describing himself as an intruder. The following day he was upset
because Frida had written to her mother and asked her to help Strindberg's
children in Finland, making his situation still more humiliating. He
informed Frida that unless she came to Mondsee within eight days, he
would go to Berlin to lecture at the Humboldt Academy and look for a job.
Should she stay away for two weeks, he would institute divorce proceedings.
On 7 August, he wrote a letter of farewell: 'Finished! Is it possible? I only
regret that I did not kill myself in London, in your arms, my head against
your bosom. I did think of it, but the sordid surroundings prevented me.'
He then accused Frida, who was trying to advance her own writing career in
England, of throwing away love for the sake of fame. 'But let me tell you,' he
continued, 'moments will come when you have achieved fame and would
like to spit it out, when all is empty and desolate around you, and you'd
gladly exchange the laurel wreath for roses.'

Strindberg left Mondsee without saying goodbye on 11 August, after
Frida, frightened by his divorce threat, had left London and gone to Berlin.
On 12 August he wrote a letter of apology to Marie Uhl, saying that he had
come to her house as a prodigal son, and that he had felt this sudden impulse
to travel on: it was not due to anger but to desperation, and he asked her
forgiveness.

After further comedies of error, Strindberg met Frida in Berlin and
settled down with her at the Pensionat v.d. Werra on Albrechtstrasse.
Strindberg's need for dramatic events in his life continued to be satisfied. *A
Fool's Apology* haunted him again, but now on an external plane. The
Swedish journal *Budkavlen*, which had supported him during the *Marrying*
case, took up the novel as soon as it appeared in Germany and started to
publish it as a serial in Swedish translation; it was entitled to do so, as there

were no publishing agreements between Germany and Sweden. The Swedish public devoured the book as a *roman à clef*, and it added considerably to its author's reputation for libel. Strindberg feigned indignation over the ruthlessness of *Budkavlen* in revealing the secrets of his marriage, yet at the same time made an attempt to collect payment from the journal. One of his more fantastic notions was that Carl Gustaf Wrangel and Sofie In de Betou, who were now married, should sue the journal for libel, but *Budkavlen* replied curtly that Strindberg was obviously panicking.

On top of everything else, the German police confiscated the novel after an anonymous report by 'A German Mother' had found the book lewd and morally offensive, and a prosecution was pending. According to one rumour, it was Frida who denounced the book in order to promote sales. She later admitted that one of her women friends had suggested something of the sort.

In early October, Frida discovered that she was pregnant. During the initial stages of their love, Strindberg had written to her that she was 'born to be a mother'. Now that nature had assigned her that role, Frida rebelled, had hysterical outbursts, wanted an abortion, called Strindberg a cowardly wretch unwilling to take responsibility. She fled from Berlin to Vienna and demanded a divorce, on the grounds of 'physical maltreatment', among other things. Strindberg defended himself in a letter to his sister-in-law, imploring her to pay as little attention to Frida's fantasies 'as I have to her threats to shoot me or have me shot'. He said that her behaviour was a natural consequence of her condition. He explained the maltreatment of which he was accused by relating an episode that had occurred in Berlin. In a fit of jealousy, imagining that Strindberg had locked himself in his room with a woman, Frida had summoned the police and the fire brigade to break down his door. On that occasion, he had used physical force to remove her from the room.

After the first difficult month of her pregnancy, Frida calmed down. Strindberg went on a short visit to Lund but found the atmosphere there oppressive; small wonder, considering that a very large number of readers devoured the instalments in *Budkavlen* every week. At the end of October, the couple was reunited in Brünn, the capital of Moravia. They rented a two-room flat. Strindberg was waiting for the child, Frida wrote, 'as a naïve and pious person awaits the perfect completion of his life'. The god of fertility was the only one he deferred to.

We do not know whether, while in Brünn, Strindberg gave any thought to Silvio Pellico, the Italian author and freedom fighter, who spent several dark years imprisoned in the fortress of Spielburg just outside the town. Perhaps it was enough for him to contemplate that he was a prisoner himself. On 16 November, he wrote to Adolf Paul: 'I'm living indescribably, I don't know whether I'm imprisoned or free, but I certainly have a gaoler!' The thought of earthly existence as a penal institution began to grow in him, though still in a semi-humorous vein. He added: 'Shitty winter here, in a town full of chimneys. I still ask: how did I get here? And what am I doing here?' According to a statement made several years later, he had a vision in Brünn: space and time disappeared, and Kymmendö lay before him in all its glory.

At the same time, his letter testified to his nostalgia for the welcoming tavern and the male companionship at the Ferkel. He could not get enough gossip about it, and tirelessly hurled implications against Aspasia. He saw himself as an outcast, doing penance for his sexual desires, by the side of an incomprehensible and unknown woman.

5

In November, the couple accepted an invitation to live with Frida's maternal grandparents, Cornelius and Marie Reischl, on the Dornach estate near Amstetten. Frida's grandfather had had a lucrative post at the imperial court and was a very wealthy man. The estate was merely a hobby; he also owned a number of buildings in Vienna and the surrounding villages. He devoted most of his time to the traditional sport of the nobility—hunting. The gourmet Strindberg, who considered hare, deer and pheasant as everyday fare, soon found them, by his own admission, a form of penance. When, in the opening chapter of *Black Flags*, he described the luxurious extravagance of Professor Stenkåhl's dinner as almost insufferable, it was, perhaps, Dornach he had in mind.

The three-storeyed castle at Dornach—it is still there, with the later addition of towers and battlements—stands only a few yards from the majestic Danube, and is a fisherman's paradise. At the back of the castle is a steep slope. The river is crossed by ferry. On clear days, it is possible to see the snow-capped Styrian Alps on the far side. To the west stretches a plain which is frequently flooded. This is where Strindberg would take his morning walks, and where for the first time in his life he saw the alpine violet: it taught him, he claimed in an aphorism, 'that all botanical systems are arbitrary and futile and that nature is not formed according to systems'. A couple of hundred yards from the estate is a stone quarry, which at that time was the gathering place for great numbers of poor labourers and gypsies. The railway had not yet been built, and the region was poor. Beggars wandered along the roads. The landscape had its own unmistakable symbolism which corresponded with what Strindberg was looking for.

Strindberg's luxurious existence at Dornach contrasted starkly with his impecunious state. His scientific pursuits did not earn money. According to a tradition that still prevails in Dornach, he was suspected of being a fortune-hunter; he was considered discourteous and rude to the servants. He needed an inflated sense of self-esteem in order to endure his existence as a pauper. The following summer, after eight months at Dornach, Strindberg gave an interesting report on life there. He wrote to his friend Littmansson about the complications involved in life as a guest and admits that he 'like everyone else soon feels a natural hatred for my benefactors'. He goes on:

> Perhaps my ingratitude is also based on the fact that I always think I have given more than I have received; when I die, I will consider that to be the cancellation of a debt people owe me. I have taught them many kinds of devilry, occupied their minds during hours of leisure, entertained them; I have avenged many injustices, liberated spirits languishing under the evil morals of others, revealed acts of oppression, torn apart false reputations which had covered up true talent in others! Is it, then, surprising that those who are so greatly indebted to me, hate their benefactor and, like true Christians, project their guilt on to me, portraying me as the 'ungrateful one' *par préférence?*

It was unreasonable of Strindberg to expect old Cornelius Reischl to realize that he owed him a debt of gratitude for having opened the eyes of humanity. Yet it was no doubt Strindberg's confidence in his own creative powers that preserved his integrity. Among those who regard themselves as geniuses, this awareness of being a 'giver', and therefore having justified demands upon one's fellow men, is probably more common that one might think.

At Dornach, Strindberg's brain seethed and bubbled more vigorously than ever before. He was excited by the knowledge that Paracelsus had been active in the vicinity, and took his first steps in the great early scientist's tracks. At this time, Bengt Lidforss was his favourite correspondent. Strindberg treated him as a complete equal, while evincing fatherly concern and tenderness. He seized his pen as soon as his thoughts turned to this unique friend who understood him so well and replied to his letters with lightning speed—and who, amazingly, as he was a scientist himself, continued to take Strindberg's efforts seriously. Lidforss was busy translating *Antibarbarus* into German, and Strindberg often thought of his drinking companions in Berlin, where Lidforss was living at this time. Strindberg had plans for a new tavern, to be called Zum August Strindberg; it was to be furnished in blasphemous 'superman' style, with, among other objects, a female skeleton with its additional tail-bone vertebrae to prove the inferior status of women, an altar with a Bible with a condom as its book-mark and a candle as a pointer. Brawling, fireworks and music were to be permitted, but decent women would be refused entry. The imaginary tavern's religion was self-adoration and veneration of the highest being, The Ego.

With the coming of spring, Strindberg's letters took on all the fragrances, sounds and colours of that season, with humorous observations on natural phenomena. He wrote to Lidforss on 13 March:

> Listen, it does seem that the alder has sexual instincts. Not the hazel, whose male catkins hang down straight like long limp pricks without a twitch next to the red females. But in *populus tremula*, the seed-wings on two twigs, one male, one female, started twisting towards each other, and I now have them drying in a coital position in one of my Bacon tomes!

After some unpleasantness in the castle, Strindberg and Frida moved to a one-storey stone cottage with small windows by the Danube at the far end of the grounds. It had been inhabited by a stubborn donkey called Lumpi, who did not like the stable; now the donkey was driven out, and Strindberg took possession, although he too was 'under guard', according to his own claim. The couple enthusiastically proceeded to paint window frames and doors and to cultivate the garden in front of the cottage. As late as the summer of 1977, residents of Dornach showed visitors a pear tree Strindberg had planted. To brighten up the white walls, Strindberg painted frescos he called 'symbolist paintings', in which it is possible to see traces of the Austrian landscape.

While the garden bloomed, and Frida prepared for the birth of her child, *Antibarbarus* was published in Berlin. Strindberg had hoped that it would explode like a bomb in the headquarters of 'conventional' science—this was his début before a scholarly élite—but the book was greeted by silence in Germany. In Sweden, however, it was reviewed on 13 April by Bengt Lidforss. Only a couple of days earlier, Strindberg had made a quick visit to Berlin to read the proofs with him. On that occasion, Lidforss had been lavish with his compliments, and even Strindberg had thought fit to tell his friend to tone down his enthusiasm. Thus he was quite taken aback by Lidforss's review: it was completely negative, and, what is more, it appeared in his own paper, *Dagens Nyheter*. Lidforss wrote: 'There is a kind of brutal grandeur in Strindberg's world of ideas that makes one think of the extinct gigantic animals of the Jurassic period; it is as if one observed gigantic fossilized thoughts wrestling and tearing up the ground.' After that grandiloquent and perhaps even flattering beginning, the review became vicious and belittling. Lidforss stated that Strindberg's comprehension of science was tainted by barbarism, intellectual brutality, and 'a stone mason's materialism', and he also made the connection between 'genius and madness'.

Nils Beyer, Lidforss's biographer, has been unable to provide a reasonable explanation for this unexpected stab in the back. It is understandable that Lidforss in his admiration for Strindberg the writer should have been driven to overlook some of the shortcomings of Strindberg the chemist; but as a career-oriented scientist, he did not want to compromise himself in public and have his name associated with someone who was regarded as a charlatan by academic circles. But why did he write the review? Being the translator of the book, he should have considered himself disqualified. In any case, there had always been explosive elements in his friendship with Strindberg—one of them being Dagny Juel, to whom Lidforss was tragically attached; he was unable to be her lover due to his syphilitic condition. Strindberg had treated Dagny Juel in a brutal fashion, and Lidforss avenged her by attacking him on a scientific level.

Naturally, Strindberg regarded the article as a most horrendous betrayal. In his letters, he cursed Lidforss with the passion of a medieval warlock, threatening to erase him by sudden death from 'the number of the living'—as if he had been omnipotent. He described him as someone in a state of moral dissolution and decay, as a pickpocket, a villain. He planned Lidforss's destruction in a future novel but did not forgo minor interim actions such as a letter to Gustav Türke containing warnings about Lidforss and trying to get him blackballed from the Ferkel, their mutual home.

Another scientist, the mineralogist Helge Bäckström—he was also closely related to Dagny Juel, being married to her sister—gave a similar review to *Antibarbarus* in *Aftonbladet*. In even stronger terms than Lidforss, he suggested that Strindberg was mentally unbalanced.

Strindberg, always quick to construct his own adversity, persuaded his friend in Berlin, Carl Ludwig Schleich, to write a letter to Ernst Haeckel asking for a statement from him to the effect that Strindberg was not a madman. At the end of May, Strindberg received a letter from Haeckel, who said that he had not found anything in Strindberg's book that could be called absolutely irrational or 'insane'; understandably, this testimonial surprised and soon irritated its recipient.

However, this setback did not depress Strindberg, nor did it slow him down. He knew how to turn almost anything to his advantage. Lidforss became one more Judas among many in his life, and so proof of his own special mission. Strindberg realized, however, that he had been addressing himself to the wrong type of audience. The academic research scholars were careful to defend their positions, and he could not expect any help from them. Furthermore, his ambitions had expanded during this year. *Antibarbarus* had been written to demolish chemistry as it was taught. Now he had a far greater target in his sights: to discover unity not only in chemistry, but in the entire created world.

Spring brought another blow: for no good reason, Strindberg wrote to his oldest daughter Karin, now fourteen, inviting her to come to Dornach, to live in his house and to instruct his wife in Swedish so that she would be able to translate his books. The letter was written in May and contained extravagant enticements. Not surprisingly, Karin wrote a cold reply, saying that it was out of the question for her to leave her mother. 'I really do not understand,' she wrote, 'how Pappa can afford to offer me 200 francs a month, with clothes and all expenses paid, when he cannot afford to provide 200 francs maintenance for all three of us.' She added that it was 'shameful' of her father not to make the payments he had promised.

Strindberg was unable to take that reproach. It cast a clear light on the absurdity of his position. He replied with a combination of self-pity and rage, saying that he had suffered deprivation, pawned his watch and books, gone without dinner in order to be able to send birthday gifts to his children. Karin's letter, he said, proved that she lacked 'compassion for the misfortunes of others' and could, therefore, 'easily find herself in a shameful position and friendless, one day'. During that summer, he was often preoccupied by the subject of ungrateful children.

On 26 May, Frida gave birth to a daughter who was christened Kerstin. Her arrival was timely, as it could fill the void left by the other children, whom Strindberg now regarded as lost. Yet he was afraid of growing attached to his daughter, being convinced that this new marriage would not last long. He knew only too well the pain involved in separation from a loved child.

Frida was not happy as a mother. There were problems from the start. Her milk ran out; local wet-nurses offered their services, but their physical condition was so poor that they could not be accepted—so great was the poverty of the region. Her mother and grandmother took matters in hand. Soon there were six women in the small cottage, and Strindberg felt out of place. He made preparations to leave, this time with Paris as his destination: there, he hoped to repeat the triumphs of Berlin.

It was a hot summer. The Danube, less than a stone's throw from the cottage, shrank, and the sand-bank in the middle of the river grew larger, spreading a stench of rotten fish. In her book, Frida wrote that the heat rendered Strindberg unfit to live. She could not have mistaken his condition more completely. *Antibarbarus* had been a failure, his best friend had become a traitor, his marriage was falling apart, his finances were in a terrible state, the dirty river brought forth all his nostalgia for the clean waters of the Archipelago, the baby was crying, the Berlin trial of *A Fool's Apology* was approaching. Ordered to appear in person, Strindberg took to his bed with an inflammation of the throat—imaginary, at any rate according to Frida—and obtained a medical certificate declaring him unfit to travel.

Instead of hampering his inner development, the mounting pressures favoured it; he made himself receptive to new ideas, formed new contacts. Littmansson in Paris became Lidforss's successor as Strindberg's correspondent of the moment, although Strindberg did not treat him as an equal, but made him the butt of his bullying and arrogance. Yet Strindberg was more candid with Littmansson than with anyone else, as an emperor is with his servant, a ready-made listener who isn't really there. Living in Austria, Strindberg often thought of Napoleon; like the emperor, he had married an Austrian as his second wife.

At the same time, Strindberg made a new friend, the theosophist Torsten Hedlund, who thought there were traces of the occult in *Antibarbarus*. Strindberg began a correspondence with him that lasted several years and was of utmost importance for his development.

Germany had lost its attraction and usefulness, and Strindberg concentrated on France, once again. He wrote to Mörner that he was now going 'like the giant Antaeus to gain strength by touching mother Lutetia'. He discovered that there were chemists in France who worked as he did, and it did not take him long to establish himself among them. Littmansson had sent him two recent French books, *La vie et l'âme de la matière* by Jollivet-Castelot, and *Les metamorphoses de la matière* by Hemel. As the titles themselves indicate, these were like guides sent from heaven, proving to Strindberg that he was on the right track.

On 21 June, he enjoyed the first fruits of his French campaign. *Creditors* was premièred at the Théâtre Oeuvre in Paris and was a success. Strindberg got ready for an attack on all fronts and negotiated about French editions of *The Red Room*, *In the Offing*, and *A Fool's Apology*, while at the same time writing a complete series of articles in French, designed to take the Parisian press by storm in the autumn.

On 14 July, he wrote to Littmansson that happiness consisted of being able to develop and rule, unhappiness, of being denied those activities. He continued:

> It is happiness, this sense of power, to sit in a cottage by the Danube surrounded by six women who regard me as a half-wit, and to know that at this very moment, in Paris, the headquarters of great minds, 500 people are sitting in a theatre quiet as moles, and foolish enough to expose their brains to my suggestions. Some may revolt, but many will leave impregnated by the seed of my intellect, and so they'll breed my young.

In letters to Littmansson and Torsten Hedlund he described his present life in terms that exuded a sense of new creativity. He admitted that writing was the only thing that gave meaning to his life—that a woman's embrace resembled the joyful birth-pangs he felt when he sired the creatures of his imagination. He called himself a man on the move, constantly prepared to break camp as soon as things got too comfortable. He felt tempted to go on enjoying the wealth Frida represented, but he chose to leave, in order to lead a life of poverty in a community of men.

He developed an idea for a convent, which was to preoccupy him for the rest of his life but was never expressed as gloriously as in the letters of that summer, complete with rules and regulations and detailed instructions as to garments and behaviour. His Utopian thoughts of the 1880s returned, but they now no longer concerned humanity at large, only the chosen one who was to liberate himself from all ties, combine philosophy and science, and produce gold and diamonds in order to break the power of money. As his own particular task, Strindberg chose the invention of the flying machine.

His convent was to be situated in the Ardennes. In July, he wrote:

> Thus I have dreamed! We will come out into the open only when we have educated ourselves to represent the highest type of humanity! Like the Salvation Army! We shall build a dragon ship, white and gold and other colours; put on white holiday raiment and row out on to the river Aisne on a pilgrimage; when the winds favour us, we shall sail with our blue silken sails down the Oise to the Seine and pass through Paris without disembarking; we shall play new instruments I have invented, new melodies I have permitted nature (chance) to invent; sing songs in keys with quarter and one-eighth notes no one has ever heard; and then sail on along the Marne and back again to Aisne where we live!

In Cornelius Reischl's library, Strindberg had found books about Buddha. He spoke of the Lord's hand who rested over him, of an impending change, of a feeling of being the mortally weary horse trotting towards home. On 22 July, he wrote:

> I have even become superstitious again, hearing ravens in my garden; weeping children on the far side of the Danube; dreams about ancient times. I feel a yearning to fly, in some cool element halfway between air and water, wearing white clothes; not to hear human voices, not to feel the humiliating sensation of hunger, not to have enemies, not to hate, not to be hated.

One moment, he was releasing a stream of blasphemies, saying that he felt an equally strong urge to behave like a swine, talking about 'the swine Buddha' and Jesus intoxicated at the wedding at Cana. The next moment, he became a Jesus again, welcoming suffering. His thoughts formed a whirlpool in his brain, and the word 'manic' might seem applicable; yet his language was always controlled and, whenever the expressions of his confidence became too grotesque, spiced with flashes of self-irony. Even in the maelstrom of his whims he remained in total, brilliant control of words, as in a grotesquely arrogant missive of 13 August in which he condemns all art forms except for his own, calls himself Champion of the Universe, and belittles the lion, who, although he is the ruler of the animal kingdom, does not know how to write tragedies. 'True, he roars and stages tragedies, but they are just trashy blood-and-thunder tales.'

While Strindberg was whirring like a dynamo on the banks of the Danube and coming close to bursting with superman thoughts, whims and notions, the same Austro-Hungarian empire that had been so good to Cornelius Reischl was developing a culture which would have decisive consequences for culture generally in the West. If new things were preparing themselves in Strindberg's brain, so were they in those of a number of men of genius along that same great river, and for many of them his contributions became important. Thus, we can imagine him in that summer of 1894 as existing in the same space with Freud, Mahler, Kraus, and Schoenberg—who was obsessed by Strindberg, according to Theodor Adorno.

While Strindberg prepared himself for Paris, his marriage deteriorated along familiar lines—conflicts, scenes, reconciliations. Frida ran away with the child and took a room at an inn on the far side of the river: Strindberg scanned the bank for her through his field glasses. Frida's family became increasingly agitated. Finally, a friend in Paris sent him money to travel. In *The Convent*, he describes his departure. As the boat leaves the pier, he suddenly feels the bond that connects him to wife and child, and he wants to jump into the river and swim back. The paddle-wheels turn a few more times, and the bond stretches, stretches—and breaks. Strindberg was to meet Frida again in Paris, and to live with her for a few weeks. Yet the parting by the steamer was a very real one. Frida's enduring dowry to Strindberg was that Danube landscape: the river, the mountains, the images of the Virgin, the ferryman. He fostered it and made good use of it in his writings.

Chapter Thirteen

'INFERNO'

I

STRINDBERG'S JOURNEY to Paris in August 1894 was beset by misadventure. The boy who carried his luggage—a yellow trunk, a basket and a green bag—on board at Grein, missed the last call ashore and had to stay on the paddle-wheeler until the next port of call. Strindberg called him a somnolent fellow, but was not much more alert himself: he left his Baedeker on Germany as well as his maps in the ship's saloon, and as he had not paid attention to the name of that particular vessel, these items were difficult to retrieve. Expecting to board a train in Linz, he found that he had misread the timetable. He missed the express and had to travel via Munich, Ulm, and Strasburg on slow trains which, according to him, stopped for a full two hours at every major station.

This was what everyday life was like for Strindberg when he had to look after himself. His pedantry was founded on the experience of constantly getting lost in the world of the senses. But he wrote a very calm report on his situation immediately after arriving in Paris:

> I come from the mountains and valleys, from down there by the banks of the Blue Danube. Behind me, I have left the cottage by the roadside, the as yet unharvested grapes, the unripened tomatoes and melons and the roses, still in bud. For the hundredth time I have tied my knapsack and emigrated to seek work in the great city, the intellectual market-place of the world—Paris!

He was formulating a pilgrim's role for himself.

At first, Strindberg stayed in Littmansson's villa in rue de Lesseps in Versailles, which its owner had vacated for the summer. The upheaval Strindberg had left behind him in Austria did not prevent him from planning a continued life with Frida, and as a token of his good intentions he wrote to her calling her 'dear Mrs Badger'. He made enquiries about the costs of room and board and sent her an extensive list of prices, with beefsteak noted at 1.60 francs per half kilogram, and oil and coal included. Frida was told that she and the child were his sole interest in life.

He still had debts in Austria—to Frida's sister, father and grandfather—but dealt with them in his usual lordly manner. He called the grandfather 'that old usurer'. 'I am no Raskolnikov,' he wrote at the end of August, as if he had been contemplating a murder, 'but I do believe that youth has a right to live and thus pay its debts.'

One of the many publishers he was lobbying for his conquest of the French audience was a young German, Albert Langen, who had established himself in Paris and specialized in Scandinavian authors, Hamsun and Brandes among them. Later, Langen expanded his northern connections by marrying one of Björnson's daughters. 'Rich, honest—at last, an ideal publisher,' was Strindberg's judgement, but he was soon to revise it. Langen had an extravagant friend and adviser, Willy Grétor, who had been born a Pedersen but changed his name to resemble that of a Swedish mistress, Greta. These two men of the world received Strindberg in Paris. They had a sense for anything new and promising, so the Swedish 'maestro' was their man—nor did they forget to please him by using that term of address when conversing with him. Langen undertook to publish *A Fool's Apology*. Grétor was a painter and art dealer. He saw Strindberg's Dornach paintings, appreciated their value, and proposed an exhibition with lucrative sales at the Champ de Mars. He also gave Strindberg the run of his wealthy wife's luxurious apartment at no. 51 rue Ranelagh in Passy, and Strindberg moved there on 6 September. The five rooms were furnished with carved furniture, Persian rugs and valuable porcelain. On the walls original drawings by Rembrandt and Rubens hung next to paintings by the new geniuses—Van Gogh's famous prison yard painting among them.

Strindberg, who always had a tendency to count his chickens before they were hatched, was taken in by Grétor's praise of his paintings and proceeded to paint some more, which included a number of his best—most of them with the same wide ocean horizon he could not tolerate in real life; one, the most beautiful, has a single flower in the foreground. But he claimed that the fashionable apartment repelled him and he described himself, two days after moving in, as 'a wild bird in a cage'. 'Passy is dreary, so dreary! but I have to stay here, since the accommodation is free,' he told Littmansson. 'I wish I were on Kymmendö, crying out like the Eagle, among the fir trees!' He told Frida that the apartment reeked of its wealthy owner's perfume, and amused himself by fantasizing a risk of arrest as a pimp, since he was, indeed, living off a woman. Then he heard rumours that Grétor's activities as an art dealer were on the shady side: this was to become a principal subject of his in years to come.

Frida, who did not find the reasonable price of coal all that exciting, was, however, interested in that apartment in Passy. She arrived in Paris in mid-September — without the child. The life-style Langen and Grétor practised is illustrated by Frida's claim that Grétor had sent Langen's servant, in full livery and white gloves, to the railway station on three consecutive days, to meet her with a coach and a bouquet of red roses.

Frida was charmed by Langen and Grétor, who were her age, and courted them with an intensity Strindberg ought to have recognized, blending the business of publication with her own sexual interest. She saw an opportunity to further her own career, and she was right in giving support to Langen, who later became one of the most brilliant German publishers, handling, among other things, the political satirical magazine *Simplicissimus*, which was the leading publication of its kind during the twilight of the empire and the Weimar Republic. According to Frida, Langen started *Simplicissimus* at Strindberg's suggestion. Frida has also told us that she made efforts to seduce Grétor, who was a man fascinating to both sexes. As he resisted, she began a love affair with Langen's secretary, Frank Wedekind, who was to become a famous playwright; in 1897, Frida bore his child. Strindberg found himself in precisely that situation, wide open to ridicule, which he had described with such empathy in *A Fool's Apology*.

The couple lived together for no more than a month. The newspaper *Les Gaulois* managed to obtain an interview in which Strindberg, his moustache in disarray, reclining in a low chair with his wife seated on one arm-rest, declared that he was momentarily unable to work because he needed to hear children's cries around him. When the interviewer touched on Strindberg's misogyny, the couple both smiled as if that was quite inapplicable to their enlightened relationship. On 22 October, after they left the apartment in Passy, Frida went back to Austria. 'Why did I feel such wild joy when you left?' Strindberg asked in a letter he wrote to Frida a month later. Those words returned three years later, at the beginning of *Inferno*, the novel about Strindberg's years in Paris. Frida and Strindberg never saw each other again. In the new existence he was planning, there was no room for anyone else — least of all, a woman. Hence his joy to be rid of her.

In the late autumn, Strindberg lived in the Hôtel des Américains in the rue de l'Abbé de l'Epée, a modest establishment close to the Jardin de Luxembourg, and frequented by many Scandinavian artists. He avoided Langen and Grétor, not only because Frida had become a spectre between them, but probably also because Langen had demanded modifications and cuts in *A Fool's Apology*. At the hotel, Strindberg met a Norwegian, Johan Fahlström, who was a man of the theatre, and his wife, who belonged to the Bosse family and had a sixteen-year-old sister — who would, seven years later, become Strindberg's third wife. Strindberg befriended the couple, and they helped him sell his paintings, where Grétor had failed.

In November, Strindberg reacted explosively against Frida, as if to ensure that she would not return, and wrote her a series of letters that totally destroyed his marriage. As with Siri, jealousy was the starting point; Langen and Grétor were mentioned—the latter as 'a pimp'—and, just as Siri had found, it was both impossible and pointless to try to force admissions or prove the accusations. In the rage that Strindberg generated from within himself, logic simply disappeared without trace.

Frida was told that Strindberg had seen through her from the very first moment, that she had caught him in a spider's web of lies, that she was a dirty human animal, doomed to perish, and that her own mother had called her a whore. Frida noticed that these insults were remarkably similar to the ones her husband had directed against his first wife, and that lessened the shock to some extent. Compared to Siri, she also had better intuitive understanding of explosive tempers such as Strindberg's. Nevertheless, she immediately instituted preliminary proceedings for divorce, and after many delays and several reconciliations, these took their course.

In public, Strindberg maintained a more dignified and sophisticated attitude. To Richard Bergh, an artist friend he liked to confide in, he wrote at the end of November:

> I don't really know much about my marriage. It was never taken too seriously, as you probably noticed in Berlin, and I think it is headed toward its dissolution—although I don't know for certain. At times, it was great fun, and good, but language, *race*,* disagreements over what is right, and bad habits did sometimes cause considerable strain.

2

The purpose of Strindberg's journey to Paris was to gain both literary and scientific acclaim in that city. Stellan Ahlström has published a richly documented study of his campaign, *Strindberg's Conquest of Paris* (1956). As in Berlin, Strindberg met with considerable success. A number of his works were translated: *The Father* had a resounding first night at the Théâtre de l'Oeuvre in December; in January 1895, *A Fool's Apology* appeared in its original French version, and a small number of the 'vivisections' written during the summer were printed in French newspapers.

Among the French cultural élite, Strindberg did not achieve a position comparable to that of Turgenev or Henry James, but he did become a peripheral star. He himself imagined that he was playing his cards with the

* Translator's note: in English in the original.

utmost shrewdness. He relabelled his works, as authors are apt to do, in order to make them fit into the leading movement of the day: Symbolism. He gave priority to French translations of those of his works that could be interpreted in that direction: *The Secret of the Guild*, *The Romantic Sexton of Rånö* and *In the Offing*.

Miss Julie, which he had proudly called the first naturalist play in 1888, now became a Symbolist one: Julie's greenfinch, as it expires in Jean's cruel hands, symbolically prefigures its owner's fate and is thus proof of the play's symbolist character. Strindberg was a protégé of Zola's, and in an interview he called Zola 'the master of Symbolism' and obviously believed that by doing so he had eliminated the danger of being regarded as belonging to a bygone literary epoch. He even made efforts to counteract the xenophobia that was so near the surface in France in the year of a president's assassination and of the Dreyfus affair: in an article, 'The Barbarian in Paris', he sought to demonstrate that French culture was created by the French and the Northmen in conjunction, and that the Gothic style had been born in Normandy, the Vikings' stronghold. In the sharp angles and shadows of Notre Dame he saw a northern pine forest; in the vault, a Viking ship turned upside down; and in the ornamental spouts, the dragon's heads on the prows of those ships.

Yet it was one of his hate articles, 'Woman's Inferiority to Man', published in the *Revue Blanche* in early January 1895, that really excited the Parisians and made Strindberg a favourite subject of conversation for several weeks. In Paris, as earlier on in Stockholm, his exotic traits and extravagant opinions were what the public concentrated on when it tried to make itself an image of him. The French did not see Strindberg, the consummate artist; rather, they saw a wild man from the North, violent, a genius, but too unpredictable for the salons, perhaps even for the literary immortality that Parisians believed was accorded exclusively by their city.

However, Strindberg had greater plans than the achievement of brief notoriety; what he produced with that short-term end in mind was careless, frivolous, half-hearted, and a target for his own disdainful comments. Generally speaking, Strindberg was never really seriously engaged in all the whims and strategies that circulated in his head because he never lost sight of his main goal, his imaginative work. This is one of many reasons why it is difficult to keep up with his day-to-day life. Four days before the première of *The Father*, for instance, he wrote to Georges Loiseau, his French translator: 'It kills me to chew the cud of old things. The same effect is caused by the punishment of social obligation—tonight—black tie, and all that! Oh, if only I had the balloon I dream of, I would fly to my island and hide in the woods by the shore of the sea—*my* sea!' 'Old things' in this case referred specifically to a revised French translation of *Sir Bengt's Wife*, but the attitude expressed had wider significance.

This was his fourth visit to Paris. On the first occasion in 1876 he had searched for the traces of the Commune. Now, he was no longer interested in the history of the city, but in its timeless aspect. In his brilliant article 'Confused Sense Impressions', quoted at the beginning of this chapter, he sees Paris as a great camp in a desert, in which 100,000 pilgrims light their fires to greet the rising sun. The following year, he continued in that vein in his article 'The Sighs of the Stones'. Paris was described as 'The Eternal City', a resurrected Rome with its own amphitheatres and catacombs, and the French language was praised as the Roman tongue in a new, rejuvenated form. In his imagination, Paris was transformed into the stage of a timeless martyr play, soon to be performed with—at least on the surface of things— himself in the main role.

3

Both Strindberg's contemporaries and posterity have found *Inferno* the hardest of his books to get to grips with. It appears to be an account of his life from the moment he parted from his second wife in the autumn of 1894 until June 1897, when he considered entering a monastic order (or so he says). In his own words, *Inferno* documents the 'great crisis at the age of fifty' with its 'revolution of the life of the psyche'. In this sense it is a sequel to his autobiography.

But if *The Serving Maid's Son* and *A Fool's Apology* are unreliable as strict autobiographical material, so is *Inferno*, and to a much greater degree. The book is completely useless as a source for the description of Strindberg's life during that period: just as in the *Apology*, the details are correct, but the overall picture is false. On the other hand, 'false' seems too strong a word: *Inferno* does have its own inner truth and will always be seen as a great human document, but its central figure, Strindberg, is not the same man we are dealing with in the present biography—he is a fictitious character.

Thus it is true, for instance, that Strindberg suffered from a rash on his hands and was admitted to a hospital in Paris for treatment, just as we are told in the first chapter of *Inferno*. For a few years, he had been afflicted by a mild form of psoriasis, possibly aggravated by his chemical experiments. After the first night of *The Father*, on 13 December 1894, he complained about both the rash and his poverty.

A French musician, William Molard, was associated with the Scandinavian colony in Paris through his marriage to the Swedish sculptor Ida Ericson; the couple lived at no. 6 rue Vercingetorix, the building in which

Paul Gauguin had his studio. During that winter, Strindberg made a number of new friends, of whom Gauguin was one. Another was the young French poet Julien Leclercq, who translated *The Romantic Sexton of Rånö* and became yet another of the attentive young courtiers in Strindberg's life.

Ida Ericson-Molard, a woman of compassion, organized fund-raising among Swedes living in Paris in order to pay for treatment of Strindberg's condition. She received help from the city's Swedish minister, Nathan Söderblom, who later became archbishop of Sweden and conducted Strindberg's funeral rites in 1912. On 11 January 1895, Strindberg was admitted to the St Louis hospital, where he stayed until the end of the month. The cure consisted of an ointment which was spread on his hands, which were then wrapped in cotton and gauze. For a few days, he was unable to dress himself, use a knife when eating or hold a pen.

That torment lasted only a very brief while. In the letters that have been preserved, his handwriting looks shaky up to 15 January, but on the 16th, five days after his admission to hospital, it is as even and finely balanced as ever, and symptomatic of a healthy mind as well as body.

Looked at objectively, Strindberg's hospitalization was of no great moment. Albert Langen, who kept in close touch with Strindberg despite their disagreements, reassured Frida, calling the damage 'negligible'. Strindberg was allowed to receive visitors and persuaded Littmansson to smuggle a bottle into his room. He was interviewed by both *Le Temps* and *Le Matin* and assured them that he had not received his injuries as a result of experimenting with explosive materials. In June 1894 the Italian anarchist Caserio had murdered the President of France, Sadi Carnot, and Strindberg was entertaining the notion that the French now regarded all foreigners as potential assassins. Caserio's name is, in fact, the only indication of any historical context at the beginning of *Inferno*: little did Strindberg realize that the coming century would be so loaded with violence that individual acts like Caserio's stood little chance of surviving in people's memory.

From the hospital, Strindberg made excursions to nearby cafés, continued his experiments with sulphur in the hospital dispensary, and wrote an essay on Gauguin, designed as a foreword to the painter's great 'final sale' exhibition before his definitive departure for Tahiti. In other words, Strindberg's life in hospital proceeded at its usual hectic pace.

It was the only time Strindberg ever spent in hospital. His tremendous ability for hard work was based on unparalleled good health. The Berlin physician Carl Ludwig Schleich, who had examined him, later wrote in his excellent book that Strindberg had a 'thick-set body with almost baroquely muscular limbs, and his chest was large, wide and superbly extended, as if he were permanently drawing in his breath'.

In *Inferno*, Strindberg's time in hospital looks very different. After seeing his wife off at the Gare du Nord, he hastens to his hotel room where the

43 Hôtel Orfila in the rue d'Assas, where Strindberg lived from 21 February to 19 July
1896, and which was the setting for most of his 'occult' experiences

sulphur concoction is awaiting him. Late at night, he discovers carbon in the sulphur and believes that he has indeed overthrown the accepted rules of chemistry. He has achieved the immortality of a great scientist — but now his hands crack in the heat of the crucible. Desperate and impoverished, he roams the streets. A compassionate woman (Ida Ericson-Molard) collects money for him so that he can afford to go to hospital. On his way there, he purchases two linen shirts, thinking that they may well be used as his shroud.

He goes on to describe his life at the St Louis Hospital and his conversations with a sympathetic and comforting elderly nun, who directs him on to the meaningful path of suffering. One day, having received permission to go out, he intends to visit his friends at the Café Napolitain, but has the misfortune to run into a man who, he believes, has contributed to the collection. Immediately convinced that he is suspected of malingering, he feels like a beggar who does not have a right to visit cafés.

> Beggar! It is the right word; it rings in my ears and brings a fiery blush to my cheeks, a blush of shame, humiliation, and fury! To think, only six weeks ago I was sitting at these tables; my theatre director allowed me to buy him drinks and addressed me as his dear master; newspapermen competed for interviews, the photographer asked for the honour of selling copies of my portrait. And now: beggar, marked man, outcast! Whipped, beaten, hounded to death, I slink down the boulevard like some nocturnal figure and retreat into my lair among the plague victims. There, I lock myself into my room which is now my home.

4

Around the turn of the year 1894–5, the beggar theme featured more and more frequently in Strindberg's correspondence. Increasingly, he described himself as a wretched, hounded creature. On 20 January 1895, in a letter to Frida, he called himself 'a sheep already attacked by the vultures', and two days later he was 'defenceless as a lamb' soon to be torn to pieces by a wolf. From that lamb, it was but a short step to Jesus, God's lamb, and it occurred to Strindberg that his wounded hands were related to the Saviour's stigmata.

A friend from his youth, Jean Lundin, came to play a peculiar part in Strindberg's assumption of his new role. Lundin had been a lieutenant of the Svea Artillery, one of Sweden's most distinguished and traditional regiments. Long into the twentieth century, its officers came almost exclusively from the ranks of the aristocracy. Lundin was a mere bourgeois, and this made his position precarious. In *The New Kingdom*, Strindberg devoted an entire chapter to describing an existence similar to Lundin's, outlining the bitter humiliations he had to suffer which finally led to his resignation from the regiment.

In the 1870s, Lundin associated with the bohemians of the Red Room, lending their circle a degree of glamour through his social standing as an officer. The regimental uniform was a splendid one: the dark blue coat, or 'attila', was adorned with corded bars, and had a light blue collar, and a cartouche or a small golden tin originally designed to contain ammunition. In *The New Kingdom*, Lundin appears as Lundqvist, but in *The Serving Maid's Son* he goes under his first name, Jean. On one occasion, related by Strindberg, the lieutenant in his splendid uniform and one of the shabbiest members of the circle had to part company and walk separately to the tavern, to avoid such an insult to the regimental honour. In another episode, Jean was due to participate in the military parade at Oscar II's coronation on 12 May 1873. His uniform, however, was in the pawnshop—a catastrophic situation. Johan (Strindberg) spent the night before the coronation with prostitutes, and Jean came and stood by the bed, in order to borrow money. The uniform was redeemed in the nick of time: it was creased, but Jean managed to make it look passable. The next day, all the newspapers commented on the magnificent spectacle the coronation had been. It was a crucial scene for Strindberg: an extravagant façade, concealing dirt and shabbiness.

Lundin's life deteriorated; he became an alcoholic, resigned his commission and emigrated to Paris where he lived in poverty, borrowing money on a daily basis, but still retaining his arrogant manner from his bohemian days. Littmansson told Strindberg about him, and the latter became fascinated by his fate, associating it with his own. Strindberg's letters to Littmansson were characterized by a wealth of puns: Strindberg amused himself by changing vowels or otherwise deforming words. *Himmel* (heaven, sky) became *hymmel*; *helvete* (hell) became *höllvete*; *kviga* (heifer) became *kvyga*. He was digging around in a linguistic mulch, trying to open up individual words as if they were oysters containing pearls. He also amused himself with a game of his own devising, the 'trimurti' game.

According to Torsten Eklund, 'trimurti' is a Hindu designation for the three deities Brahma, the creator, Vishnu, the sustainer, and Shiva, the destroyer; it has also been adopted by the Theosophists.

Strindberg used the concept to characterize people. He drew up equilateral triangles either resting on one side or standing on one point. In each corner there was a word: reading the three words—they had to rhyme—in a certain order, one witnessed a drama in miniature. Here is an example, a trimurti Strindberg sent to Littmansson in mid-August 1894:

Örnen

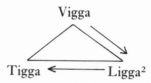

Børnen ←——— Törnen[1]

Under this trimurti, Strindberg wrote: 'That ys my trymurty, the tragyc part.' As a counterpart, he then provided Lundin's trimurti:

Vigga

Tigga ←——— Ligga[2]

Time and time again, Strindberg returned to the subject of Lundin in new trimurtis or other references. 'Lundin exists here and borrows his way like a devil! Just like me!' he wrote on 30 November 1894. On 6 December he returned to the subject.

> What's more, he is damned impudent, so that when he has borrowed from the minister of the local congregation and then breakfasts on some Beaune wine, and the minister happens to come by and humbly walks up to greet him, Lundin denies both his own identity and his acquaintance with the man. That is true greatness!

In other words, Lundin found himself in precisely the situation Strindberg placed himself in at the opening of *Inferno*—being surprised by a benefactor in a tavern. While Lundin retained his arrogance, Strindberg (in *Inferno*) wished the earth would swallow him up.

Strindberg toyed with the idea of inviting Lundin to the banquet held after the first night of *The Father*. Had he done so, it would have been a rehearsal for the wedding feast in his play *Erik XIV*: as the noble guests fail to appear, beggars and riffraff are asked in. Lundin became one of Strindberg's many *Doppelgängers*, a mirror that was both true and distorted. In the play *To Damascus*, a beggar plays a leading part, and when the play's protagonist, The Unknown One, meets him he realizes that he has come face to face with himself.

---

[1] The Eagle, the Thorn, the Burn (or Bruin).
[2] Borrow, Lie (prone), Beg.

5

Strindberg's many *cris de coeur* that winter led to further collections in addition to the one Mme Molard had initiated. One of them was started by Knut Hamsun who was living in Paris at that time; an appeal to the Scandinavian public spoke of Strindberg's 'helpless condition' and said that he 'was going through a crisis that could lead to his ruin'. The signatories, among them Jonas Lie, Albert Edelfelt, and Andreas Zorn, acted in good faith. In March 1895 Edelfelt wrote to his mother that Lie had told him Strindberg was insane, suffering from persecution mania and obsessive notions. Thus the myth was created—and it still persists today—that Strindberg was undergoing a severe crisis that winter. He contributed to it himself, first and foremost in *Inferno*.

In reality, he was furious about what he called, in a letter to Mörner, 'that disgusting begging appeal'. He found himself in exactly the same situation as on his arrival in Berlin, when Ola Hansson had raised the alarm. He treated Hamsun savagely and in April sent him a postcard saying: 'Keep the thirty pieces of silver, and let us be done with one another for the rest of our lives.' A few days later, he wrote to the kindly Lie that he had not refused assistance, 'but I have expelled Hamsun who took advantage of my need and subjected me to moral violence'. To redeem himself from the indignity he felt he had suffered, he decided that the collected funds should go to his children in Finland. When a German theatre—this, too, was Hamsun's doing—gave a charity performance for him, he ordered the money to be sent to his daughter in Austria; Friedrich Uhl, being a wealthy man, took this as an insult.

In the course of March and April, yet another collection was organized, this one under the aegis of F. U. Wrangel, whom Strindberg had known since his schooldays. The appeal was worded more carefully: 'ill and hard-pressed' had to suffice. Strindberg put the 1,795 kronor he received to good use. In 1895, his finances were reasonably good, and during the summer he was able to purchase a number of instruments for his research, among them an expensive microscope.

After his discharge from hospital, Strindberg did not return to the Hôtel des Américains, which he called 'a place of horror'. Instead, he took lodgings in a small family-run *pension* at no. 12 rue de la Grande Chaumière just by the Jardin de Luxembourg, and stayed there for over a year. On the other side of the street was a *crèmerie*, a small, crowded restaurant run by Mme Charlotte Futterer. Strindberg ate his meals here and became the object of the lady's maternal attentions. Gauguin also frequented the place, as did the Polish painter Slewinski, who painted a portrait of Strindberg. The 'begging appeal' alienated him from the local Scandinavians to some extent, and he benefited from a wider international circle of new friends, among whom were the British composer Frederick Delius and the Czech poster artist Alphonse Mucha.

On 1 February, Strindberg completed and signed his foreword to the Gauguin catalogue. In it, he declared that he detested 'Christ and his crown of thorns', had no use for 'that pitiful God who allows himself to be maltreated', and paid homage to Gauguin who had created a new heaven and new earth in his art. Gauguin was 'the Titan who envies the Creator and in his spare time makes his own little Creation'. Gauguin was delighted by this characterization, which also expressed Strindberg's own feelings.

Strindberg spent the entire spring and summer of 1895 on his chemical experiments, encouraged by the fact that a number of French journals and several French scientists had paid attention to him and seriously discussed his results. Marcelin Berthelot, professor at the Ecole de Pharmacie of Paris, wrote him a long, respectful letter. Strindberg established close contact with François Jollivet-Castelot, whose book *Life and Soul in Matter* had captivated him the previous summer. In April, he travelled to Rouen to meet a new friend, the chemist and engineer André Dubosc, and to enjoy — he told Mörner — round-the-clock discussions of scientific matters, comparable to those he had had in Lund with Bengt Lidforss. That same month, he also received permission to work at the analytical laboratory of the Sorbonne. He believed that he had now conclusively proved to those sceptical professors that sulphur was not an element.

He frequently found himself in excellent spirits and deferred the role of beggar-lamb for the time being — without forgetting it: on 12 May, he wrote to Mörner that he possessed only one pair of trousers, with a hole in one leg 'so that I had to hold my hat in front of it when I went to the Legation'. His reason for that visit was to receive an advance on the monies collected in Sweden, from F. U. Wrangel's brother Herman Wrangel (the brothers were very remotely related to Siri's first husband). Once again, he wrote to his children in Finland with amicable interest, and even Frida received milder words than before. On 16 May, he wrote to her that she had never been able to solve the riddle his sphinx-like, enigmatic soul presented, and which was far more complicated than she could even suspect. He said that he had been following the laws of nature which compelled him to love her although he detested her — 'Can you understand such things?' He continued:

> It seems to me, that my esoteric person remains a stranger to you. Perhaps you still believe that I was a fortune hunter. . . . When I married, I knew very well what I brought with me and what I hoped for. I have suffered from misfortune and plain bad luck. Forgive me! Despite your cruelty, you relieved my life of vexations. That is a great deal, and I am not ungrateful. You have eased my existence, but have made it bitter at the same time.

During that spring, Strindberg saw Gauguin every day until the painter departed in June. A Dr Eliasson in Ystad, Sweden, whom Strindberg had met in Lund in the early 1890s, invited him to stay at his home for the summer. When the hot summer weather began in Paris, Strindberg wrote to him and asked him for 300 kronor for his journey home. He received the money by return of post and wrote to thank Eliasson for it on 7 June, adding by way of explanation:

> There was a word in your first letter that perturbed me a little! You spoke of my broken-down soul. My soul is not broken down, has never been as lucid and clear, on the contrary, I have myself broken down souls of a lower kind that threatened my soul's more justified freedom. And I have even broken down old scientific prejudices, made my way into the Sorbonne itself, thrown the burning torch of doubt into it, gained supporters, admirers, detractors. . . . Beware of the legends, keep your faith in me, and do not try to disturb the freedom of my soul, for that would cause me to flee.

Strindberg left for Sweden immediately and arrived in Malmö on 12 June. In Ystad, he was allowed to conduct his experiments in a kitchen. He stayed there until mid-July, and then returned to Paris for new enterprises in chemistry.

6

In the summer of 1895 Strindberg began to connect his writing with his scientific pursuits. He called himself a 'poet chemist' and his chemical formulae 'chemical sonnets'. If everything is contained within everything else, the poet with his totally engaged senses is the true discoverer of this hidden unity and does not really need crucibles or microscope to do so. In September, Strindberg published a short paper in Paris, titled 'Introduction à une chimie unitaire', in which the monistic doctrine was presented with a proliferation of formulae. On 28 September, Louis Pasteur died; Strindberg consoled himself with the thought that the commotion caused by that event was the reason why no one paid attention to his article. But, as so often before, in terms of his development he was really far ahead of his published writings.

In October, he took a step that was important for his progress. He remembered his occultist correspondent from the summer of 1894, Torsten Hedlund, put on his beggar's hat, and wrote to him that he needed financial assistance in order to write a new book about 'a new universe, like the one I started in *Antibarbarus*, but several notes higher, since suffering and fighting have given me courage to be myself, courage not to mock those who mock me.'

What Strindberg had in mind was to present all the kingdoms of nature, the entire universe, as seen in the light of the new doctrine of unity. Torsten Hedlund responded to his appeal and provided funds. For a year, he became Strindberg's favourite correspondent—the last in a long succession. Strindberg chose him as a heaven-sent guide, and made use of a number of his theosophical speculations; but Hedlund's main task was to listen and bear witness, just like all his predecessors.

The first result of the new project was *Sylva Sylvarum*, published in French in Paris, in January 1896. In addition, Hedlund published two small pamphlets entitled *Jardin des plantes* in Göteborg that year. For the most part, the texts of the two titles are identical. The cheap printing of these little brochures contrasts pathetically with the imaginative power that finds its expression in them. *Sylva Sylvarum* starts out with Dante's 'In the middle of the journey of our life I came to myself . . .' and continues with Strindberg's description of how he had grown weary of the deadly monotony of a world in which God had been abolished and science claimed to have solved all riddles. So weary, in fact, that he resolved to take his own life. He has prepared some cyanate, its fumes already constrict his throat, a stinging pain runs through his spinal cord. Then he has a vision of a flowering almond tree by a garden walk, and he hears an old woman's voice say: 'No, child, do not believe in that!'

The feeling of salvation from death and destruction and of a happy rebirth expressed in that scene is the starting point for the essays that follow, and also for the powerful literary works that Strindberg created during the following years.

The essays are 'rambles', somewhat in the manner of *Flower Pieces and Animal Stories*, but—as Strindberg had promised Hedlund—on a considerably more elevated plane. One brilliant observation followed another; Strindberg's intuitive awareness that everything is infinitely interconnected fired its lightning bolts into the great chaos—the starting-point of it all. Strindberg's imagination had gained a new resilience, a new confidence in his ability to see correspondences and parallels between different areas of knowledge. He connected all the kingdoms of nature, but never in a generalizing, pantheistic way: the connections are palpable, concrete. The kingfisher, he claimed, had evolved the brightly coloured, scale-like feathers on its neck and wings by spending many hours sitting and staring down into the water at its prey—the fishes. The mackerel's moiré back reflected wave motions in water, to the extent that one could copy and present them as waves on a canvas. The hoar-frost crystals on trees and blades of grass resembled caterpillars, roses and cauliflower heads: the observation is presented as evidence for a connection between the organic and the inorganic world. The pattern on the wings of the death's-head moth was generated by the fact that the insect frequented sites of execution and graveyards, where it laid its eggs in corpses. The forms of plant-life recur in metals. The sunflower reflects the image of the sun with its disc, rays and spots. Flowers and animals mistake themselves for one another and exchange forms.

Sylva Sylvarum—the title (The Forest of the Forests) was borrowed from Bacon, but it also refers to Dante's 'dark wood'—did not win acclaim for Strindberg, nor did *Jardin des plantes* do any better later in the year. But he was not discouraged: he knew he was on the right path. On 24 January 1896, while sending out copies of *Sylva Sylvarum*, he wrote to Hedlund that he had regained his faith in a personal God, and that he now believed that the soul's immortality was a self-evident fact. He offered his own proof:

> The butterfly larva crawls around and eats just as we higher animals do. Then, one fine day, it falls ill, its powers wane, its body is consumed, yet, in a final effort, it weaves its own shroud and builds its grave. Then, it decomposes—necrobiosis! Death-life! Life-death! Because there is no difference between life and death! I have opened up cocoons, examined them through a microscope. All that is in there is a white, unformed, inchoate substance that resembles the saponification of a corpse and smells like one. Out of that slime, from 'growth points', the butterfly or moth develops and leaves its grave. It is a symbol—and more!—if the creator is an artist who amuses himself by speaking in exquisite sign language to people who understand even a little of what he is trying to say!

The personal God is, in fact, a natural consequence of monistic philosophy. God is an artist, and his intentions can be deciphered from his creation. This is an ancient concept, but for Strindberg it was a new and fresh discovery, and it suited him all the better since that creative God worked his ways on nature in a manner similar to that of the writer, who created living beings by his words.

7

On 21 February 1896, Strindberg moved from the rue de la Grande Chaumière to the Hôtel Orfila, at no. 60 rue d'Assas. The Orfila was an unpretentious family hotel with narrow corridors, wooden stairs and passageways. It was owned and run by M. and Mme Ginguet. Room and service cost 40 francs a month; Strindberg was served breakfast and lunch for 66 francs a month, and coal for heating came to 20 francs. His evening meal was still provided by Mme Futterer. His finances were relatively stable for some time, as Hedlund undertook to pay his hotel and restaurant bills directly: a wealthy patron of the arts in Göteborg, August Röhss, had provided the sum of 1,200 kronor for that purpose.

One of Strindberg's visitors at the Orfila, F. U. Wrangel, found the room less than congenial. A simple iron bedstead stood diagonally in an alcove, and there was a large table covered with papers, journals and various utensils. On the marble mantelpiece stood a row of bottles, and small porcelain crucibles were ranged along the windowsill. Wrangel found Strindberg looking pale and red-eyed—there are many indications that he was drinking more heavily than usual at this time—and said that there was a 'searching' expression in Strindberg's eyes which he had not seen before. Yet when the two of them went to the Closerie des Lilas to drink absinthe, Strindberg became his old self and was friendly, almost exuberant.

Strindberg stayed at the Orfila for five months, and the hotel became more closely connected than anywhere else with the mental crisis which he is believed to have undergone during this time. It was there that Strindberg started the *Occult Diary*, which for over fifty years after his death lay sealed with a double seal in Stockholm's Royal Library. The few scholars who were allowed to see it were regarded as brave explorers in an underworld filled with sulphurous fumes and demons. On its cover, Strindberg had written in 1908: 'This diary must never be printed! This is my last will! which has to be obeyed!' Those words were reproduced in facsimile on the cover of the complete diary, printed and published in 1977: Strindberg had made sure in other ways that it would not remain unpublished.

During this period, Strindberg was fond of employing the occult terms 'exoteric' and 'esoteric'. The exoteric is someone who is uninitiated and displays himself to the populace at large. Strindberg's exoteric first person is the author who visits friends every day, writes cheerful letters and pursues his literary career. This was the person who reported to Eliasson in May 1896 that Paris was a lovely place to be in, that one could live on the pavements, that there was 'room for every kind of idea, especially new ones, even mine'; he also surprised his sister Anna and her husband who had come to visit him because of the alarming rumours they had heard, by appearing 'unusually harmonious in his behaviour'.

The esoteric Strindberg, however, was a secret figure, an initiate. The diary is a collection of observations about him. Strindberg had been looking for the unity of nature in his laboratory experiments. Now, he was looking for that unity—God—in his everyday life. The esoteric first person became the hero of a new, and overwhelming drama.

For the outsider, the uninitiated, the *Occult Diary* and Strindberg's letters to occultist friends would appear as frequently ridiculous and even boring. Strindberg recorded birds who were nesting in his chimney, pebbles shaped like hearts, his own glasses falling off his nose and ending up in his coffee, pendulum clocks which struck a greater number of times than they were supposed to, pigeons heading either east or west, a rooster weather-vane that seemed to flap its wings, playing cards found in the gutter. Amidst all this, there are notes about books, contemporary political events—the Dreyfus affair figured prominently, and Strindberg regarded Dreyfus as guilty—and records of dreams in which his father appeared frequently, as well as Siri and Frida.

All these pieces of information, sometimes copious, sometimes sparse, relate to the scientific discoveries in that the primary impulse behind them is a vision of connectedness and a creative deity. Thus each individual observation does not have to be proof in itself. The connection is there, but human beings find it hard to see. Mere mortals often make mistakes and then become objects of ridicule. It is—and this is important—the exoteric ego who keeps the diary and is not always able to keep up with what happens to its initiated *Doppelgänger*.

In the summer of 1896, Strindberg received more concrete material for his exoteric ego to work on. His Polish friend from Berlin days, Przybyszewski, had a mistress, Marthe Foerder, who died in June. Przybyszewski was arrested and charged with her murder and that of their child. At first, Strindberg started a plan for his rescue, together with Edvard Munch who now had his studio in Paris. However, Przybyszewski was released when it became evident that Marthe had taken her own life. Strindberg then imagined that Przybyszewski was on his way to Paris in order to murder him because he suspected Strindberg of having had a relationship with his wife. Strindberg thought that he was hearing the strains of Schumann's 'Aufschwung' played on a piano—this was one of Przybyszewski's favourites which proved that the assumed murderer was on his way.

During the summer, Strindberg wrote a number of letters to Torsten Hedlund, that were similar in tone to the letters to Littmansson in the summer of 1894—highly strung and incredibly inventive. To Hedlund he confided details of murder plots, strange knockings on the wall, electric currents beamed through his room in order to kill him, and his fear that the police were looking for him, suspecting him to be a forger of works of art—this last form of paranoia was caused by Grétor's having been arrested for some dubious transactions. These letters constitute the main evidence at the disposal of those who want to be convinced that Strindberg did indeed suffer from extreme paranoia, that he was driven out of the full use of his senses in the summer of 1896, and that *Inferno* is an accurate report of a shattering crisis from which Strindberg was then miraculously saved.

Strindberg's drama reached its climax on 19 July. On the 18th, he wrote to Hedlund—and it is remarkable that his command of language and intellect remained intact all this time—that it seemed to him that hallucinations, fantasies and dreams possessed a high degree of reality.

> If I see my pillow taking on human shapes, then those shapes are there, and if someone says that they are only (!) generated by my imagination, I'll reply: 'Only', you say?—What my inner eye sees, is more to me! And what I see in that pillow, made out of the feathers of birds who once were carriers of life, is a soul, the power to create forms, and, out of linen which once carried the life force in its fibres, reality, since I am able to draw these forms and show them to others. There are times when I hear a cricket singing inside that pillow. The sound made by the grasshopper has always seemed magical to me. It is a kind of ventriloquism—it has always seemed to me as if it came from some empty hall down below, underneath the surface of the earth. Now, assuming that these creatures once sang in a field of flax, do you not believe that Nature or the creator could use the vegetable fibre as a phonograph, so that it plays to my inner ear which through suffering, deprivation and prayer has become willing to hear farther than before? But that is where 'natural explanations' do not suffice, and I abandon them instantly!

Those eloquent and inspired words may be seen as providing a key to the so-called 'Inferno crisis'. Strindberg was listening with his inner ear and admitting his fantasies and dreams, which he did not confuse with the reality of his exoteric life.

On 19 July at 11.15 am, Strindberg fled from the Hôtel Orfila after 'a night of horror', according to the diary. He rented a room at a pension in the rue de la Clé. That afternoon, at 3 pm, he wrote Hedlund a long and beautifully lyrical letter in which he said that he had been convinced someone was trying to murder him by means of lethal gas. He gave a detailed description of the preceding twenty-four hours: he had heard mysterious voices in the room next door; he had looked for and found consolation in the Bible; he had gone for a walk in the Jardin de Luxembourg and suddenly felt his legs paralysed; then he had taken a hansom cab from the hotel, and now, at the moment of writing, he was lying on a bed in a pavilion in a garden. The doors were open, hollyhocks and acacias were flowering outside, and he knew it was truly summer. He went on to give Hedlund instructions in case of his demise: he wanted to be buried at Montparnasse, a place he had been visiting continually. The letter ended with a description of how he had opened his window on the first night in his new room and seen the Big Dipper with the Pole Star, and how his thoughts had turned north, homewards.

The letter is, in fact, a sketch for *Inferno*—not a report but a poem about the esoteric being who would soon go on a great journey through hell and interpret the signs he saw there.

8

The peace at the rue de la Clé did not last long. Strindberg fled again, this time first to his friend Fritz Thaulow in Dieppe and then—as the stars had predicted—homewards. On 30 July, he arrived at the residence of Dr Eliasson in Ystad.

He had, in fact, reached the end of his quest. On 20 July, he wrote to Hedlund that he had discovered he was born under the sign of the Ram—as mentioned on the first page of this book. Thus he represented the Sacrifice chosen by God, and all that had happened to him was designed as an education for something new. 'I would like to write a book about it all, in order to free myself from it,' he told Hedlund on 12 August. A few days later he wrote that his 'researches into the hidden'—his choice of words is significant—had been impermissible. The persecution he had suffered had to be understood as punishment. He had been immersed in 'selfish enjoyment of the growth of my self' and had neglected to work for a living and meet his obligations. He said that he wanted to discover a way to divide his person, 'to create a worker, sober, conscientious, and then, if I'm capable of it, let a silent, esoteric *Übermensch* go on growing by the side of the field'. On 23 August, he mentioned *Inferno* for the first time. He wrote to Hedlund:

> You said recently that there is need for a Zola of Occultism. I hear that call, in a grand and elevated sense. A poem in prose: called *Inferno*. The same subject as *In the Offing*. The annihilation of the individual when he isolates himself. Salvation through: work without fame or gold as reward, duty, family, ergo—woman—mother and child!

From Ystad, Strindberg travelled via Berlin to Austria. Frida's mother had invited him to come and stay with her, in order to spend time with Kerstin. In *Inferno*, he immortalized that journey in a couple of memorable sentences. 'A hansom cab takes me from Stettin to Anhalt Line's station in Berlin. That journey of half an hour feels like one through a hedge of thorns, as the concrete reminders sting my heart.'

In Austria, he lived first in Saxen, a small village, where his mother-in-law had an apartment, and then in Klam, a few kilometres from Dornach. His mother-in-law's sister Melanie put a room at his disposal: it had red wallpaper, and Strindberg called it 'the Rose Chamber', after a notorious and legendary torture chamber in eighteenth-century Stockholm. Later, he rented a room in a cottage only a few yards away.

The surrounding landscape was a distinctive one, of relatively high wooded hills and wide fields stretching between them. The village of Klam was dominated by a medieval castle, complete with a tall tower, a Renaissance yard surrounded by pillars and an enormous cellar quarried out of the mountainside: it had been the hereditary residence of the Counts of Clam for centuries. Below the castle lies a ravine with a rapidly flowing creek

44 (*top*) The ravine road in Klam with the Turk's head. 45 (*centre*) The pigsty. 46 (*bottom*) The house by the Danube where Kerstin Strindberg was born. It has been added to, and the windows have been enlarged (*Photographs on this page taken by Olof Lagercrantz*)

at the bottom; in the ravine, there used to be a mill, a smithy and a pigsty, all of these overshadowed by a cliff resembling a huge human head with wild features.

Strindberg had a tract printed in the main town of the region, Grein: its subject was the making of gold. It was basically a farewell gesture: as he wrote to Hedlund on 18 August, he was now leaving the natural sciences, or at least trying to do so. He took walks in the great ravine and spent time with his young daughter, although he found it hard to have to let his psyche descend to such an infantile level. He read Swedenborg and Dante's *Commedia* and felt a strong sense of growth.

All this time, he was working on his 'sacrificial' role, for which the landscape of Klam proved a suitable background. He persuaded himself that while conducting chemical experiments in Paris, in his zinc tub, he had seen the same outline of mountains visible from the window of the Rose Chamber. He recognized the entire region as identical with the hell he read about in Swedenborg. The ravine resembled the entrance to the nether world in Dante. A pigsty by the road with its seven gates (which is still there) led his thoughts to the red-hot sarcophagi in the Canto X of Dante's *Inferno*. It was a correspondence in the spirit of Swedenborg. Strindberg did not believe in it as a genuine identification: in his diary, he drew an entirely different building with six doors; it was a coach-house built out of stone which he used to pass in the summer of 1894 while walking by the Danube. He arranged things, and was not a victim of delusions. He was looking for metaphors and symbols to use in his novel.

Marie Uhl, a remarkably talented woman, saw Strindberg daily during that autumn. She testified later that he often acted in peculiar ways. Once he grabbed a knife and started stabbing the air behind his back, in order to fend off hostile spirits (so he claimed). Another time, he dressed in black and lay on his bed as if in state. Marie Uhl commented:

> My sister and I have often wondered if these dramatic and frequently theatrical events were not so much expressions of an occasional abnormal idea but rather experiments designed to create a good theatrical effect and, also, to test its impact on an audience, ie ourselves, for whom these scenes were performed. It is difficult to decide how much was fantasy, how much reality, hard as it is to imagine how Strindberg really saw the real world. It is certain that, despite all the moments of anxiety we lived through because of him, he also provided us with many amusing and even pleasing ones, by means of his natural talent for comedy.

9

On 27 November 1896, Strindberg left Klam and travelled home via Berlin and Denmark. As we can see from his diary, the new novel was now taking shape in his mind. In Copenhagen, he looked up Georg Brandes. One evening, the two of them were sitting in the Theatre Café on Kongens Nytorv, sharing a bottle of wine and discussing occultism, the fashionable subject of the day. According to Brandes, Strindberg offered to destroy his enemies by means of black magic: he would stick needles through their eyes in photographs. Brandes could have made use of some of Marie Uhl's scepticism; the episode is often quoted to support the argument for Strindberg's insanity. That kind of talk about voodoo had simply become a part of Strindberg's intellectual and artistic invention, and he did not care if people were shocked by it or not.

In December, Strindberg arrived in Skåne. After a few days in Skurup with his friend Dr Lars Nilsson, he settled in Lund, moving on 7 February into a furnished apartment at no. 8 Grönegatan. He made new friends and contacted old ones—all of them a great deal younger than himself, and devoted admirers. The *cher maître* of Paris now became *Den store* (The Great One), a designation which Strindberg even used himself. Many of his new friends were unsophisticated in their affection and naïve acceptance of their master's peculiarities. They generated a comfortable, almost *petit bourgeois* atmosphere around him.

A key figure of that circle was Waldemar Bülow, an editor of *Folkets Tidning* (the *People's News*), a great joker and story-teller. Strindberg found a close friend in Nils Andersson, a lawyer, collector of folk music and a man of steadfast and affectionate character, who remained close to Strindberg until his death. Another friend was Håkan Gillberg, who like Andersson, was a lawyer practising in Lund: he became the model for the unhappy attorney Edvard Libotz in Strindberg's novel *The Scapegoat*. Bengt Lidforss was living in Lund, and there was a reconciliation between him and Strindberg, although they never returned to their former, almost lover-like intimacy.

These friends assisted Strindberg in matters great and small. Bülow's housekeeper Elna cleaned his house for him and even cooked his meals when he complained that the hotel menu offered too many monotonous roasts. In the evenings, people congregated at the Åke Hans Tavern to drink, gossip and conduct ingenuously 'occult' conversations, in which everyone tried to add to 'The Great One's' collection of strange coincidences.

Strindberg's time in Lund, which lasted until the spring of 1899 with the exception of a stay in Paris during the winter of 1897–8, proved calm, harmonious and almost idyllic. These were years of extraordinary inner growth for Strindberg and he realized that he was approaching a time of heightened artistic creativity. He had already set his imaginative powers in motion: all that had previously appeared madness soon vanished, just as his jealousy had disappeared when it no longer served its purpose, to generate *A Fool's Apology*.

Strindberg wrote the most charming letters to his daughter Kerstin and her grandmother, playing a Napoleonic game with them, in which Kerstin was his princess and he an emperor who, like Bonaparte, had a second marriage to an Austrian woman, and a child by her. He was blissfully unaware that his Marie-Louise, Frida, was at that time expecting Frank Wedekind's child, and was eager to obtain a divorce quickly. There were admittedly occasions, as on 6 December 1896, when he told Kerstin and her grandmother that he was being hunted like an animal and that his compatriots avoided him like a ghost. But on 11 December he reminisced about happy days in Klam and about the ducks in the ravine that used to follow them on walks like the swans of Lohengrin. In that letter, he drew a picture of himself wearing an elegant new tweed suit, captioning it *Prinz Hamlet oder der kranke Giegerl* (Prince Hamlet or The Sick Dandy).

In Copenhagen, Brandes had noticed how elegant Strindberg was. The young literary historian Johan Mortensen, who belonged to the circle in Lund, was particularly impressed by a tweed suit, dark grey with white dots like the feathers of a sparrow-hawk, which Strindberg wore with Argyll socks, yellow shoes, knickerbockers and a shirt with a strap-collar.

Strindberg agreed to write a series of articles on Skåne for Gustaf Gullberg, editor of *Malmö-Tidningen*, the local affiliate of *Dagens Nyheter*. In December and January, he travelled in the area and wrote the articles, under the collective title 'Landscapes of Skåne'. He included light-hearted childhood memories in them, and they are tinged in general by a gentle, rosy glow—with not a trace of the past summer's excitements and murder plots, unless one chooses to count among the symptoms of madness a carefully proposed hypothesis that a number of strange-looking rocks in the Ystad region were idols from pagan times. Bülow, who accompanied Strindberg on some of his rambles through the beech woods, spoke of the 'happy humour' that brings joy to life. There is a healthy sheen on these articles, which can be found today in the collection *Swedish Nature*.

One evening—17 February 1897—August Lindberg came to Lund, and he and Strindberg met in Bülow's home. They discussed plays, gossiped about actors and actresses and Strindberg made Lindberg perform the gravedigger scene from *Hamlet* three times in a row. At 5 am, Strindberg lit the fire and made coffee, while Lindberg set the table and prepared breakfast. The party ended only at 7 am, when Elna arrived to congratulate the gentlemen on having risen so early.

During these months, Strindberg was not sending out his usual complaints with the same degree of intensity as before. Some strange entries were made in the *Occult Diary* as on 1 February: 'A gentleman fired his revolver at me.' On 19 March, Strindberg saw in the flames of his tile stove a skull wearing a monk's hood. His imagination was generating images, but this did not prevent him from also noting that the chaffinch was heard in Lund on 28 February, for the first time that year.

Mortensen has given an account of an episode belonging to this period. After an enjoyable evening at the Åke Hans, Strindberg accompanied Mortensen to his apartment. There, on a chair, he discovered some soft eiderdown cushions covered with brightly coloured silk. Strindberg picked them up, threw them about and shaped them in different ways, with a little smile on his lips. In his imagination, the cushions were assuming human and demonic shapes. Mortensen went and fetched his large white bed-pillow, and the friends succeeded in throwing that one and a green silk cushion in such an inspired fashion that they formed a face of Zeus next to the visage of a suffering Christ.

Then Strindberg proceeded to act as though he were participating in a spiritual seance. He knelt down and addressed the white god in a low, imploring voice, then waited for a reply, which he believed came when the pillow subsided and altered its shape. The experiment continued until the morning sun obliterated the light of the table lamp. Disappointed, Strindberg rose from his knees, but said, 'I have never experienced a night like this.'

The anecdote illustrates how Strindberg's imagination worked. The entire *Occult Diary* is a kind of pillow fight in which Strindberg tried to make the leap from observation of his senses to that of the supernatural; he was aware all the time that everything would evaporate in the light of morning, but the experience would provide him with new materials for his writing.

10

On 3 May 1897, Strindberg began work on *Inferno*. Just as when he wrote *A Fool's Apology*, he was aware of the enormity of his undertaking, and, as then, he was writing in French.

It was yet another autobiographical work, but it differed from its predecessors in a number of respects. August Strindberg was writing about August Strindberg, but the two were not the same person. Let us, therefore, call the hero of *Inferno* the Sacrificial Victim, or Victim for short, and the writer, the Narrator. Contemporary Dante scholars use a similar distinction when they analyse the *Divine Comedy*: there is Dante the Pilgrim, and Dante the Narrator.

Strindberg called his book *Inferno*: all the more reason to refer to Dante, who, like Homer and Virgil before him, descended into the underworld to visit the dead. At the same time, his journey was an imitation of the greatest Occidental *muthos*—Christ's descent into Limbo, and his Resurrection. The Victim in Strindberg's *Inferno* makes the same journey, although the hell he visits is located here on earth, and to a large extent consists of conditions of psychic pain.

In the *Divine Comedy*, the fictional proposition is that Dante himself, citizen of Florence, has journeyed through the realms of death. His readers obviously realized that the work was a poetic vision, not a piece of reportage. Yet, according to tradition, Italian women used to regard Dante's swarthiness as proof of his having endured the flames of the underworld. Thus Dante discovered that his voyage of the imagination was understood by the common populace as one made in reality.

Strindberg returned to Dante's approach, and like Dante in the Canto I of the *Purgatorio*, he was able to claim that he had resurrected an extinct poetic form—*la morta poesi risurga*. His work was then misunderstood in the same way Dante's had been: people actually believed that he had been to the same places, in similar conditions. He had spent the years preceding the writing of *Inferno* collecting material for his creative journey, as one must assume Dante did for his.

Just as Dante the Pilgrim is small, weak and frightened, sometimes riding on Virgil's hip like a child, while Dante the Narrator is proud, arrogant and courageous, the Victim in Strindberg's work is a poor wretch, superstitious and easily frightened, while Strindberg the Narrator is able to compete in races with horses and is brave and indomitable. The Victim will also be familiar to anyone who has followed Strindberg down the years, with his complaints and suicide threats, while the Narrator is the arrogant trickster and strong-willed writer who is determined to leave his mark on the world. Strindberg's whole life passed in a state of tension between these two, and in the book he was able to make them interact successfully.

The extinct poetic form Strindberg was attempting to bring back to life obliged him to use certain devices. In order to sustain the sense of illusion, he frequently connects Victim and Narrator. He even provides a note in which the reader is assured that the Victim was the author of *Sylva Sylvarum* and other Strindberg works. This was Jonathan Swift's method: precision in details enables us to accept the incredible whole. The Victim of *Inferno*, reduced to a state of nervous collapse, was unable to write anything.

When Strindberg reached the final page of his book, he brought out his big guns. 'The reader who believes that this book is a fiction', he wrote, 'is invited to examine my diary which I have kept daily since 1895, and of which the present text is only an expanded and organized extraction.' The statement contains much that is misleading. The diary was begun in 1896, not 1895. Very little of the contents of *Inferno* can be found there. Strindberg took a calculated risk in offering the sceptic access to the secret diary; he knew that no one would ask him to keep that promise. Incidentally, a Khmer folktale uses exactly the same device.

Who, indeed, had doubted the veracity of *Inferno*, and claimed that it was fiction? When Strindberg wrote those words, the book had not even been published. Only he knew that the Victim and the Narrator were not the same person—yet he realized that the book's success would depend on its readers perceiving them as one.

Thus *Inferno* is not a forgery, even though Strindberg feared that he would be discovered as a liar. It is a confessional book. The Victim is an inner Strindberg, whom he had carried within himself during his entire writing career; he is the one who, in the voice of the daughter in *A Dream Play*, laments the pain of existence—'to feel my sight weakened by an eye, my hearing dulled by an ear, and my thought, my airy light thought bound in the labyrinths of coils of fat'; a stranger who does not feel at home here on earth and yearns for another, better land.

From the very beginning, the narration of *Inferno* has a strangely poetic sense of elevation. Strindberg applies the expression 'purity of the soul'—*pureté d'âme*—to the Victim's condition. The disturbed, suffering creature we are confronted with now sets out on his journey towards clarity and insight. We are invited to observe an education of the human soul, one of the most memorable in our history, resembling the *Pilgrim's Progress* in ardour and longing for salvation.

It does not matter in the least that the Victim appears a little ridiculous in his superstition: it is part of his weakness. As we follow him day after day, from the hospital in Paris to the Hôtel Orfila, from France to Skåne and on to Austria, he becomes less and less Strindberg and more and more a timeless, nameless representative of humanity. He is liberated from his biographical prison and allowed to live outside time. The absurd element is there, but the sublime takes over. When the Victim, convinced of his impending death, bids farewell to the animals in the Jardin des Plantes, the Narrator extends this leave-taking into every departure from a life that is so rich in forms and appearances. It is the Victim's tremendous alertness, his eagerness to explore secrets, his willingness to experience everything for the sake of the belief that everything is connected, that moves us and makes us recognize something within ourselves that also yearns for liberation and is now seized by awareness of flight and strength.

Farewell, vultures, dwellers of heaven, enclosed in a dirty cage; farewell, bison bull, farewell, hippopotamus, fettered demon; farewell, seals, you well-matched couples, consoled for the loss of the ocean and the wide horizons by your marital love; farewell, stones, plants, flowers, trees, butterflies, birds, snakes, all created by one benevolent God's hand. And you great men, Bernardin de Saint-Pierre, Linne, Geoffroy Saint-Hilaire, Haüy, whose names stand carved in gold on the lintel of the temple—farewell! No: until we meet again!

And when, later in the autumn, the Victim walks down the road to the ravine, sees the pigsty's gates as red, glowing sarcophagi, the mill boys as faithless angels, the workers in the smithy as devils attacking a tree-trunk that looks like a tortured giant, it is indeed a great vision of hell that opens up before us. The animals, plants, stones and great names of the Jardin des Plantes constitute the earthly paradise and its yearning for purification—the ravine, everything that degrades, terrifies and tortures.

I I

Inferno was finished on 25 June 1897, and Strindberg sent the manuscript to Gustaf af Geijerstam on the same day. Early that year, Geijerstam had been appointed literary director of Gernandts Publishing Company, and one of the first things he did in that capacity was to contact Strindberg. This came at the right moment. Strindberg's relationship with Bonniers was not over, but it was strained, since strong personal and financial bonds connected the publishers to the 1890s, so triumphant in a literary sense, but so hateful to Strindberg.

Gernandts and Strindberg came to an agreement which lasted until the company went bankrupt in 1903. It proved beneficial to both parties. For *Inferno*, Strindberg demanded and received 50 kronor per sheet and 1,000 copies—which was good payment for that time. Eugène Fahlstedt was entrusted with the translation, which in spite of Strindberg's complaints about minor mistakes turned out to be excellent: Fahlstedt had a sense for the rhythms of Strindberg's language that dated back to their youth. Danish and Russian editions were being prepared: the book's German translator was a 26-year-old German poet, Christian Morgenstern.

Strindberg remained in Lund for the summer within his circle of friends. His cousin Johan Oscar Strindberg, the first of his favourite correspondents, had a son, Nils Strindberg, born in 1872. Strindberg was his godfather. Nils had chosen to study science, and was invited by the explorer-engineer S. A. Andrée to participate in an expedition by balloon to the North Pole. The enterprise was inspired by Nordenskjöld's journey on the *Vega*, and Strindberg followed the preparations with intense interest. The voyage had first been projected for 1896, and it is mentioned in *Inferno*.

The balloon was called the *Eagle*. In 1896 there were rumours that the Strindberg who was to be among the voyagers was in fact the writer, who had chosen this original way to get rid of his wife. Frida reacted with horror and a message of supplication—also recorded in *Inferno*. Their children in Finland received a telegram in May 1896 in which 'Daddy' asked them to come to Stockholm immediately for a farewell banquet: this was, in fact, a message Oscar Strindberg had telegraphed to his son who happened to be in Helsinki—by mistake, it had been delivered to August Strindberg's children. Their father registered the event in the *Occult Diary*, among other inexplicable but secretly meaningful signs.

In the summer of 1897, the North Pole voyage got under way. On 11 July, Andrée and his two companions in the *Eagle* departed from Spitzbergen and disappeared over the Arctic Sea. Thirty-three years later, their scattered bones, chewed by polar bears, were found on White Island, which they had managed to reach after a three-month trek across the ice.

Strindberg followed the daily progress of this dramatic exploit, noting the serial numbers of the returning carrier pigeons and cutting out and pasting up newspaper reports on the journey. On 16 July, he noted in his diary: 'This afternoon saw two pigeons heading north–south (in Åke Hansson's Garden). Said Herrlin: "There go Andrée's pigeons!" ' On 17 July: 'At 3.45 this morning I woke up hearing a cry from somewhere up in the air, like someone dying: haw—haw—haw.... It went on for a while, moving from north to south. I thought of Andrée's balloon! Don't know why, but it was terrifying.' On 28 July, he noted that according to a telegraphed message the balloon had been sighted in the White Sea on 17 July, with birds circling over it, and he immediately combined that information with his dream of that morning.

On the 19th, Strindberg wrote his cousin Johan Oscar a letter of consolation, reminding him how he had used 'The Eagle' as his signature in earlier days, and adding, in reference to his godson: 'A premonition of mine tells me that all will be well, and these past few years I have been right so often! Especially since the Powers who control our fate have given me the clearest evidence of their existence and good intentions, even in the adversities we encounter.'

In the shadow of that dramatic sequence of events, Strindberg wrote the continuation of *Inferno* entitled *Legends*; in it, he proceeded with his 'autobiography', including his friends in Lund and their supposedly occult experiences. It turned out to be a feeble sequel.

At the end of August, he returned to Paris, to the Hôtel Londres in rue Bonaparte. He told his friends and children that he was living a sober life alone in a garret, 'like Marie Antoinette in prison' (in a letter of 11 October to his daughter Kerstin in Austria). He was awaiting the publication of *Inferno* in Sweden with some excitement. It appeared on 1 November 1897, with a simple typographical cover: Strindberg's name and the title in black Gothic lettering, with the initials A, S, and I in red—the darkness and fire of hell. Strindberg anticipated that he would either win the Nobel Prize (which was being deliberated at this time), or be crucified. As it turned out, neither of these events took place. Many of his old friends were revolted by what they saw as a personality in a state of disintegration. Everybody read the book as an account of a crisis and an illness. Some were deeply moved, among them Ibsen and Hjalmar Söderberg; others merely laughed.

The book sold well, and a second printing had to be issued as early as the end of November. At Christmas, Strindberg was able to send a substantial contribution to his children in Finland, and his letters and diary indicate that he was in a comparatively cheerful mood all winter. He saw much of Marcel Reja, who had undertaken the task of editing *Inferno* for a French edition to be published by Mercure de France, combined with the 'Postlude' of *Master Olof* (the version in verse), to indicate the continuity of Strindberg's literary progress. Even a couple of the essays from *Sylva Sylvarum* were added to this edition—which do, as we have seen, belong to the corpus of *Inferno*.

Chapter Fourteen

THE FORTY DAYS

I

DURING A FEW days of intensive work in February 1898 at the Hôtel Londres in Paris Strindberg wrote the first half of his play *To Damascus*. 'Burst into tears several times today, wrote the end of Act 3,' he noted in his diary on 3 March. Reading the play, one understands those tears, which were obviously caused by his joy that everything was working out right, that scenes and lines were coming to him in a natural and spontaneous fashion. The play was completed on 6 March, and on the 10th, he wrote to Axel Herrlin in Lund that it seemed to him he had 'regained the grace to write for the theatre'.

This marked a fundamental change in his situation. He now wanted to return to Sweden in order to engage in research for his historical plays, and to attend to his interests in the theatrical world of his homeland. Since Strindberg's last stay in Sweden, that world had acquired a new protagonist, Albert Ranft. Ludvig Josephson, who had 'discovered' *Master Olof*, was in a decline and died in January 1899. Strindberg sent a wreath to his funeral and always remembered him with gratitude, even on his own death-bed. Ranft was of a different breed, an industrialist of the theatre, with a growing theatrical empire at his disposal. Strindberg had had a disagreement with him about *The Keys to the Kingdom of Heaven*, which Ranft had disparaged. Now, however, Strindberg was eager to let bygones be bygones, and even considered working as a reader for the great man.

At this time, another important change took place: Strindberg abandoned both the occult and chemistry, explaining to Herrlin that 'the powers' had told him to do so. Strindberg's 'powers' were pragmatic ones, who never interfered with his work as a writer, least of all as a writer of plays. As early as 2 March Geijerstam was told that 'the religious battles are over, and the whole *Inferno* saga has come to an end.'

47   Strindberg in Lund, January 1897

Yet a belief in God and an interest in the occult, as well as in chemistry, remained with Strindberg to the end of his life. He continued to record and reflect upon noteworthy coincidences, and to see his own life in a cosmic context. It was part of his everyday existence, a kind of spiritual calisthenics, which was designed to maintain his ability to make connections. He also devoted much time to pondering whether there was a personal divine will at work in history. But the most important activity in his life now consisted of the artistic exploitation of his experiences during the *Inferno* period: he was heading into his most intense years of creativity, one of the most fertile periods known in literary history.

On 3 April, Strindberg left Paris. A few days before that—15 March, according to the diary—he was visited by the 23-year-old Swedish writer Marika Stjernstedt, who brought him a bouquet of white lilac. Her mother was from Poland, and her grandmother's aunt was Countess Hanska, Balzac's mistress and, later, wife. In Strindberg's hotel room, this admirer with her large radiant eyes and raven hair—she was regarded as one of the most ravishing beauties of her day—must have been a delightful apparition. According to her, the visit ended with Strindberg asking her 'with a certain inquisitorial gravity in his voice' whether she did not consider her visit contrary to what was regarded 'proper behaviour for a young lady'.

'Please forgive me, if it is,' she replied.

'Forgive yourself. I don't have anything to forgive,' were Strindberg's parting words. One might hazard a guess as to what he was thinking; a secret tremor may have been concealed in what the visitor saw as 'inquisitorial gravity'. Anyway, it was a near thing. The next time a young woman with dark eyes stood before him, he succumbed.

On 7 April, Strindberg arrived in Lund and was warmly received by his friends, who were not particularly concerned about the indiscretions in *Legends*, which appeared in May. Strindberg had taken pains not to offend them, and was proud of having done so. Axel Herrlin had even been permitted to read a section of the book in proof and to delete a piquant episode about how he had injured himself by contact with a brooch in the ruffle-collar of a café waitress and had suffered blood-poisoning by way of punishment.

Strindberg stayed in Lund for a little over a year, working continuously in a happy, lucid frame of mind. He wrote his plays *The Folkunga Saga*, *Gustaf Vasa*, *Crime and Crime*, and *Advent*, as well as the novel *The Convent*. He spent his evenings at the Åke Hans, enjoying the gossip, observing, listening and gathering material for the novel *The Scapegoat* (1906). He sent out peace missives in several directions, to Ibsen among others, who had stated that he was 'deeply moved' by *Inferno*. He also showed greater interest than before in his children in Finland, and advised Karin never to discuss religion with any other person. When Karin told him that she was considering a writer's career, he wrote to her that she would be wise to choose a pseudonym 'since the public is such that it does not like to have to deal with two subsequent editions of the same author. You would gain a more independent position.' Karin followed that advice.

At this time, the inner circle of Lund friends included Emil Kléen, a young poet who wrote melodically pleasing, passionate verse, made a living as a journalist and belonged to the radical group centred around Lidforss. He and Strindberg became close friends despite an age difference of almost twenty years. Strindberg treated Kléen with a consideration and tenderness that was unparalleled in his life. Kléen had visited him in Paris in January— Strindberg had written the most seductive letters about that city's beauty and how it was possible to live there inexpensively—and now, back in Lund, they would meet on Saturdays, which was Kléen's day off from his job at *Malmö-Tidningen*.

In the autumn, Kléen was diagnosed as having cancer of the throat, and in November he was admitted to the hospital in Lund. Strindberg visited him frequently; when the patient's condition grew worse, Strindberg, according to his diary, saw him twice a day, advising him on treatment and doctors. Kléen died on 10 December. Strindberg noted in his diary that he had said goodbye to him the previous evening, and that he had woken up during the night and experienced 'the last agony'. Strindberg attended the funeral in Höör and, what is more, was one of the pallbearers—a unique action in his life, as he always avoided any association in which his originality was not clearly distinguishable. On the funeral, he noted: 'A magpie flew up in the cemetery. A dog howled. A pig was being slaughtered at the beginning of the ceromony. An icy wind met us in Höör. The bells of the church could not be heard, although they were ringing.'

A few days later, Strindberg described Kléen's death to Gustaf Uddgren, who had come to Lund to interview him on the occasion of his approaching fiftieth birthday, as if he had really been present when it occurred, instead of merely experiencing it in his imagination. In Strindberg's account, the image of the cocoon and the butterfly reappeared. The dying Kléen

> was violently moving his head back and forth, not because of the pain but as if he had been feeling birth-pangs, as if he was gradually being transformed into a new creature which was generated out of his human frame. When, at last, death came, it happened imperceptibly and quietly; one corner of his mouth turned down in a half-bitter, half-amused expression of surprise—as if he had wanted to say: I see, so that's all it was.

On his fiftieth birthday, Strindberg received some splendid tributes, indicating that the icy winds of the 1880s were dying down around him. In *Svenska Dagbladet*, where a great number of the country's leading cultural figures outside the academies paid homage to him, there also appeared a poem by Heidenstam, his old friend and enemy. The poem was not without a certain ambiguity; in it, Strindberg was celebrated as a champion of the truth, yet the final lines read:

Ej fagrare lager
i aftonens dager
två händer fått pressa
kring diktarehjässa
än den du har burit.
Ett löfte du svurit:
du skulle ej slita
från hår, som bli vita,
om dagen än sprunge
i mörker och släcktes,
den tistel som räcktes
till krans åt den unge.

*No fairer laurel
in the evening's light
two hands have been able to press
around a poet's crown
than the one you have worn.
A vow you took:
you would not tear
from hair that turns white,
even if the day would leap
into darkness and be extinguished,
the thistle that was given
as a wreath to the young one.*

Reading between and behind such adulatory lines, one can discern that the martyr's crown—the wreath of thistles—no longer seemed appropriate in Heidenstam's view, and that Strindberg was cultivating to an absurd degree the disappointment he had experienced in his youth. It is possible that Strindberg was also annoyed by the two not so delicate allusions to his age— the evening light and the white hair.

   In Lund, his birthday was celebrated at a dinner in Waldemar Bülow's home. A couple of photographs of that occasion have survived. In one of them, for once, Strindberg had not had time to strike a pose. He sits, stooping a little, in the Bülows' drawing-room, wearing a black frock-coat. He is wearing what looks like a rosebud framed with lilies-of-the-valley in his buttonhole, and his gaze is not as stony and hard as usual; it seems inspired more by good wine than by visions of hell. Uddgren, in his interview mentioned above, thought that Strindberg looked like 'a rogue with a lust for life'.

Hjalmar Branting sent a birthday telegram, in which he expressed his wish that the writer would 'return to the side of the eighties' again. Strindberg took this as a question and replied the next day:

I have never been anything but a writer, and I think that we writers overstepped our authority when we wanted to become prophets and politicians during the recently ended period. 'No programme' was my password, and it still is. I retained the same right to develop that I granted to others. Thus it is mere coincidence that I am struggling in your company as a champion of peace and suffrage, and you should not regard me as a political person. Some people have a need for religion, some do not. I need contact with 'jenseits' in order to gain perspective and a sense of distance in my paintings, and I cannot breathe in your physical vacuum. So: that is where we differ, and consequently have different points of view on life and things.

2

On 20 June 1899, Strindberg left Lund for ever. On the day of his departure, he wrote a line from Jeremiah, the prophet who had been Master Olof's guiding light, in his diary: 'For I will surely deliver thee, and thou shalt not fall by the sword, but thy life shall be for a prey unto thee.' To see his own life as a prey to pursue and capture was what he had learned during the *Inferno* period. Next to the biblical quotation, Strindberg pasted in a cutting from a review by Georg Brandes, in which he heaps scorn on the occultists and Strindberg himself is termed a madman who 'sees portents in a dog in a gateway and in a little girl sitting on some stairs with a pack of cards'. Brandes continued:

Never has such idiotic worship existed before. Perhaps no such touching hatred of the intellect ever flowered before, but it has never been demolished as triumphantly. The few old-fashioned souls who still celebrate the intellect are rightly regarded as outmoded objects of scorn. Trussed and gagged, intellect is made to lie on the ground, to be stamped on by cheering Spiritualists, Protestants, and Catholics.

Strindberg wrote a single word under the cutting: 'Idiot!' Thus two old allies applied the same epithet to each other on the same diary page.

Strindberg went to Furusund in the Stockholm Archipelago, where his sister Anna and her husband Hugo von Philp had a summer house, and rented quarters in a red house from a shoemaker, Andersson. Writing to Bülow on 29 June Strindberg called the landscape 'the most beautiful in Sweden'—it was, after all, the Archipelago. 'My years of wandering seem to be over, now I intend to stay in my country and make an honest living,' he wrote to Håkan Gillberg in July, and this was the plan he followed. Since 1883, he had been on the move; now he returned to the stationary life of his youth, and Stockholm and its environs welcomed him and became the frame of the rest of his life.

This last summer of the century became one of his happiest. He was working calmly, saw friends, went bowling in the afternoons. There was music at the von Philps' home—Anna played the violin. One afternoon, she burst into tears for no apparent reason: her marriage was under strain, and this was to provide details and actual lines for *The Dance of Death*, Strindberg's most horrendous play about marriage. Georg and Kata Dalström—Kata was soon to be a famous Social Democrat agitator and strike organizer—and their daughters were also living there, and they, too, would serve as models in later work.

Carl Larsson visited Strindberg for two days and drew his picture. Strindberg's daughter Greta, now seventeen, came to visit her father after her confirmation. Strindberg, who had been apprehensive about this visit, was moved by her kind blue eyes, her dimples and her way of calling him *lilla pappa* ('little daddy'), 'which I had not heard for seven years'. Carl Larsson and he must have recalled celebrating Greta's christening on Kymmendö in 1881 with fancy dress, fireworks and theatricals.

In Furusund, Strindberg wrote *Eric XIV*, one of his most tightly constructed plays, and had good reason to write in his diary on 15 August, the day he left: 'Looking back on it, this sojourn seems like a beautiful midsummer night's dream. Yet there were dreadful details.' He was thinking of his sister Anna.

In Stockholm, he first rented a room on Narvavägen and on 13 October moved into two furnished rooms at no. 31 Banérgatan. From his ground-floor windows he saw the Gustaf Adolf Church and the barracks of the Svea Guard. The street was named after Johan Banér, a hero of the Thirty Years' War, whom Strindberg included in his play *Gustaf II Adolf*, which he had recently begun. Naturally, he entered all these facts in his diary as good omens. He was living in the very midst of the history he was dramatizing.

Strindberg lived at Banérgatan for nineteen months and continued his calm, confident, productive flow. He later described his quarters in the novel *Alone*, which is so mild, serene and lucid that it became one of his most popular books in Sweden. He worked at a huge desk, marked, as he claimed with his usual sense for significant detail, by 'the awful cyanide-blue ink' his landlady's deceased husband had used. In his study there was a portrait as well as a bust of Shakespeare, his only admitted rival.

Now as ever, his 'loneliness' was a myth, existing only in his mind. In his exoteric life, he socialized more than ever, played cards at the von Philps or with Richard Bergh, arranged soirées of Beethoven's music, visited

Geijerstam in Saltsjöbaden, indulged in theatrical gossip with actor friends, visited the taverns almost every day, and was well on his way to being devoured by the Swedish Establishment, which, like all others of its kind, has a perennial hunger for returning prodigal sons—each one of them representing one less painful witness.

3

It was Strindberg's intention to make his post-*Inferno* debut as a playwright in the autumn season of 1899. Crafty as ever, he gave Geijerstam instructions as early on as during his time in Lund, on how best to deal with various theatrical directors. The Dramatic Theatre accepted *The Folkunga Saga*. Ranft, encouraged by this, agreed in July to put on *Gustaf Vasa*: he made a special journey to Furusund to draw up a contract and discuss casting.

On 17 October 1899, *Gustaf Vasa* had its first night at the Swedish Theatre, and became an instant hit with both the critics and the public. It ran to many full houses until 1902, and to this day remains in the national repertory. In November, *Erik XIV* had its première and, in February, *Crime and Crime* at Dramaten. August Palme, a good friend of Strindberg's, played Maurice, and the role of the fatal Henriette, modelled on 'Aspasia', was played by August Lindberg's wife Augusta who received tremendous acclaim. The season was, indeed, Strindberg's: his name was red-hot.

What was the reason for this success? Sweden was enjoying a heyday of national pride, and audiences liked to see themselves reflected in their own history. Strindberg's plays were cleverly and tightly constructed. In *Gustaf Vasa*, the rebels' bloody threats are met by the king's bloody revenge. In *Erik XIV*, the Sture murders provide an appalling and gripping climax.

The life and attraction of these plays is due to the liberation of Strindberg's imagination as a result of his voyage through hell. Looking at Gustaf Vasa in the play that bears his name, one does indeed see the Swedish Renaissance monarch, clad in his magnificent historical garments which were provided by Strindberg's 'store-house', *The Swedish People*. Yet the historical king is only one of the personalities present in the Gustaf of the play: among the others are the ancient Nordic god Thor, terrible in his wrath, and Abraham of the Old Testament, willing to sacrifice his own son to the cause. To indicate the king's relationship with these mythical figures, Strindberg makes him strike his desk with a steel hammer whenever he is aroused, and hang a painting of Abraham on his wall.

Behind Gustaf, behind Erik XIV and all the historical figures in

Strindberg's new plays, we can see the hero called The Unknown One in *To Damascus*, the play Strindberg wrote immediately after *Inferno*. The Unknown One is a pilgrim, a stricken man, a changeling, but he is also a saviour who sustains the world. On innumerable occasions, he has been made to look like Strindberg on the stage—yet, every time, the actor concerned has thereby missed the most essential aspect of the role, locking The Unknown One into Strindberg's biography.

The reason this character has no proper name is just because he is a meeting ground of different figures: like Cain, he bears a mark on his forehead, like Jacob, he walks with a limp, and within him are beggars, emperors and criminals. All of humanity has been crowded into him. When The Unknown One's counterpart, The Lady—also nameless, as an indication of her representative character—takes such pity on him, we understand why: he is a timeless image of struggling humanity, and in him we recognize ourselves.

4

Among the many who witnessed, and were excited by, the rising of Strindberg's dramatic star, was the 22-year-old Norwegian actress Harriet Bosse. Since the autumn of 1899 she had been working at the Dramatic Theatre; rumour had it that she had been sent to Sweden because her sister Alma, wife of the Norwegian theatrical director Fahlström, feared the attraction she exercised on her husband. This was the couple Strindberg had met in Paris in 1894. On New Year's Eve 1899, by her own account, Harriet Bosse walked past Strindberg's apartment on Banérgatan and whispered 'Happy New Year' through the unlit window. Like Frida, she was a young woman of initiative.

In the spring of 1900, Harriet Bosse played Puck in Shakespeare's *A Midsummer Night's Dream*. In the part, she was 'a perfectly magic apparition of charm and roguishness, the essence of poetry and more!' as Strindberg wrote a year later to his German translator, Emil Schering. She had black hair, large brown eyes and an exceptionally well-proportioned figure.

That same spring, the Dramatic Theatre finally accepted *To Damascus* for its autumn repertory. August Palme, who was a close friend of Harriet Bosse, suggested her—presumably with her active consent—for the part of The Lady. Palme invited Strindberg to a performance of *A Midsummer Night's Dream*, and that decided the matter. From that moment on, an awareness seems to have existed between Strindberg and Harriet, who obviously knew who was in the audience. Later, Strindberg confided to her that she got the part because she had 'such sweet legs', a polite euphemism for all that was meant by 'and more'.

On 31 May, they met in private for the first time. Harriet Bosse visited the apartment on Banérgatan to discuss her part, and found that Strindberg had made an artistic arrangement of flowers, fruit and wine, as was his custom on such occasions.

It was not until the following winter that they started having an affair, which would culminate in the spring of 1901. On one level, it was an ordinary, almost banal, liaison. An ambitious young actress and a fifty-year-old genius with influence in the theatre had a relationship which was to their mutual advantage. Strindberg found himself separated from Harriet by an age gap of three decades, but his success had fortified him. Yet, as with Siri and Frida, his affair with Harriet was conducted on several levels simultaneously, only this time the turns it took were even more numerous and more complicated—it was impossible to be sure just when they were being playful or serious, lyrical or down-to-earth.

If Strindberg had already deprived Frida Uhl of her identity, so that she was never able to get close to him as an individual, this was true to a far greater degree of his relationship with Harriet Bosse. She became the object of his desire and his affection, but was at the same time seduced by his imagination and transformed into a figure of his art. While twenty years earlier, the blonde, passionate Siri von Essen took the place of his work to such an extent that he later complained about the time he had lost, Harriet Bosse intervened between her lover and his writing only for brief moments.

The summer of 1900 became as stormy as the previous one had been calm. Strindberg travelled out to Furusund the day after Harriet Bosse's visit, but after a few days he fell out with the von Philps and broke off relations with them for the next four years—a not uncommon kind of event in the Strindberg family. He returned to Banérgatan. The presence of Harriet Bosse in Stockholm probably affected his decision; on 5 July, she visited again, this time to tell him that she was taking the part of The Lady (as if she had ever felt any hesitation).

Strindberg had not spent a summer in Stockholm for a long time. In his diary entry of 15 July he described a ride round Djurgarden in a cab during which he had seen only cripples, drunks and demonic-looking children. 'A dog wanted to jump up on the driver's seat; the driver chatted about revolting subjects; finally I found myself driving behind two harlots, one of whom seemed to be in love with the other; one was dressed like a nun, all in black with a tall white collar.' Strindberg was seeing the city's poor and its eccentrics, emerging now that the well-to-do citizens had moved out to their summer residences. Two years later, Strindberg included the episode in *Alone*.

During the autumn, while waiting for the opening of *To Damascus*,

48 Harriet Bosse as Puck in *A Midsummer Night's Dream*

Strindberg wrote the plays *Easter* and *The Dance of Death*. His sister Elisabeth, who had become mentally disturbed in 1898, now believed that she was being persecuted and that attempts were being made to poison her. Strindberg consoled her, recognizing his own experiences in hers, and advised her to do as he had done, to discover the hidden significance of everything that happened to her. He made use of her fate in *Easter*. As always, he himself played the characters he created, and in his diary quoted Ezekiel 23:32: 'Thou shalt drink of thy sister's cup deep and large: thou shalt be laughed to scorn and had in derision; it containeth much.' Eleonora, the disturbed young woman who is the play's main character, is a female counterpart to The Victim in *Inferno*. Perhaps Harry G. Carlson is right in his analytical assumption that the daffodil (in Swedish, *påsklilja* (Easter lily)) which Eleonora cannot resist stealing from the florist's window, with such fatal consequences, is the same flower that Persephone plucked, and which caused her to fall into the kingdom of death where she was compelled to marry Hades. In any case, The Victim undergoes the same sequence of events, and behind both of them stands Jesus with his journey into death and his Resurrection.

On 15 November, *To Damascus* had its dress rehearsal, with Strindberg in attendance. Two days later he wrote to the director of the theatre, Nils Personne, who had accepted *Easter*, asking him to give the part of Eleonora to Harriet Bosse; he stressed that she had powers of poetic expression and a seriousness which the others lacked, and he suggested that the first night should be on 19 February—a secret compliment to Harriet, since that was her birthday. On the first night, he sent her a bouquet of red roses and a letter in which he thanked her for the great and beautiful experience the dress rehearsal had been for him, and expressing one reservation which she was free to interpret as a further compliment if she wished: he had imagined the part 'a little lighter, with small touches of roguishness and more expansiveness. A little more Puck!'

His nascent feelings for Harriet Bosse reminded Strindberg of the ecstatic experiences of his youth, and in his diary entry of 21 November he mentioned the lighthouse of Korsö which had made an indelible impression on him in the early 1870s. After his return to Stockholm, his imagination increasingly returned to the years of his youth and the parallels they presented with his present situation. In December, he quoted Kellgren's translation of Voltaire's famous poem about pleasure soon turning from sweetness to bitterness, and about fame that is but vanity. He re-read his love letters to Siri and found 'many strange things' in them. He drew Harriet into his world by letting her join his sister as Eleonora in *Easter*. On 12 December, he wrote in his diary that he felt he was in telepathic communication with her, and that he had had a strange dream that night.

An account of that dream appears in the diary under the date 15

November the day of the dress rehearsal, but it is obvious that it was written later. This is the entry in its entirety:

> First dress rehearsal of Damascus. The inexplicable scene with Bosse. This is how it happened! After the first act I went up on stage and thanked (Bosse). Made a remark about the final scene, in which the kiss is given through the lowered veil. As we stood there in the middle of the stage surrounded by a lot of people, and I was speaking seriously about that kiss (Bosse's) little face became transformed, grew larger and assumed a supernatural beauty, seemed to approach mine, and her eyes were ensnaring me with black lightning flashes. Then, for no reason, she ran off, and I stood there crestfallen as after a miracle, with the impression that I had received a kiss that intoxicated me. Then (B) haunted me for three days, so that I felt her presence in my room. Later I dreamt about her, like this: I was lying in a bed; B came in her costume of Puck; she was married to me. She said about me: 'See there, my brewer,' gave me her foot to kiss. She had no bosom, absolutely none.

It is impossible to determine what is invention and what is fact in the entry. Harriet Bosse did not experience the meeting on 15 November as particularly noteworthy: in her account of her love story with Strindberg, admittedly written twenty years later, she has not one word to say about it. She did not have access to the *Occult Diary*.

Harriet Bosse accepted the part of Eleonora, and this led to more visits to Banérgatan. Strindberg's amorous feelings reawakened his interest in the occult. He noted in the diary that he was pursued by the odour of celery and was unable to decide whether it meant chastity or profligacy. The telepathic connection continued, and on 13 January he noted that Harriet Bosse visited him at night and that he had 'possessed' her. He prayed to God—at particularly solemn or 'secret' times he used the Greek alphabet—to save him from this passion. He did not let Harriet Bosse know of its occult aspect.

On the contrary: he treated her with old-fashioned courtesy, sometimes taking the role of an older, more experienced friend. When she confided to him that she was able to portray on the stage only things that she had experienced herself, he asked her in rather a fatherly way if she believed she really had experienced Puck's pranks and The Lady's journey to hell in *To Damascus*. Although she obviously had not, she had received great praise in those roles. This was an aspect of art which Strindberg knew very well.

Harriet continued to visit him telepathically at night, and he lived 'with only her in my thoughts' and feared 'a catastrophe' (12 February). At the same time, he began to hope that she would love him in a more tangible way. He called her his angel who would reconcile him with life and with women. We do not know whether that reconciliation referred to him as the writer August Strindberg, or to his invented persona. In his diary entries, the smell of celery was replaced by the scent of incense, which he connected with the object of his desire. After one of Harriet's visits on 8 February, he writes that she had asked God to bless him for having written so beautifully in *Easter*: 'I felt like Faust regretting his youth, before this masterpiece of a woman child.' The same day, he sent her a letter in which he analysed the figure of Eleonora. 'Due to a tragic event in her family,' he wrote, 'Eleonora has entered a frame of mind, which some consider pathological, in which she finds herself in communication (telepathic) with her relatives, then with all of humanity, and finally with the lower tiers of creation, and thus she shares the suffering of every living creature, or, to put it another way, realizes the idea of 'Christ in Man'.

It is hard to explain the exact significance of the telepathic intercourse Strindberg believed he was having that spring with Harriet Bosse, and which he was to resume after his marriage to her had foundered. It is entirely in keeping with the occult experiments he involved himself in during the Inferno period, and which provided such a rich artistic harvest. Strindberg often used the term 'incubus', an ancient concept related to erotic nightmares and to intercourse between demons and humans. It has been suggested that these were Strindberg's masturbation fantasies, but this seems extremely unlikely, especially since the telepathic couplings were practically unlimited in number in the course of a single night. Considering Strindberg's methods as a writer, it would seem more reasonable to regard them as imitations, poetic exercises, preparations for creative work.

While Harriet Bosse had seemingly invaded his imagination, Strindberg continued to work with undiminished energy on various projects throughout the year. On 26 February 1901, he noted in the diary: 'Entire day spent in an intoxication with the idea of Swan White.' *Swan White* is a fairytale play, reminiscent of Kipling and Maeterlinck, whose works Strindberg was studying and admiring at the time. It is one of the most studied plays Strindberg ever wrote, and there is an air of depravity about it—a word not usually applicable to Strindberg. It presents, among other things, a cleverly set love trap. The play's heroine, Princess Swan White, is a romanticized portrait of Harriet Bosse seen as a symbol of goodness and innocence in an elegantly decadent medieval setting. On the red and white tile floor lies a lion's skin, the symbol of Hercules; there are rose bushes in bloom; the bed is covered with a light blue counterpane. A sleeping peacock and a golden cage containing white pigeons complete the Art Nouveau background.

In keeping with fairytale convention, Swan White has an evil stepmother who wields a steel whip. But her grey-haired father comes to the rescue. He calls her 'the joy of his old age' while referring in the same breath, somewhat less paternally, to her 'little purple snail of a mouth'. Swan White uses equally ambiguous expressions: 'You are like a royal oak', she says, 'and I cannot get my arms around you; but . . . I want to swing on your branches, like a bird. . . . Raise me up, and I will clamber into your crown.'

The cynical observer, initiated into Strindberg's private life, may well surmise that Swan White in another form had whispered to another prince: 'Free me from the supporting roles and let me be the leading lady in your dramatic crown.' We have a letter from Harriet to Strindberg, to that effect. Swan White's lines can also be seen as an enticement: 'Come and swing in my roles and ——!' In *Gustaf Vasa*, the queen accuses her stepson, Prince Erik, of hating her, to which he replies: 'I am not permitted to love you! It is forbidden to love one's stepmother, yet one should love her; that, too, is madness.' Swan White's words to her father, that she cannot put her arms around him, are similarly equivocal, while the audience is invited to assume that she is an *ingénue* who is not really aware of what she is saying. In the manner of Shakespeare, innocent young women make shameless proposals.

Another point which can be given a personal interpretation is the way Strindberg consigns the Prince (who wins Swan White in the end) to a dungeon, where his hair turns grey overnight. In a letter, Strindberg made a deliberate connection between Harriet–Swan White and the hero in *Inferno* who had to conquer the mountain in Klam before he was allowed to hear the strains of the wedding march.

Yet *Swan White* was not intended only to symbolize the woman whom Strindberg the father-prince desired; it also provided the young actress Harriet Bosse with a fine role. It was one in which she was not intended to be cloyingly sweet: Strindberg made every effort to provide sudden changes of mood, wit, and irony in the part, again with Shakespeare's heroines in mind. He was out to achieve several goals simultaneously.

5

In February, it became clear that a decision had to be reached. Strindberg continued his telepathic communion but also made rapid advances on a more down-to-earth level. On 20 February, he noted that Harriet Bosse during her visit to his apartment kept her veil down the whole time, and that she wore a fur round her neck 'with two small claws, black and sharp'. Six days later he considered the consequences of 'relinquishing my power and my property, my freedom and my fame to a hard, calculating woman belonging to an enemy race'. However, that consideration did not keep him from devising a ruse to discover how the land lay. This occurred after another visit by Harriet on 28 February: 'She came at 3 pm, dressed in black, lovely, amiable and kind. We conversed intimately! Intimately!' He had picked up the *To Damascus* motif again and was working on the third part of the play. He gave Harriet the unfinished manuscript and asked her for her opinion: should The Unknown One enter the monastery, or should he attach himself to a woman who is able to reconcile him to life? It was a masked proposal, made in true dramatic fashion. Strindberg lived through days of great suspense, waiting for her answer; he did, however, give himself a little advance taste of happiness by leafing through the well-known Bodafors Furniture Company's catalogue, looking for furniture suitable for 'The Mrs's' room. Was he preparing a play or a real marriage? Invention and reality were mingling in combinations known only to himself. 'What if it is and will be no more than a fiction?' he wrote on 1 March, immediately after looking at the furniture. 'So what? So then I will write a fiction, and a great one! And the pain of her loss will be transformed into song. Dante never won Beatrice, which was why he remained faithful to her; even though she was married to another man!'

On 4 March, Harriet Bosse replied: 'I can well imagine the little woman's jubilation if The Unknown One—despite all her misgivings—would only quietly take her hand in his and with her wander on towards—the goal. And forgot the monastery!' Thus her answer was clearly 'yes'. The following day, the lovers abandoned the *To Damascus* game but instantly assumed new disguises. Harriet Bosse came to Banérgatan, and it was on this occasion that Strindberg is claimed to have uttered the question quoted even in brief accounts of his life: 'Miss Bosse, will you have a little child with me?' Harriet Bosse said that she curtseyed and replied, in a trance-like state: 'Yes, thank you.' But she certainly knew what she was doing.

On 6 March, the lovers purchased engagement rings and compiled the notice that appeared in the newspapers the following day:

> August Strindberg
> and
> Harriet Bosse
>
> Announced only in
> this manner, without
> cards or visits.

The engagement of these two celebrities became the talk of Stockholm. They did not avoid the public gaze. On 6, 7 and 8 March, they dined in the city's most fashionable restaurants and took carriage rides around Djurgården. Strindberg was showing off his beautiful fiancée to all the world. If we can trust his diary, even the King himself saw them; perhaps His Majesty then pondered a few of his memoir comments on Strindberg, whose muse he called 'a whore' who 'washes herself and sprays everyone within reach with the greenish-brown liquid of the gutter'.

After the engagement, there were no diary entries until 18 April. As complications arose, Strindberg considered how his wedding ceremony should be formulated. To the door of the Gustaf Adolf Church, which he could see from his window, he wanted to affix a proclamation stating that he and his beloved 'had exchanged vows of fidelity and rings in view of the All-Seeing and prayed for God's blessing of our union as husband and wife!' 'Wanderer, go and do thou likewise!' were the final words of the document, dated 19 April 1901, 'Master Olof's Day'. Strindberg was fired by the thought that he was creating a new law, like Master Olof, who broke the Catholic Church's ban against marriage for priests. However, Harriet Bosse did not go along with that symbolic action, nor is it certain that Strindberg himself ever intended it seriously.

On 6 May 1901, Strindberg entered the state of matrimony for the third time. After the wedding, the couple dined at Hasselbacken in Djurgården. They rode there in an open landau, and Strindberg had arranged for Karl Otto Bonnier's eighteen-year-old son Tor and a few friends to wait for them by the bridge to Djurgården in order to throw bunches of violets into the carriage as it passed.

Their home was a five-room apartment on the fifth floor of no. 40 Karlavägen, a brand-new building. The bills for furnishings have been preserved, and they give an indication of the kind of change this marriage brought to Strindberg's lifestyle. He had been living in furnished accommodation for almost twenty years. Now he surrounded himself with innumerable objects and knick-knacks. There was a large oak sideboard, carved in German Renaissance style, that cost 265 kronor and was deemed hideous by Harriet; there were mahogany chairs and tables in Empire style, a dining table, window table, night tables, washbasins, a large mirror and a smaller one, a pendulum clock that struck the hour, three spittoons, and hundreds of smaller items, from curtain rods and steam-irons to buttermilk bowls and corkscrews. On the wedding day, a purchase was made of two small statues, one representing Venus, the goddess of love, the other, Jason—a copy of the Thorvaldsen statue used as a centrepiece in the first play Strindberg ever had performed, *In Rome*. The bride was surrounded by products reflecting her husband's taste. He had set the scene: she would be the leading lady, he the hero, but also the director.

As the hefty tailor's bills demonstrate, even the groom himself had been refurbished. An overcoat and a suit made in April, together with a felt hat, came to 120 kronor, and in May, for roughly the same amount, two new suits. In addition, there were numerous other articles of clothing, including two embroidered shirts with detachable collars and cuffs.

Strindberg lived longer in this apartment than in any other place: from May 1901 to July 1908. It was integrated into his life and work to a greater degree than anywhere else, immediately becoming a part of the drama of his life and almost a living being, as his surroundings always did. It was situated in an expanding suburb, and was rich in symbolic associations. Outside, there was Gärdet ('The Field'), where at this time demonstrations of an increasingly grim and serious nature were held on 1 May. The red lectern where the speakers stood reminded Strindberg of an execution scaffold. Round Gärdet towered the barracks guarding the threatened city. In the distance shone the water of Lake Värta, and behind the Lidingö woods there was the Archipelago.

6

Strindberg provided posterity with a wealth of details about his third marriage. At first sight, it seems possible to reconstruct the whole sequence of events. We are even invited to be present on the wedding night. The bride had a haemorrhage—not the result of the loss of her virginity—and her husband possessed her twice, providing little enjoyment for either her or himself. Before dawn, they had had their first argument. Nevertheless, all the wealth of material is really more of a hindrance than a help, because it is impossible to distinguish between what Strindberg invented and what actually happened.

On one of their very first days together Strindberg was seized by a desire to 'flee and rent a room in a garret' and this does not seem surprising in view of the great readjustment the marriage entailed. Harriet understood, Strindberg noted.

In May and June, the couple made efforts to adjust to one another, planned a honeymoon trip to Germany and frequently received company at home—mostly people from the theatre. His energy undiminished, Strindberg wrote his play about Karl XII, the king who renounced women. At the end of May, a 'Press Week' was celebrated in Stockholm, and Harriet wanted to go to its fancy dress ball; Strindberg refused, and this led to a confrontation, which, according to the diary, ended in Strindberg purchasing trunks and threatening to leave. In early June, Strindberg received a reminder of his past. Dagny Juel, 'Aspasia', was shot and killed by a young lover in Georgia, in the Caucasus. Strindberg pasted the notice of her death, signed by Przybyszewski, into his diary without comment, although it would have been suitable for inclusion in one of his lists of enemies who had gone to their deserved ends.

On 23 June, Strindberg noted in his diary that his play was finished. In the last act, the king dies in despair, abandoned by all, struck down by the mysterious bullet which, according to the Frenchman who witnessed the event, entered his brain with a sound like that of a rock thrown into a marsh. One of the king's last lines in the play concerns the women 'who hated me

because I did not want to admit their sovereignty'. It fits appropriately into
the other drama which was being enacted on Strindberg's homefront.

On 25 June, the diary was exultant. Harriet, who had been on a visit to the
country, returned 'radiant', and read *Karl XII*. 'We are now convinced that
our union will last for ever, because we are living in complete harmony.'
Harriet is said to be 'overjoyed' to be back in the yellow room (the bedroom).
It is likely that a child was conceived that day: Strindberg certainly believed
so. His daughter Anne-Marie was born on 25 March 1902.

A few days later, disaster struck, and it is hard to resist the thought that
Strindberg engineered it himself. Instead of the honeymoon journey his
young wife had been looking forward to, Strindberg decided to spend the
summer on Kymmendö, and sent a telegram to enquire for lodgings. He was
compelling Harriet to return to his youth, where she would be reminded of
Siri at every turn. However, there was no free accommodation on the island,
and the trip to Germany was reinstated on the agenda. Tickets were
purchased, suitcases packed, and the day of departure arrived. Strindberg
declared that 'the powers' forbade him to travel. Harriet became 'wrathful'.
She was not mollified by the offer she claimed Strindberg made her of a
Baedeker, with the suggestion that she should travel in her imagination
instead, 'thus avoiding all the factual vicissitudes of the journey'.

In his diary, Strindberg wrote that Harriet fled their home that same day,
'without a farewell, without telling me where she was going'. 'What a night
of sorrow!' he added, continuing the following day: 'Horrible morning.
Yearning, sadness, desperation.' Thus the precipitation from the heights of
happiness to deepest pain occurred here as rapidly as in the plays written
after *Inferno*, and, as in classical drama, hubris is the cause of that
downfall. Yet the viewer-reader has reasons for scepticism. To take just one
detail: Strindberg did know where his wife had gone, as they had discussed
the possibility of spending the summer in the Danish seaside resort of
Hornbaeck. On the day Harriet left, Strindberg sent a telegram to her there
and offered to meet her in Sassnitz, which meant that he and the powers had
given in. The diary entry is an exaggeration for dramatic effect.

After Harriet's departure, Strindberg resumed work on the third part of
To Damascus, which he had set aside after using it in his proposal of
marriage. As Harriet Bosse had suggested, The Unknown One is allowed to
leave the monastery and celebrate his wedding to The Lady. Thus, this
time, only a month elapsed between reality and fiction. In one of the stage
directions we recognize the dining-room on Karlavägen, complete with its
carved sideboard. When the couple enter their home after the wedding, The
Unknown One acts as brazenly as Strindberg himself had done, using the
same words.

Disaster is imminent. The Lady realizes that her husband does not see
her for herself. He has killed and disembowelled her, in order to use her as a

receptacle for his dreams. The Unknown One defends himself. He offers her everything he has won during a long life 'through the deserts and groves of art and poetry'. The Lady replies that the only thing wrong with all that wealth and fame is that it is not hers. The bitter but loving exchange concludes with the mutual insight that they cannot live together.

While Strindberg was composing that scene, which is part-invention, part-analysis of his relationship with Harriet Bosse, he wrote her a letter on 27 June presenting the same thesis in somewhat veiled terms:

> Beloved, Beloved Wife, So many tears, so many tears, and so hot that they burn out my eyes! And why? Mostly because I am tortured by the thought of all the suffering I have caused you; but at the height of self-reproach I cry out: 'But I was not able to act otherwise! I was not!' And yet, as I enter the golden room, I see you, see you as I found you that day sitting there weeping—and then my heart wants to burst from pain! I thought myself experienced in suffering, but this—I could not bear. And last night—I thought I would choke on my tears—and in the dark I searched for the little hand that made me feel so safe when the night's horrors frightened me! The sense of loss, the sorrow, the uncertainty, the pangs of conscience! I do not go through the door! but stay in the monastery! Not alone! Because you are here, everywhere, with your regal beauty, your kindness, your innocent smile.

On the same day Strindberg wrote this tremulous missive of love, he asked his brother Axel to help him exchange the grand piano he had bought for Harriet—'it totally destroys the room: the dining table does not fit under the light fixture'—for a small upright, and discussed the most economical ways of doing so. Was this revenge? Or was it simply that Strindberg, after shedding all those tears in his letter, rose brisk and cheerful from his desk, ready to discuss details of interior decoration, just as after his literary labours he was left unmoved by the sufferings he had described?

It is likely that Harriet Bosse realized even during the time of her engagement to Strindberg that she had taken on more than she could handle. Edvin Adolphson, the brilliant actor who became her third husband, once said that Strindberg was a person who was unable to disclose his inner self and therefore remained a stranger to her. It was an interesting statement, made independently of Marcel Réja, and quite contrary to the prevailing image of Strindberg as a confessor and self-revealer. It is also natural that Harriet Bosse—Adolphson was echoing one of the insights she had early on—did not like to bring up the matter in later life, as it tended to show her powers of intuition in an unfavourable light. Marriage to Strindberg was obviously a formative event in her life. 'There is no woman born who would not be happy to be elevated above her own sex,' Edvin Adolphson said, and Harriet was certainly accorded that elevation. In a letter written two days after the one quoted above, Strindberg told her how he held her 'inner image so pure, so chaste, that no evil may touch you!' and compared her, like Eleonora, to Christ.

At the same time, by all accounts, it was the sexual foundation of this marriage that was shaky and ultimately made it impossible. It seems that Strindberg—here again Edvin Adolphson is the source—entrenched himself behind the philosophy he had championed during his most actively anti-feminist years: according to it, a woman should not seek sexual pleasure in intercourse, which is designed only for procreation. A woman's pleasure consists in bearing a child and giving birth, and she has to be content with that. Had he forgotten what he had written in *A Fool's Apology*—that only the golden moments of sexual cohabitation enabled husband and wife to get through this thorny life on earth?

Despite everything, they spent a honeymoon summer together: in July, Strindberg travelled to Copenhagen, where Harriet met him. As planned, they went to Hornbaeck on the east coast of Själland, a fashionable beach resort with sand dunes. They rented a small red brick house, overgrown with ivy, and bathed in the sea. Sneaking up behind a dune, a photographer for a Copenhagen newspaper tried to get a picture of the beautiful bride. Stringberg attacked the man and broke his camera, thereby causing a press debate throughout Northern Europe on the sacredness of privacy and the rights of the mass media.

Strindberg made efforts to please his wife—his concessions were later held against her—and even wrote to the Dramatic Theatre imploring them to let Harriet play Juliet in the Shakespeare play. He remembered how he had made similar pleas on Siri's behalf. He even abandoned his resistance to a German tour, and on 1 August, the couple travelled to Berlin, taking lodgings at the Aachener Hof. But here, in the heat of the summer, things took a turn for the worse. In his diary, Strindberg called 3 August 'a day of horror' after a quarrel with Harriet. 'She wanted to go to a prostitutes' café, but I didn't want to.'

That day, Strindberg, in a state of insensate rage, had called his wife a whore. The word would recur in his writings during the years to come. Harriet Bosse felt wounded and defiled and regarded any further cohabitation impossible. The atmosphere of catastrophe was enhanced by her suffering from nausea and realizing that she was pregnant. The couple hurried home, and on 9 August a physician confirmed the pregnancy. For a few days, the couple attempted to continue their life together; but it did not work. On 20 August, Strindberg noted: 'She said the child should be called Bosse. I gave her what for! Crash!' Two days later, Harriet left home and sent a letter saying she had gone 'for ever'. Strindberg recorded that he felt drowsy several times that day, that he read about Beethoven, and that it was his father's birthday.

Harriet stayed away for forty-five days, until 5 October. With his usual tendency to dramatize, Strindberg changed that to forty, the number of days Jesus suffered temptation in the desert, the number of years the children of Israel wandered there, and the number of weeks a child spends in its mother's womb. Those forty days became a central theme in his work, representing a painful time of preparation for the greatest growth-period of his life.

7

For the third time, Strindberg had failed as a husband and a lover. This time, the situation was aggravated by Harriet's pregnancy and the fact that his life was open to public scrutiny. The entire Swedish nation was watching the drama unfold. 'How do you write?' an interviewer for *Bonnier's Monthly* asked Strindberg in 1909. He replied that he composed in 'a kind of pleasant fever, which changes into ecstasy or intoxication'. 'But,' he added, 'it does not come on command, nor when it pleases *me*. It comes when it pleases *it* to do so. But best and mostly after some great disaster.' Indeed, Strindberg's life and work provide many examples proving the accuracy of that description, and many artists have reacted in the same way—Wagner and Joyce are well-known instances. The difference, at this juncture in Strindberg's life, was that he had achieved some measure of control over his inspiration and knew how to guide it to a certain extent. We cannot always establish what was genuinely experienced pain, but now more than ever we should recall what a man who became close to Strindberg a few years later once said of him: 'Besides, he was truly happy only when he was deeply unhappy, diabolically, triumphantly unhappy.'

During August and September, Strindberg expressed his pain in a series of letters to Harriet Bosse and in diary entries that were unusually detailed. He described in convincing terms how he walked around in the apartment, caressing the things she had touched. 'Outwardly, I have cried so much that my eyes have been drained, and inwardly, so much that my soul has been washed clean!' Harriet was told on 1 September. 'I have kissed your picture and called your name, so that, if you were dead, I would have "grieved you out of the ground".' His diction was so ardent that he had good reason to allude to Orpheus who made the stones weep and the dead rise.

Now Lovisa is packing your belongings into crates like coffins! Young corpses of such young memories! This is the bitterest thing I have experienced, because I love you— Now comes the hard work—to bury the memories and to forget you. I imagined that I would be able to cry myself rid of you in eight days, but I was mistaken! My child. It is mine, but will never be, for when it sees the light, its mother will be a stranger, known to the entire city but not to me! Last letter. Last farewell! Farewell for ever! How prodigious!

But while addressing his beloved in these terms, the swooning singer of Swan White also rose from his knees. He reasserted himself, called the marriage a ghost story, accused his wife of having played with him, described her as cruel and wretched, and stressed once again that she was his creation and as such had to submit to the roles he had written for her. He regretted everything he had sacrificed for her. She had degraded him as Omphale degraded Hercules. He compiled a veritable catalogue of his sufferings in the course of the marriage:

> Did I not suppress my antipathies, in order to please you? You got a grand piano, although I detest grand pianos; you had your room furnished in green and yellow, although I hate green and yellow; I bought Grieg, although he was too old-fashioned for me, and I asked for Emil Sjögren, although I do not like him. I followed you to Denmark, the worst country I know; I ate at the table d'hôte which is torture; I bathed off the sandy beach which is something that figures in my worst nightmares. . . .

and so on.

As always in such situations, and despite the ironic comments on the habit he makes in *To Damascus*, Strindberg then resorted to suicide threats. On 9 September, he declared that the end was near, 'death by my own hand'. He wrote his last will and testament and ordered his headstone to be engraved with the words 'O Crux Ave Spes Unica'. At the same time, he negotiated with Harriet for a meeting on neutral ground, and offered to move out and leave the apartment on Karlavägen to her. In the midst of this whirlpool of emotions and projects he continued his orderly everyday life, took his walks and sat at his desk even more regularly than ever. During the summer, he had been busy with a play on the medieval freedom fighter Engelbrekt. The hero, however, turned out far too sunny a figure, and the play was a failure, but as soon as Strindberg had finished it, he drafted a new large-scale historical play about Kristina, Gustaf II Adolf's daughter, who abdicated for the sake of her faith. It became one of his most successful plays.

It was also a repetition of his *tour de force* in the spring, *Swan White*: a play that was a portrait of his beloved, and an enticement for her to return to him. Queen Kristina did, indeed, become one of Harriet Bosse's most famous roles. To make the part even more tempting, Strindberg gave detailed instructions for the queen's wardrobe. In the play, she appears as a natural actress and charmer, surrounded by men who love her and who represent various stages of Strindberg's own feelings for Harriet: Tott, in the first flush of love; Magnus Gabriel de la Gardie, betrayed but faithful;

Oxenstierna, who has renounced her. Each received his share of words Strindberg himself had spoken to Harriet.

Immediately after Harriet's return on 5 October, the end of the forty days—'Light! G.v.t! [*Gud vare tack*: 'God be thanked]' he wrote in his diary—Strindberg returned to work on the play he regarded as his masterpiece and which has become his best-loved work: *A Dream Play*.

In a 'Remembrance', with which he prefaced the play when it was printed the following year, Strindberg says of the characters in *A Dream Play* that they 'divide, split in two, become doubles, evaporate, coalesce, flow outward, gather together'. The terms are almost identical with those he used in the 1890s, in regard to the elements—all of which were merely the occasional and provisional forms of existence assumed by a single basic substance. Now, he had advanced further in his representation of human beings. Everything is contained within everything else. This being the case, then all are contained in all. But one consciousness, Strindberg wrote, stands above all others—that of the dreamer, within whose creative consciousness these shifting figures are moving. The poet is to them what God is to the world.

One of the main concepts of *A Dream Play* had already appeared in *Kristina*. Tott, the young nobleman, sees his beloved, the queen, as 'a higher being'. For him, she is 'an eagle, born out of air in the air, and thus she finds it difficult to breathe down here'. In *A Dream Play*, Indra's daughter descends to earth, and there is a strong emphasis on her similarity to Jesus, also a child of Indra. She is incarnated on earth, and the play's action deals with her experiences there—as the glazier's daughter, as a door-keeper at the opera, as the lawyer's wife.

Indra's daughter finds it difficult to breathe the heavy air of earth. Throughout the play, she repeats the words: 'It is pitiful to be a human!' Should this be understood as a complaint concerning the conditions of human existence in general? The two best-known episodes do seem to indicate this. The Officer, who vainly waits for his Victoria in front of the opera house, has to become a student all over again, although he has already graduated, and in front of the stern master he cannot remember what two times two is. He represents the curse of repetition. The Billsticker, who dreams all his life about a green hoop-net, discovers when he finally acquires one that it does not please him as much as he had expected. He illustrates the vanity of all hope.

Yet, on closer examination, one realizes to one's surprise that *A Dream Play* also provides a concrete image of the society Strindberg had been satirically attacking all his life. The Lawyer, who becomes the husband of Indra's daughter, dedicates himself to the cause of the poor, which results in the laurel wreath being removed from his brow in the very act of promotion. He is told that the judiciary is everybody's servant, except the servants'.

In his marriage, he discovers that poverty is the heaviest burden. The housemaid Kristin who seals windows and doors in order to keep the house warm, does so with hatred, and her 'I'm taping, I'm taping' sounds like a call to revolution. Lina, the servant at the spa, does not even dare to complain, since her situation would worsen if she did. The three serving maids are not invited to the great society ball. When Agnes and the Lawyer travel to see the paradise of the Mediterranean shore, they encounter two coal-heavers, who experience that paradise as an inferno. When Agnes asks the Lawyer why people do not do anything to improve their condition, he replies that all 'improvers' end up in prison or the madhouse. When she asks him who it is that puts them in prison, she receives the answer: 'All the right-thinking, honest people.'

She insists: 'Has it never occurred to anyone that things are as they are for secret reasons?' The Lawyer has a reply to this as well: 'Yes, those who are well-to-do always believe that!'

8

After Harriet's return to Karlavägen, the couple spent the winter in relative harmony, even though the word 'whore' was used once in a while. 'Good and considerate toward me', was Harriet's opinion of her husband. As she found it difficult to tolerate tobacco smoke, Strindberg made an attempt to stop smoking. He encouraged his wife to sculpt and paint, and she made a small statue of herself as Puck. Strindberg had it cast in an edition of twelve, which was distributed among friends. During arguments about women's rights—'Strindberg's whiskers vibrated, I wept'—Harriet's husband, by her own account, would nervously and furiously wash his hands in a basin that stood in his room; this calmed him down.

The couple did not lead an isolated life. They often received callers, and went to visit friends. *Engelbrekt* opened on 3 December and proved a complete flop. Strindberg could afford that setback: he had stronger works than ever before, to throw into the breach in his battle for fame. In February, *Karl XII* had its first night at the Dramatic Theatre, with August Palme as the king. The part of Emerentia Polhem had been intended for Harriet, but she was unable to play it because of her advanced pregnancy. This play was a success, and Strindberg immediately went on to write *Gustaf III*, finishing it on 16 March, the day that monarch had been shot at the famous masked ball at the Opera in 1792.

On 8 March Harriet 'raised the alarm during the night'. Strindberg made haste to call the midwife and managed to set fire to his dressing-gown as he tried to light the lamp: according to the diary, flames were running up and down the fabric. But it was a false alarm.

On 25 March, the day of the Annunciation, a girl was born and christened Anne-Marie. Harriet's sister assisted the midwife at the birth. To convince Strindberg that he was wrong in his claim that women bore children with pleasure, the sister opened the door to the bedroom. Strindberg closed it. She opened it again. According to Harriet, this went on for at least an hour.

The arrival of the child disturbed the balance of life on Karlavägen. For some time, Strindberg's diary became quite laconic—thus, under 5 April 'Explication! Dark!' The wedding anniversary, 6 May, was celebrated 'without flowers', and the entry for 15 June reads: 'Argument at table'. In July, Harriet took the child to Räfsnäs, and Strindberg stayed in Stockholm. In the autumn Harriet resumed her career, and realized her ambition to play Juliet. During the winter, the marriage proceeded by fits and starts, but in March 1903, after a dispute about Ibsen's *Peer Gynt*, there was an unusually vicious scene, and on 20 March, Strindberg noted in his diary that he had returned his wedding ring to Harriet. In June, she and their daughter moved to Blidö in the Archipelago, and that marked the end of the marriage, although it was to have a long 'Indian summer'.

9

Strindberg wrote some of his greatest poetry during the year that followed the forty days. Until then, he had used verse forms mainly as tools for satire, polemics, witty attacks in the tradition of the eighteenth-century Enlightenment poets. Now he turned his attention to lyrical subjects: nature, love, freedom.

In the cycle *The Night of the Trinity* he created an idyllic framework for a series of widely divergent pieces, in the manner of *The Canterbury Tales* or *The Decameron*. In Fagervik in the Stockholm Archipelago, which was also the setting for parts of *A Dream Play*, a number of gentlemen congregate in a tavern one early summer's day, to enjoy food and drink and to engage in friendly bardic competition. Most of them are civil servants and summer visitors to the island, several of them being associated with seafaring. There is a clergyman among them, and also The Poet. It is the world of the *petit bourgeois* which Strindberg never really left. His father and grandfather would have felt quite at home in this cosy, peaceful circle. The hexameters employed by several of the gentlemen roll off their tongues so naturally that one might think they had been sitting there since the days of Homer.

The notary and the toll-collector sing the praises of summer in Sweden, while the former dwells extensively on one of Strindberg's favourite subjects, Swedish summer cuisine, with particular emphasis on the crayfish, the lamb and the herring, all of them enhanced by 'the indispensable dill weed'. The curate of Skägga, piously following in the footsteps of Linnaeus, describes how fertilization takes place in a field of rye. The postmaster chooses a less ambitious subject, rhyming about what a weathercock on the roof of a barn might be thought to be singing in the wind; the toll-collector retaliates with a skilful verbal imitation of the song of the nightingale.

As is only fitting, The Poet surpasses all these lyrical gentlemen with his poem 'Chrysaëtos'. Throughout his career, Strindberg had referred to Sven Nilsson's book *Scandinavian Fauna*, which had been part of his father's library, and which he found a useful adjunct to his prose. Nilsson's book contains a great number of echoes from earlier days when popular myths and superstitions regarding animals still prevailed: the author, a man of the Enlightenment, attempted to disprove these things, but at the same time perpetuated them. Strindberg paid due attention. In his youth, Sven Nilsson had believed that there were two kinds of golden eagle in Sweden, and one of these he gave the Latin name *Falco chrysaëtos*. Later he realized that he had merely mistaken the young golden eagle for a different bird, and *chrysaëtos* disappeared from Swedish zoology.

Strindberg retained the term. Nilsson had described the bird as black on its throat, breast and stomach, but with an admixture of rust-brown, which gave it that golden sheen. Those were Harriet Bosse's favourite colours. In February 1901, Strindberg had removed an eagle feather from her hat and made a pen out of it, and in a poem he had remembered his youthful nickname, The Eagle, and promised to protect her under his powerful wings. Now he named her Chrysaëtos.

The poem is a virtuoso performance on a theme that Strindberg had formulated over a quarter of a century. The first time he had fallen in love, (how long ago it seems), he had fled from the object of his emotion to Dalarö. There, he had described himself as a madman, had followed Siri von Essen's tracks through the woods like a hound, and had finally thrown himself into the ice-cold sea to die. At the time, he had not had sufficient artistic means at his disposal to do justice to such a tremendous surge of emotion; now, he did.

The poem links Dalarö to the forty days. It deals with a man who loses his lover. Agonized, he starts searching for her, first in the apartment they had shared, then on the heath outside, and finally on the ice, where he meets his death in the form of an ice-breaking steamer. In the moment of his death, memories of his former happiness cascade through his consciousness, which expands to include the whole of creation: the darkness of the night, the howling dogs, the migrating crows, the whirling snow all stream into his soul. Thus his death becomes not only the demise of an individual, but a cosmic catastrophe.

The idyll in hexameters, 'The Journey to the City', reaches similar heights of lyricism. When its hero, a rural sexton, exchanges his old upright piano for a grand, and inaugurates it with Beethoven's 'Appassionata', he reflects Strindberg's own artistic development: like the sexton, he has chosen an instrument with a deeper tone.

Of the poems in the cycle, 'The Wolves Are Howling' is the most remarkable. As Gunnar Ollén has demonstrated in his erudite study of Strindberg's poetry of the 1900s, the poet was able to hear the caged wolves on Skansen howling on winter nights: in the course of the poem, a great fire breaks out in the city, colouring the sky red. The Skansen hilltop is illuminated, and the wolves, howling out their hatred against the humans who have deprived them of their freedom, redouble their fury. The other animals wake up: the foxes' lair resounds with echoing laughter, the bears get up on their hind legs and grunt like slaughtered pigs, the lynxes' fangs gleam in the dark, and the seals cry woe over the city.

In this poem the animals become representatives for an enslaved humanity. The elks start butting against their cage bars; the eagles shriek and beat their worn-out wings against their cages; the swans swim silently between the ice floes on the lake and snap at the reflected flames that resemble goldfish.

The world conflagration which the caged wolves hope will free them is one that Strindberg had surmised in his youth when the Commune in Paris set fire to the Tuileries. Sparks from this wolf poem fly back as far as the first version of *Master Olof*, in which Gert appears as the victor and forerunner of the many upheavals and revolutions to come. Europe was closer to her downfall than anyone guessed—except for the wolves.

Chapter Fifteen

'BLACK FLAGS'

I

FROM THE SUMMER of 1903, Strindberg lived alone. Harriet rented a furnished apartment at no. 30 Biblioteksgatan, near Stureplan. 'What do you want of me? You are free now, and enjoy peace and happiness, things you had to do without while you lived with me. . . . Capture the joy I denied you, but allow me to keep my sorrow intact. Pursue your destiny, which you believe you control, but do not interfere with mine, it is guided by another,' Strindberg wrote to her on 25 August. He visited her and Ann-Marie, taking flowers and presents, acting the part of a father-at-a-distance—the one best suited to him during that phase of his life. No demands—but, now and again, the pleasure of watching the beautiful mother tuck her child into bed for the night.

Harriet and Anne-Marie used to go to Karlavägen for Sunday dinner, and occasionally Harriet stayed in the yellow room after the nanny had taken Anne-Marie home. 'Fear of pregnancy' was Strindberg's regular comment in his diary after these wifely visitations.

In October 1903, the young Austrian philosopher Otto Weininger took his own life. He had formulated thoughts about women that resembled Strindberg's. Weininger's book *Geschlecht und Charakter* (*Sex and Character*) had attracted tremendous attention. Strindberg sent a wreath to his funeral, and that same month wrote an article whose subject was a variation on an old theme of his: submission as the price man has to pay for woman's love. A loving woman wants to debase, dominate and humiliate the man, thereby sapping his psychic strength:

> According to the latest analysis, a woman's love consists of 50 per cent rut and 50 per cent hatred. It sounds strange, but it is true. Quite apart from differences of taste, inclination, opinion and so on, one finds that when a woman loves a man, she also hates him; hates him because she feels tied to

him, and inferior to him. There is no continuous flow in her love, but a continual reversal of polarity, a perennial alternation of current; this is a sign of the negative, passive aspect of her nature, as opposed to the man's positive and active one.

It is positively astounding how close Strindberg came here to describing his own behaviour pattern in love: every word fits into it—and particularly that 'alternation of current'. Was he really not aware of it? He must have been, but it went against the grain to admit it.

On 18 April, Strindberg signed the preliminary documents for divorce proceedings. The same day, he replaced the statue of Venus, purchased on his wedding day, with portraits of his children: an attempt to substitute the father for the lover.

Nevertheless, physical relations with Harriet continued. As summer was approaching, he offered her Isola Bella in Furusund, which he had once again rented for the season. He declared that she could live there by herself if she wished—he would be content with occasional visits. He clarified the situation in a letter of 27 May:

> But we will have to live in matrimony, because I love your body as I love your soul, and I know that our relationship has triumphed, although it took time, as I told you on our first night. And we must take the risk of having another child, but then try to have a son, so that you won't be displeased later. Now I believe that we will get one after such long privation. And I believe that when my yearning reaches out to your beauty as it does now, you will find what you have been seeking for so long. Let us tempt fate once more! What will the world and the lawyers say about it? They will rejoice in their hearts.

Strindberg's turns of phrase seem to indicate that he was prepared to modify his sexual philosophy, and that even less chaste embraces might produce good children.

On 1 June, Strindberg moved out to Furusund with Anne-Marie and her nanny. Harriet joined them after three weeks, on her return from Paris, where she had been studying. The novel *The Roof-Raising* (1906) is Strindberg's record of the happiness of that summer. 'I knew how precarious it was,' the protagonist declares in Strindbergian tones, 'but for just that reason I received and gave back, living in a state of intoxication that had to come to an end.' The images of bliss he conjured up can be completed with an entry from the *Occult Diary*:

> Harriet's return from Paris to Furusund is one of my happiest memories. When she left my bed at night, she did not look like herself but had a long oval face . . . and she gave off a scent so powerful and lovely that I became ecstatic and almost lost consciousness. It was supernatural, and sometimes I believe that she belongs to a very elevated sphere, and is not an ordinary human being.

49 Harriet Bosse with her daughter Anne-Marie

50 Strindberg in Furusund

Like every other extended period spent with Harriet, this one, too, ended abruptly. On 9 August, Strindberg left Isola Bella without saying goodbye, and soon after the interrupted divorce proceedings were resumed. That autumn, Strindberg's mood was a sombre one, ane he was seized by extreme pessimism. He wrote in his diary on 3 September:

Life is so abominably ugly, we humans so abysmally evil, that if a writer were to describe *everything* he has seen and heard, no one could bear to read it. There are things I remember seeing and hearing, in the company of good, respectable, popular people, that I have deleted, have never been able to discuss and do not want to remember. Education and culture seem like mere masks worn by the beast, and virtue merely dissimulation. Our highest achievement is to conceal our vileness. Life is so cynical that only a swine can feel comfortable in it. And whoever is able to see this ugly life as beautiful *is* a swine! Life is certainly a punishment! A hell; for some, a purgatory, but a paradise for no one.

A few days later he dreamt that he was executed by hanging. 'Saw the scaffold and the cart. Was not particularly sorry.'

On 27 October, the divorce was declared absolute in the municipal court, and he was free again. Nevertheless, his relationship with Harriet continued along its old lines: friendly words, sexual contact, mutual support, insults, explosion! A reasonably balanced state of affairs prevailed after the divorce. Strindberg was still preoccupied with Harriet, but he showed some restraint, as he did not want to risk losing his privileges. There is a vast difference between what he told the world about his marriage to Siri, and what he revealed about Harriet.

2

Back to what was more or less a bachelor's existence on Karlavägen, Strindberg returned to social satire in the two novels *The Gothic Rooms* and *Black Flags*. They are darker in tone than *The Red Room* and *The New Kingdom*, written twenty-five years earlier.

During the 1880s, Strindberg directed his satirical scourge against the wealthy and powerful society of the Oscarian era. Now, Strindberg directed his main attention to the literary establishment.

At the turn of the century, Strindberg's whole situation had changed decisively. His plays had proved popular with the general public—but more importantly, the works of his youth and middle years finally also found a wide readership.

51 Arthur Sjögren's drawing of Strindberg as a chemist—Faust?—in *Antibarbarus*, 1905

His *Collected Novels and Stories* appeared between 1899 and 1902, and the *Collected Dramatic Works* in 1903 and 1904. New individual editions followed in rapid succession, and even the more esoteric works like *Somnambulist Nights* and *Poems 1883* became available. Books in popular cheap editions, selling for 1 kronor or 25 öre, first appeared in Sweden at the beginning of the century, and Strindberg soon became the most widely read author in that market. *The Red Room*, *The People of Hemsö*, *The New Kingdom*, *Utopias*, *Swedish Fates and Adventures* were published in large editions, and read particularly by young people. *The People of Hemsö* appeared in seven editions, at 25 öre each, between 1904 and 1909.

At the same time, more lavish illustrated editions of Strindberg's works were produced for the wealthier book-buying public. In Arthur Sjögren, Strindberg found a congenial illustrator in the Art Nouveau manner he himself was fascinated by. Sjögren had the same initials as Strindberg, a fact which the latter acknowledged graciously. Particularly famous, and for good reason, are Sjögren's illustrations for *Wordplay and Small Art* (1905), a collection of the lyrical writings of the forty days. Strindberg managed to make its first printing into an unrivalled collector's item. In one of the poems, 'The Dutchman', he had drawn a delightful portrait of Harriet Bosse, in which the female form was described with a wealth of metaphors from heaven, earth and sea; yet, at the end, he uttered a number of maledictions against Harriet, accusing her of having deprived him of his manly strength, and in the final lines she is called 'a small, nasty woman'. As fate would have it, one of his many periods of reconciliation with Harriet coincided with the week the book was to appear; Strindberg made the publisher cut the offending passage from every copy of the edition. Thus the few extant uncut copies are very rare collector's items.

Surrounded by such a plethora of editions, Strindberg realized that he had a powerful weapon at his disposal, which he could wield to his own advantage with publishers and journals: through his writing, he had access to a large audience which merely by its existence lent what he had to say a new degree of authority. For a long time, he had approached his publishers humbly, cap in hand—so far as he was capable of such an attitude. Now he was able to dictate terms, and his freedom to criticize and satirize was unlimited. He made use of some of his long-hoarded literary 'capital' when he proceeded to examine the literary world.

The beginning of *Black Flags*, which describes a meal at Professor Stenkåhl's home, presents a wonderful caricature of the conditions of existence prevailing among artists and writers as Strindberg had experienced them in Berlin, Paris, and Stockholm. The guests in Stenkåhl's influential salon detest one another—their host is no exception—but have to attend because this is where reputations are launched and destroyed, prices registered on the literary stock market, personalities scrutinized. Rendered almost inert by food and drink, the invited authors attempt to spy on each other, rob each other, and run each other down while at the same time spreading a layer of flattery over it all. Details such as the hands which like crawling crabs roll pellets of bread across the white beach of the tablecloth make one think of a human bestiary whose members are always ready to tear and devour one another.

'Yes, here we sit among murderers and thieves,' says Dr Borg to Falkenström, and the latter, Strindberg's alter ego (his name can be associated with Falk in *The Red Room*), replies: 'How right you are, it is a den of murderers.'

Black Flags was received very much as *The New Kingdom* had been in its day. In the eyes of the public, the universally applicable satire was obscured by the book's malicious individual portraits, and those were seen as acts of personal revenge. First and foremost, the novel's main character, the writer Lars Petter Zachrisson, was understood to be a caricature of Gustaf af Geijerstam who was a strong rival of Strindberg's, not least in Germany.

There is a repulsive figure in one of E. T. A. Hoffmann's tales, a vampire who cunningly usurps the merits of others, 'Klein Zachris genannt Zinnober' ('Little Zacharias called Cinnabar'). Zachris or Zinnober are the nicknames Strindberg chose for his hero. Acting like a public prosecutor who had for ever joined the criminal to his deed in this book, Strindberg repeatedly referred to the portrait as a just verdict on Geijerstam. Zachris is the evil genius of the literary establishment.

But he is more than that: he is a professional writer, and Strindberg fed his own experiences into the character. As Jean Lundin is a double of Strindberg's on a comic level, Zachris is one in the realm of the frightful and grotesque. After *Inferno*, Strindberg was incapable of creating characters who were merely individuals; no matter who his models, they turned into representatives of himself, and of many others. He no longer saw what distinguished people, only the features they had in common.

Zachris is beside himself with worry that someone else may surpass him. He is constantly on the lookout for dangerous competitors, whom he attempts to ensnare. As Anni Carlsson, the German Strindberg scholar, has skilfully demonstrated, Zachris's modus operandi is close to Strindberg's. The most important subject in his work is his wife Jenny, and images from his marriage continually recur in his consciousness. When something that had previously appeared innocent is seen in a new light, it is as if some invisible force had injected poison into his body, and he is consumed by hatred. The only way he can get rid of it is by writing about it. He pursues Jenny like a bloodhound. She takes to drink, and he rejoices at her disintegration and tries to hasten it. When he realizes that an overly hateful portrait of her would cause a scandal in his own country, he decides to publish the book in Germany.

Thus Strindberg characterizes Zachris in ways that are entirely his own. He had even used the word vampire about himself. In March 1885, he wrote to Heidenstam, who was considering a writer's career:

> Just a word before you become an author! There is no profession as crude, so devoid of sensitivity as this! If only you knew what life looks like afterwards to a writer, whose profession has forced him to strip off his clothes in a public place, or suck the blood of close friends or even that of his own kin, like a vampire! Ugh! And if one does not do those things, one is not a writer.

The New Kingdom pilloried the writer Carl David af Wirsén, the prototype of a literary career hound. As a portrait, this is no more than a caricature: the character has no inner tension or life of its own. Zachris, on the other hand, demonstrates Strindberg's development as a human being and as an artist. True, Zachris is scum—but he is also an unhappy creature who deserves our compassion. Although Strindberg writes about him with loathing, the expression 'the desperate one' escapes from his pen: Zachris is said to be incapable of enjoying any innocent pleasure in life, and to regard anyone able to do so as belonging to the Golden Age. Compelled to transform everything he encounters into poetry, he is an outcast from normality.

In *The Blue Book*, Strindberg discusses, à propos of Swedenborg, an ancient religious experience which he calls devastation. There are human beings, he says, who are gripped by a sense of damnation. Their bad conscience invents malicious persons who persecute them and are the cause of all their misfortunes. In actual fact, that sense of being damned is a gift from God, a trial leading to salvation. He who understands that he is not being persecuted, but rather punished for the sake of his own improvement, is on his way to salvation and a state of blessedness. The evil within him is being devastated. His life grows lighter, and peace returns to him.

This was the form of 'devastation' Strindberg believed he had experienced during the *Inferno* period. He stated explicitly that the damned 'invent' evil persecutors for themselves, and this was exactly what he had done himself: herein lay his so-called persecution mania.

Zachris is one of those damned who do not reach the redeeming state of devastation, yet his pain indicates that he is capable of achieving it. He can be seen as one of Strindberg's self-portraits. If one wishes to do so, one can see an implicit prayer inherent in the make-up of his character, a prayer to be released from the role of author. 'I am not permitted to exhibit my person, which I have self-sacrificed for my work,' Strindberg wrote in 1907 to his friend Tor Aulin, the musician. Indeed, he was unable to show himself openly to anyone, and thus could not testify to the pain caused by being excluded from an ordinary life and forced by the demon to devote everything to one's art.

He employed a sophisticated ruse when he made another writer—Geijerstam—draw the fire intended for his own sins. He justified this by the notion that he had recognized in Geijerstam traits of a kind that he condemned in himself. It is difficult to venture an opinion as to whether he also really believed that he had been saved by the experience of devastation, while Geijerstam had remained among the damned. No one can avoid a certain degree of self-deception, not even those who have penetrated the depths of their own consciousness. It is certainly possible to forgive Strindberg's readers for failing to understand the code of ethics he employed in his relationship with Geijerstam.

In *Black Flags*, Strindberg makes Jenny pronounce severely on the entire guild of authors. She says on her deathbed:

> Do you know, I sometimes wonder if your books do more harm than good. You poets stand outside life and society, you are like the birds that live in the air, looking down on the world and its people. Can you see things right? Can your ethereal teaching have any relevance to our burdened life on earth? When your work is play, and your life, a feast? You despise the bourgeois and their way of life. You call those who are dutiful and law-observing servile blackguards, those who are patient, lacking in courage, or who suffer, hypocrites. I curse the hour I entered your gypsy world with its criminal code, and I praise God who has opened my eyes, and given me hope and a belief in a better one.

Twenty years earlier, in *Somnambulist Nights*, Strindberg had allowed his spirit to rest, like a bird, on the Observatory roof, and look down upon the society he wanted to serve as an author. Now the image returned, only this time he condemned even the 'fire-fighter's' role he had once offered to fulfil.

In *Black Flags* he created, as a counterpart to the 'gypsy world', a convent (an idea dating back to 1894), to which outstanding men of letters can retire for meditation and self-searching.

3

During 1905 and 1906, Strindberg lived on Karlavägen, with the literary bombshell *Black Flags* lying temporarily defused in his desk drawer. Every publisher to whom he had sent the manuscript had refused it. One of his young friends, the writer Gustaf Janson, warned him that to publish the book would be a form of suicide.

In the autumn of 1905, Richard Bergh painted his great portrait of Strindberg. 'He really resembles a wounded yet proud old lion,' Bergh wrote, in November, to his friend the Danish painter Viggo Johannssen,

52 Richard Bergh's portrait of Strindberg, 1905

adding: 'He is the most interesting model I have ever had. His face with its many fate-lines reads like a fascinating book.'

Ever since 1899 and his final return to Stockholm, Strindberg had held regular musical soirées at his home, mostly dedicated to Beethoven, with a good supper to follow. He called his guests 'the old Beethoven boys'. In 1906, he wrote: 'It makes me happy to see how Beethoven endures; everything else is transient.' With advancing age, he felt an ever greater need to belong to only the most select élite.

The actual music was initially provided by his brother Axel on the piano, but later on, some of Sweden's most outstanding musicians participated, such as the violinist Tor Aulin and occasionally Wilhelm Stenhammar. Strindberg felt protective towards his brother, who ran the risk of being superseded by such virtuosi.

A touching friendship developed between Strindberg and Aulin. One reason Strindberg was so dangerous as an enemy was that he recognized his own weaknesses in the adversary. But, the same capacity for empathy also made him a wonderful friend. He dreamed his own genius into others. He urged Aulin to compose, and the latter did set several of his works to music. Before the first night of *Master Olof* in the early spring of 1908—for which Aulin had composed the music—Strindberg wrote:

> You were born with music in your soul and hands . . . I know that you have succeeded, and even believe it will be a success with the audience. And the reason for that, I believe, is that you are not weighed down by erudition (Lindegren) and that you approach your art in the spirit of play, but a divine kind of play, distinct from research or mathematics or algebra.

Lindegren was a composer famous for his proficiency in counterpoint. Time and again, Aulin received expressions of Strindberg's deep gratitude for playing for him; Strindberg even dreamed about him. When Strindberg lay on his deathbed, Aulin, then a resident of Göteborg, offered to come to Stockholm to alleviate his agony with violin music.

During these years, Strindberg associated to some degree with younger writers—Henning Berger, Algot Ruhe, Albert Engström, Hjalmar Söderberg—and they treated him with due respect. Yet, as always, he felt most at home with painters and sculptors. A new friend was Carl Eldh, who became the most proficient of those who sculpted Strindberg. In 1904, Eldh had returned from Paris and rented a studio on Narvavägen next door to Strindberg's apartment. In the early mornings, Eldh used to see Strindberg walk by, one hand behind his back, the other swinging a cane. In 1905, the two became acquainted, and Strindberg promised to sit for a bust. They became close friends; Eldh helped Strindberg with his studies of cloud formations—Strindberg had the notion that these were actually reflections of distant countries, and Eldh took photographs of them, for verification.

Eldh received a commission from the Nordic Museum to execute bas-reliefs of representatives of the Swedish working class, and in February, he asked Strindberg to provide texts for them. Strindberg made an attempt which demonstrated his knowledge of various styles, of the history of the Swedish language, and also his empathy for the subject. Thus, his epitaph for *The Logger*:

> Skrynkligt skinn och krumpna knogar,
> tjocka fingrar, trumpen uppsyn,
> lutad rugg och långa hälar
>
> *Wrinkled skin and shrunken knuckles,*
> *thick fingers, sullen countenance,*
> *bent back and long heels*

and for *The Old Woman*:

> Vakna Du Groa!
> Vakna, goda kvinna!
> Lång är färden,
> vägarna så långa
> lång är mänskans saknad.
>
> *Wake up, You Grey One!*
> *Wake up, good woman!*
> *Long is the journey,*
> *the roads so long*
> *long is man's regret.*

Both of these short poems are based on the Elder Edda.

In April 1906, San Francisco experienced its Great Earthquake. Strindberg noted in his diary that Gustaf Eisen, a friend from student days, had come from California to visit and told him that earthquakes were presaged by birds of an unknown kind, black on top and white below, resembling waders and popularly known as earthquake birds. Two days later, Strindberg saw a large bird with black top feathers that looked like a stork or a big seagull, and this gave him cause for reflection. No earthquake occurred; as ever, the omens he was watching out for were not fulfilled. But he was prepared.

In May, Ibsen died, leaving more scope for Strindberg. During a visit to her husband, Harriet Bosse lost her engagement ring; later it turned out that it had been stolen by the housemaid Ebba. Many scandalous events took place in Sweden, all noted in the *Occult Diary*. Strindberg's old friend and benefactor F. U. Wrangel was a chamberlain to Queen Sofia, whom Strindberg in the 1880s had regarded as the main force behind the women's crusade against him. Wrangel used to accompany Her Majesty to the Riviera every spring. One evening in 1906 he made an excursion from Nice to Monte Carlo and lost all the Queen's travelling funds, 50,000 kronor, at the tables. He was forced into exile after the King had offered to ensure there was no public scandal, provided the money was returned. For a while, Wrangel was reduced to an impecunious state, becoming another Jean Lundin in Strindberg's life.

During 1906, Strindberg devoted much of his time to photography. In January of that year, Röntgen published his great discovery, which Strindberg treated with scorn. Generally, he took a jaundiced view of the scientific discoveries of the day. Thus he was sceptical in regard to the Curies and their radium; like Röntgen, he saw them as members of the scientific establishment, rewarded with Nobel prizes, which he doubted as a matter of principle.

Emil Kléen had put him in touch with the photographer Herman Anderson who had started out as a portrait painter but then established himself in his own studio on Klara Vattugränd as a portrait photographer in 1886. As Per Hemmingsson relates in his book *Strindberg As Photographer*, Anderson was a worthy fellow, somewhat reserved, but with an artistic, Bohemian temperament and Socialist sympathies as well. He took many pictures of Strindberg, among them the well-known one with the eagle quill, dated February 1902. He assisted Strindberg in his photographic efforts. The two men constructed a darkroom on Karlavägen, and also devised a camera which made it possible to take life-size photographs. Strindberg had a life-size copy made of Harriet Bosse as Puck and installed it in his apartment behind a curtain. Occasionally, while talking to a friend, Strindberg would disappear to contemplate this picture for a while in an emotional, agitated state.

When Herman Anderson was dying of cancer in 1909, Strindberg visited him in hospital; after his death, he organized a collection for the destitute widow and her four young children.

4

1906 was memorable in Strindberg's life mainly because this was the year that he embarked on his largest prose work, *A Blue Book*, which was to occupy most of his time for the following two years. In its final version, the book runs to 1,200 pages; its fourth and final part, complete with a detailed index, appeared posthumously.

Initially, Strindberg's intention was to call the work *A Breviary*, in accordance with classical and Roman Catholic tradition—a volume of extracts from larger works. The Latinate title was replaced by a Swedish one, *A Blue Book Issued to Whom It May Concern, and Being a Commentary on 'Black Flags'*. Below the book's complete title stands a line from Isaiah (24:18) as an epigraph: 'He that cometh up out of the midst of the pit shall be taken in the snare.' The reference is to Strindberg's idea that in his novel he had parted from the black flags, the 'gypsy world' of literature condemned by Jenny, and that now he had to face a time of persecution. To a considerable extent, *A Blue Book* is a discussion of the ethical stance expressed in the novel.

When the first part of *A Blue Book* appeared in 1907, it bore a dedication to Emanuel Swedenborg, to the 'Teacher and Leader' from the 'Disciple'. Swedenborg had preoccupied Strindberg since his *Inferno* days, not so much as a master—he had not read his writings systematically—but as an example of how to pursue one's own way with independence and courage even if mocked by the entire world.

Swedenborg had died in London in 1771 and had been buried in the Swedish Church there. Now plans were made to bring his mortal remains back to Sweden. Strindberg, referring to these plans, added to his dedication: 'A wreath on your grave, upon your return from a century's rest in foreign soil. Resurgat!' In April 1908 Swedenborg's remains were transported from London in a Swedish man-of-war and placed, with solemn and stately ceremony, in a sarcophagus in Uppsala Cathedral on 19 May.

Strindberg combined all kinds of material in *A Blue Book*. He had grown weary of literary invention and arrangement, and finally gave in to his old wish to be more of a sage than a poet. The book consists of fictitious conversations between Swedenborg and himself, of short essays and aphorisms, personal portraits, fragmentary short stories, reminiscences and polemics. It is a gathering-place for all the various subjects Strindberg had been interested in; one might call it a larger, wider occult diary. When he read the proofs of the first volume, he wrote in his diary that he felt his mission in life had been completed: 'I have been allowed to say everything I had to say.'

5

1906 was also the year Strindberg published his last narrative prose works, two small novels: *The Roof-raising* and *The Scapegoat*. A year later, he had a dream during his customary early afternoon nap, and recorded it in his diary:

I dreamt that I walked in Loviseberg (one of my childhood homes) and saw that the largest pond had dried out. This pond had always been dangerous for children, as its edges were quagmires, and the stinking water itself full of toads, leeches and lizards. Now, in my dream, I walked on its dry bottom and was surprised to find it so clean. Thought: that's the end of the toad marsh, now that I have taken my leave from the 'black flags'.

Strindberg's interpretation of that dream, the drained pond as an image of a Sweden he had dried out and purified, may well be a reasonable one: but a dried-out pond from childhood is also an excellent symbol for an imagination that has begun to wilt and become barren. Strindberg's incredible ability to open up the great realms of the subconscious in his art, to enter the kingdom of death where preceding generations dwell, to penetrate humanity's collective experiences as preserved in myth and tales, contributed to the greatness and universal validity of his work. His dream about the pond can be seen as an expression of his fear that his links with the subconscious were about to terminate, that the great reservoir was in the process of drying out.

The two short novels demonstrate that he no longer had his old powers. Yet *The Roof-raising* has its own particular interest, not least because in it Strindberg introduced a new technique that was to leave its mark on twentieth-century literature. The main character is a conservator, approaching death in his apartment in Stockholm after an accident. Through his morphine-drugged consciousness stream images from his life, a river without beginning or end, and we are invited to listen to his interior monologue. This was the method Joyce used in the triumphant ending of *Ulysses*, Molly Bloom's extended and sensually vibrant soliloquy.

The conservator is the last example in Strindberg's *oeuvre* of a Renaissance man doomed to be ensnared by a woman's cunning. To remind us of his mythical origins, there is a lion's skin on his living-room floor. As mentioned above, his marriage is based on that of Strindberg and Harriet Bosse, but the wife is a sketchy figure; it is her husband who is the focus of interest.

In his apartment on Karlavägen, Strindberg had a series of reproductions of Rembrandt's self-portraits. In *A Blue Book* he stated that he became intimate with Rembrandt by constantly having these pictures before his eyes. The unfinished play *The Dutchman*, which was to include the great hymn to the female body, had Rembrandt as its main character.

In *The Roof-raising*, Strindberg attempted to take his self-analysis further, with Rembrandt as his guiding light. He hinted at the possibility that his protagonist, who embraces a Strindbergian view of science and believes that he has made a number of revolutionary discoveries, was, in fact, a victim of delusional misconceptions.

The description of his death is particularly remarkable. We read that his being is in the process of dissolution and that new personalities begin growing out of him, 'whether these were "residues" of ancestors or reflections of all whom he was thinking about'. He becomes mean and vicious one moment, and arrogant and superior the next. 'Then there appeared an old wise man, a child, a rudimentary woman. His own ego dissolved, and the innate character was seen to have been the mask behind which he had played his part, created by assimilation or conditions of life, and according to the law of the greatest exchange of psychic elements.'

The rudimentary woman Strindberg saw gliding past in the mirror of self-examination was one of the many roles he carried within his creative self.

Chapter Sixteen

OUTCAST

I

DURING THE FIRST years of the new century, Strindberg's plays were being widely performed in Europe, especially in Germany. Previous productions at experimental theatres had been brief and sporadic, but now the times seemed to have caught up with him. Max Reinhardt had embarked on his brilliant theatrical career, and he put on a number of Strindberg's plays. *Miss Julie*, with Gertrud Eysoldt as Julie, was a great success at Kleines Theatre in Berlin in 1904. The Germans moved faster than the Swedes to present new Strindberg works. *Easter* had its world | première| in the Schauspielhaus of Frankfurt-am-Main in 1901—with Gertrud Eysoldt as Eleonora. *The Dance of Death*, too, had its first performance in Germany, at the Residenztheater in Cologne in 1905, and toured forty German towns the following year.

Strindberg, who had a good nose for youthful talent, followed with interest Reinhardt's work in particular, through the mediation of his translator Schering; he tried to adapt his own writing to the new principles proposed by Reinhardt.

There were developments in Sweden as well. In 1906, the young Swedish actor-director August Falck mustered sufficient courage to take on *Miss Julie*, and the play had its Swedish première in Lund on 18 September. August Palme, who had introduced Strindberg to Harriet Bosse, played Jean, and the part of Julie was taken by Manda Björling. The play was a considerable success and, during the autumn, Falck's company toured Sweden, arriving in Stockholm in December.

Ever since the Copenhagen experiment Strindberg had nurtured the idea of a theatre of his own, making plans for one in both Berlin and Paris. When Falck came to Stockholm, Strindberg invited him to Karlavägen, and in his book *Five Years with Strindberg* Falck gives an account of that first visit.

Strindberg was so eager that he stood waiting for him by the window, and threw the door open before Falck had had time to ring the bell.

'Your name is August! Your name is Falck! Welcome!' were Strindberg's first words. Falck, as yet unfamiliar with the great interpreter of omens and portents, did not immediately understand the reference to the shared first name and the name 'Falk' from *The Red Room*.

At this first meeting, Strindberg and Falck discussed the possibility of creating a *théâtre intime* in Stockholm, modelled on those in France and Germany. The following year these plans became more definite. Having declared himself tired of drama, Strindberg returned to it immediately and in rapid succession wrote four plays which he called 'chamber plays' after Reinhardt, who had his Kammertheater (Chamber Theatre) in Berlin. In homage to Beethoven, whose mask hung on his wall, he gave the plays opus numerals: Opus 1 was *Storm*, followed by *The House that Burned*, *The Ghost Sonata*, and *The Pelican*. 'Small subject, thorough treatment, few characters, mighty viewpoints, free play of imagination, yet founded on observation' was his verdict on these plays, according to a letter to Adolf Paul of 6 January 1907.

The chamber plays are dark, like *Black Flags*. Many of their characters are spiritual relatives of Zachris, caught in various stages of damnation. The Student in *The Ghost Sonata* calls the world a madhouse, a house of correction, a mortuary—this is the hell to which humankind was doomed, and into which Jesus descended.

While the historical plays and *To Damascus*, *Crime and Crime*, and *Advent* express a preference for open-air locations like cemeteries, gardens and beaches, and frequently change scenes in a Shakespearean manner, the chamber plays take place in small rooms or by the outer walls of buildings. Domestic infernos are described, with memories streaming in from Strindberg's own childhood—which tended to grow darker as he grew older.

As always, Strindberg arranged his life to harmonize with his work: this had become second nature by now and occurred automatically. His tendency to complain and find fault to an intolerable degree grew stronger than ever, with the result that his maid Ebba, who had served him for two and a half years, resigned in a fury on 6 March. Before that she had made sure that Strindberg led a reasonable everyday existence. In the following weeks, while the chamber plays were being written, a succession of new servants came and went, all of them equally incapable of satisfying such a demanding employer. These are the entries from the *Occult Diary* between 26 March and 3 April 1907:

26: Anna left! Alma came. Calm, clean, a good girl. Well-prepared food for lunch. Lillan and Ruth visiting. Telephone call from Harriet! Aversion towards strong spirits in the evening.

27th: Started drinking beer with wormwood!

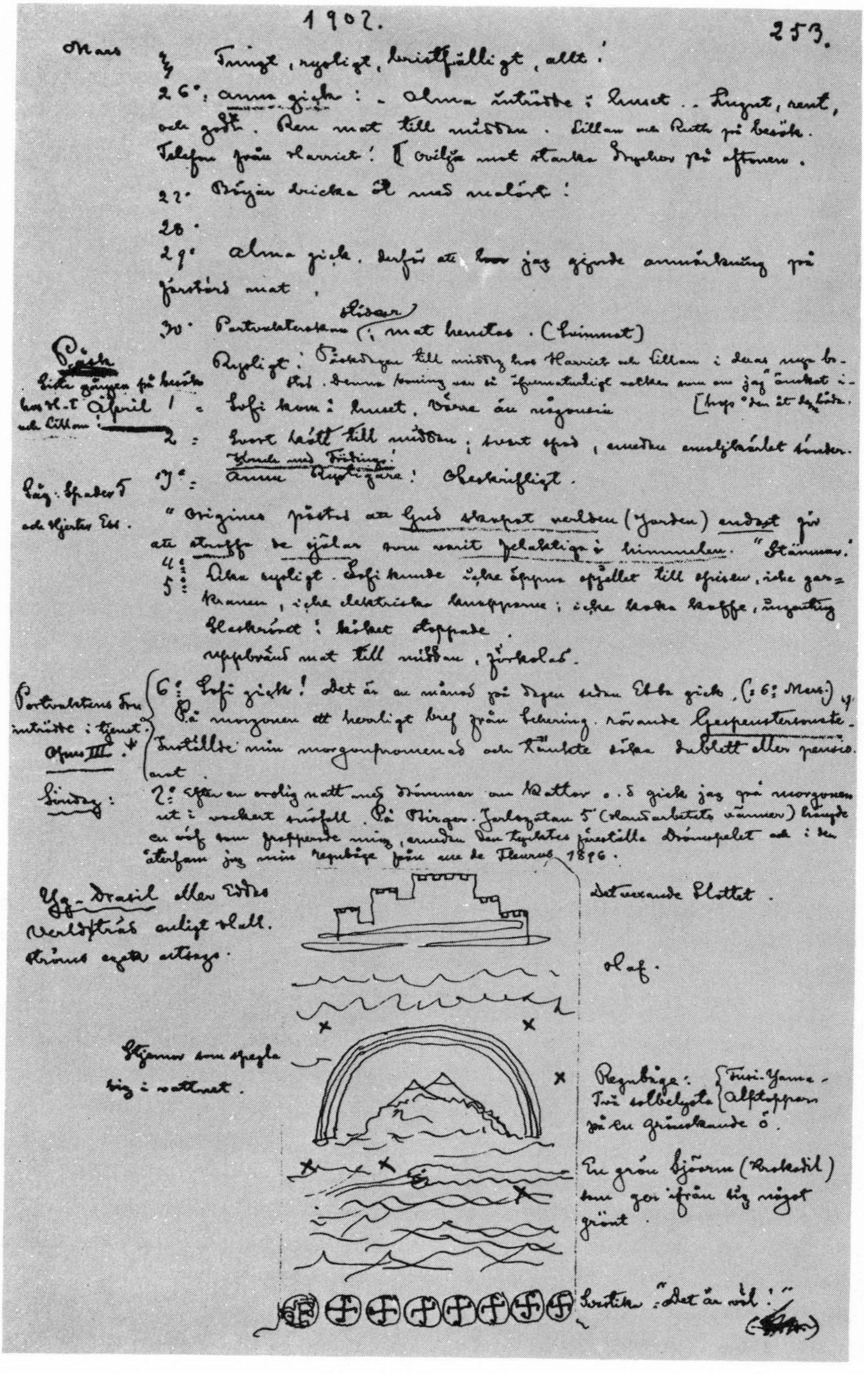

1902. 253.

Mars 25. Tungt, [illegible], [illegible], allt!
26°: Anna gick: - Alma inträdde i huset. - Lugnt, rent, och godt. Ren mat till middan. Lillan och Ruth på besök. Telefon från Harriet! Ovilja mot starka drycker på aftonen.
27° Började dricka öl med malört!
28°.
29° Alma gick. derför att jag gjorde anmärkning på [illegible] mat.
30° [illegible] i mat hemtas. ([illegible])
Påsk. Sista gången på besök hos H. och Lillan! Rysligt: Påskdagen till middag hos Harriet och Lillan i deras nya bo. [illegible]
April 1: Sofi kom i huset. Värre än någonsin.
2: Svårt lått till middan; svart spad, [illegible]
3°: Anna [illegible]: Oskrifligt.
"Origines påstod att Gud skapat verlden (Jorden) endast för att straffa de själar som varit felaktiga i himmelen." Stämmer.
4: 5: Allt rysligt. Sofi kunde icke öppna [illegible] till spisen, icke gas-kranen, icke elektriska knapparne; icke koka kaffe, ingenting [illegible]! Köket stoppade. Uppbränd mat till middan, förkolad.
6: Sofi gick! Det är en månad på dagen sedan Ebba gick. (6: Mars) På morgonen ett herrligt bref från [illegible] rörande Gespenstersonate. Inställde min morgonpromenad och tänkte söka dublett eller pension[at].
7: Efter en orolig natt med drömmar om Katter o. s gick jag på morgonen ut i vackert snöfall. På Birger Jarlsgatan 5 (Handarbetets vänner) hängde en väf som frapperade mig, emedan den tycktes föreställa Drömspelet och i den återfann jag min regnbåge från rue de Fleurus 1896.

53 Page from the *Occult Diary*

28th: (no entry).

29th: Alma left, as I made remark about spoiled food.

30th: Concierge cleans house, food is brought in. (Pig-food.) Terrible! . . .

1 April: Hired Sofi. Worse than ever.

2nd: Black meat for lunch; black gravy, as the enamel bowl had cracked. Argument with Frödings

3rd: Even more terrible! Indescribable.

Three days later, Sofi also left, and so things continued. Strindberg's sister Anna, widowed since 1906, moved in, but matters did not improve, and after a week, the removal van stood in front of the house to take away her belongings.

The central figure in *The Pelican* is a monstrous mother who makes their home a living hell for the family. Typically, Strindberg let it be known that this was a portrait of his sister, Anna von Philp. He also claimed to have had her and her husband in mind when he wrote his most shattering marriage play, *The Dance of Death*, in which most of the blame is placed on the husband. Now that Hugo von Philp had died, he felt regret and redressed the balance.

The mother in *The Pelican* sucks her family dry, devours the best titbits, half-starves her children. While her daughter is ill, she attends the performance of an operetta (for Strindberg, a deadly sin) and she believes herself to be young and desirable, making shameless advances to her son-in-law. Observed more closely, she is a Zachris, a female variation of the author in the depths of the hell of damnation, possibly the most repulsive of all of Strindberg's self-portraits. It is he who battens on the lives of others; who, while advanced in years, pursues love and neglects his children. It is he who constantly demands the very best in the house, and who uses all life within the family for his writing. It is he who is the pelican, claiming to shed his blood for others, while, in fact, he devours all he can for himself. Even details demonstrate how close to himself Strindberg was getting. When the son in the play tells his mother: 'Father said that if you were tortured on the rack, you would not admit to a single error or lie'—we are hearing a confession. With her deep insight into her father's psyche, Karin Smirnoff has rightly stressed how impossible it was for Strindberg to ever admit a mistake.

2

It was painful for Strindberg to have finished a work and then to find that no one wanted to publish it. He experienced his own creativity as an elemental force which had to make its way into the outside world, had to find a response. In his later years, he made much of never reading reviews, or even newspapers: that, however, needs to be taken with a grain of salt. He was perfectly well aware of what was being said about him. His letters and his diary prove it, time and again. He lived in a close relationship with his readers and could not have done without them.

By 1907, *Black Flags* had been languishing in its manuscript state for two years, but in February of that year Strindberg discovered a new publisher, Karl Börjesson, the thirty-year-old proprietor of Björck & Börjesson, Antiquarian Book Dealers, who was working his way towards a leading position in his field. Börjesson was a radical and a devoted reader of Strindberg. He had gone into publishing in 1903, and he accepted *Black Flags* for immediate publication although he was aware that this involved a certain risk for his firm. He paid Strindberg 1,500 kronor for a first edition of 2,000 copies. He also liked the book. 'I understood so well', he wrote to the author the following year, 'what this book cost you and what it meant for our communal morality and a new sense of justice.' He became a staunch supporter of Strindberg, acting as his private banker and financial adviser, and tirelessly providing him with books: Strindberg was an avid reader.

'Now there'll be some fresh air again,' Strindberg told August Falck the day he received Börjesson's positive reply. He felt released, which was probably one of the reasons why his productivity increased during that spring. The book came out on 29 May 1907. The next day, Strindberg was standing at his window, looking over Gärdet, where a fire brigade exercise was in progress. In the distance, people were constructing something that Strindberg thought looked like a pyre or a small building, possibly an outhouse. It was set on fire but did not burn down; it was set on fire again, but remained standing, although by now it was blackened. Around it stood people holding scarlet objects that looked like bowling-pins. In his description of this event in the *Occult Diary* Strindberg claims that he did not understand what it was he was observing, but came up with an interpretation: it was he who was to be burned, but refused to be destroyed—or, alternatively, Sweden itself would undergo the same trial. Strindberg concludes: 'I saw it as a pyre, erected for me.'

The incident is an amusing demonstration of how his imagination worked. The bowling-pins or cones were, most likely, hand-held fire extinguishers filled with chemical foam. In *A Blue Book* Strindberg returned to the scene, calling it 'symbolic', and adding: 'In such concrete images I receive my admonitions and exhortations.'

Black Flags had a plain grey cover on which the author's name was printed in red, and the title in black: the colours of *Inferno*. The letter F looks like a dragon with a spiky spine, rearing up, ready to attack. A conciliatory note appeared on the last page: 'This book has been published in a limited edition. It will not be reprinted.' That promise, however, was not due to any tenderheartedness or compassion for the victims on Strindberg's part. On the contrary, it annoyed him that he had to renounce further income in this manner. He wrote on a scrap of paper, preserved in the huge Strindberg Archive of the Royal Library in Stockholm:

> When I published *Black Flags*, my description of the mores of the turn of the century, a time of renascent decadence, I agreed to the publisher's insistence to limit the edition. But I never understood such considerateness toward bandits, nor did I understand why I should break off the point of *my* sword in a time of battle.

The novel sold out within a few days. Just like *Marrying*, twenty-three years earlier, it became a hot property on the black market. It was rumoured that it was possible to purchase copies with the 'real' names spelt out.

3

The critics were merciless, justifying their indignation by claiming to feel compassion for the book's victims. Consciously or not, they were certainly affected by the fact that Strindberg's target was their own world.

It is said that the fish in a shoal improve if a shark has been pruning their number. All his life, Strindberg was just such a vitalizing shark in Sweden's cultural life, acting as an antidote to apathy. This became evident in the way *Black Flags* was received. Bo Bergman, normally a sensible, level-headed poet, reviewed the book in *Dagens Nyheter* with unaccustomed warmth and eloquence, describing how once upon a time Sweden's youth had rallied to Strindberg's flag of defiance and liberation. 'Red and beautiful, it unfurled against an overcast sky,' he continued, 'but now it has lost its colour. So many flags have turned grey in time. August Strindberg's has turned black, and he will have to sail on alone under that spiritual burial banner.'

Many reviewers took the line that the book did not deserve attention. In *Stockholms Dagblad*, Sven Söderman found it unique in its infamy, 'a filthy act', and exclaimed: 'He defecates like a dog. Tschandala. It is nauseating.' Tor Hedberg, in *Svenska Dagbladet*, felt that the book should be accorded the 'quiet burial given to personal excrement'. Yet he differed from his colleagues in admitting that the satire, in all its horror, achieved dimensions of greatness. 'And then,' Hedberg continued, 'he [Strindberg], knowingly or unknowingly, strikes deep into his own heart; for all his boundless self-love he has equally boundless self-hate.' Hedberg concluded his review by saying:

Yet a book such as this is its own punishment and doom. Whether it also contains within itself its own reconciliation, the reconciliation of self-sacrifice and the blind, ruthless urge to confession, the future will decide, as it will be in a better position to do so than we who are witnessing, in astonishment and pain and not without disgust, the convulsions of a great genius.

For a long time the Swedish public regarded *Black Flags* as no more than a vicious lampoon. Strindberg's enemies made good use of Geijerstam's death two years after the book's publication, pointing to its author as Geijerstam's murderer. Even close friends hesitated, and one of them was lost for ever.

Over the years, Strindberg and Carl Larsson had remained in touch. Now and again, Larsson would attend the Old Beethoven Boys' soirées. In 1905, he painted Anne-Marie's portrait and also arranged for Ernest Thiel to purchase three Strindberg canvases for his gallery; but the two friends were not as close as before—Ernst Josephson, among others, had come between them.

In June, Carl Larsson visited Karlavägen and distanced himself from what he called Strindberg's 'hatred'. According to the entry of 12 August in the *Occult Diary*, a bumblebee flew in through the window and circled the chair on which the painter was sitting: Strindberg commented that Larsson 'really stung before he left'. Then, as was his wont, he terminated the friendship abruptly. For *A Blue Book*, he wrote an essay on Carl Larsson which is a masterpiece of characterization. In it, he called Larsson a 'synthetic person', in every respect the very opposite of what he pretended to be. He is the friend who praises you to your face but slanders you behind your back. In his art, he depicts himself as the happy paterfamilias in the warmth of his home, but as soon as he joins a group of men, he introduces a sordid note, and discusses subjects belonging to 'such low regions that boys would blush'. He pretended to be shy, Strindberg continued, while secretly nurturing 'the most immoderate ambition'. Although his beard was real, it looked like a false one, and the grease-paint had permanently fused with his skin. We are presented with an entirely self-forged character.

Long before the reader reaches the end of this venomous description, he has asked himself if that synthetic person has not been studied at even closer quarters than in the case of Larsson. The same thought occured to Strindberg, and he concluded the essay with this surprising reflection:

Perhaps all people in this life, in their pursuit of happiness, are like this? Perhaps he has seen me as equally mendacious and lacking in character? What if I were, indeed, such as I have described him to be? After all, there are many who like to see me in that light, and thus it is always possible that I really am one of these. That would be a calamity. But it would be hopeless if everybody was like this insincere character.

54 The house on Karlavägen where
Strindberg lived from 1901 to 1908

55 The cover of *Black Flags*

The commentary testifies to Strindberg's profound self-knowledge, but also to his reassuring understanding that all judgements passed on people are relative. Carl Larsson, however, was not placated. In his autobiography —entitled *I*—he gave an account of his reaction. Upon perusing the essay, he rushed off, armed with a costly knife given to him by Anders Zorn, to despatch 'the revolting skunk'. The murder did not take place, but the friendship was over. Perhaps this was inevitable, according to the axiom Strindberg set up after his encounter with Björnson: friendship between strong personalities is an impossibility. From the mid-1890s, Carl Larsson had been an artist, soon to win international acclaim, who depicted his domestic happiness—his wife, his children, their home—in words and pictures. His books, *A Home* and *My People*, offered counterparts of paradise, in contrast to the infernal interiors Strindberg provided from his home life. Like so many fellow artists of the nineteenth century, Larsson was a Utopian and wanted to show a home as it should be in ideal terms; in fact, however, he simply glossed over all the problems and created a lie, while Strindberg described life without cosmetics, dipping his brush into hatred for the sake of truth.

4

While the storm continued to rage in the press, the Intimate Theatre was taking shape. Falck later claimed that *Black Flags* hung like a dark veil over the enterprise, and that people transferred their dislike of Strindberg to him (Falck) and his ensemble. Nevertheless, the enterprise started in a buoyant mood. On 27 June, Falck signed a lease for a warehouse space on Norra Bantorget that was to be converted into a theatre. That evening, Strindberg invited Falck and the two Lindroth brothers—builders who were to make the conversion—to his home for supper. In his diary, the host noted: 'As we were sitting there drinking, petals fell off the peonies every time the clock in the hall struck,' and as the guests did not leave until 5 am, quite a few of those petals must have fallen.

Strindberg attended to the preparatory work daily—which meant many late nights—and made a few not-so-occult comments in his diary on zoning decisions, fire laws and licensing matters. The conversion was expensive, 45,000 kronor. Strindberg contributed with 'loans' to Falck, and in October, the total of these was 10,120 kronor. Strindberg raised money as best he could, feeling more annoyed than ever that he had consented to limit his now highly marketable book to only one edition.

As in Copenhagen, the initial idea was to present works by other dramatists as well as Strindberg. Again, his own works irresistibly gained

56 *The Father* at the Intimate Theatre, 1908

57 Strindberg at the Intimate Theatre. Drawing by Gunnar
Widholm in *Stockholms Dagblad*, 6 December 1907

precedence; the question soon became a bone of contention between him and Falck. As a symbol of his omnipotence, a portrait bust of Strindberg was placed in the foyer. It was a small, literally intimate theatre, with a cramped stage that made it difficult to create illusions of depth. The auditorium, with green walls and dark green carpeting, had fifteen rows of seats, 161 seats altogether. A young painter, Carl Kylberg, who was to become famous one day, painted copies of Böcklin's *The Island of Death* on both sides of the proscenium; it was Strindberg's idea, obviously indicating that the plays presented here would deal with souls awakening from the infernal dream of life on earth, and arriving at their true home. Kylberg also designed posters and programmes in black and white, the *Inferno* colours. In order to pay the first instalment of rent, Strindberg pawned the *Occult Diary* with Bonniers for 2,000 kronor.

The Pelican was chosen to be the opening play, and rehearsals began in August. Around this time, Strindberg was searching with increased intensity for omens and portents, and recorded blackouts, strange cloud formations, falling stars in Capella, the numbers of streetcars, a red flag on a wagon carrying gunpowder, a haxel-hen being maltreated in his kitchen and reminding him of the culinary hell of his play. In a stereotyped way—something new to Strindberg—he repeated over and over again in his diary this prayer gleaned from one of the devotional books he was using 'O Lord! We pray to Thee, have mercy on us all, deliver us from evil and sin and take us with Thee through eternity. Amen.'

The Intimate Theatre was inaugurated on 26 November. Strindberg could not muster the courage to attend but had promised a 'prologue', which Falck received just before the curtain rose. Quiet in tone, almost humble, it reminded the audience that they were sitting in safe darkness while the actors stood 'revealed by a hundred lights'. The prologue ended:

> 'Medlidande och fruktan' var de Gamles fordran
> för sorgespelet, deltagande för dem som prövas,
> när gudarna i dolda rådslag skaka
> på mänskobarnens skilda öden.
> Vi nyare ha ändrat något ton
> Humanitet. Resignation—
> på resan ifrån Livets ö till dödens!
> *'Compassion and fear' was the Ancients' demand*
> *upon the tragedy, sympathy for those who are tried,*
> *when the gods in secret councils shake*
> *the various fates of humankind.*
> *We recently have changed some notes*
> *Humanitarianism, Resignation—*
> *on the voyage from the Isle of Life to the Isle of Death!*

After the performance, Falck went to Karlavägen to present Strindberg with a laurel wreath from the actors. He was greeted with an embrace: Strindberg confessed that he had spent the whole day pacing back and forth in the apartment in a state of anxiety.

But the play was not successful. The reviewers were niggardly in their response, and the audience stayed away. 'The theatre is not doing well! Dark!' Strindberg wrote in his diary the following day. On the third night, the box office had taken only 39 kronor. It became necessary to replace the play with *Miss Julie* and then to rush forward the next first night, *The House that Burned* on 5 December. It got no better a reception. In *Dagens Nyheter*, Bo Bergman considered the performance a 'soupy concoction of endless babble and cheap profundities'. With trepidation, Falck and Strindberg watched the approach of 1 January, when the next quarter's rent was due. This time, Strindberg mobilized Bonniers, and noted on New Year's Eve that Falck owed him 18,190 kronor, spelling out the sum in words as well as figures.

While the Intimate Theatre in its initial stage was fighting for its life, King Oscar II died, who in Strindberg's world had been the dark and bigoted counterpart to the radiant and generous Karl XV.

After the relative failure of the chamber plays, the Intimate Theatre became a fairly successful enterprise, and at its best, an extension of Strindberg's home and his world. There were times when objects from Karlavägen—a palm tree, a gilded pedestal—found their way into the theatre, to serve as props once again. Strindberg showed some interest in the personal lives of the actors and tried to protect them when the press was inveighing against the theatre. On 27 March 1908, *Kristina* was premièred. It was a big hit with the public, but the critics were merciless, and Sven Söderman surpassed his record-breaking review of *Black Flags*, saying: 'All that remains for this viewer is a juvenile, inept and inartistic work by an author who is defective both intellectually and ethically.'

Strindberg, who followed the progress of *Kristina*, noted on 19 March that he had that day seen a serving-maid come running out of the entrance to no. 38 Karlavägen, screaming, her clothes on fire. 'It was a horrifying sight! She fell down in the snow, and I took off my coat, beating out the flames with it. The most awful thing I have ever seen.' No further comments were made on this strange experience; perhaps it could not be used? The newspapers made no mention of the event. *Kristina*'s bad reception was merely another misdeed of 'the Black Gang'.

August Falck was the last in a series of young men friends in Strindberg's life, and it seems that Strindberg was less guarded with him than he had been with others. Falck later said that Strindberg was the vainest person he had ever met: he was constantly concerned about his appearance, incessantly straightening his moustache, taking at least half an hour to get dressed in the morning. He had the notion that water from the mains made his hair darker, and gave himself innumerable rub–downs. Falck made these observations without comprehending that it was Strindberg's shyness which caused him to behave like this.

Falck also provided instances of Strindberg's incredible frivolity in important matters, contrasted with his pedantry about trivia. Strindberg was becoming more and more like his father as his childhood resurfaced into his consciousness; this is particularly evident in the chamber plays. In his autobiography, he complained about his father's stinginess, exemplified by the way he would check the level in an uncorked bottle of wine. By all accounts, Strindberg himself provided others with many bitter memories of his own suspicious pettiness. Falck relates how Strindberg gave him a lesson in exactly how cigarettes, cigarillos and cigars had to be dealt with, in accordance with a certain system, on his large ashtray. When he served his guests crayfish, he requested that the plates should look just as appetizing after the meal as they had looked before, personally providing a good example.

In the summer of 1908, Bernard Shaw travelled to Stockholm to see Strindberg, who proudly took him to the theatre and compelled Falck and Manda Björling, who were on holiday in the Archipelago, to return to Stockholm in order to perform *Miss Julie*. According to Falck, Strindberg had never seen the play on stage and asked Manda Björling to 'do it with somewhat of a light touch, or else I'll get so agitated'. He obviously remembered his experience of watching *The Father* in 1887 in Copenhagen. After the performance, Strindberg came on stage and kissed Manda Björling's hand, with tears in his eyes. This did not prevent him from writing to her a few days later to comment on her diction and provide this instruction: 'Do the exit of the final scene like a sleepwalker, slowly, arms outstretched in front of you, gliding out as if looking for support in the air so as not to trip over rocks or such; irresistibly out into the last great darkness.'

It should be added that when Erik Palmstierna, Swedish Ambassador in London, asked Bernard Shaw about his recollections of Strindberg in 1926, Shaw did not remember the performance of *Miss Julie*. It had been given in Swedish, a language with which he was not familiar. He did, however, say that he had visited Strindberg at home, and that their conversation had become complicated, as it was first conducted in French and then in German, of which Shaw had little command. Then, suddenly, Strindberg wound his watch and said solemnly: 'Um zwei Uhr werde ich sehr krank sein!' ('At two o'clock, I shall be very ill!') Shaw merely stared at his host and then proceeded downstairs with all dispatch. It seems likely that he had misunderstood Strindberg's words, perhaps with an eye on humorous effect. The anecdote is widely known and often quoted in support of the view that Strindberg was half–crazed.

His initial delight in Falck soon changed into suspicion and antipathy. As early as April 1908 he wrote to Börjesson that Falck suffered from 'moral feeble-mindedness'. Their clashes about loans and bills of exchange became increasingly acrimonious. Yet Strindberg was older and more cautious than he had been when he rejected his collaborator Gustaf Steffen, and this time the joint enterprise was of more concern to him. In letters to Börjesson he predicted that Falck would end up at Långholmen, the state prison, but shrank from forecasting the public execution as he was often wont to do in such cases.

However, it was against his nature to keep entirely silent. He was tirelessly engaged in work on *A Blue Book*, whose first volume had come out in the autumn of 1907 and had been a success in terms of sales. In the second volume, published in 1908—while his collaboration with Falck was at its height—he included a lampoon of Falck. In two extended sections of the book, he gave an account of an aristocratic explorer, Lord Wilkins. During his sojourn on the African Gold Coast, the lord makes the acquaintance of a musically gifted native, whom he invites to his house to play for the local gentry. The man's talent is nothing out of the ordinary, but his social success makes him conceited and arrogant, and when a genuine virtuoso comes to the region, he prevents him from playing. The native suffers, we are told, from the 'nature-child's' lack of memory, intelligence and self-knowledge, and is therefore so blind that he cannot even conceive of the existence of his rival, the virtuoso. Nevertheless, Lord Wilkins does not punish his ungrateful and self-centred friend.

The same gentleman, now in Zanzibar, encounters yet another problematic native by the name of Pongo. Pongo offers to build a house for him and claims to have both the capital and powers of construction to do so. They enter into an agreement for five years, and this leads to a series of calamities. Pongo keeps asking for more money; he cheats on bills of exchange—it is implied that some of the money goes to pay for jewellery for his beloved—and finally threatens Lord Wilkins with a libel suit when the latter intimates that he is a thief.

It is not hard to see Falck in the Gold Coast musician and the Intimate Theatre in Pongo's house. Perhaps Falck, mercifully, did not see himself in this Strindbergian mirror; or perhaps it was his pride that kept him from mentioning this attack in his book.

5

Strindberg wrote notes and instructions for the benefit of the members of the company, published by Börjesson as small, plain pamphlets: they have been collected into a volume titled *Open Letters to the Intimate Theatre*.

Almost everything Strindberg ever wrote was a link in a chain of creative process. Even in seemingly simple communications to friends and relatives he was simultaneously busy transforming his reality into fiction. When writing about matters of the theatre, he himself became transformed: he was entirely professional in a straightforward, unambiguous and quiet way, and without resorting to any tricks.

Strindberg had had some stage experience as a youth. He had been married twice to actresses, and a number of the country's foremost actors were close friends of his. Interviewed in January 1909 for *Bonnier's Monthly*, he replied, when asked why he had chosen the dramatic form for his first ventures as a writer: 'I found it easiest to write plays; people and events took shape, wove themselves together, and that work gave me such pleasure that I found existence to be sheer joy while I was writing—and still do. Only then am I alive!' The theatre was Strindberg's natural home; one could even say that it was his life, in a world where everything—dreams, costumes, stage sets—was unreal; however, when one encounters him around the actual world of the stage, he appears alert, soberly instructive, knowledgeable and shrewd. As a theatrical commentator, he reminds one of Hamlet who, addressing his speech on the actor's art to the visiting group of players, momentarily forgets the tragic conflict in which he is involved. As a theorist of drama, Strindberg is close to Shakespeare: like Shakespeare, he pleads for measure and balance and stresses that playwrights and actors must learn to listen to their fellow men—in the street, in the tavern, in bed.

The strength of Strindberg's plays lies in their emphatic simplicity. The actress Aino Taube once said that there was always a connection between 'head and guts' in everything Strindberg wrote, which made it easy to familiarize oneself with his roles. What his characters say echoes through their whole being: it does not merely appear in comic strip balloons above their heads, as is the case with many other playwrights.

Strindberg's commentaries on a number of Shakespeare plays are of particular interest, providing important information on Strindberg himself. Of Hamlet's relationship with Ophelia he says that Hamlet kills Ophelia by his scepticism, treating her with scorn in the first acts and extracting from her noble nature all that is base in it. This is not due to his madness, which is merely feigned, but to his warped vision; he commits a kind of murder of her soul by pretending to be mad.

This reads like a confession in disguise. Had Strindberg himself not feigned madness to Siri in order to write *The Father* and *A Fool's Apology*? And had this not been a murder of her innocent soul, which he did not understand? And, come to that, had he not driven Harriet Bosse away in the same manner? He had, at any rate, extracted the 'evil' from her substance, just as with Siri.

As Strindberg proceeds to discuss Hamlet's love for Ophelia, so violently expressed at her graveside, he asks himself how Hamlet's demeanour can be reconciled with his calling her a whore. He replies:

> He loved her despite everything! There is no inconsistency, merely different ways of seeing; changes of level for the viewpoint, like a surveyor seeking to gain a true, overall picture of the terrain. Simple minds always talk about contradictions and inconsistencies, but every living creature is composed of elements which are not homogeneous but have to be opposites in order to cohere, just like the forces that attract unlike to unlike. Thus Hamlet himself is composed of contradictions that only seem to be such; he is evil and good, he hates and he loves, he is cynical and fanciful, malicious and forgiving, strong and weak, in one word: a human being, different every moment, as human beings are.

In the 'letter' entitled *King Lear's Wife*, Strindberg returned to Hamlet, asking who Hamlet is, and answering:

> He is Shakespeare; he is humanity, as it steps out of childhood into life and finds everything to be quite different from what it had imagined. Hamlet is the alert youth who discovers that the world is out of joint and feels himself called to set it to rights. He becomes desperate when he applies all his strength to the great boulder and discovers that it will not budge.

Strindberg goes on to describe Hamlet as a young man pure of heart who experiences his mother's degradation as unnatural and demeaning to 'the father's memory and the mother's majesty'. He continues:

> But in the very disposition of this youth, never really at home down here in the 'prison' and 'the vale of tears', there is a truly divine trait: for him all men are equal. Although he is heir to the throne, he knows his people intimately. He has associated with the court jester Yorick, with actors and students, and when he speaks to the lowly gravediggers, he is polite, not arrogant. Thus he is adored by the humble, by the people, so that the King grows to fear his popularity; yet this does not make Hamlet into a democrat, one who grovels in front of the 'wild mob' in order to gain power. His viewpoint is so universally human that he is above it all, throne and court, society and laws; had he been of a more brutal disposition, he would not have murdered his stepfather, but would have started a revolution, overthrown the monarch and ordered the legal execution of the murderer.

This characterization of Hamlet is applicable to Strindberg himself. The longer he lived, the more the universal became apparent to him and in him. Perhaps, given a 'more brutal disposition', he would not have written books but would have joined those who tried to destroy society and create a better one out of its ruins.

6

In the spring of 1908, Strindberg lived through the epilogue of his real-life drama with Harriet Bosse. On 4 April, she informed Strindberg by letter of her engagement to a fellow actor, Gunnar Wingård, who was her age. The news can hardly have come as a surprise: on 20 January 1907, almost eighteen months earlier, Strindberg had noted in his diary that Harriet had stayed the night in 'the yellow room'. Some time afterwards, he added to the entry the words: 'For the last time.'

The former husband and wife had met occasionally during 1907, but Strindberg's comments in his diary about Harriet had grown more jaundiced: he called her evil, stupid, black, arrogant, venomous. In June 1907 he sent her a 'final letter', but this elicited an amorous response, indicating that Harriet was reluctant to lose touch with him entirely. Between the lines, one senses new developments: 'I think very highly of you,' she wrote, 'and whatever may happen—I love you, perhaps because you have, by causing me extraordinary sorrow, given substance to my life.' Strindberg must certainly have pondered over those words 'whatever may happen'—or did he, as so often before, see only what would fit into his dreams.

Despite these forewarnings, her engagement turned out to have astounding consequences. The same day Strindberg received Harriet's letter, he resumed his telepathic connection to her of the winter of 1900, and lived with her for three months in an imaginary tempest of passion. What he had written in *Alone* about telepathic communion with friends was now triumphantly crowned by a love relationship.

In his imagination, Harriet visited him at night, and her arrival was heralded by the scent of incense and roses. He merged with her physically more profoundly than was possible in human coitus. In his waking dream, he felt her heart beating in his own chest, and thought her and himself one being; one night, her heart stopped, and he was afraid she had died. She was resting on his shoulder. They embraced. All the painful rivalry between them was gone, and only the sweetness, the celestial delight remained.

Here Strindberg was attempting to recreate the love story of 1901, which had become one of his prime sources of 'capital' for his writing. Every year he had noted and 'celebrated' the great memorial days in his diary—the wedding, the day Harriet left, and the day, 5 October, when she returned; and he had pondered the mystery of the forty days.

It is quite possible that what he had in mind was a new, even more grandiose, work on this subject. The old vivisectionist within him awoke, and he started experimenting with love, after a year of celibacy. As usual, it is impossible to determine what was living, spontaneous emotion, and what was calculated fiction.

This time, he is no longer content with diary entries, as he was in the initial stages of the love story, but expounds his thoughts in letters to Harriet. He assails her with declarations of love and falls back into the exact pattern he always resorted to in emotionally agitated situations. Thus he declared that he would not survive her wedding night with another, and although in *To Damascus* he had satirized his own mania for threatening people with suicide, he wrote to her on 11 April: 'Well, then I'll celebrate my blood wedding!'

On the basis of his own experiences, he had, in *Gothic Rooms*, described the behaviour of the newly betrothed Count Max: he ate little, drank less, took greater care of his wardrobe than before. Strindberg imitated his character down to the least detail, even returning to the idea that had so angered Siri: that he brought misfortune to everyone who crossed his path. Thus, he threatened Wingård.

Read together, the diary and the letters become a love poem, grandiose in conception and full of ambitious fusions. Strindberg had returned to the triangle drama he had experienced in the home of the Wrangel family. Wingård replaced Wrangel; Harriet replaced Siri. It was the same fascination, the same terror. Strindberg was intruding between two lovers. Twenty years earlier, in *Creditors*, he had analysed what occurs between such an intruder and the beloved. The two feel 'that someone is staring at them in the dark', where they have sought refuge.

> He becomes a nightmare to disturb their amorous sleep, a creditor who knocks on the doors, and they see his black hand between their own when they dip into the bowl, they hear his disagreeable voice in the stillness of the night, which only their throbbing pulses were to disturb. He does not prevent them from joining one another, but he does disturb their happiness. And when they recognize his invisible power to disturb their joy, when they finally flee—but flee in vain from the memory pursuing them, from the debt they have left behind, and the opinion that frightens them, and they do not have the strength to carry the burden of guilt, then they have to go to the pasture to find a scapegoat and butcher it!

This was the situation Strindberg was trying to recreate. The forbidden, the taboo was exercising its fascination again. And who would be more closely protected by the gods of society and eternity than the newly-wed?

A further absurd refinement was provided by a new infatuation. In April 1908 Strindberg had noticed a seventeen-year-old extra at the Intimate Theatre, Fanny Falkner, and instantly convinced himself that not only was she right for the part of Eleonora in *Easter*, which was in rehearsal at the time, but also that she had the makings of a great actress. He then instigated one of those parallel actions that appealed to his imagination so strongly. Fanny Falkner was to replace Harriet by stepping into her role. Thus she became the fourth partner, as Sofia In de Betou had once done. Strindberg wrote to Harriet Bosse, telling her to take Fanny under her wing, and to adopt her as a foster-daughter. Why? In order to arouse Harriet's jealousy? Or to give Wingård a chance to exchange Harriet for a younger woman? Admittedly, questions like these cannot do justice to the finesse of the problems revealed here; yet it was all poetry and fiction, and even the most fleeting impulses were granted entry.

In the letters as in the diary, Strindberg introduced occult notions which gave this strange event a wider framework. Once again, Harriet appeared as Agnes in *A Dream Play*. He imagined her as the daughter of the god Indra, and thought that they could conceive a child by spiritual means. She was his divine wife, destined to bear him heavenly children.

On 16 April, Maundy Thursday, Strindberg's six-year-old daughter Anne-Marie came to visit him, wearing a bracelet given to her by Gunnar Wingård. In his diary, Strindberg understood this as a demonstration of Harriet's evil nature, 'the most evil ever created'. On the same day, *Easter* was performed at the Intimate Theatre, and the bracelet found its place in a passion play Strindberg drafted in his diary. In it, his esoteric ego is the protagonist. The following day, he wrote to Harriet saying that the 'slave bracelet' had made him feel the child was no longer his; he also called her 'you black Swan White'. On Good Friday, however, he began to suspect that the bracelet was merely an innocent toy without significance. 'Was it all a show put on by the demons, to make me suffer through Good Friday?' he asked himself. The incident unusually illustrates clearly how his imagination worked.

Strindberg begged Harriet to join him again, to have another child with him. The idea of spiritual children had been abandoned. He claimed to be suffering pangs of conscience for having written such cruel things about her, but consoled himself with the previously tried notion that he had, by setting forth her 'evil nature' on paper, liberated her from it. Now she visited him every night, always preceded by the scent of roses.

On 24 May, Harriet Bosse and Gunnar Wingård were married. In the mystery play of Strindberg's love, the event caused no interruption: on 25 May, he visited Harriet telepathically, and they embraced six times. This adulterous existence caused him both pain and delight. 'Praying to God to die rather than to live in sin,' he wrote on 26 May. But Harriet haunted him, and he confided to the diary that he was weeping a great deal. He fantasized that Harriet's marriage to Wingård was possibly only a formal affair, and that that was why she visited him at night. 'Cried so my soul almost flew out of my body!' he wrote on 29 May. The following day, Miss Falkner paid him a visit and told him that Harriet had taken a room at the Grand Hotel. At this time, Strindberg noted that he had stomach cramps, suspected that he had ulcers or worse, and connected this sense of malady with Harriet, believing that he was close to death. On 13 June he wrote: 'After being tortured for sixty years! I beg God to let me leave this life! The little joy there was, was illusory, or false! Work was the only thing! but even that was wasted, in part! or useless, or harmful. Wife, children, home, all of it, false! The only thing that gave me an illusion of happiness was wine! That is why I drank!'

On Midsummer's Day, he once again asked God to let him die. A physician was called, but the examination revealed no serious disturbance. He had stayed in touch with Fanny Falkner, sensing that a new phase of life was about to begin, and he accepted her proposal to move into an apartment on Drottninggatan which her parents had rented. On 11 July, he left Karlavägen, and never made another entry in the *Occult Diary*.

Chapter Seventeen

THE GREAT DEBATE

I

No. 85 Drottninggatan, at the intersection of that street with Tegnérgatan, was to be Strindberg's last address. He lived there from 11 July 1908, until his death on 14 May 1912. The building was new at that time, constructed in typical Art Nouveau style, but roofed with tin and bearing fanciful botanical ornaments above the entrance and in the stairways. There was a lift—a new-fangled invention which Strindberg, according to the concierge, did not use—central heating and shower rooms. For the first time in his life, Strindberg was able to take showers instead of his customary cold rub-downs with a towel.

In 1907, the Falkner family had rented two apartments in this building, intending to take in lodgers. Strindberg was given his own furnished apartment of three rooms on the fifth floor. He sent the furniture he had acquired when he married Harriet Bosse to a pawnbroker, and consequently arrived on Drottninggatan with very few belongings, although the laurel wreaths did come along. He was proud to have been able to make such a decisive move.

His meals were served to him on a tray brought down from the upstairs apartment, where the Falkner family lived. Full room and board cost Strindberg 240 kronor a month. Communication between the apartments was conducted via the maid Mina Boklund and a private telephone, and demands and orders were written on pieces of paper which were religiously preserved. They could consist of no more than 'Ice, ice' or 'Food for pigs!' but as the years passed, their tone grew sweeter.

At this time, things had turned out for Strindberg the way he had always wanted: he had a family, without any of the responsibilities; he enjoyed intimacy, yet everything proceeded according to his wishes and nobody else's. Fanny had three young sisters, Ada, Eva and Stella, whom he could rest his eyes on from a distance, feeling like a paternal protector.

58–59 Interiors from the Blue Tower. Strindberg in the library and sitting
below a bust of Goethe

'Come and have a good time with me in my "Green Tower" at the top of Drottninggatan,' he wrote to Nils Andersson in Lund on 21 August 1908. 'It has a view of the Parliament Building, has a green roof, laurel wreaths and cornucopia of gold, balconies, shower rooms, everything! And I have the urge to write, good food to eat, and Beethoven.'

After a while, Strindberg renamed his dwelling 'The Blue Tower'. On the ground floor of the building, there was a coffee shop, and the proprietor had pictures of the 'tower' printed on the coffee bags. Once in a while, Strindberg cut out the picture and pasted it on to his letters, and so 'The Blue Tower' became a name associated with him. Today, it is a Strindberg museum, sponsored by the Strindberg Society.

Both in practical and symbolical terms, the apartment was very well situated. A little farther down Drottninggatan, towards Strömmen, was Björck & Börjesson, the antiquarian book dealers. It was only a couple of hundred yards from the Intimate Theatre, and Strindberg made a habit of passing by on his morning walk, to see what its billboard announced. Drottninggatan could be called the street of Strindberg's life. It extends from Klara, where he first awoke to consciousness amid the ringing of church-bells, past the Adolf Fredrik Church, where he had been confirmed with the 'piccardong' and Lettström's maize wafers, and past the Observatory above the 'ore mansions' of his youth. Continuing north, one arrives at the North Cemetery, where Strindberg himself was to be interred. It was on Drottninggatan, three decades before, that Siri's veil had wafted across her hair. When Strindberg called his last play *The Great Highway*, it was Drottninggatan—and Norrtullsgatan—that provided the model.

The move seemed to do his health good. During his first summer in the tower, he wrote three grandiose historical plays—*The Last Knight*, *The Director of the Kingdom* and *The Earl of Bjälbo*. The first two were set in the sixteenth century, Strindberg's favourite: to read or attend a performance of these plays is to participate in a dinner at Strindberg's table. They teem with characters that had occupied his imagination since the 1870s, Olaus Petri and Gustaf Vasa among them.

Strindberg scholars have little regard for these plays. The protagonists are stereotyped fairytale heroes. Sven Sture, in *The Last Knight*, is insufferably virtuous, drawn like an icon against a golden background. It is impossible to muster any interest in him. Nevertheless, his counterpart and stepmother, Lady Märta Dyre, is forcibly seen and heard, and it is she who saves the play.

Märta Dyre is Strindberg's last witch, a study in evil and damnation, drawn with a mocking glance at the greatest talent among Swedish writers in the 1890s, Erik Axel Karlfeldt. Two years earlier, Karlfeldt had published a collection of poems entitled *Flora and Pomona*, which was triumphantly received. The major poem of the book was 'The Witches'; in it, Karlfeldt concentrated on sexual obsession and described secret, evil waterspouts blowing through the young women's virginally sweet dreams. A Don Juan in devilish garb appears to entice these innocents with unfathomed pleasures which disintegrate their personalities and lead them to the stake.

Strindberg had no difficulty in surpassing Karlfeldt's vision. All his life, he had feared the raven-black antagonist of the innocent Virgin Mary figure he used to praise in the initial stages of his love affairs; but Märta Dyre developed into something far more than an Aspasia, a sexual vampire. She is related to the witches of *Macbeth*, and to Phorcyas in *Faust*. In ecstatic moments, she can see into the future, and in her consciousness the gates are wide open to the underworld and the teeming life of the subconscious. She calls herself a warrior bride of hatred and revenge, and feels that she is riding over black waves on a demon's back. In the midst of all that fury and malice, a yearning for reconciliation survives in her, like a spark in a dark and billowing cloud of smoke. In damnation itself lies her chance to be saved. She is a sister to Zachris—and to Strindberg.

In *The Director of the Kingdom* it is Gustaf Vasa's sinister counterpart, Gustaf Trolle, the Archbishop, who attracts attention. Like Märta Dyre, he is fleeing from his guilty conscience: it was his denunciations that led to the great massacre in Stockholm, in which a number of Swedish nobles were executed by the Danish king, Kristian the Tyrant.

In the greatest and most significant scene of the play, Gustaf Trolle is vanquished. He flees and seeks refuge in Uppsala Cathedral, locking himself into the sacristy. He is threatened by both his external enemies, who will soon enter the church, and the accusing voices within himself.

On the sacristy walls hang the portraits of archbishops from past centuries; his own portrait is there, too, but it has been covered with a green cloth. Perhaps it has been painted recently, and has not yet been unveiled? Gustaf Trolle pulls the cloth aside and sees himself. He is seized by horror. 'Is this me? Do I look that terrible? This has been painted by the Devil!' And a voice, possibly emanating from within himself, replies: 'In his own likeness!' The Archbishop looks around to discover who is speaking, but there is no one there, and a desperate outburst follows: 'And this is me! A human being, born of woman, suckled at a mother's breast, yet unlike a human being! It is not possible! I have seen my fylgia, I have seen myself—I must die! But it is not me, it is someone else! I am not like that!'

Trolle takes a looking-glass from the wall and looks at himself, but finds his reflection even more frightful than the portrait. He wants to take his life, fall on his sword like Saul in the Bible, but there is no one there to hold it for him. At that moment, Trolle's father enters the sacristy and see his son's despair. An ambiguous conversation ensues: his father tells him that there is mercy for the condemned and hope for the despairing, referring both to the salvation born out of despair and to a secret passage out of the cathedral through which his son can escape. The scene ends with the father opening that door and saying, with tears in his eyes: 'I shall follow my child, afraid of the dark! My grown up, lost child!'

It is one of the most moving scenes in Strindberg's dramatic *oeuvre*. Behind Gustaf Trolle contemplating himself in the portrait one can see Gustaf af Geijerstam staring at the picture Strindberg painted of him in *Black Flags*. Nevertheless, Trolle is obviously also Strindberg himself, looking at the self-portrait he presented in disguise in that novel—the 'grown up, lost' child.

2

During Strindberg's first year in the Blue Tower, his well-being was enhanced by Fanny Falkner, who had enticed him there. She was delicate, slender, blonde and shy—Harriet Bosse's opposite in every respect. She had studied painting at a technical academy and ended up at the Intimate Theatre more by accident than design. After the Strindberg episode, she returned to painting, specializing in miniature portraits. She moved to Denmark and painted members of the Danish royal family. It was a far cry from the artistic tastes of her first admirer.

Strindberg was annoyed when Falck did not consider Miss Falkner suitable for the part of Eleonora: he had been moved to tears when she had played the part for him. But in the autumn of 1908 he succeeded in getting her the part of Swan White, originally written for Harriet Bosse. He wanted to see her in Harriet's costume—and so exorcize the woman who had betrayed him. Contrary to his usual habits, he participated eagerly in the staging of the play, trying first and foremost to persuade Fanny to project, to counteract her introverted nature. The first night was on 30 October, and Fanny Falkner was acclaimed. Sven Söderman wrote that 'in her slender virginality' she gave 'an indescribably delightful impression of the Swan White of the fairytale'.

There is very little material by which to evaluate the relationship of Strindberg and Fanny Falkner, especially by comparison with the tremendous torrent of words that surrounds Harriet Bosse. There are few letters—Strindberg and Fanny lived in the same house—and the *Occult Diary* had been finished and sealed. We know that she became his secretary and received a modest salary of 60 kronor a month. She prepared fair copies, assisted in the design of the books and ran errands. Strindberg was concerned about her wardrobe, and for Christmas 1908 he wanted to give her a fur coat. Her parents became alarmed, and he withdrew the idea. 'It is

60 Fanny Falkner

61 Fanny Falkner's pastel portrait of
      Strindberg, 1911

possible that my innocent gift was improper,' he wrote to Fanny on 29 December. 'Therefore, and to avoid anything that could contribute to a disruption of the peace, I ask you not to visit me in my quarters by yourself any longer. Our old agreement about salary stands.'

In August and September of 1908, while Strindberg was writing the historical plays in which the dark, demonic characters were so dominant, he also spent time on another fairytale play, *Abu Casem's Slippers*. Like *Swan White* seven years earlier, it can be read as a proposal in disguise.

In *The Arabian Nights*, a favourite with Strindberg since childhood, he found the tale of the Baghdad merchant Abu Casem, notorious for his hardness and meanness. Haroun al-Rasheed, the Caliph, wanders about his capital in disguise, in order to observe and judge his subjects. He leaves his beggar's slippers, part of his disguise, in front of Abu Casem's gate; in his greed, the latter takes them, and thereby becomes the victim of a series of calamities. Abu Casem has a beautiful daughter, Suleyka: in a dream, she has been warned against the insincerity and treachery of men, and has decided never to get married. A prince falls in love with her and languishes when his feelings are not returned. A shrewd shoemaker devises a plan to lead the two into each other's arms.

Disguised as an ailing old man, the prince is placed in front of Suleyka's gate, lying prone on a bed. She walks by, is roused to compassion, but as a precaution asks how old the sick man is. 'Oh, he's an old dog,' declares the shoemaker, who just happens to pass by.

'If he is truly old, I want to go and see if I can do anything to alleviate his state,' Suleyka says, and the shoemaker replies, 'I am sure you can, you and no one else.'

Suleyka walks up to the bed, calls the patient 'poor old man', and takes his hand to feel his pulse. As it seems too fast, she puts her hand on his heart: that sweet touch so excites him that his heart stops for a moment, then resumes its beating again. Suleyka concludes that the man is dying, and at the same instant, her eyes meet his—and she is lost, in love.

It is possible to regard this scene, with Suleyka at the prince's bedside, as an allegory of Strindberg's relationships with Fanny Falkner. Simone de Beauvoir has said that age is a mask life forces us to wear: behind it, the ageing person remains as he was before. Suleyka has only to meet the disguised prince's glance to fall in love with him. Fanny Falkner had one such disguised prince in her house, but he was no ordinary love-sick man—he used his life for his fictions, and was always ready to retreat inside them.

3

The Falkner family was hard-pressed, financially and in other ways. Fanny's father was an alcoholic, and one of her brothers a delinquent.

Strindberg tried to enlist the legal aid of the attorney Nils Andersson for him. The Falkners were for ever making grandiose plans to increase their fortunes—one of these was the lodgers scheme. Strindberg probably recognized some of his traits in them—in some ways they were living as he had over the years. Now he was a Haroun al-Rasheed at a distance, exercising power over his subjects.

In the summer of 1909, his interest in Fanny intensified. She was sent to Dalarö for a holiday; Strindberg recommended her to his friends on the island and probably paid her expenses during her stay. She wrote to him about her worries, and received a consoling letter in reply, although it also contained a reproach:

> As long as you remain close to your immediate family and discuss everything with them, I cannot speak to you frankly. You need to emancipate yourself. I am glad that you did not come home, where they deprive you of clothes and money and subject you to beatings. Try to find a way to leave home without making a complete break.

It is not clear what Strindberg meant exactly by 'speak to you frankly', but during the autumn he alluded in his letters to the 'pelican system' in Fanny's home. Fanny understood, of course, that Strindberg was implying that her mother devoured what was really her daughter's.

On 7 September 1908, Strindberg wrote another letter to Fanny sounding a warning note. A couple of admirers she had met during the summer had wanted to take her to see an operetta, *The Bells of Corneville*, but Strindberg reminded her of the high, pure standards which he always evoked in the initial stages of a love affair. 'It [the operetta] will leave a bad taste in your mouth,' he wrote, 'and the young gentlemen only want to show you off and later brag about it in the taverns, which will not enhance your reputation. My own standing is not high, but I am delighted to see that yours is: please, do not lower yourself.'

Strindberg's letters to her during this period are inadequately dated. When, some ten years later, Fanny wrote (or dictated) her little book about the relationships, she did not have access to these letters, which explains her numerous lapses of memory. It was probably in the beginning of September that Strindberg wrote:

> Tired of sitting and growing grey in the Tower, I yearn to return to my Djurgården, which I have not been able to do since 10 July last year. But as long as the bridge is watched from number 57, I cannot bring myself to go there. What I need to know now, is: has the separation begun, ie, is my last beloved child still in another man's hands. You who helped me leave Karlavägen, please help me leave the tower to which you brought me.

Ever since Harriet Bosse had married Gunnar Wingård, Strindberg had regarded himself as cut off from Djurgården because the bridge leading there could be seen from no. 57 Strandvägen, where the Wingårds lived. Now, hearing rumours that the marriage was falling apart, he started to hope for a reconciliation with Harriet, disguising this as a yearning for their child. Fanny had assisted him in gaining information before, and he turned to her again.

However, when Fanny Falker refers to that letter in her book, both Harriet and the Djurgården bridge have disappeared from her memory: all that remains is that Strindberg had pleaded with her to liberate him from the Tower, and that she had understood the plea as a disguised proposal. According to her narrative, she rushed to see Strindberg, in a state of agitation, to find him pale and trembling in the doorway, steadying himself with one hand on a coat-rack. 'I did not know,' she writes, 'what he wanted, what he really meant, but only thought that what he had written was beautiful and moving, this outcry from a human being who sat there, confined and alone. . . .'

According to Fanny Falkner, Strindberg proposed to her a little later, and she accepted. He purchased two rings, made plans for their move to a country estate, and told her that marrying him would be like entering a convent. They decided to keep their engagement secret; after a few days, Fanny expressed regret, frightened by the idea of the convent. Strindberg reacted with equanimity. He was willing to wait.

Strangely enough, Strindberg has left us no version of these events. There is a letter to his sister Nora, written in September 1909, in which he said he was thinking of settling in Kolmården. Possibly this was the location of the estate where Fanny and he were to live.

Some evidence provided by Fredrik Ström, a young radical politican and journalist, has been given some credence; however, it dates only from the following year, as that was when Ström and Strindberg first met. During the great Strindberg controversy, which was to ensue shortly, Ström would be one of Strindberg's allies. One day he ascended to the Blue Tower and found Strindberg, who normally received him in a dressing-gown and slippers, attired in a lounge suit, ruffled shirt and shoes with heels. 'The Master', as Ström reverently addressed Strindberg, asked his visitor to sit down and give him advice: 'What would the public say about a marriage in which the groom was over sixty, the bride, eighteen or nineteen? Please give me a frank reply.'

Ström thought that Strindberg was working on a new marriage play, and that by public he meant the audience. He replied: 'Well, I think people would think that such a marriage is against nature.' Later, Ström told the Strindberg scholar Matte Schmidt that his reply had, in fact, been even more acrimonious. 'That would be bestiality,' is what he claimed to have said—in other words, using the very expression which the publisher Seligmann had found so offensive in *Miss Julie* that he compelled Strindberg to delete it.

According to Ström, Strindberg turned ashen and 'sort of collapsed' and then excused himself. It is hard to tell whether Ström's account is an accurate one. It is reasonable to assume that Strindberg vacillated between paternal and other feelings for Fanny. In a letter, he called her 'Ma Mouche', the pet name used by the ageing and ailing Heinrich Heine for his young friend Camilla Selden.

At this time, Goethe was an important influence in Strindberg's life. The Blue Tower contained an entire Goethe library, and numerous underlinings testify that Strindberg studied the book assiduously. In Philipp Stein's volume *Goethe als Theaterleiter* (*Goethe as Theatrical Director*), he read what Goethe once said to Eckermann about his position as theatrical director. Goethe said that he was threatened by two enemies: one was his passion for talent, which could tempt him to be unfair, and the other—the young, beautiful and even spiritually graceful women he met in the theatre. 'I felt passionately attracted to several of them, and they were frequently willing to meet me halfway.' Goethe then went on to say that he had resisted temptation, as he thought that the success of the theatrical enterprise was more important than his private happiness.

If Strindberg gained moral strength from this (underlined) passage, he also had access to other instances from Goethe's life that pointed in the opposite direction. It is no accident that he called the heroine in *Abu Casem's Slippers* 'Suleyka': he owned several copies of *West-östlicher Diwan*, and his underlining pen was very active in 'Buch Suleika', which reflects the ageing Goethe's love for the young Marianne von Willemer.

Nevertheless, one hesitates to take this last love story of Strindberg's entirely seriously. There is a surviving letter form Strindberg to Fanny in which he speaks simply and realistically. Fanny claimed that it had been written before the 'proposal', but we cannot trust her on that score. These were his words:

Do I really have to write this letter? Only eight days ago I found out that there was talk about my intention to get married once again, this time to a young girl. I found it so absurd and so poorly invented that I, old and ailing, should try to chain a young person to my heavy fate, which will soon be completed according to the dictates of nature. It is none of my doing that your name was involved. When my last child was taken from me, I lost interest in life and only sought someone to care for in an unselfish way. That was all! Do not reply to this, only have the same trust in me as before; then the gossip will subside.

Strindberg's relationships with Fanny Falkner changed tone and faded, but he tried to support her in various ways. He arranged for her to have a studio at the very top of the Blue Tower, allowed her to paint his portrait, and commissioned a portrait of Hjalmar Branting's wife, which he then gave to Branting as a gift. At that time, the Falkner family had already moved out of the building, and Strindberg remained in the Tower by himself. As he lay dying in 1912, Fanny Falkner came and asked to be admitted, but was not allowed in. Mina returned from the bedroom with a message: 'He said that Miss Falkner should not be sad, because he has been thinking of her.'

In 1911, Strindberg wrote to Nils Andersson: 'These last three years have taken their toll; in this "tower" there was nothing beautiful; in the previous one, there was some beauty—the child, and a couple of Christmas Eves.' These words cannot be regarded as a condemnation of Fanny and his relationship with her: to the end, Strindberg retained his habit of describing every period of his life as pure hell. Nor is the letter any kind of confirmation of the claim that he intended to marry her.

4

On 22 January 1909, Strindberg had celebrated his sixtieth birthday. Since *Black Flags*, he had consolidated his popularity with his readers. Almost all of his important works were available in popularly priced editions of tens of thousands of copies. His youth and maturity were thus present and standing guard, as it were, over his old age.

The sixtieth birthday was ample demonstration of this: poems of homage—dealing with 'the courage of sacrifice' and 'the proudest flag of our poetry' (Gustaf Ullman)—appeared in the press, along with flattering anecdotes, idealized drawings and public opinion polls. Strindberg fêtes were held all over the country in lecture halls and clubhouses, and the Socialist youth organizations were particularly active in this respect. The newspaper *Social-Demokraten* dedicated an entire issue to Strindberg, and he wrote a letter of thanks in which he called the paper's editors 'the spokesmen of the common people'. He added: 'To whom I will always belong, being *The Serving Maid's Son*.

Even the Swedish establishment paid tribute. The Dramatic Theatre premièred *The Last Knight*, with August Palme in the title role, and the royal box was occupied by the new King, Gustaf V, who, in contrast to his two closest predecessors on the throne, did not compose verses but dedicated his long life to playing cards and hunting. Strindberg was not present, but received reports of the performance. The next morning, Carl Eldh arrived at the Tower with a bust modelled especially for the occasion.

The painter Per Ekström, with whom Strindberg had mourned the death of Karl XV, accompanied Eldh, bearing blue anemones picked at Lilljans, where the Bohemians of *The Red Room* used to congregate. The youngest Falkner daughters arrived with flowers and songs, and the newspapers were able to report that this was the tribute that had pleased the author most of all. In the evening, after Strindberg had retired, the participants in a Strindberg fête at Berns conducted a torchlight procession past his house. He got dressed again and stood on the balcony for a while, receiving the homage. It seems as though he would be able to end his life in an atmosphere of reconciliation, but his nature did not allow that. Soon he was to engage in actions that guaranteed new dramatic events.

In Sweden, 1909 was a year of political unrest. In August, a general strike—the only one in the country's history—broke out: at its height, it involved 290,000 workers, of whom 45,000 lived in Stockholm. The country had been governed since 1906 by a cabinet of the Right headed by Arvid Lindman, who was both a factory owner and a naval admiral—a symbolic combination, as the government's prime concerns were industry and the armed forces. The government took drastic measures against the strikers, who suffered a defeat and were forced back to work in the autumn. However, the labour movement had had a significant opportunity to demonstrate what could be achieved by union solidarity and cohesion, weapons which Strindberg had questioned in the 1880s, to Branting's annoyance.

During the strike, Strindberg remained remarkably silent. At its culmination in August and September, he was in the midst of his emotional crisis with Fanny Falkner. In addition, he had become engaged in philological speculations that were to occupy him until his death. He even tried to return to playwriting, but in vain.

It is not impossible that his silence was to some extent connected with his anticipation of a Nobel Prize, although it was said that Alfred Nobel had been angered that Strindberg had praised him as a producer of ammunition for terrorists, and that this would count against Strindberg: in addition, the Swedish Academy's practice until then seemed to exclude writers of Strindberg's kind. Nevertheless, he was expecting a prize, noting in the *Occult Diary* that his stars favoured a monetary reward in December. As is well known, the Prize is awarded on 10 December, the anniversary of Nobel's death.

In the autumn of 1909, the Literary Nobel Prize was not awarded to Strindberg, but to Selma Lagerlöf. Thus Strindberg knew that he would not receive it during his lifetime, and he was no longer tempted to remain silent for opportunistic reasons—if he had ever really experienced such a temptation.

5

In April 1910, Valfrid Spånberg, editor-in-chief of the brand new paper *Afton-Tidningen* (the *Evening Paper*), which had offices at no. 83 Drottning-gatan, next door to the Blue Tower, received a letter from Strindberg in which the latter offered to contribute free material to the paper, on condition that everything would be printed without censorship. Spångberg, a thin, gangly man with a forked reddish beard that made him resemble King Erik XIV, had already received a promise of collaboration from Strindberg earlier in the year, and was delighted to hear that matters were proceeding. Little did he guess in what direction. . . .

Strindberg's first article was published on 29 April, under the heading 'Pharaoh Worship', and its subject was one of the most hackneyed in his repertoire—the absurdity and uselessness of Karl XII, and the nation's stubborn insistence on congregating to sing the praises of his memory and that of other royal corpses. These were the 'pharaohs'.

Karl XII had, indeed, become a recent topic of public discussion. A leading Swedish historian and politician, Harald Hjärne, had presented Karl XII as the guardian of Western civilization, of which he was himself the embodiment. According to Hjärne's thesis, it was Sweden's historical mission to stand guard at the eastern frontier of culture, against barbarism and despotism. The Greeks, engaging with the Persian tyrants at Thermopylae, were cited as a parallel. Hatred of Russia was an ancient Swedish tradition. Since 1868, the statue of Karl XII had been standing in Stockholm's Kungsträdgården, pointing an exhortatory finger toward the East. In Tegnér's popular poem, the hero-king did battle with the Russians, and now he was being given renewed and heightened significance: at the end of the 1890s, Heidenstam had gained vast popularity with his heroic collection of stories, *The Karolinians*.

Strindberg perceived all this as a challenge. In a story contained in *Historical Miniatures*, a collection of historical tales he had published in 1905, he paid homage to Peter the Great as a Renaissance genius. It was he who had brought civilization to Russia, and no Swedish assistance was required in that direction.

'Pharaoh Worship' was the first shot to be fired in what became a genuine barrage of acerbic articles. During the next seven months, Strindberg wrote fifty-four pieces for *Afton-Tidningen* and *Social-Demokraten*—an impressive demonstration of the energies Strindberg released now that he no longer needed to devote them to *belles-lettres*.

By and large, Strindberg expounded the radical ideas of his youth, sharpening them with selected material from the contemporary literature of the Left. He had, however, extended his range: he wrote about constitutional matters, often following Adolf Hedin. He took a stand against proportional representation, wanted to abolish the right to inherit property, poured scorn on the royal family and the court, attacked bureaucracy and judiciary in the best manner of the 1880s, held fast to the small farmer as the pillar of a sound society, and declared that Socialism as a doctrine was infused with the spirit of Christianity, even though individual Socialists still had not seen the light.

The ensuing feud—'the Strindberg feud' has become an expression in its own right in Swedish, and has its own entry in Swedish dictionaries—was the most resonant literary battle ever conducted in Sweden. It became evident that Strindberg was in full command of his talent for provocation. From the very beginning, violent attacks *ad hominem* raised the temperature of the discussions considerably. Yet the debate gained its importance from the fact that the persons involved represented central and fundamental differences in their views of the world.

The controversy that surrounded *Marrying* in 1884 had been conducted within a limited social sphere. *Dagens Nyheter* had been obliged to invent excuses for the lack of interest on the part of the working class. This time, the entire nation was mobilized. Unrest throughout the country after the great strike, the Rightist government's enthusiasm for defence as opposed to the workers' aversion to militarism, the advance of Social Democracy, seen by the middle classes as menacing and ominous—all these factors contributed to a heightening of the tone and methodology of the debate. The full history of the Strindberg feud has still to be written. Here, we shall deal with only one of its aspects—a decisive one for Strindberg.

The leaders of the two opposing factions were the erstwhile friends, Strindberg and Heidenstam. They were well suited to their symbolic roles: the rebel, a self-styled 'serving maid's son', versus the aristocrat, who regarded power and wealth as his unquestioned right. In actual fact, however, Heidenstam was not the leader of his camp: behind him stood a man equipped with a more powerful intellect and a more scintillating prose style: Oscar Levertin.

By the time of the feud, Levertin had been dead for three years, yet that made him an even more dangerous adversary. Legends were being woven around his memory, and he was a literary saint. 'You were the priest within our singers' temple,' Heidenstam intoned at Levertin's grave, 'the ever wakeful priest with his wistful, gentle smile and finely honed sword.'

At the time of his death, Levertin was Sweden's foremost literary critic. He seldom used the sword Heidenstam saw in his hand. His principal means of expression were fiery mimesis and enthusiasm. He burned incense before Sweden's national heroes—not least Bellman and Linnaeus—but he also poured entire hecatombs of praise over poets of his day. The gratitude of all the nonentities whom he had declared geniuses contributed substantially to the legend surrounding him.

Sweden's critics, Levertin included, had heaped incredible praise on Strindberg: clouds of superlatives surrounded his name in contemporary articles. Yet all those tributes share one reservation: Strindberg was a genius but not a great poet. Levertin wrote a number of articles on Strindberg which made a deep impression on public consciousness and determined the way Strindberg is perceived to this very day. Without any doubt, the most brilliant of these pieces was the one Levertin published in *Svenska Dagbladet* on 3 May 1899. Strindberg was, he declared, at once genius and plebeian 'natural man', combining the purest and most ethereal desire for infinity with the basest instincts. Strindberg, according to Levertin, lacked natural nobility and the ability not to take oneself seriously that distinguishes the truly cultured person.

Levertin concluded:

August Strindberg could be called August the First, the Confessor, for it would be hard to find a more ruthless writer. I cannot help it, but sometimes while reading him I am reminded of childhood visits to the zoo at feeding-time: in Strindberg's books, all the wild beasts of the human spirit roar and shriek behind their bars—and they include not only the majestic lion and the enchanting tiger with his gold-speckled fur, but also the dirty monkeys.

It was only natural that Levertin understood Strindberg's work to be primarily autobiographical, and that he had difficulties in seeing what was universally human in the characters Strindberg created. What was more damaging to Strindberg was that Levertin denied him artistic consciousness and deep human insight. The world's greatest poets, above all Dante, had used their own experiences, without sparing their enemies. On those counts, it was possible to muster understanding and forgiveness. But a writer described as merely a battleground for forces he could not control stood no chance of being counted among the truly great, and could be suspected of having contact with those anarchic elements in society and the human psyche that have to be kept firmly under control if chaos is to be prevented.

Georg Brandes, who may be regarded as a spokesman for the entire European cultural élite of the day, expressed the matter in his great essay on Strindberg in a more courteous but even more explicit way. 'Strindberg was', Brandes wrote, 'a great writer without being a guiding spirit.' He is not a teacher, Brandes continued, in the difficult art of life, 'as there is no *one* Strindberg but many and they are engaged in combat with each other'.

During the Strindberg feud, Levertin's characterization was repeated and varied *ad infinitum*. Heidenstam, who entered the controversy late, followed in his dead friend's footsteps when he called Strindberg 'the full-blooded barbarian', 'an escaped serf', whose world is dominated by 'confusion, suspicion, superstition and fear'. Heidenstam declared that

Strindberg had never 'enriched my soul, never truly opened up a new vista, never in any single matter given the fully valid answer which is the true genius's gift to mankind'.

From the first, Strindberg had realized what a deadly menace Levertin's interpretation was to him and his work: it was, indeed, a matter of life and death. In the final analysis, the Strindberg feud concerned the question of who exactly is to determine what a great writer is, and consequently to determine what a human being is, and what society that human being is to live in.

Strindberg saw clearly where the enemy's main line of defence lay and did not hesitate to attack. In his first book of poems, Heidenstam had published a number of short, 'centrally lyrical' works under the title *Thoughts of Solitude*. These conformed exactly to Levertin's definition of greatness in poetry. They were lofty words of wisdom, vying with Goethe's 'Über allen Gipfeln' ('Above all the treetops'), and received inordinate acclaim. Strindberg exposed them to ridicule, compared them to greeting-card verse, and took them apart, bit by bit, punctuating the operation with scornful sarcasm.

This really set the debate in motion: as so often in the past, Strindberg incensed people by means of strong personal attacks and concrete examples. During the following months the debate deteriorated somewhat into a squabble about whether Heidenstam was a good poet or not, and whether Strindberg's way of analysing poems was valid or not. It is not hard to understand why Strindberg was so angry. His rich and varied life's work, and his lifelong struggle to create it, were being rejected in favour of a few supposedly profound verses—an evaluation that was symptomatic of a warped concept of culture.

Levertin, the main enemy, was protected by posthumous legend, but that did not cramp Strindberg's style. Even before the feud began, he had overcome his scruples and pronounced a condemnation of Levertin that was invisibly present throughout the debate. Strindberg had found support in Goethe: in one of his Goethe volumes he underlined a pronouncement of the German poet to the effect that one who does not hate what is evil runs the risk of falling into the habit of considering everything relatively good, with the result that all genuine feeling dies within him.

On the day of Levertin's death, 22 September 1906, Strindberg had written a notable entry in the *Occult Diary*. He included a slightly edited version of it in *The Blue Book*, thus bringing it to the notice of initiates. In it, he claimed that on the morning of Levertin's death, but before he had received the news of it, feelings of relief and liberation flooded through his consciousness. During his morning walk, he saw his life pass before him as it is supposed to do in the moment of death, and he imagined that this took place simultaneously with Levertin's demise.

In *The Blue Book* he called Levertin his 'worst enemy': 'He was a sinister man with an old-fashioned, materialistic view of the world which he thought was modern, a literary usurer who reviewed garbage written by marchionesses in order to be invited to their castles; who praised his acquaintances as long as they remained acquaintances; a coterie man, and a company man.'

During that morning walk he had thought of buying a bottle of perfume for Harriet Bosse. Later, he gave this a symbolic interpretation: the perfume was to counter the stench of the dead man, who was so decomposed when he died that he had to be buried immediately.

The burning hatred expressed in this diary entry becomes comprehensible if one considers that Levertin's court of of literary justice had deprived Strindberg of everything he had worked to achieve.

6

The Strindberg feud encompassed another debate as well. In *Afton-Tidningen* of 1 July 1910 a housepainter, Adolf Lundgrehn, suggested that the nation should prove its love for August Strindberg by creating for him 'a green oasis of peace, where he could grow old, dream, and die—without financial worries'. In other words, he was proposing a national fund-raising scheme for Strindberg.

It proved to be a viable proposition, especially since Strindberg had not been awarded the Nobel Prize. He declared himself willing to accept an 'anti-Nobel Prize', as it could not be considered one of those worldly distinctions he had, in *Inferno*, vowed to refuse. Soon many other voices joined in to support the idea, and this opened up another battle-front.

Per Hallström, one of the leading writers of the 1890s, since 1908 a member of the Swedish Academy (he told Heidenstam that he had accepted the invitation to become a member in order to work for an award of the Prize to Heidenstam), wrote in *Svenska Dagbladet* that the suggestion of such a prize to Strindberg was scandalous: it would mean honouring a libellous pamphleteer. This view also found numerous supporters, and it took a long time to realize the fund scheme.

Nevertheless, the Social Democrat Youth Alliance under its chairman Zäta Höglund, one of the labour movement's most distinguished figures, made an initiative in the matter in January 1911. In order to gain the widest possible support, its origin was kept secret. A fund-raising committee was formed, its leading members being the actor August Lindberg, Richard Bergh and Karl Nordström, Strindberg's close painter friends, Nathan Söderblom, now a professor at Uppsala, and Hjalmar Branting. The young critic John Landqvist, who had fought with verve for Strindberg during the feud, now wrote an appeal which was distributed throughout Sweden at the beginning of April 1911. He took great and ingenious pains to phrase it so that it would be acceptable to the greatest possible number of people. By way of hidden rebuff to Levertin and Heidenstam, it stressed that Strindberg's *oeuvre* extended 'over the depths and heights of the human soul', that he had 'penetrated the fiery and painful abysses of life, to rise again up into the ethereal realms of reconciliation and love'. 'Throughout his work we find an ethical trait of self-searching, and a feeling for humanity's rights as well as for its need.'

The appeal was published in practically every newspaper, even though some of the conservative papers indicated their disapproval by printing it in the Letters to the Editor section. It was signed by 217 names representing a wide range of social strata and opinions, even though, as was to be expected, the majority of the signatories had Leftist leanings. But the establishment was certainly represented: a director general; a governor; bank director Ernest Thiel; Hjalmar Lundbohm, general manager of the great mining company of Lapland, which was contributing so importantly to Sweden's advance towards prosperity at that time; Nathan Söderblom and two other representatives of the Church.

Significantly enough, Söderblom was attacked for his participation, as if it had been obvious that a man of the cloth had no business supporting Strindberg's cause.

7

The debate subjected Strindberg to heavy attacks. As an example of what was permissible in public debate at that time, here is the final paragraph of a long article by Sven Hedin in *Dagens Nyheter*, 22 July 1910:

Like the jackal, he prefers corpses, but will even attack the living as long as they do not bite. Oh, he is such a pitiable man! One walks by his dwelling here in Stockholm with the feeling of passing a house of mourning in which the bier has already been prepared. And yet he is still sitting there, writing, alone with his hatred and consumed, day and night, by envy, worse than a woman's jealousy. A pale reflection of former, brighter times is the only laurel crowning his silver hair. The darkness has already started rising around him. Soon the black bats will come, and his heart grow cold. Then, it will be too late to confess. Then comes the judgment. Will Strindberg's Christianity be approved by his judge? Poor, desolate, lonely pilgrim, who lives on the ruins of his own tragic life! It is

62 The Strindberg feud. Drawing
by Carl Jacobssion in *Stormklockan*,
1910

63   Stockholm's   Workers'
Commune   pays   homage   to
Strindberg   with   a   torchlight
procession,   22 January 1912.
Illustration   from   *Social-
Demokraten*

as if, led by noisy pipes and flutes, he had already begun his march under the *Black Flags* that point the way to Hades.

Strindberg, however, who was quite capable of similar effusions, had become invulnerable: his mind was occupied by other things. He had embarked on yet another scholarly quest, which was to be his last, in the field of philology. He was writing his articles with his left hand.

Words were Strindberg's medium, and he was exceptionally skilled in their use. He could easily have written a volume entitled *Open Letters to Young Writers*, comparable to the ones he had written to actors. But like many other writers before him, he preferred not to expose the craft of his profession.

Strindberg often wrote in an exalted state, in which words appeared fresh and new in his imagination, yet he was always conscious of language itself, never resorting to mechanical means or prophetic incantation. He prepared himself for the act of writing, frequently collecting loose sheets of paper with words and lines that might come in handy. He expanded his vocabulary tirelessly, and, as Karl-Åke Kärnell has shown in his exceptional work *Strindberg's Imagery*, he continuously introduced terminology and imagery created by the new modern technology. The submarine, the flashlight, the gramophone, new techniques of photography, the airplane, and the names of new medical drugs appear in his vocabulary more or less simultaneously with their introduction on to the market. The freshness of his language is often due to the fact that he got there first. While the gramophone was still called the 'graphophone' and used cylinders instead of records, he let his dying protagonist in *The Roof-raising* repeat his memories over and over as if they had been recorded on cylinders which started turning at the approach of death.

Although Strindberg claimed that he trusted in his inspiration and never revised anything he wrote, it is clear that he kept the flow of his words under strict intellectual control. He avoided repetitions at all costs, aware of their debilitating effect on any text, even rejecting fairly remote assonances for that very reason. Lars Dahlbäck provides many interesting examples of this procedure in his erudite dissertation on *The People of Hemsö*. Strindberg replaced '[he had] taken a seat' with 'settled down' because the preceding line had included the expression '[it had] taken to blowing'. The words 'A warm dampness rose from the bear-moss' was amended to 'The bear-moss exuded a warm dampness', because the line above contained the parallel construction 'blue anemones rose'.

Early on, he learned to prefer the specific to the general and to use exact terms for any occasion of nature—which may be seen as similar to his polemical method which examines sinners under their given names rather than sin in the abstract. His reading of Linnaeus and Sven Nilsson played an important part here. His writing involved hard work and constant attention to detail. Dahlbäck provides some good examples of this. In *The People of Hemsö*, Rundqvist, the hired hand, says that he doesn't 'give a shit for anybody'—and to make the statement more specific, Strindberg adds 'not even the Queen Mother herself'.

Now, his own creative writing done, Strindberg's attention shifted. Words were no longer bricks with which to build, but objects worthy of examination in their own right. He began an enormous examination of the linguistic material at his disposal and studied dictionaries, grammars and books on linguistics with the same enthusiasm and in the same subjective manner as he had studied chemistry books in the 1890s. Now as then, his aim was to discover a lost connection and coherence. His imagination never contented itself with anything less than great comprehensive solutions. One might say that he disdained adversaries who were less than God himself.

As a chemist, he had searched for the original matter from which the world had been created. As a philologist, he decided that the sacred language, Hebrew, was the mother of all other languages. That notion had been widely embraced during the Renaissance, and Swedenborg had adopted it.

Strindberg immediately went to work, despising empty speculation that was not followed by experiments and vivisections. From 1910 to 1912 he published scores of articles and an entire series of books with titles like *The Roots of World Language*, *Ancestors of the Mother Tongue*, *The Origins of Chinese*. In these, he pursued his vision of unity by demonstrating linguistic similarities and thereby linking all the world's languages to one another. Oceans, deserts and mountain ranges presented no obstacle to him; he relied on his ability to perceive associations where all before him had rushed blindly past. He had discovered the inverted Viking ship in the Gothic cathedral and proceeded to draw conclusions about those who first employed this mode of construction. Now he claimed to see a kinship between the graphic signs of Hebrew and Chinese. In North American Indian languages he found proof in terms of geographical names for the thesis that the Indians were the people expelled from Canaan by the Israelites. Thus Idaho was Yehuda; Minnesota, the Hebrew Minasoth— 'places of refuge'; Canada was the Hebrew *kam*—'market town'. Northern Europe was not left out of this worldwide community. The ancient Nordic king Urbe was, perhaps, none other than Orpheus; and song itself was possibly of Nordic origin.

No philologist has ever examined Strindberg's language studies, and such an examination would probably lead to an even harsher judgement than Svedberg's on his chemistry. Strindberg himself often made apologies for his work, complaining about lack of time and his waning strength. Yet his perseverance is touching. Day after day, month after month, he sat poring over his tomes, annotating and compiling endless word-lists.

In *The Swedish People*, Strindberg had made some fairly contemptuous remarks about Olaus Rudbeck who had located the Pillars of Hercules at Öresund and claimed to have discovered the lost continent of Atlantis in Sweden. He wrote that the Swedish scholar had allowed himself to be intoxicated by the glory of the country's era as a great power. Rudbeck had started out from unproven assumptions in order to prove his facts, although Strindberg himself employed a similar method as chemist and philologist and indeed had expressed his admiration, in *The Swedish People*, for Rudbeck's ability to find parallels. Now he regretted his scornful words and fully perceived the congruence between Rudbeck and himself.

Chapter Eighteen

DEATH

I

In HIS LAST years, Strindberg established increasingly strong relations with the children of his first marriage. Greta completed her training as an actress, moved to Stockholm, and in 1907 married her cousin Henry von Philp, the son of Strindberg's sister Anna. Strindberg found a refuge in the young couple's home. In 1911, when Greta bore a child which died on the day of its birth, Strindberg followed the tragedy with strong emotion. He never saw a grandchild of his own.

The death of Greta's child brought Siri von Essen to Stockholm. She spoke to Strindberg on the telephone on one occasion; according to Karin Smirnoff, his voice 'became low and had a tremor in it'.

At this time, Strindberg required medical care, and it was of some importance to him that his son-in-law was a doctor. The symptoms of his illness of 1908 had never quite disappeared, and in the summer of 1911 he began to feel seriously unwell. As a result, he decided to set his affairs in order. Karl Otto Bonnier had noted with relief that Strindberg had not sent the manuscript of *Black Flags* to him: he would have found himself in an awkward situation, as he was the publisher of so many of the writers attacked in the book. Nevertheless, he had long tried to acquire the rights to Strindberg's entire production. Gernandt's publishing company had gone bankrupt in 1903, and Strindberg no longer had a main publisher. In June 1911, he started intensive negotiations, which he conducted shrewdly and energetically. Bonnier offered 150,000 kronor for the rights to the *Collected Works*. Strindberg did not accept and, on 28 June, the offer was raised to 200,000 kronor. 'That is a lot of money for me as I have never owned anything, and I accept, on the conditions you suggest,' Strindberg replied in a letter.

This transaction removed one of the reasons for the nationwide fund-raising scheme. Karin Smirnoff has described Strindberg's delight over the money. She travelled to Stockholm with her brother Hans, and with Greta they went to the Blue Tower:

> The dining-room table was covered with bank-notes. He had divided these into four piles, which were slowly toppling as he was fidgeting and fussing and closing doors and ordering doors to be closed, afraid that someone might come in and steal all that wealth. Then he took the money, one pile at a time, and handed them to each child with a little admonition to be frugal, was kissed on the cheek with 'thank you *so* much daddy', and then picked up the fourth pile. Obviously wanting to get the matter over with as quickly as possible, he cast a shy glance at Karin and said, in a low voice: 'This is for Mama', adding, in an even lower tone: 'It is an old debt.' Perhaps he understood the chords he was touching at that moment—but then there was no time for anything else: bright-eyed again, he gave orders for a joint march to the Bank of Sweden where the money was to be deposited.
>
> When Karin returned to Finland and delivered the money, a total of 6,000 kronor, to her mother, Siri stared at her as if this was some kind of practical joke. 'To me!' she exclaimed, a hot flush rising to her cheeks. She listened calmly to Karin's account, and then said, in a tone of soft pride: 'Please, Karin, write and thank Daddy from me.' 'I accept it as payment of an old debt,' she added in the same tone of voice and rose to her feet.

That summer, Karin was preparing to get married to Wladimir Smirnoff, professor of Russian at the University of Helsinki. Strindberg wrote her a warm letter and offered to act as host at the wedding 'for my firstborn, who once brought the first joy into my life'. His offer was accepted, and the wedding was celebrated in the Blue Tower dining-room with a champagne supper and a cake 'topped by a sugar angel with two red hearts in its outstretched hands, as the confectioner, to everyone's amusement, "had thought that it was Mr Strindberg who was getting married".'

Strindberg spent Christmas Eve 1911 at Greta's and Henry's home on Hornsgatan. A photograph was taken that evening. When it was time for him to leave, no cab could be found, and he walked home. It was quite a long walk, and he caught a cold; and the next day he fell ill with a high fever and pneumonia.

The illness was a sign of his lowered resistance. In April 1911 he had written to Nils Andersson, his favourite correspondent of the time 'Old age is here; I have had warnings and premonitions.' In June, he was more explicit:

> Poorly for a couple of months now; probably a still unknown, not full-fledged, internal ailment the physician (my son-in-law) cannot diagnose.

All my innards in revolt, and feel like bursting; don't seem to fit into my skin, although I am half-starved and have given up my evening grog (the regular one). It is as if a mad soul inhabited the wrong body—it has always felt that way—that is why I have needed wine to make my soul feel at home. Fasting and sobriety cause pusillanimity, downright cowardice. Self-searching, *conscientia scrupulosa*, which reproaches one with every-thing, even crimes one never committed. Even, when the last great interest came to an end—the roots of world language—life became insipid—Gigantic labours without encouragement are not edifying.

At the end of the letter, Strindberg said that he had rented a fisherman's cabin in the Archipelago, but that he was unable to 'change location'. 'I just sit here and wait—for something unknown! and feared, but with a certain calmness!'

Shortly before writing this letter he had amused himself by combining various dates of his life and had worked out that the year of his death would be 1912. A few days later he declared that he would be gone in less than a year.

His memory dwelled on the summer in Denmark that produced *Miss Julie* and on the affair with Ludvig Hansen in which he had played such a deflated part. In a letter to Nils Andersson he gave an account of the story with the girl and repeated that he had been 'ambushed'. 'If for no other reason, I should be vindicated for my children's sake; but privately, secretly perhaps.'

In the autumn of 1911, his condition grew worse. On 8 November he wrote to Nils Andersson:

I am ill! Sometimes go to bed at 7, as I cannot fit into my clothes. Worst in the daytime! All right in bed and at night. Best when I have visitors. No physician understands what it is. Almost the same symptoms as in 1896—(Inferno). Personally I believe that it is the people's dreadful hatred. The presence of visitors seems to deflect the hate-currents. I must have made some great discoveries that certain people have noticed, but they remain silent and—hate.

It is strange that he should have fallen back on the idea of persecution, after so energetically demonstrating that such notions arise in those who have fallen from grace and who invent enemies instead of understanding that their trials are a gift from God. As we have seen on so many occasions, nothing is ever definitively fixed with Strindberg: he offered different interpretations of life which existed simultaneously and side by side, and not one of them was ever given full precedence over the others.

At the end of 1911, Strindberg was bedridden for a couple of weeks. The first thing he did when he was able to get up again was to write an article about his experiences. *Afton-Tidningen* published it on his sixty-third birthday, 22 January 1912, under the heading 'Reflections on my birthday with regard to my illness'.

On Christmas Day, when the fever first struck him, Strindberg (according to the article) had felt that he had gained peace at last, that he had been liberated from his driving urge to work. He went on to quote from something he had written in his diary five years earlier: 'It seemed to me that I had completed the day's work of my life, had said all I wanted to say.' That was how the diary functioned in his life: it was a gathering place for words and reflections to be used at the right moment.

His illness was a prologue to the drama of his death, but contrary to his belief, it had not freed him from his urge to express himself, which remained with him to the end. In 1911, his philological ruminations had taken up almost all his time. Now he returned to politics with a sense of obligation towards those who paid him homage primarily in his capacity as a social conscience.

Early in 1912, Sven Hedin published a tract entitled *A Word of Warning*, disseminated in an edition of a million copies, the premise of which was an impending attack by Russia. The message was than Sweden must arm and join the Triple Alliance. It was a new version of the philosophy of Karl XII. Strindberg owed Hedin something for the 'jackal' and the 'bats'. The reason for Hedin's attack in 1910 was that Strindberg had negated Hedin's Asiatic explorations and discoveries on the basis of the maps of Siberia he had brought to light in the 1800s (see Chapter 4). Hedin had received fantastic acclaim and had been knighted in 1905—the last Swede ever accorded that distinction. He was a concentrated embodiment of everything Strindberg hated.

Strindberg renewed his attacks. During the spring, he managed to publish a polemical pamphlet entitled *Courier of the Tsar, Or: The Secrets of the Saw-sharpeners*. It was published by Frederik Ström's publishing house Fram (Forward), and the lettering on the title page was in red, like the workers' flags. The 'Courier' was Sven Hedin, whom Strindberg satirically accused of importing Russian spies, disguised as saw-sharpeners, in order to frighten the Swedish public and make it more willing to bring sacrifices to the altar of war.

Strindberg exhorted the government—a liberal one since the autumn of 1911, with Karl Staaff, Pehr Staaff's brother, as prime minister—to refuse to accept the armoured cruiser for which the Swedish people, eager to defend themselves, were raising money. And he wrote apropos of the products of barracks and drill-grounds: 'Learning how to become in-susceptible to one's own sufferings has the drawback that one also becomes insensitive to those of others. . . . If one learns to endure injustice in silence, one becomes unjust oneself: and blind obedience creates slaves or tyrants.'

He certainly did not remember that he had expressed the same views, in almost identical words, thirty-six years earlier in an article in *Göteborgs Handels- och Sjöfartstidning*. At that time, Carl Gustaf Wrangel's uniform of the Svea Guard and the military philosophy that went with it had provided the emotional impetus: now he had far more abundant material to deal with, in a world that was preparing for the greatest military explosion in history.

Strindberg's sixty-third birthday, his last, was celebrated as if it had been his sixtieth again, or his seventieth. A delegation, led by Hjalmar Branting, presented him with the proceeds of the fund-raising scheme. After deductions had been made for expenses, the final sum was about 45,000 kronor, with 20,000 donations listed, of which 11,000 were less than 50 öre. Several of the major listings involved many donors, as collections had been made at places of work or by means of lectures and festivities. It was estimated that the total number of donors was around 40,000—and so undoubtedly, a broad-based popular manifestation. Strindberg gave away most of the money, which he no longer needed.

On his birthday, he was again honoured by a torchlit procession of Stockholm's workers who marched past the Blue Tower with bands and red union banners. The police estimated that 10,000 people participated in the event. Strindberg appeared on the balcony, holding the hand of his daughter Anne-Marie, and listened to the *Marseillaise* and other anthems of liberation, punctuated from time to time by cheers for 'The People's Strindberg' and 'The King of Poets'. According to *Dagens Nyheter*, Strindberg's son-in-law Henry von Philp held up a candle so that those passing below were able to see Strindberg's face. It was emaciated.

During these tributes, Strindberg maintained his civilian stance. In a note of thanks published in *Afton-Tidningen* the following day he reacted caustically against the 'overrated importance' he felt he had been given. In the birthday article mentioned above he had discussed the hazards of public homages:

> Finally, I believe that their 'object' himself feels the profound disharmony between what he considers himself to be and what he is made out to be at that moment. Deep down in every human being, whether he has been beaten down by life or not, there is, after all, a dark sense of unworthiness which falsifies his position at the moment of ovation, and thus he feels ashamed rather than arrogant. That is what happened to the great French singer Nourrit after a performance, when the torch-bearing mob arrived in front of his house to cheer him. He was seized by the notion that they had come to mock him, as he had not been in good voice that night, and in his despair he jumped out of the window to his death.

It was a precise summary of his own attitude. What he had asked from life was to be crucified and to triumph, in the same moment. Behind these twin roles lay a Strindberg who felt unworthy, and perhaps he felt tempted to follow Nourrit's example, as he stood on the balcony above Drottninggatan.

2

Early in April, Strindberg fell ill again. The symptoms this time were stomach pains and vomiting. Nils Andersson, who visited him, consulted a mutual friend from Lund, the distinguished physician Karl Petrén, to whom Strindberg wrote on 7 April:

> Now I am in pain round the clock, no matter what I ingest; sometimes the pain is dull, sometimes more intense, but I am never free of it, whether I sit, walk or lie down. I take to my bed in order to get rid of my clothes, but that no longer makes any difference. The pain does cease when I lie on my stomach; my left side is better than my right, but lying on my back is the worst. I am losing my appetite; I have an aversion to all kinds of food; and am growing increasingly weary of life. Sleep may come for an hour or two, then the pain wakes me up. A night of twelve hours (8—) is endless!

The physicians who attended Strindberg in addition to his son-in-law were Gunnar Nyström, university lecturer in medicine, and Henrik Berg. According to Strindberg's words to Petrén, they were thinking in terms of 'gallstones, inflammation of the stomach lining, Benike's worm, etc.' However, the physicians felt that the diagnosis was cancer with progressive metastases. Fluid was drained from Strindberg's belly on three separate occasions.

There was nothing else to be done. Strindberg was informed of his condition, and the newspapers, which started running daily bulletins on his condition, openly discussed his impending demise. Strindberg, who had always been a great complainer, showed no fear, remained calm and even joked with those friends who did not desert him. He sent his scientist friend, Vilhelm Carlheim-Gyllensköld, who became his indefatigable and much-maligned executor after his death, on a hundred errands; he enquired about some altar stones at Skansen which he connected in his mind with the Ystad stones of the *Inferno* period; and according to his first biographer, Erik Hedén, he was even contemplating a play about a coalminers' strike that had occurred in England in the early spring.

Despite pain and attacks of suffocation, he still took delight in the use of words. 'Thank you for your roses in the iodine and morphine,' he wrote to Anna and Hjalmar Branting, reminding them of joint memories of the 1880s, not forgetting Kymmendö. On 19 April, he wrote to Anne-Marie, then ten years old: 'My dear little daughter! Thank you for your red flowers! But you mustn't come and see me. There're so many bottles of medicine and doctors and such a general rumpus going on here that it's no fun at all. Enjoy yourself in your youth, with your young friends, and do not grieve for the old, whose only wish is to depart.'

64 Strindberg taking his last walk, April 1912

During the month Strindberg lay dying, the greatest international event was the sinking of the *Titanic*. The 'unsinkable' ship quickly became a symbol of the times. It was a blow to the triumph of industrialism, and marked a brutal ending to the utopia which the nineteenth century and Strindberg had dreamed of. By way of confirmation, the First World War broke out two years later, and from that moment through decades of chaos, humanity would see the future through Zamyatin's, Huxley's and Orwell's eyes—as a prison, not a paradise.

Strindberg had good reason to reflect. The liner had taken his own life and its dreams down into the depths of the ocean. He got out of bed and played variations on 'Nearer my God to Thee' on the piano, the hymn allegedly played by the *Titanic*'s orchestra while the ship was sinking.

A few days later, he received the news of Siri von Essen's death. She died on 21 April, twenty-three days before him. Karin Smirnoff has given an account of what happened when her sister Greta read the letter announcing her mother's demise to Strindberg:

> Utterly emaciated, with his sparse and almost white hair damp with the strain of staying upright, he sat there in his old brown-checked dressing-gown and listened. The letter was matter-of-fact, restrained, almost cold in the dryness of its style, yet he sobbed while listening to it, and blew his nose incessantly. When Greta had finished reading, he went into the next room and returned wearing an old black dressing-gown and a white opera scarf. In that quiet way he wanted to honour the woman whom he would soon follow into death.

He sent a wreath decorated with lilies and two white ribbons, without any message, to Siri's funeral.

A few days before his death he had confirmed his will in the presence of two witnesses. Its stipulations had been worked out over several years, as he tended to write a new 'testament' every time he found himself in a crisis. The final document began:

> My body must not be dissected or laid out in state, only shown to my relatives. No death-mask can be made, no photographs taken. I want to be interred at 8 in the morning, to avoid any curious bystanders. I do not want to be buried in a crypt, much less in a church, but in the new cemetery; not in the section for the wealthy, however. At the grave, there shall be no playing of music, no singing, no speeches. The clergyman should simply follow the words of the ritual.

At the beginning of his love story with Harriet Bosse, Strindberg wrote in the *Occult Diary*:

> Thought about my life this way: is it possible that all the terrible things I have experienced were specially staged for me, so that I could become a

playwright, capable of describing all manner of psychic conditions and situations? I was a playwright at the age of twenty, but if my life had proceeded in a calm and orderly fashion, I would not have had anything to render into drama.

He wrote several versions of this notion of life as a play. When he was about to begin his new life with Harriet Bosse, he wrote a tender letter of consolation to his young Austrian daughter, telling her that she should not worry that he would forget her, his Beatrice, who had guided him through the inferno and the ravine in Klam. He continued: 'In all plays there are changes of scene, even changes of characters, but in the last act, all of them reappear, and the author is not allowed to forget a single one. Such is the eternal law of drama, and of life. And woe unto him who forgets it. Now you know it! God bless you and all who love you.'

We do not know if Strindberg recalled that train of thought as he lay on his death-bed. If it is a law of drama and life that all must be remembered by their author in the final act, then he was not alone during those last days. A teeming mass of characters must have surrounded him: the father with his pipe; the ailing mother, her skin transparent as the petals of pelargonium blossoms; Siri on Drottninggatan, the veil over her hat; and, mingling with those from real life, all the figures of his own creation—the captain who died in a straitjacket, Miss Julie who could not endure the squalor her passion had driven her into, and Zachris, locked into the prison of his damnation and longing to be freed. All of them moved within Strindberg, just as he himself felt that he was part of an entity, the Great Human Being, who was his God.

Strindberg died on 14 May at 4.30 in the afternoon. According to his nurse Hedvig Kistner, who sat up in his room the night before his death, in his last words he encouraged her to go and take a rest: 'Don't worry about me, I am no longer here!' *Svenska Dagbladet* recorded his final comment as: 'Now I have spoken my last words, now I won't speak again!' After he had died, his daughter Greta, obeying his wish, placed upon his chest a crucifix which he had kept on his desk.

Wladimir Smirnoff, who saw the body, thought that Strindberg's face bore an amiable expression: 'But it was not a common amiability, directed towards the outside world; the pale face on the white pillow had a strange expression that is hard to forget, a beautiful, almost impish little smile.'

3

Strindberg had asked Hjalmar Branting to arrange the funeral, which was held on Sunday, 19 May, at the stipulated early hour. Despite Strindberg's instructions, it became a grand popular occasion, even though there were no saturnalia as at Victor Hugo's funeral. Members of the government were present. The country's student corps, the Authors' Association, the theatres of Stockholm, the Association for Peace and Arbitration (which Strindberg had publicized in his last articles), and a number of other organizations from all the countries of Northern Europe were represented. All the Social Democrat members of the Swedish Parliament attended. Above all, the workers' organizations, beneath more than a hundred red flags, lent colour to the vast funeral procession as it wound its way along Drottninggatan and Norrtullsgatan—the Great Highway—out to the Northern Cemetery.

Strindberg's coffin had been placed on an ornate hearse with a baroque roof crowned by a golden cross. The horses wore long black veils. At the cemetery, eight sturdy members of Stockholm's Workers' Commune carried the coffin to the grave, and Nathan Söderblom performed the funeral rites. One of the quotations from the Bible which he read out came from the Sermon on the Mount: 'Blessed are they which do hunger and thirst after righteousness: for they shall be filled' (Matthew 5:7).

For a year, the grave remained unidentified. Then it was marked with a black, tarred cross, probably carved by Strindberg's friend, the sculptor Christian Eriksson. The cross is inscribed only with Strindberg's name, the years of his birth and death, and the Latin words he had so often read on gravestones in the Montparnasse cemetery in Paris and which he had wanted to be inscribed on his own: *O Crux Ave Spes Unica!* ('O Cross, Be Greeted, Our Only Hope!')

BIOGRAPHICAL NOTES

Almqvist, Carl Jonas Love, 1793–1866: Prolific Romantic novelist, journalist, clergyman-adventurer. Fled Sweden in 1851 under suspicion of murder by poison and lived in various parts of the United States until 1865.

Andersson, Nils, 1864–1921: Noted collector and recorder of Swedish folk music; compiled a collection of 7,900 traditional tunes.

Andrée, S. A., 1854—1897: Engineer, physicist, Arctic explorer.

Bäckström, Edvard, 1841–1886: Poet, music critic, editor, translator.

Bellman, Carl Michael, 1740–1795: Poet, author of elegant and still popular Swedish songs in the Rococo mode.

Bergh, Richard, 1858–1919: Painter, student of Bastien-Lepage.

Björnson, Björnstjerne, 1832–1910: Norwegian novelist, short-story writer, playwright.

Bonnier, Albert, 1820–1900: With his brother Adolf, the founder of one of Sweden's oldest and most prestigious publishing houses.

Bosse, Harriet, 1878–1961: Norwegian-born dramatic actress, Strindberg's wife 1901–4.

Brandes, Georg, 1842–1927: Noted Danish literary critic and historian.

Brandes, Edvard, 1847–1931: Brother of George B., politician, author, newspaper editor.

Branting, Hjalmar, 1860–1925: Father of Sweden's labour movement, leader of the Social Democrat Party, editor, essayist.

Buckle, Henry Thomas, 1821–1862: Author of *History of Civilization in England*, proponent of 'naturalist' approach to history.

Dehmel, Richard, 1863–1920: German Symbolist poet.

Essen, Siri von, 1850–1912: Actress, Strindberg's wife 1877–91.

Fröding, Gustaf, 1860–1911: Swedish poet, critic.

Geijerstam, Gustaf af, 1858–1903: Naturalist author, playwright popular in his day.

Hansson, Ola, 1860–1925: Poet, short-story writer, novelist of rural life.

Hedin, Sven, 1865–1952: Swedish explorer in Central Asia, author of numerous books on his travels. Nazi sympathizer during World War II.

Heidenstam, Verner von, 1859–1940: Poet, novelist, aristocratic aesthete.

Josephson, Ludvig, 1832–1899: Theatre director, playwright.

Josephson, Ernst, 1851–1906: Ludvig J.'s nephew, one of the foremost Swedish Neo-Romantic painters of his day.

Karlfeldt, Erik Axel, 1864–1931: Poet, awarded posthumous Nobel Prize in 1931.

Kielland, Alexander, 1849–1906: Norwegian novelist, journalist, social critic.

Klemming, Gustaf Edvard, 1823–1893: Head of the Royal Library, mysticist.

Lagerlöf, Selma, 1858–1940: Swedish novelist, awarded Nobel Prize in 1909. Author of popular children's book, *Nils Holgersson's Wonderful Journey.*

Lange, Algot, 1850–1904: Opera singer, writer on musical theory.

Larsson, Carl, 1853–1919: Swedish painter whose idyllic picture books (*A Home* in particular) have gained renewed popularity in recent years.

Lidforss, Bengt, 1868–1913: Botanist, political writer, social critic.

Lindberg, August, 1846–1916: The greatest actor of his time, close friend of Strindberg.

Nordström, Karl, 1855–1923: Impressionist landscape artist.

Palme, August, 1856–1924: Actor who performed in many of Strindberg's plays.

Paul, Adolf, 1863–1943: Finnish–Swedish–German novelist, short-story writer, student of music (under Busoni).

Personne, J. V., 1849–1926: Theologian, bishop of Linköping (Sweden).

Staaff, Per, 1856–1903: Swedish journalist and playwright.

Uhl, Frida, 1872–1943: Austrian-born, Strindberg's second wife, 1893–1894.

Vult von Steijern, Nils, 1839–1899: Swedish jurist, Minister of Justice 1880–8.

SELECT BIBLIOGRAPHY

I Primary Sources: Editions of Strindberg's Works

Samlade skrifter. 55 volumes. Edited by John Landquist. Stockholm: Bonniers, 1912–20. The standard edition.

Samlade otryckta skrifter. 2 volumes. Edited by Vilhelm Carlheim-Gyllensköld. Stockholm: Bonniers, 1918–19. Supplements the Landquist edition.

Skrifter. 14 volumes. Selected and edited by Gunnar Brandell. Stockholm: Bonniers, 1945–6.

August Strindbergs brev. Edited by Torsten Eklund. Stockholm: Bonniers, 1947ff. His letters.

August Strindbergs dramer. 3 volumes. Edited by C. R. Smedmark. Stockholm: Bonniers, 1962–4.

Strindbergs brev till Harriet Bosse. Stockholm: Natur och Kultur, 1932. Letters to his third wife.

Vivisektioner. Translated by Tage Aurell, with foreward and notes by Torsten Eklund. Stockholm: Bonniers, 1958. Essays in French from 1894.

Det sjunkande Hellas. Edited by Erik Gamby. Uppsala: Bokgillet, 1960. Early version of *Hermione.*

En dåres försvarstal. Translated from the French by Tage Aurell. Stockholm: Bonniers, 1962.

Klostret. Edited by C. G. Bjurström. Stockholm: Bonniers, 1966. A previously unpublished novel from the Berlin period.

En dåres försvarstal (Le plaidoyer d'un fou). Translated from the French by Hans Levander. Stockholm: Forum, 1976.

Ockulta dagboken. Stockholm: Gidlund, 1977. Facsimile reprint with an appendix by Harry Järv.

II English Translations
(In chronological order of publication)

Gustafson's *A History of Swedish Literature,* pp. 651–4, has a fairly complete list of pre-1961 translations; see, also, the annually published bibliographies in

Scandinavian Studies, the publications of the Modern Language Association, and *Samlaren* for more recent translations and studies.

By the Open Sea. Translated by Ellie Schleussner. London: Palmer, 1913.

The Son of a Servant. Translated by Claud Field. London: Rider, 1913.

The Red Room. Translated by Ellie Schleussner. New York: Putnam; London: Howard Latimer, 1913.

Zones of the Spirit: A Book of Thoughts. Excerpts from the *Blue Books*, translated by Claud Field. London: Allen, 1913.

The Growth of a Soul [*Tjänstekvinnaus Son*—The Son of a Servant]. Translated by Claud Field. London: Rider, 1913.

Advent. Translated by Claud Field. London: Holden and Hardingham, 1922.

Eight Famous Plays (*The Link, The Father, Miss Julie, The Stronger, There are Crimes and Crimes, Gustavus Vasa, The Dance of Death, The Spook Sonata*). Translated by Edwin Björkman and N. Erichsen. London: Duckworth, 1949. (Reissued 1979 as *Eight Best Plays*.)

Queen Christina, Charles XII, Gustav III. Translations by Walter Johnson. Seattle and London: University of Washington Press, 1955.

Six Plays (*The Father, Miss Julie, The Stronger, Easter, A Dream Play, The Ghost Sonata*). Translated by Elizabeth Sprigge. Garden City: Doubleday, 1955.

The Last of the Knights, The Regent, Earl Birger of Bjälbo. Translated by Walter Johnson. Seattle and London: University of Washington Press, 1956.

Gustav Adolf. Translated by Walter Johnson. Seattle and London: University of Washington Press, 1957.

The Road to Damascus. Translated by Graham Rawson. London: Cape, 1958; New York: Grove, 1960.

Three Plays (*The Father, Miss Julie, Easter*). Translated by Peter Watts. Harmondsworth and Baltimore: Penguin Books, 1958.

Letters of Strindberg to Harriet Bosse. Edited and translated by Arvid Paulson. London and New York: Nelson, 1959.

Open Letters to the Intimate Theater. Translated by Walter Johnson. Seattle: University of Washington Press, 1959; London: Peter Owen, 1967.

The People of Hemsö. Translated by Elspeth Harvey Schubert. London: Cape, 1959.

The Saga of the Folkungs; Engelbrekt. Translated by Walter Johnson. Seattle: University of Washington Press, 1959.

The Vasa Trilogy: Master Olof, Gustav Vasa, Erik XIV. Translated by Walter Johnson. Seattle and London: University of Washington Press, 1959.

Five Plays of Strindberg (*Creditors, Crime and Crime, The Dance of Death, Swanwhite, The Great Highway*). Translated by Elizabeth Sprigge. New York: Doubleday, 1960.

Seven Plays (*The Father, Miss Julie, Comrades, The Stronger, The Bond, Crimes and Crimes, Easter*). Translated by Arvid Paulson and introduced by John Gassner. New York: Bantam, 1960.

The Chamber Plays (*Storm Weather, The Burned House, The Ghost Sonata, The Pelican*). Translated by Evert Sprinchorn, Seabury Quinn and Kenneth Petersen. New York: Dutton, 1962.

Inferno. Translated by Mary Sandbach. London: Hutchinson, 1962.

Twelve Plays (*The Father*, *Miss Julie*, *Creditors*, *The Stronger*, *The Bond*, *Crime and Crime*, *Easter*, *The Dance of Death*, *Swanwhite*, *A Dream Play*, *The Ghost Sonata*, *The Great Highway*). Translated by Elizabeth Sprigge. London: Constable, 1963.

Eight Expressionist Plays (*Lucky Per's Journey*, *The Keys to Heaven*, *To Damascus I*, *II*, *and III*, *A Dream Play*, *The Great Highway*, *The Ghost Sonata*). Translated by Arvid Paulson. New York: Bantam, 1965.

From an Occult Diary: Marriage with Harriet Bosse. Translated by Mary Sandbach. Edited by Torsten Eklund. London: Secker and Warburg; New York: Hill and Wang, 1965.

The Son of a Servant. Translated by Evert Sprinchorn. Garden City: Doubleday, 1966; London: Cape, 1967.

A Madman's Defense. Translation (based on Ellie Schleussner's 1912 translation *Confession of a Fool*) and introduction by Evert Sprinchorn. New York: Doubleday, 1967; London: Cape, 1968.

The Natives of Hemsö; The Scapegoat. Translated by Arvid Paulson. New York and London: Bantam, 1967.

The Red Room. New translation by Elizabeth Sprigge. London: Dent; New York: Dutton, 1967 (Everyman's Library).

Inferno, Alone, and Other Writings. Edited and translated by Evert Sprinchorn. Garden City: Doubleday, 1968.

The Cloister. Translated by Mary Sandbach. London: Secker and Warburg, 1969.

Strindberg's One-Act Plays. Translated by Arvid Paulson. New York: Washington Square Press, 1969.

Pre-Inferno Plays (*The Father*, *Lady Julie*, *Creditors*, *The Stronger*, *The Bond*). Translations and introductions by Walter Johnson. Seattle and London: University of Washington Press, 1970.

World Historical Plays (*The Nightingale of Wittenberg*, *Through Deserts to Ancestral Lands*, *Hellas*, *The Lamb and the Beast*). Translated by Arvid Paulson. New York: American–Scandinavian Foundation, 1970.

Play by Strindberg. *The Dance of Death* choreographed by Friedrich Dürrenmatt. Translated from the German by James Kirkup. London: Cape, 1972.

Getting Married. Edited and translated by Mary Sandbach. London: Gollancz; New York: Viking, 1972.

A Dream Play. Adapted by Ingmar Bergman, introduced and translated by Michael Meyer. London: Secker and Warburg, 1973.

A Dream Play, and Four Chamber Plays (*A Dream Play*, *Stormy Weather*, *The House that Burned*, *The Ghost Sonata*, *The Pelican*). Translations by Walter Johnson. Seattle and London: University of Washington Press, 1973.

The Plays of Strindberg (*The Father*, *Miss Julie*, *Creditors*, *The Stronger*, *Playing with Fire*, *Erik the Fourteenth*, *Storm*, *The Ghost Sonata*, *To Damascus*, *Easter*, *Dance of Death*, *The Virgin Bride*, *A Dream Play*). Introduced and translated by Michael Meyer. New York: Vintage Books, 1973.

The Plays. Translated by Michael Meyer. Revised edition. London: Secker and Warburg, 1975. 2 vols. (Previous edition of vol. 1, 1964.)

Three Experimental Plays (*Miss Julie*, *The Stronger*, *A Dream Play*). Translated by F. R. Southerington. Charlottesville: University of Virginia Press, 1975.

The Dance of Death. Translated by Arvid Paulson. New York: Norton, 1976.

Dramas of Testimony (*The Dance of Death*, *Advent*, *Easter*, *There are Crimes and Crimes*). Translated by Walter Johnson. Seattle and London: University of Washington Press, 1976.

Inferno, and From an Occult Diary. Translated by Mary Sandbach. Harmondsworth and New York: Penguin Books, 1979.

Plays of Confession and Therapy (*To Damascus, I, II*, and *III*). Translations by Walter Johnson. Seattle and London: University of Washington Press, 1979.

Apologia and Two Folk Plays (*The Great Highway*, *The Crownbride*, *Swanwhite*). Translations by Walter Johnson. Seattle and London: University of Washington Press, 1981.

INDEX

INDEX